GROWING UP WITH Girl power

mediated youth

Sharon R. Mazzarella
General Editor

Vol. 15

The Mediated Youth series is
part of the Peter Lang Education list.
Every volume is peer reviewed and meets
the highest quality standards for content and production.

PETER LANG
New York • Washington, D.C./Baltimore • Bern
Frankfurt • Berlin • Brussels • Vienna • Oxford

Rebecca C. Hains

GROWING UP WITH **Girl** *power*

Girlhood On Screen and in Everyday Life

PETER LANG
New York • Washington, D.C./Baltimore • Bern
Frankfurt • Berlin • Brussels • Vienna • Oxford

Library of Congress Cataloging-in-Publication Data

Hains, Rebecca C.
Growing up with girl power: girlhood on screen and in everyday life /
Rebecca C. Hains.
p. cm. — (Mediated youth; v. 15)
Includes bibliographical references and index.
1. Mass media and girls—United States. 2. Girls in mass media.
3. Girls—United States—Social conditions. 4. Feminism. I. Title.
P94.5.G572H35   305.23082'0973—dc23   2011028990
ISBN 978-1-4331-1139-6 (hardcover)
ISBN 978-1-4331-1138-9 (paperback)
ISBN 978-1-4539-0244-8 (e-book)
ISSN 1555-1814

Bibliographic information published by **Die Deutsche Nationalbibliothek**.
Die Deutsche Nationalbibliothek lists this publication in the "Deutsche
Nationalbibliografie"; detailed bibliographic data is available
on the Internet at http://dnb.d-nb.de/.

Cover design by Lauren Minco

The paper in this book meets the guidelines for permanence and durability
of the Committee on Production Guidelines for Book Longevity
of the Council of Library Resources.

© 2012 Peter Lang Publishing, Inc., New York
29 Broadway, 18th floor, New York, NY 10006
www.peterlang.com

Printed in the United States of America

Table of Contents

List of Figures

List of Tables

Acknowledgments

It takes a village to raise a child—and I've learned the same is true of writing a book. This project was helped along by many people. I would like to thank the community of colleagues, friends, family, and participants who supported this project's evolution from dissertation to book.

At Temple University, my dissertation chair and adviser, Carolyn Kitch, and my dissertation committee members, Fabienne Darling-Wolf and Renee Hobbs, offered a range of helpful insights that shaped my study of girl hero cartoons and my research with young girls. I thank them for their methodological and theoretical contributions to this project and their years of intellectual support.

I first met Sharon Mazzarella, this book's series editor, after presenting my initial textual analysis of *The Powerpuff Girls* at the International Communication Association's conference in May of 2004. I was already a fan of her work with Norma Pecora in *Growing up Girls* and appreciated her enthusiasm for my research. She has maintained an ongoing interest in my work and has become a valued collaborator and mentor. I am grateful for her support and feedback at every stage of this book's progress—as well as the ongoing help of Mary Savigar, Bernadette Shade, Sophie Appel, and other great folks at Peter Lang Publishing.

I would also like to thank Lauren Minco, the artist whose illustration graces this book's cover. Her depiction of a real girl looking dubiously at the normatively feminine girl hero flying overhead skillfully sets the tone for this book. I am a fan of her work (see laurenminco.com), and I am so grateful for her engagement in this project.

As I set out to develop the proposal for this book, Dafna Lemish of Southern Illinois University-Carbondale, Jody Lyneé Madeira of Indiana University, and Claudia Mitchell of McGill University all offered excellent guidance and a range of helpful hints. I am also grateful to my Salem State colleagues Guillermo Avila-Saavedra, Robert Brown, William Cornwell, and Chris Fauske for providing feedback on my book proposal draft.

During the early stages of drafting this book, Jody Madeira and my fantastic sister, Sarah Jackson, were generous with their time, reading early drafts of the first few chapters. Sarah and my friend Tom Dawkins also kindly read a later chapter draft when I was seeking some quick feedback. Finally, April Logan of Salisbury University and Tiffany Chenault of Salem State University offered invaluable suggestions regarding my work on Chapter Nine. I am grateful to them for their time and advice.

A majority of this book is based on qualitative human subjects research, and when analyzing hours upon hours of interview data, quality transcripts are essential to the process. A huge debt of gratitude goes to my friend and transcriptionist Florrie Marks for the care with which she treated and presented my data. Her impeccable work is bar none.

I am also grateful to the undergraduates who helped me with a few additional transcripts. At Emerson College: Maxwell Peters, Benjamin Bradley, and Hyojin Sonia Byun; at Salem State University: Christopher Ethier and Amy Latka. I am also grateful for the literature review provided by some Communications Laboratory Practicum students at Salem State: William Addison, Ryan Freeman, Joseph Ialuna, Logan McClory, Laurie Moon, Olivia Swanson, and Johnson Tang.

I was delighted when my student Jenna Austin, now a Salem State alumna, wished to conduct a directed study in girlhood studies the summer before she graduated. As part of her directed study, she trained in interviewing techniques and acted as a research assistant, collecting half of the data I used in Chapter Three of this book. I have such gratitude for the dedication with which she approached this work. In locating interviewees for that data set, I am also indebted to my colleague Jennifer Jackman at Salem State, who helped me reach to the Feminist Majority Foundation for recruitment purposes. It was a delight to interview some of the young feminists from their National Young Feminist Leadership Conference, and I am thankful that the FMF responded so positively to our request.

Special thanks also go to Salem State's College of Arts and Sciences Dean Jude Nixon and the School of Graduate Studies for providing me with a semester-long research assistant while I wrote this book, and to my department chair Judi Cook for her ongoing advocacy for my research projects. I am grateful to graduate student Timothy Magill for the quality and utility of his work during his research assistantship and wish him the best of luck in his continuing studies. I am also thankful to have received funding for my research from Salem State's Faculty Research Mini-Grant program; the Provost's Office; the Department of Communication; and the School of Graduate Studies.

The International Central Institute for Youth and Educational Television (IZI) in Munich, Germany, supported the publication and presentation of an earlier version of part of this work in their journal, *Televizion*, and their "Heroes and Heroines of Children's Television" conference in 2007. I am grateful to IZI and their director, Maya Goetz, for this support, as well as for their permission to include a revised and expanded version of this work in Chapter Eight of this book.

Throughout the years, the Girls' Studies Scholars group on Yahoo has been a helpful resource. The group is located at http://groups.yahoo.com/group/Girls_Stud ies/ and moderated by Ilana Nash of Western Michigan University. To Ilana and the group members, thanks for the ongoing exchange of information.

On a more personal note, I would like to thank my parents, Anthony and Lucie Consentino, for fostering my intellectual curiosity by raising me to ask questions and look for answers. I would also like to thank both my mother Lucie and my friend Mira Clark for countless hours of childcare while I worked on this project. My toddler Theo is the delight of my life, and I could not have asked for better babysitters to dote upon him. I am also infinitely grateful to my husband, Tyler Hains, for believing in my studies and scholarship through the years. With his loving support, anything is possible.

Finally, I would like to thank the women and girls who so generously shared their lives and perspectives with me. This book is dedicated to them.

This book was written on a MacBook Pro with Scrivener.

Introduction

"It's not every day that girls show boys they're strong, but girls are real strong. Like me."

—*Angela, age 8 (Euro-American)*

"We can be as strong as we want."

—*Bobbi, age 10 (Euro-American)*

"It doesn't matter what the boys think!"

—*Roshanda, age 6 (African-American)*

In the 1990s, girl power saturated the marketplace, infusing empowerment rhetoric into all aspects of girls' culture. Exclamations such as "Girls rule!" and "You go, girl!" became commonplace. Along with "Girl power!", these phrases appeared on countless products available for purchase—everything from pop music to pillowcases; clothing to car seat covers; eyeglasses to embroidery patterns; pocketknives to posters (Hains, 2009). For a generation of girls, girl power discourse has always existed, promoting the ideas that girls are strong, smart, and empowered and that their interests are of cultural value. Girl power rhetoric has also been full of contradictions, however; it has often implied that there is a limited range of acceptable physical behaviors and appearances for girls, and critics have argued that girl power's mode of empowerment problematically targets slender, white, middle-class girls above all others (Durham, 2003; Hains, 2004). Thus, girl power is empowering but also constraining; feminist but also postfeminist; progressive but also regressive (e.g., Banet-Weiser, 2004; Driscoll, 1999; Lemish, 2003; Newsom, 2004). What have real girls—girls like Angela and Bobbi and Roshanda, quoted in the epigraph—made of all these mixed messages?

Growing up with Girl Power addresses this question, focusing in particular on girl power's manifestations in children's popular culture. It considers music (particularly the Spice Girls), then prioritizes television in light of cultural critics' argument that television serves a socializing function in our society. As social learning theory (Bandura, 1977) suggests, when we watch television, we learn. When television characters are shown being rewarded or punished for their actions and attitudes, we learn about cultural norms: what behaviors, roles and expectations are appropriate for various people—including ourselves—within the existing social order (Gerbner and Gross, 1976). In this context, television's girls are symbolic models (Ormrod, 1999) through which viewers—male and female, adults and children—learn about girls' status in society, their relationships to others in our social structure, and the possibilities and limitations culturally proscribed of girlhood.

Forty years of studies have confirmed that children's programming is rife with gender stereotypes, influencing cultural ideas about girlhood. Time and again, girls have been depicted as passive and uninteresting, as objects instead of subjects—as people whose stories are less attention-worthy than those of boys. Boys have been depicted as having agency, status, and power while girls just looked pretty. In children's television programs and advertisements, boys have been featured more frequently, more prominently, and in a wider range of settings and activities than girls (i.e., Barner, 1999; Browne, 1998; Larson, 2001; Seiter, 1992; Signorielli, 1989; Sternglanz and Serbin, 1974). This constituted a symbolic annihilation (Tuchman, 1978) of girls, who were omitted from or trivialized in a range of story lines, and condemned if they failed to meet a very narrow range of standards for acceptable female behavior and appearance.

In the 1990s, pro-girl rhetoric gained traction in U.S. culture and many other countries, lessening girls' symbolic annihilation and the perpetual reinscription of restrictive female sex roles. Children's television networks began airing shows internationally about complex, interesting female protagonists, such as Nickelodeon's *Clarissa Explains It All* (1991–1994), *The Wild Thornberrys* (1998–2004), and *As Told by Ginger* (2000–2009). Sarah Banet-Weiser (2004) considered these programs to be girl power texts in which "empowerment and agency define[d] girls more than helplessness and dependency" (p. 136). This was the opposite of much prior children's television programming. Banet-Weiser (2004) noted that despite this progress, these girl power shows have been criticized as commercial texts devoid of real political engagement (p. 137)—but she argued that they nonetheless "provide[d] a different cultural script for both girl and boy audience members, a script that challenge[d] conventional narratives and images about what girls are and who they should be" (pp. 135–136).

This positive change also extended into action-adventure television cartoons—a remarkable improvement, given that in this genre, story lines consistently had trivialized or omitted girls altogether. As Ellen Seiter (1992) observed, in the 1970s, action-adventure children's television included girls on only a token level, and by the early 1990s, girls were typically excluded altogether. Yet in the late 1990s and early 2000s, many action-adventure cartoons featured girls and teams of heroic girls who would always save the world—fists first, if necessary, harnessing and owning their anger. In programs like Cartoon Network's *The Powerpuff Girls* (1998–2005), *Totally Spies* (2001–2007) and Disney's *Kim Possible* (2002–2007), girls were superheroes in their own rights—smart, strong, and savvy. Their acts of strength and bravery were the rule, not the exception, in their behavior. It was an unprecedented televisual representation.

This book documents how girl hero cartoons emerged and contributed to cultural discourse about pre-teen girls. It begins by situating girl hero cartoons within other major discourses about girlhood. Chapter One considers studies by the American Association of University Women, books by popular authors such as Mary Pipher and Peggy Orenstein, and the riot grrrls' creative output, including the concept of girl power—as well as their media reception. Chapter Two explores the mainstreaming of girl power effected by the Spice Girls and what it came to mean in their hands, while Chapter Three describes how young feminists who grew up with the Spice Girls recollect receiving the band's discourses on girlhood. Through retrospective interviews, I consider whether and how they feel the Spice Girls' mainstreaming of girl power influenced them and informed their feminist identities.

Chapter Four builds upon the first three chapters by unpacking the stories girl hero cartoons have told, examining their discourses about girlhood and empowerment. Then, Chapter Five describes the research methodologies used for the studies described in Chapters Six through through Nine. These latter chapters explore what the girl hero cartoon's discourse on girl power meant to pre-adolescent girls in the cartoons' target audience while the cartoons were popular. In the research that underpins these chapters, I viewed and discussed girl hero cartoons with real girls. We explored what it meant to grow up with girl power, contradictions and all. Through these conversations, I learned how girls have negotiated the cartoons' representations of sexism, strength, intelligence, identity, femininity, and race, and how they related these readings to their everyday lives. Chapter Nine moves beyond the girl hero cartoons to investigate other modes of girl power preferred by the African-American girls in my study. It focuses especially on the Bratz brand of diverse dolls that many of the girls loved—and used in surprising ways. Thus, *Growing up with Girl Power* both analyzes discourses on girlhood and reveals how real girls have drawn upon girl power discourse while negotiating pre-adolescent identities.

Although *Growing up with Girl Power* examines girl power within a U.S. context, it may be read in relation to the girl power literature previously published in other nations. The Spice Girls were a British pop music act who gained global popularity, making girl power a truly international phenomenon. As such, scholars beyond the U.S. have published numerous internationally situated interrogations of the Spice Girls and other girl power vehicles. These publications include the works of Catherine Driscoll, Anita Harris, Dafna Lemish, Valerie Walkerdine, and Rebecca Willett, among others. *Growing up with Girl Power* provides a perspective on girl power's reception by U.S. girls that both informs and is informed by studies in Australia, Canada, Israel, the United Kingdom, and other nations.

This book also has deeper implications beyond our understanding of girl power alone. Its overarching goals are to enhance our understanding of girls as audience members and of girls' identity development processes. How do girls negotiate the media's representations of girls, and how are these negotiations influenced by their broader cultural context? How do girls then inform their self-images and identity construction through the consumption of these representations and related social influences? Engaging with feminist theory and cultural studies scholarship, *Growing up with Girl Power* offers answers to these questions.

1

The Girl Crisis and the Riot Grrrls

"Schools set girls up to fail."
—*The American Association of University Women, Shortchanging Girls, Shortchanging America (1991)*

"We are angry at a society that tells us Girl=Dumb, Girl=Bad, Girl=Weak."

—*Bikini Kill, 1991*

"Math is tough."

—*Teen Talk Barbie, 1992*

Where did girl power come from, and why did it emerge? With its focus on girls' empowerment, girl power's existence points to long-standing problems with the socialization and enculturation of girls. After all, in an ideal world, girl power would not exist. Girls would have always considered themselves strong, smart, and empowered—making pro-girl rhetoric irrelevant. Our culture would have always valued girls' interests—making discourses supporting those interests redundant. Girls would have always been represented fairly and engagingly on film and television—making depictions of powerful girls neither new nor trendy.

Given the reality, however, girl power can be understood as a discourse that emerged in response to a popular set of discourses I call "the girl crisis." The girl crisis centered upon the societal devaluation of girls in U.S. culture, a circumstance that gained widespread recognition in the 1990s. Parents, academics, and cultural critics became concerned that girls were being treated inequitably, in profound ways, on a daily basis, with dire psychological and material consequences. Their activist movements and best-selling books shone a spotlight onto girls' issues and attempted to work on girls' behalves to reconstitute their damaged self-esteem.

At the same time, a grassroots movement of young feminists arose from the punk rock counterculture. Its members, called riot grrrls, railed against widespread misogyny in ironic and subversive ways, making headlines with their startling tactics. Their countercultural work presented an alternate discourse of girlhood, in which girls were not constructed as helpless victims; rather, they knew they are mistreated by society and were angry about it. The riot grrrls' approach pointed to a problem: many concerned adults were over-emphasizing girls' vulnerability, failing to recognize the full range of girls' efforts to grapple with a toxic culture.

Soon, the marketing industry followed the cultural gaze towards girls. Sensing an opportunity, savvy marketers pursued routes into girls' pocketbooks (and their parents' wallets), hoping to maximize sales in this hitherto untapped market. Their successful efforts proved girls were profitable, paving the way for more media designed for girls. In this context, mainstream girl power emerged—and became embraced for the cultural support it offered girls.

The Girl Crisis

In the early 1990s, girls' cultural devaluation sparked national attention and outrage. A new discourse of girlhood coalesced—the discourse of the girl crisis. As people spoke and wrote more about the inequities girls faced at school, in the media, and even in the home, a paradigm shift occurred. Sex biases became visible everywhere, making it more obvious when girls were trivialized, treated chauvinistically, or ignored. This change in perception was prompted by the release of a series of seminal research reports and books, written from a feminist perspective, which argued that adolescent girls keenly felt these inequities. Adolescent girls became broadly understood to be in crisis: routinely wounded and rarely recovering the confidence and assurance of their pre-adolescent selves. Though this discourse sometimes overgeneralized girls as being victimized, failing to recognize the ways in which girls had agency to negotiate or resist societal inequities, the research reports and books were at the center of a quickly expanding national conversation about girls' well-being. They documented the nature and sources of girls' problems and demanded solutions, prompting activist campaigns on girls' behalf.

The AAUW's Research-Based Activism

In documenting and critiquing the girl crisis, the American Association of University Women (AAUW) led the pack. The AAUW is a feminist organization dedicated to activism, education, and research in support of equity for women and girls. The AAUW has a long history: founded in 1881 by a small group of female college graduates, they sought to make higher education more accessible to women (AAUW Online Museum, n.d.). A century later, in the aftermath of the women's liberation movement and the passage of Title IX, women had achieved basic equity in higher education. Within certain disciplines, however, disparities were startling; women lagged far behind men in the high-paying, socially prestigious, often highly satisfying science, technology, engineering, and mathematics (STEM) fields (Brush, 1991; Dix, 1987; National Science Foundation, 1990). Therefore, the AAUW began working to achieve parity between the sexes in STEM education. In this pursuit, they focused not on college-aged women but on girls.

In comparison to schoolboys, schoolgirls fared poorly in the math and science classes that serve as gateways to STEM majors in college. It was not a matter of aptitude; studies had shown that many girls simply could not see the usefulness of science and math courses, choosing to eschew them early in life (The U.S. Department of Education, 1984; National Science Foundation, 1990; Eccles, Adler, and Meece, 1984; Eccles, 1984; Eccles, 1987). This decision significantly narrowed later career choices. Adult support and encouragement could make a difference, though, especially on the home front: children whose parents played an active role in their career planning were more likely to pursue a science or technology career (Hilton et al., 1991; Farmer, Anderson, and Brock, 1991).

In 1988, the AAUW founded the Eleanor Roosevelt Fund for Women and Girls, which focused on teacher development, research, and activism related to science and mathematics (AAUW Online Museum, n.d.). Then, in 1991, the AAUW launched their Initiative for Educational Equity in an "effort to get girls onto America's education agenda" (AAUW Online Museum, n.d.). They kicked off this initiative by publishing a research report, *Shortchanging Girls, Shortchanging America*, in January of 1991. Based on a 1990 nationwide poll of 9- to 15-year-olds that the AAUW commissioned, the study revealed that among girls, self-esteem decreased much more in adolescence than among boys; so did girls' confidence in mathematics and the sciences. The report further argued that girls' self-esteem, life goals, and success in math and science were interconnected—so that all three could be improved with better cultural and educational support in math and science. This report would prove influential.

The AAUW announced the report's results at an AAUW Educational Equity Roundtable, held on January 9, 1991 in Washington, D.C. Members of the media and professionals from the fields of education, policy, and the corporate workplace attended (AAUW Online Museum, n.d.). After the roundtable, the mass media helped bring the AAUW's findings to national attention. The *New York Times* immediately raised the alarm on the girl crisis with an article titled "Little Girls Lose Their Self-Esteem on Way to Adolescence, Study Finds" (Daley, 1991, B6). This article reported with concern on *Shortchanging Girls* and featured interviews with experts, including Carol Gilligan, author of *In a Different Voice* (1982), who offered support for the study (she had served as a project adviser). Responses to the *Times* article included a letter to the editor whose writer posited a link to the media, arguing that society would need to change the representation levels of women on television to address the problems outlined in the report (Dean, 1991).

A few months later, with a prominent front-page *New York Times* headline that declared, "Children's TV, Where Boys Are King," journalist Bill Carter (1991) exposed the matter-of-fact, cavalier way in which industry executives privileged boys' viewing interests as they vied for top ratings. Carter's article spelled out the connections between this form of sexism and that reported by the AAUW. ABC television had just announced their fall line-up for 1991, deciding to cut the shows that most appealed to girl audiences. Their rationale was that boys consti-tuted a 53% majority in the Saturday morning viewing audience—a difference that, slight as it was, ABC executives feared could make or break their odds of success in the so-called ratings war. Carter quoted ABC's vice-president for children's pro-grams, Jennie Trias, as unapologetically explaining that the girl-favored *New Kids on the Block* cartoon was being canceled because "Only girls were watching the show. And you have to have boys watching a show for it to succeed" (qtd. on p. A1). Carter also noted that ABC had chosen to cancel *Little Rosey*, its only series with a girl protagonist, because "It is well known that boys will watch a male lead and not a female lead. But girls are willing to watch a male lead" (qtd. on p. A1).

Interrogating the lack of girl characters on other networks, Carter spoke with CBS Vice President for Children's Programs, Judy Price, who argued that in the net-work's focus group research, "The boys certainly didn't want to be seen liking the things the girls like. Barbie is the most popular character for young girls probably of all time, but she would never succeed as a Saturday morning show. The boys would refuse to watch her" (qtd. on p. A1). CBS Senior Vice President for Research David Poltrack neatly summarized the issue, saying, "Children's television has always been male dominated" (qtd. on p. A1). In other words, this was just busi-ness as usual—but the AAUW report had provided a lens through which to view this institutionalized sexism. In her interview for Carter's article, AAUW executive director Anne Bryant underscored the damage caused by such sexism, criticizing industry decisions for playing a role in girls' low levels of self-esteem. "They say things like, 'My opinion may not matter'" (qtd. on p. A1)—which Bryant claimed was "an attitude being reinforced by the choices made by television programmers" (p. A1).

Building on the momentum the *Shortchanging Girls* report generated, the AAUW released a follow-up report, *The AAUW Report: How Schools Shortchange Girls*, in February of 1992. Released to coincide with the AAUW Educational Foundation's new National Education Summit on Girls, the new report synthesized research about girls' schooling. It argued that although girls attended the same schools as boys, they were not receiving the same education: teachers' unconscious gender biases and established curricula favored boys' learning styles and interests, while some boys' comments and actions made the classroom a hostile environment for girls. Compared with boys, girls scored poorly on tests in math and science— and when they scored evenly, boys were given preference in scholarship awards. Girls from minority and low-income backgrounds fared even worse than their white and/or socioeconomically advantaged peers. Against these challenges, the AAUW demanded work to improve the quality of girls' education and increase their career options in STEM fields. The report therefore concluded by offering 40 recommendations to improve girls' experiences in school, ranging from better enforcement of Title IX, to removing sex bias from standardized tests, to improving the quality of health- and sex-education programs. Promisingly, the summit and report "brought commitments of support to end gender bias in schools from leaders of education organizations, associations, and government agencies" (AAUW Online Museum, n.d.).

The media covered the release of *The AAUW Report: How Schools Shortchange Girls* even more prominently than it had covered the previous report. The *New York Times* declared in a front-page headline, "Bias Against Girls Is Found Rife in Schools, with Lasting Damage" (Chira, 1992, p. A1). In the article, AAUW executive director Anne Bryant called the study "a wake-up call to the nation's education and policy leaders, parents, administrators and guidance counselors." She argued that "unless we pay attention to girls' needs today, we will find out 15 years from now that there is still a glass ceiling" (qtd. in Chira, 1992, p. A1).[1]

Barbie Hates Math

In the midst of growing interest in the AAUW's research-based activism about the girl crisis, Mattel committed a gaffe. The company released Teen Talk Barbie, the first Barbie with a voice chip, and programmed some of the dolls to say "Math is tough." This drew the AAUW's ire for reinforcing a cultural stereotype that undermined girls' confidence in mathematics. In October 1992, the AAUW campaigned for Mattel to recall the dolls and reprogram them with more empowering statements, like "We should start a business" ("Critics Question . . . ," 1992, p. D3). Mattel executives balked, but within two weeks, the company succumbed to the pressure of the growing negative press. Although Mattel executives refused to authorize a full recall or program new phrases into the dolls, they invited customers to exchange any Barbies that doubted their math skills. They further removed the offending phrase from the database of 270 possible phrases that a Teen Talk Barbie might be programmed to say. (Any individual doll only said four phrases in total.)

Regarding Mattel's response to the AAUW demands, Mattel president Jill Barad told *The New York Times*, "The last thing we would intentionally do would be to have Barbie convey anything but the most aspirational of messages" (Kurtzman, 1992, p. C2). In a letter to the AAUW, Barad admitted, "In hindsight, the phrase 'math class is tough,' while correct for many students both male and female, should not have been included. We didn't fully consider the potentially negative implications of this phrase, nor were we aware of the findings of your organization's report" (qtd. in the Associated Press, 1992, p. D4). In its campaign against Teen Talk Barbie, the AAUW succeeded in not just changing the voice chip programming of future Teen Talk Barbies. It also raised awareness on girls' behalf among parents reading the press coverage, who could now exchange the doll. Moreover, it brought the AAUW's original reports to the attention of Mattel executives—no mean feat.

The Ms. Foundation Sends Schoolgirls to Work

The longest campaign related to the AAUW reports on the girl crisis is Take Our Daughters to Work Day, established in 1993 to teach girls about the work world and broaden their horizons. Inspired by *Shortchanging Girls, Shortchanging America* and *The AAUW Report: How Schools Shortchange Girls*, Take Our Daughters to Work Day was developed and organized by the Ms. Foundation for Women. Originally planned as a one-time New York event, it gained such traction that it was immediately reconceptualized as an annual national event, held on the fourth Thursday of April. The campaign urged people to bring girls into the workplace, helping them to learn about and aspire to a wide variety of professional fields—and, with the companies' support, to see that girls are valued and welcome in a professional environment. To this end, the Ms. Foundation encouraged girls' parents, family members, and friends to bring girls ages 9 to 15 to work with them.

When the campaign was first announced, many misunderstood it as a day when girls would trail their parents at work, instead of a day when any girl could go to a participating workplace with any adult—family or not. Writing for the *Pittsburgh Post-Gazette*, Kalson (1993) admitted to this misconception: "When I first heard that the Ms. Foundation for Women had designated April 28 'Take Our Daughters to Work Day,' my immediate reaction was: And do exactly what with them—bore them into stupefaction? No daughter of mine or anyone else's would be able to watch what I do all day without falling dead asleep in the first 20 minutes. [. . .] But then I saw a couple of articles about the concept, and it didn't seem so dumb after all" (p. D1).

As the *New York Times* explained, Take Our Daughters to Work Day was about more than just trailing. It relied on employers' participation, using resources available from the Ms. Foundation if desired, to organize activities for girls. In describing the campaign, the *New York Times* noted, "The [Ms.] foundation recognizes that visions of a workplace invasion by hordes of preadolescents, each perhaps with a favorite My Little Pony, are, to use its own word, daunting. It will provide [employers] a sample schedule and a list of activities, all written in a soothing, anxiety-lowering tone" (Noble, 1993, p. C25). An article in the *Christian Science Monitor* also underscored that Take Our Daughters to Work Day required organizational planning in a detailed explanation of the event, which emphasized the potential for exposure to STEM careers in the examples it offered:

> Across the country, participating employers are planning activities that range from one-on-one conversations to carefully organized seminars and group tours of the premises.
>
> In New York, Merrill Lynch will bring 120 girls onto a trading floor and into offices to show them how the stock market works. At Liz Claiborne, participants will visit the areas where clothes are designed. "They'll find out that you can't just design something by drawing it," explains Ms. Wilson. "You have to know math. So girls will realize, 'Oh, there's a reason to know math.'"
>
> In Washington, women in Congress and the Cabinet will give girls an inside view of government. And at the Environmental Protection Agency in San Francisco, 45 girls will take part in activities that range from testing water to sampling air quality. (Gardner, 1993, p. 11)

The campaign further functioned as a consciousness-raising event. The Ms. Foundation prepared a curriculum guide for teachers to use in schools the week prior to Take Our Daughters to Work Day:

> Women, it informs students, make up almost half the work force, but hold only 3 percent of top positions. The average salary of an African-American female college graduate in a full-time job is less than that of a white male high-school dropout. And in the category of information that galls no matter how often it is repeated, students learn from the guide that wives employed full time outside the home do most of the housework, too. That last bit of information may pique the girls' interest in one of the guide's exercises, devising a personal bill of rights. (Noble, 1993, p. C25)

The campaign received the support of many celebrities: Gloria Steinem, founder of *Ms. Magazine*, held a press conference on her 59th birthday to promote Take Our Daughters to Work Day, where she was joined by several actresses and singers including Judy Collins and opera star Jessye Norman (Bourgoyne, 1993, p. A23). Linda Ellerbee, co-chair of the campaign, reported that after the first Take Our Daughters to Work Day, the Ms. Foundation heard from many corporations, who said "it was one of the most successful and rewarding programs they ever took part in, that it was, in fact, something with no downside" (Ellerbee, 1994, p. A13).

From this promising start in 1993 and 1994, Take Our Daughters to Work Day became a long-running and successful campaign that made great contributions to cultural discourses of girlhood. Its inroads into workplaces grew so strong that within a decade, it expanded to include boys and was renamed the Take Our Daughters and Sons to Work Day in 2003.[2] By 2007, the program had grown so large that the Ms. Foundation transitioned it to the newly created Take Our Daughters and Sons to Work Day Foundation.

The Girl Crisis Hits Bookstores

During the early 1990s, consensus grew: more needed to be done to save girls, and quickly. The successes of the AAUW and the creation of Take Our Daughters to Work Day were only first steps. From the start, the AAUW argued that addressing the girl crisis would require change across all institutions that contribute to girls' sense of self worth: family, education, government, and mass media (AAUW, 1991, p. 17).

In 1992, Lyn Mikel Brown and Carol Gilligan released *Meeting at the Crossroads: Women's Psychology and Girls' Development*, which unpacked from a psychological perspective why girls suffered so much in adolescence: they silenced their own voices in fear at damaging their relationships with others. Based upon five years of longitudinal research with 100 girls, *Meeting at the Crossroads* built upon Gilligan's seminal earlier book, *In a Different Voice: Psychological Theory and Women's Development* (1982; re-released in 1993), which argued psychology had long misunderstood women and posited a new perspective. Specifically, Gilligan used *In a Different Voice* to critique the ideas of Kohlberg (1969), the developmental theorist with whom she had worked during her graduate studies; in his research on the stages of moral development, he had found that women's moral development was weaker than men's. Gilligan argued that the issue was with his definition: He viewed moral reasoning as being about following the rules, but the women she studied often viewed morality as making decisions in people's best interest—caring, not rule-following. Positing that multiple dimensions of moral reasoning could coexist, she argued that society had been privileging the thinking and moral approaches of men, when it needed to value both men's and women's perspectives as having equal validity. In *Meeting at the Crossroads*, by focusing specifically on girls, Brown and Gilligan employed Gilligan's psychological theories to better understand adolescent female development and posit ways in which society could better support girls.

In the debut issue of *Girlhood Studies: An Interdisciplinary Project*, Lyn Mikel Brown reflected on this work. She explained:

> Our goal then was to interrupt the prevailing academic and public conventions that placed boyhood at the center of child and adolescent development, and provide the means for girls to give voice to their thoughts and feelings. We did so in the mid-80s when 'girl' was synonymous with unimportant, and, except for those few private girls' schools which funded our early work, listening to girls was considered a waste of time and money. We did so through the early- and mid-nineties when popular books misconstrued our findings and took up the 'girls in crisis' call; and grant money was more available, both for research and for empowerment programs designed to 'save' girls from a tsunami of all things bad. (Brown, 2008, p. 2)

The tsunami Brown described began in 1994, when a bumper crop of key works on girls' problems were published by the popular press. In *Reviving Ophelia: Saving the Selves of Adolescent Girls*, Mary Pipher (1994) shared the stories of many adolescent girls from her psychotherapy practice, making a case that society damages girls—and also noting that the behaviors girls found normal (including drinking and engaging in sexual behaviors) were interpreted as deviant by the adults in their lives. In *Schoolgirls: Young Women, Self-Esteem, and the Confidence Gap*, published by Anchor Books under the imprimatur of the AAUW, Peggy Orenstein (1994) reported on her fieldwork with girls at two California middle schools, breathing life into the AAUW data. Myra and David Sadker's (1994) *Failing at Fairness: How Our Schools Cheat Girls* detailed the inequities girls endured at school, and Judy Mann's (1994) *The Difference: Discovering the Hidden Ways We Silence Girls* cast a broader net, considering parenting and religion in addition to education. Dovetailing with the AAUW reports, these books cited several major causes for concern: As girls hit adolescence, their academic achievement dropped, their self-esteem plummeted, and their comfort with their appearance decreased. In short, the books made a case that girls faced an all-consuming crisis of adolescence, with serious and devastating consequences.

The authors argued that this crisis of female adolescence had no analog among boys, and they suggested multiple intersecting causes for this difference. One proposed cause was gender bias in education. Teachers, despite their best intentions, unconsciously gave preferential treatment to boys (Orenstein, 1994, pp. 12–17; Sadker & Sadker, 1994, p. 1; Pipher, 1994, pp. 62–63). Another proposed cause was the disintegration of the family; divorce was on the rise, and more children were being raised in single-family homes (Pipher, 1994, p. 65). Adding complexity to this fact, cultural norms positioned nuclear families as "normal," leading some girls to worry they were wrong to feel happy being raised by a single parent (Brown & Gilligan, 1992, pp. 129–130). Another was gender role socialization: Girls were primed—by dozens of seemingly small daily interactions—to believe themselves more fragile than boys, less skilled at mathematics, and so on (Orenstein, 1994, pp. 18–26, 48–49; Mann, 1994, p. 94). This socialization often privileged above all else the idea that girls should be "nice": not direct and honest, but gentle, polite, submissive, and cooperative (Brown & Gilligan, 1992, pp. 53–62, 200–203; Pipher, p. 39). The overall effect was a silencing of girls (Mann, 1994). This socialization also encouraged a limiting manner of dress. Girls' dresses and skirts, sometimes required as school uniforms, restricted free movement during play in ways that boys' outfits never did (Mann, 1994, pp. 73–74).

An additional proposed cause for the girl crisis was media content. Children's television cartoons and commercials teemed with sexist content (Mann, 1994, pp. 48–51). Depictions of women were even worse, and with much classic literature equally sexist, books offered little escape from on-screen offenses (Pipher, 1994, p. 42). Furthermore, the sexualization of girls promoted by media culture encouraged girls to engage in dangerous sexual behavior (Pipher, 1994, p. 12), and society's increasingly unrealistic beauty ideals were "intense and damaging" (p. 56), resulting in eating disorders and self-loathing (pp. 184–185). Any girl who did not present and carry herself in just the right way might be condemned and ostracized by peers, labeled a slut (Orenstein, 1994, pp. 51–58). Some boys were especially quick to sexually harass girls, contributing further to the crisis of female adolescence (Orenstein, 1994, pp. 111–132, 148–154). To walk this fine line with success, girls monitored themselves carefully and silenced themselves from communicating their true feelings (Gilligan and Brown, 1992), often cutting themselves off from their "true selves" in a way that was damaging to the psyche (Pipher, 1994, pp. 36–37). Pipher (1994) argued that our culture bore responsibility for this splitting (p. 37). Sexual abuse and violence sometimes played a critical role, as well: By adolescence, girls faced a very real, statistically significant danger of being sexually assaulted (Pipher, 1994, p. 205), and in urban communities, low-income girls were at particular risk of being harmed (Orenstein, 1994, pp. 205–213).

Taken altogether, these books formed the backbone of a useful and fruitful national conversation about girls and their status, condemning many social practices and institutions as poisonous to girls. U.S. newspapers published hundreds of articles about adolescent girls' issues while these books were on bestseller lists, and the topics and tones were influenced by the books' discourse on girls' issues (Mazzarella and Pecora, 2007). Many parents could see their daughters struggling through adolescence, and concerned adults quickly propelled the books onto bestseller lists. This owed in part to strong reviews from publications including the *New York Times* Book Review, which assigned the review of *Schoolgirls* to David Halberstam, a Pulitzer Prize-winning journalist. Halberstam (1994) concluded his review with this resounding endorsement:

> There is a certain sadness to "Schoolgirls," a sense of young gifted children slipping away from the possibilities that might be theirs, a sense of lost talent and lost confidence. While the academic and political debate about biology and behavior continues, for parents and other tax-paying adults "Schoolgirls" is a valuable glimpse of reality. This important book should be read by parents raising children of all ages and of both sexes. (para. 22)

In a recent telephone conversation with Peggy Orenstein, she explained to me that because of Halberstam's credibility, his review helped *Schoolgirls* become perceived as an important book. "Suddenly," Orenstein reflected, "everybody wanted to talk to me. *Fresh Air, Good Morning America, Morning Edition, Nightline.* His review was the overwhelmingly exciting, positive, important piece that I think made the book become taken seriously. That isn't to say that it couldn't have been taken seriously otherwise—but it might not have gotten out there in the same way."

Later, when Orenstein saw Halberstam at a book festival, where they were promoting their respective books, she learned why he had so strongly endorsed *Schoolgirls*. When she introduced herself to him, she recalled, "He actually jumped over a table and pumped my hand. He had a fourteen-year-old daughter, and as it turned out, these issues were just really intense for him right then. He was really struggling with what was going on with her, what was going on with the relationship, what was going on with her school—you know, all the things that were in the book were like his daughter's life. So he had been very drawn to it."

In sum, the discourses presented by these books served a valuable purpose, opening broader conversation about how society could better treat girls. At the same time, however, many of them have been criticized (especially *Reviving Ophelia* and the "Ophelia industry" that followed it) by scholarly publications for presenting all-consuming "vulnerability discourse" about girlhood (Aapola, Gonick and Harris, 2005, p. 44). As Umberto Eco (1986) has noted, "Crisis sells well" (p. 127)—and the concept of the girl crisis indeed sold well. Scholars problematizing this discourse have cautioned that by positing girls as victims, the Ophelia industry failed to do justice to the complex ways in which girls actually negotiate the world. In a study of news articles that contributed to girl crisis discourse in *Ophelia*'s wake, Mazzarella and Pecora (2007) reached a similar conclusion; a majority of the news articles in their sample (N=169) implied that girls themselves were an issue that adults needed to do something *about*—"a social problem of crisis proportions" (p. 21). As the authors noted, the girl crisis's dominant discourse on girlhood failed to recognize that girls can have agency. This was a serious shortcoming, and Lyn Mikel Brown has since lamented that *Reviving Ophelia* mainstreamed a "'girls in crisis' interpretation of our work in *Meeting at the Crossroads*" (Brown, 2008, p. 5). Although Brown and Gilligan "never set out to worry about or fix girls" (Brown, 2008, p. 2), the broader culture took an interest in this project—with both positive and problematic outcomes.

Overall, these bestselling books about girls in crisis could also be read in dialogue with other popular feminist books at the time. Naomi Wolf's *The Beauty Myth* (1991) and Susan Bordo's Pulitzer-Prize-nominated *Unbearable Weight* (1993) offered critiques of feminine beauty ideals; Deborah Tannen's *You Just Don't Understand* (1990) explored gendered differences in communication styles; Susan Faludi's *Backlash* (1992) exposed the antifeminist backlash by conservatives against all women; and Carol Gilligan's *In a Different Voice*, first published in 1982 and re-released in 1993, considered female self-esteem. Books such as these, though not specific to girls, presented arguments about femininity and gender, useful as context for better understanding problems with how girls are socialized. With concerned adults seeking solutions for the girl crisis, these books helped set the right climate for a mainstream version of girl power to emerge just a few years later.

The Grrrl Riot

Before becoming a mainstream concept, girl power emerged from a countercultural feminist movement called "riot grrrl." While the AAUW mobilized researchers and activists to work on girls' behalf, teenagers and young adults were trying to improve girls' lives at a grassroots level. To these riot grrrls, "girl power" was a rallying cry—a slogan that promoted the self-actualization of empowerment among girls. To understand what girl power originally meant, and how it ultimately became reborn as a mainstream concept, requires understanding the riot grrrl scene from which it emerged.

The term "riot grrrl" originated as the title of a zine[3] in 1991, inspired by the race riots occurring around the U.S. in response to police brutality.[4] Jen Smith, a musician and zine writer who was living in the Mount Pleasant neighborhood of Washington, D.C. during the three-day-long race riots that occurred there in May 1991, felt charged by the riots' energy. After fighting her way through the riots to get home, she declared to her housemates, "What we need is a girl riot" (qtd. in Meltzer, 2010, p. 5). She then wrote about the riots to the punk-feminist zine *Girl Germs*, suggesting that a "girl riot" should be next. Inspired, *Girl Germs* co-editors Allison Wolfe and Molly Neuman moved to D.C. for their summer break from the University of Oregon, where they were undergraduates. They asked Smith to join their band, Bratmobile, and she agreed. The three decided to collaborate on a new zine, which Smith proposed calling *Girl Riot* and was ultimately published as *riot grrrl*—the words inverted, and "girl" rendered as a growl ("Jen Smith," 2011).

Riot grrrl swiftly became the name for a coalescing movement of young women and girls across the country, who used self-produced music—especially punk rock—to address girls' issues from a young feminist perspective. Leaders in this scene included Bratmobile and the band Bikini Kill (see Figure 1.1), which was formed in 1990 by Tobi Vail, Kathi Wilcox, and Kathleen Hanna, students at Evergreen State College in Oregon. Bikini Kill's members published an eponymous zine that focused on topics related to punk rock, feminism, and politics, and they also contributed to the *riot grrrl* zine. Issue two of the *Bikini Kill* zine offered this brief history of riot grrrl's start:

> 'Once upon a time . . . ' last spring ('91), Molly and Allison (Girl Germs, Bratmobile) went to Washington D.C., shook things up and got shook up, and

connected with this radsoulsister Jen Smith who wanted to start this girl network
and fanzine called Girl Riot. (This was also inspired by the Cinco de Mayo riots
occurring in her neighbourhood at the time.) So that summer a bunch of us
Olympia kids (Bratmobile and Bikini Kill) lived in D.C. to make something happen with our friends there. Tobi (Bikini Kill, Jigsaw) had been talking about doing
zines in the spirit of angry grrrl zine-scene, and then one restless night, Molly made
this little fanzine stating events in the girl lives of the Oly-D.C. scene connection—
and Riot Grrrl was born. (Bikini Kill #2, 1991, qtd in "Riot Grrrl," n.d.)

**Figure 1.1: Tobi Vail (left) and Kathleen Hannah (right), two members of Bikini Kill.
Copyright Pat Graham, patgraham.org**

Issue two of *Bikini Kill* also included a lengthy manifesto, reproduced in
Figure 1.2. This manifesto outlined the reasons why the band members felt riot grrrl
needed to exist. It suggested that creating a riot grrrl community, whose members
were non-hierarchical and mutually supportive, could effect real change in the
world. Riot grrrls could own their anger and deploy it against the status quos of
capitalism and patriarchy, becoming self-sufficient cultural creators who know
they can do anything. Riot grrrl was thus conceived as an egalitarian but angry feminist movement that would "save the psychic and cultural lives of girls and women
everywhere, according to their own terms, not ours." (See Figure 1.2.)

BECAUSE us girls crave records and books and fanzines that speak to US that WE feel included in and can understand in our own ways.

BECAUSE we wanna make it easier for girls to see/hear each other's work so that we can share strategies and criticize-applaud each other.

BECAUSE we must take over the means of production in order to create our own moanings.

BECAUSE viewing our work as being connected to our girlfriends-politics-real lives is essential if we are gonna figure out how we are doing impacts, reflects, perpetuates, or DISRUPTS the status quo.

BECAUSE we recognize fantasies of Instant Macho Gun Revolution as impractical lies meant to keep us simply dreaming instead of becoming our dreams AND THUS seek to create revolution in our own lives every single day by envisioning and creating alternatives to the bullshit christian capitalist way of doing things.

BECAUSE we want and need to encourage and be encouraged in the face of all our own insecurities, in the face of beergutboyrock that tells us we can't play our instruments, in the face of "authorities" who say our bands/zines/etc are the worst in the US and who attribute any validation/success of our work to girl bandwagon hype.

BECAUSE we don't wanna assimilate to someone else's (boy) standards of what is or isn't "good" music or punk rock or "good" writing AND THUS need to create forums where we can recreate, destroy and define our own visions.

BECAUSE we are unwilling to falter under claims that we are reactionary "reverse sexists" and not the truepunkrock soulcrusaders that WE KNOW we really are.

BECAUSE we know that life is much more than physical survival and are patently aware that the punk rock "you can do anything" idea is crucial to the coming angry grrrl rock revolution which seeks to save the psychic and cultural lives of girls and women everywhere, according to their own terms, not ours.

BECAUSE we are interested in creating non-hierarchical ways of being AND making music, friends, and scenes based on communication + understanding, instead of competition + good/bad categorizations.

BECAUSE doing/reading/seeing/hearing cool things that validate and challenge us can help us gain the strength and sense of community that we need in order to figure out how bullshit like racism, able-bodieism, ageism, speciesism, classism, thinism, sexism, anti-semitism and heterosexism figures in our own lives.

BECAUSE we see fostering and supporting girl scenes and girl artists of all kinds as integral to this process.

BECAUSE we hate capitalism in all its forms and see our main goal as sharing information and staying alive, instead of making profits of being cool according to traditional standards.

BECAUSE we are angry at a society that tells us Girl=Dumb, Girl=Bad, Girl=Weak.

BECAUSE we are unwilling to let our real and valid anger be diffused and/or turned against us via the internalization of sexism as witnessed in girl/girl jealousism and self defeating girltype behaviors.

BECAUSE self defeating behaviors (like fucking boys without condoms, drinking to excess, ignoring true soul girlfriends, belittling ourselves and other girls, etc. . .) would not be so easy if we lived in communities where we felt loved and wanted and valued.

BECAUSE I believe with my whole heartmindbody that girls constitute a revolutionary soul force that can, and will change the world for real.

Figure 1.2: Riot Grrrl Manifesto

Bikini Kill, which arguably became the best known of the riot grrrl bands, produced many self-released singles and records with such titles as "Revolution Girl Style Now!" (Bikini Kill, 1991). Revolution Girl Style Now became an organizing concept for the movement. In an interview with *The Houston Chronicle*, one riot grrrl further explained the phrase's meaning:

> "Revolution Girl Style Now is about reclaiming all the rights you should have had since the day you were born—to be respected, to have a guaranteed place in society as opposed to being left out," says Tiffany Fabian, 19, of San Francisco. "It's 'girl style' because we're not playing by boys' rules anymore. And 'now' because we're not waiting." (qtd. in Busico, 1992, p. 3)

The riot grrrls' feminist aims and intentions manifested in song lyrics, in which bands like Bikini Kill sang about their admiration for other girls, expressed anger about the betrayals of lovers, explored lesbian and heterosexual desire and agency, and grappled with feminist politics. As Kearney (1998) noted, "The songs of performers associated with riot grrrl courageously assert the bold voice lacking in many adolescent girls, thus challenging them to speak out and fight back" (Kearney, 1998, p. 159). Many riot grrrls spoke out by creating their own zines and even forming bands, regardless of musical training—reflecting the punk ethos that one need not have experience to be a punk musician.

The riot grrrls' anger about the societal subordination of women and girls was also palpable in their performance practices, which often included outrageous acts. For example, some would leave their midriffs bare and scrawl words like "slut" and "whore" across their stomachs with Sharpies or lipstick. Riot grrrls would also sometimes wear clothing and accessories for little girls—such as bright plastic barrettes—alongside punk accoutrements, such as combat boots. These stylings were intended to be subversive and ironic. Girls were protesting their own objectification, disrupting the male gaze and claiming ownership of their own bodies and sexualities.

Two excerpts from riot grrrl zines, quoted by Chideya, Rossi, and Hannah (1992), underscore the feminist implications of riot grrrl practices for female sexuality. "[Riot grrrl] Hopper writes, 'SEX ISN'T DIRTY . . . AND IT ISN'T UNLESS SOMEONE IS FORCING IT ON YOU.'" The fanzine *Hungry* is even more explicit: "'SLUT. Yeah, I'm a slut. My body belongs to me. I sleep with who I want . . . I'm not your property'" (p. 84). Seen through this lens, scrawling "slut" or "whore" on one's body is a way of taking ownership of a slur in an attempt to deflate it—much the same as embracing the word "girl," rescuing it from trivializing connotations. Despite this logic, the riot grrrl fashions and trend of writing on oneself would lead to unwelcome notoriety in the media, which fixated on their surprisingly non-normative behaviors and outfits, as we will see later.

Some riot grrrl bands also declared the mosh pits at their concerts female-only in an expression of separatist politics (Kearney, 2006, p. 82). This resulted in some amount of backlash from men in the punk rock scene, but Kearney (1998) explained, "Though their 'don't need you'/'grrrls only' stance is often misinterpreted as 'male bashing' and reverse sexism, as Dawn writes in her zine *Function*, '[R]iot G[rrrl] is meant to be empowering for grrrls, having a safe comfortable space to speak out openly against anything'" (p. 156).

Within the riot grrrl movement, music was not its members' only interest. Some riot grrrls were not that interested in punk, focusing primarily on zines and activism. Thus, many riot grrrls—punk rockers or not—drew upon feminist practices from the 1960s and 1970s, holding meetings to discuss current issues and politics in feminist consciousness-raising style. As Kearney (2006) summarizes:

> Much like the consciousness-raising groups initiated by feminists in the late 1960s, these Riot Grrrl meetings allowed female youth to explore their experiences of sexism, misogyny, and homosexuality, often considered taboo discussion material in mixed company, much less the various clubs they frequented that were dominated by straight male punks. Indeed, for many of the girls involved, these meetings presented the first opportunity to connect personal experience to larger systemic problems, such as patriarchy and heterocentrism. By helping to construct a community built on female solidarity, Riot Grrrl meetings were a powerful rejection of dominant society's encouragement for girls to compete with one another. (p. 60)

In areas where such meetings were held, riot grrrl "chapters" formed. Local chapters communicated their ideas with other chapters through zines and, eventually, via conventions and conferences (see Kearney, 2006, p. 64), creating a loose-knit nationwide network. This loose-knit nature was a defining characteristic of riot grrrl; as a movement, riot grrrl was relatively fragmented—especially in comparison with mainstream organizing efforts going on around the same time, such as those spearheaded by the AAUW and the Ms. Foundation. Bikini Kill singer Kathleen Hanna, who found herself "the face of riot grrrl" (Halpin, 201 though she didn't intend to be, has offered insights about this fragmentation recent interview, she asserted, "I can't really define riot grrrl, because the whole idea is that each person gets to define it for herself. In the '90s, it was a loose-knit group of feminist artists, musicians, writers, punk-rock instigators, and promoters who were all pushing politics back into punk rock" (Halpin, 2010, p. 73).

Although there were many differences among riot grrrls, they frequently railed against the status of girls in the broader society. Many riot grrrls were from white, middle-class families (Chideya, Rossi, and Hannah, 1992; Snead, 1992; Kearney, 2006, p. 67; Meltzer, 2010). Although women of other races and social classes were involved in riot grrrl, they seem to have been in the minority. Mimi Nguyen (2010) has reflected that, problematically, retellings of the riot grrrl story have often included women of color "as an afterthought, as additive, as interruption, as reactionary" (para. 2). Perhaps because of the most visible riot grrrls' relatively privileged backgrounds, members of the movement often "felt like they had the higher calling of rescuing girls' lives and identities and trying to restore the self-esteem of women at a young age" (Meltzer, 2010, p. 31). As Tobi Vail recalled, "We really did sit down and say, 'How can we change what it means to be a girl?' and 'How can we reinvent feminism for our generation?' and we actually came up with a plan and implemented it" (qtd. in Meltzer, 2010, p. 13). Recently, Vail (2010, Oct. 13) also reflected on the limitations of these efforts:

> It is important to ask who felt included in riot grrl* and who didn't. It was not for everybody. There was this idea that it was inclusive because 'anybody could do it' and anybody could decide what a riot grrl was (in theory at least), but because not everyone has equal access to information, resources and leisure time, dominant hierarchies reproduced themselves in riot grrl, just as they have throughout the history of feminism. (para. 11)

Kearney (1998) has noted the earnestness of the riot grrrls in their mission of rescuing girls and reinventing feminism. She wrote, "Sarah, a riot grrrl from Washington, DC, interviewed by *off our backs*, indicates how riot grrrl's political activism begins with individual responsibility: 'I want a revolution, but that's too big for me . . . So I'm going to do my own personal revolution. If every girl does her own personal revolution, we don't need a big one'" (p. 161). Elsewhere, Kearney (2006) has quoted Corrine Tucker, a member of the riot grrrl band Heavens to Betsy, as speaking of riot grrrl's political agenda: "The whole point of riot grrrl is that we were able to rewrite feminism for the 21st century. We took those ideas and rewrote them in our own vernacular" (p. 64). part of this vernacular, the reclamation and reconceptualization of the word "girl" held significance. Leonard (2007) has argued that the invention of the term "grrrl" was of central importance to this riot grrrl network:

> The utilization of the neologism 'grrrl' sets the agenda for this network. The traditional feminist insistence on the use of the term 'woman' has, it can be argued,

to some extent reduced the value of the term 'girl'. Where 'woman' has been equated with an empowered feminist adult, 'girls', defined by their immaturity, have been depoliticised. Riot grrrl was then a reclamation of the word 'girl' and a representation of it as a wholly positive term: 'she [a grrrl] can do anything she wants . . . she (you) are [*sic*] a powerful person to the degree that you can hold the powers that enable you to be free of a lot of things—sexism, phat-ism, racism, homophobia' (*Notta Babe!* #1: 46). The term 'grrrl' was invested with a new set of connotations. It signified a feisty, assertive girl or woman, who relished a political engagement with feminist issues. [. . .] Those involved with the network celebrated the use of the term riot grrrl as an empowering label. (p. 117)

Overall, the riot grrrls' tactics defied the cultural scripts expected of girls. Their discourse on girlhood was something new. Disrupting the mainstream presentation of girls as passive, weak, conventionally pretty, and in need of saving, they asserted that girls had power—the ability to do it all themselves. As Kearney (1998) notes, the Bikini Kill song "Don't Need You" made this stance clear:

"Don't need you to say we're cute / Don't need you to say we're alright / Don't need your protection / Don't need no kiss goodnight / Us girls don't need you . . ." Although the song is directed to boys, I would argue that we can also hear these words as an address to others who feel it is their role to both protect girls and affirm their behavior. Heard this way, the song can be understood as representative of riot grrrls' separatism not only from males, but also from adults, especially older women who all too often (and all too problematically) speak for girls in the name of "women," "feminism," and "sisterhood." (p. 148).

Tobi Vail and Kathleen Hanna of Bikini Kill coined the phrase "girl power" in this context. It was a slogan meant for use on concert flyers and zines (Meltzer, 2010, p. 17). The idea was not intended for the mainstream marketplace; it circulated within the riot grrrl and punk rock countercultures. When the riot grrrl movement went international within a year of its formation, "girl power" spread alongside it, appearing in the phrase "Totally Girl Powered" on British riot grrrl band Huggy Bear's 1993 tour t-shirt (Leonard, 2007, p. 156).

As a slogan, "girl power" signified that girls had true power. "Girl power" was about solidarity and girls' self-worth. Protesting girls' conceptualization as immature, helpless, and lacking feminist consciousness, riot grrrls argued that they could take care of themselves. They could assert themselves, be political, and heal their own wounds. They didn't need males or older women to guide or tend them; they could do it for themselves. Realizing oneself as an individual with agency and power is one of the true benefits of feminism, and riot grrrl's self-actualizing potential suggests that for those who had access to riot grrrl, it often felt positive and healthy to engage with the movement.

Misrepresentations: Riot Grrrls in the News

Music journalists on the lookout for the next hot trend noticed the spread of riot grrrl from its provenance in Olympia, Washington. [5] With the work being undertaken by the AAUW, however, the mainstream media and their readers were becoming primed for the idea that girls were in crisis. Therefore, because the punk rock manifestations of riot grrrl defied societal expectations of girls—they dressed provocatively to make a statement about girls' objectification, they ejected boys from grrrl-only spaces, and they screamed obscenities in their lyrics—they were misunderstood by many journalists and readers as girls in crisis themselves. Their performance practices were meant as a protest against their own objectification, a disruption of the male gaze, but they contained so many levels of irony and cultural criticism that their intended meanings became garbled, made unintelligible by many media outlets. It is easy to understand how the uninformed might have read the riot grrrls' ironic gestures as manifestations of deep psychic pain.

The major articles about riot grrrl directed negative attention towards the movement. In August 1992, a *USA Today* article opened: "Better watch out, boys. From hundreds of once pink, frilly bedrooms, comes the young feminist revolution. And it's not pretty. But it doesn't wanna be. So there!" (Snead, 1992, p. 5D). After this trivializing lead, the article proceeded to dwell on a scene observed at a riot grrrl event that seems intended to shock and titillate readers:

A punk girl musical group called Cheesecake screams a full-throttle manifesto: "Better watch what you say! I might have a gun! Don't make fun of my hair! Don't make fun of my clothes! Better watch what you say! I might have a knife!"

A scrawny boy stands by, watching the group and the bouncing sea of mohawked female fans in Pucci-print minis. They sport hairy legs, army boots and tattoos.

Finally, he yells: "Punk rock is just an excuse for ugly girls to get on stage!"

In seconds, he's surrounded by an angry mob of girls, hopping and slam-dancing in a frenzy. He bolts to safety, chased by their jeers. (Snead, 1992, p. 5D)

By calling the boy "scrawny" and describing the girls in masculine terms—hairy-legged, tattooed, and wearing army boots—readers were led to sympathize with the boy. Because of this rhetorical strategy, the boy's comment was not interpreted for the reader as a signal of male privilege, which afforded this youth the opportunity to bring misogynistic taunts to a feminist event. Nor was his comment interpreted as part of the reason riot grrrl existed—as a response to the sexism girls faced in daily life, constantly judged against impossible beauty ideals. Instead, the writer suggested the wildness of the girls with a sort of *Lord of the Flies* sensibility, encouraging readers to fear what havoc these otherworldly, brutish girls might wreak upon boys.

Other news articles would similarly foreground the image of uncouth, threatening young women, failing to frame the coverage in terms of girls resisting sexism. An October 1992 article in *The Oregonian*, describing the ascendence of riot grrrl in Portland, began:

> Think of Gloria Steinem with a nose ring: That's the image that Riot Grrrls conjure up with their anger, their energy and their direction.
>
> It adds up to feminist punk and it's coming, just maybe, to a young woman near you. (Schraw, 1992, p. L10)

The next summer, a *Rolling Stone* article upped the ante on the "young woman near you" theme. In an article called "Grrrls at war," Kim France's (1993) lead paragraph addressed parents:

> Like she devils out of Rush Limbaugh's worst nightmare, a battery of young women with guitars, drums and a generous dose of rage stampeded into popular consciousness earlier this year. They do things like scrawl SLUT and RAPE across their torsos before gigs, produce fanzines with names like *Girl Germs*, and hate the media's guts. They're called riot grrrls, and they've come for your daughters. (p. 23)

These provocative descriptions demonstrate how riot grrrls' potential as a means to feminist liberation was invisible to many outside the counterculture. The descriptions once more set riot grrrl up as a threat—not to scrawny boys who like to jeer at girls, but to the readers' innocent little daughters. Fixated on the grrrls' provocative appearance, but devoid of context, such discourse created exploitative, sensationalist effect—a reminder of how difficult it is for young women to attempt to critique sexual objectification while simultaneously communicating their rights as sexual agents. As Aapola, Gonick, and Harris (2005) have noted, "A young woman can, in the sexual discourses available, either want sex or love; not both; she is presented as either a good girl or a bad girl; it is difficult to find a position that would not exclude one or the other" (p. 151). And indeed, the media presented the riot grrrls as bad girls, dichotomously opposed to readers' daughters—who presumably are good girls.

Note further the penultimate sentence of the last blockquote—that the riot grrrls "hate the media's guts." This was one of the paradoxes of the riot grrrl movement: although the riot grrrls presented themselves in ways that seemed calculated to provoke attention, the grrrls rejected attention as unwanted. [6] On the one hand, many riot grrrls had a positive relationship with *Sassy* magazine, a mainstream teen magazine seen as a feminist alternative to *Seventeen* and its ilk, which helped deliver riot grrrl ideas to a broader audience of interested young girls (Part of the appeal was that *Sassy* gave riot grrrls a voice in the magazine's production; it even published several reader-produced issues, sometimes featuring riot grrrls as guest editors.) But on the other hand, in mainstream news media and music magazines, the coverage had been rampant with errors, assumptions, and incorrect conclusions. For example, a *Newsweek* article incorrectly reported that Kathleen Hanna represented "the extreme edge of the Grrrls' rage" because she was "a victim of rape and child abuse" (Chideya, Rossi, and Hannah, 1992, p. 84).

Between such mischaracterizations and a desire to maintain underground credibility, the most popular riot grrrl bands declared a media blackout, denying all interview requests. One reporter for the *Houston Chronicle* who telephoned Kathleen Hanna to request an interview quoted Hanna's response:

> Hanna won't answer any questions. She and other Riot Grrrls take the revolution very seriously, and they have instituted a "press block," she explains angrily.
>
> "Our integrity is being taken away by the media and the powers of exploitation," she says. "You should respect us as an underground movement. The nicest thing you could do is not write an article about us. Or have a blank space where the article would be—that would be even nicer."
>
> And then she hangs up. (Busico, 1992, p. 3)

The riot grrrls thus found themselves in a double bind. They would not speak with the media because they were tired of being misrepresented and exploited; but unless they spoke with the media, they would nevertheless continue to be misrepresented and exploited. Feminist authors who had been writing about girls' issues were sympathetic to the situation, however. Naomi Wolf expressed support for the riot grrrl form of activism in a *Newsweek* article (Chideya, Rossi, and Hannah, 1992), as did Lyn Mikel Brown in a *New York Times* article. She explained, "To be openly resistant is to invite trouble. These are the girls who get sent to therapy or get kicked out of school" (qtd. in Japenga, 1992, p. 30). In the end, however, the

riot grrrls chose to stick with integrity. Besides ignoring the media, they also rejected the advances of major music labels. As McDonnell (1993) noted in *Billboard*,

> Large record companies are not seen as such safe spaces. "Most girls who ID them-
> selves as Riot GRRLS, I don't think any of them would want to be on a major,"
> says Candice Pedersen, who co-runs the Olympia-based indie K Records, home
> to such women-led bands as Mecca Normal and Tiger Trap. "The ultimate polit-
> ical statement is they're not for sale.'" (p. 1)

In short, riot grrrl protests—especially those of the visually shocking variety—
could be repackaged into compelling sound bites that sold newspapers and magazines, but these frequently lacked complexity and context. Thus, in many cases,
riot grrrls were misinterpreted and sensationalized, presented as angry girls to be
worried *about*: good (white) girls, from good (middle-class) families, who had
turned foul-mouthed and provocative—flaunting deviant sexualities in a cry for
help, not an act of resistance. Any diversity among them was flattened in the
interest of a compelling narrative, scalable to sound-bite size. It appeared the riot
grrrls were not empowered and speaking for themselves; instead, they were misrepresented as another type of girl in crisis. Adults had been advocating for girls'
empowerment, but many never expected it to look like *that*.

This points to some problems with girl crisis as a dominant discourse of girlhood. Although chronologically the riot grrrls' media coverage occurred before the
girl crisis hit bookstores, the cultural reception of the riot grrrls suggests that the
concept of girlhood as a time of crisis was too flexible a concept—capable of
explaining too much. Acts of strength and empowerment could too readily be misinterpreted as acts of girls in crisis. It was too easy to pathologize girls who subverted normative femininity, rather than recognize that perhaps they had found a valid
way to demonstrate that not all girls are vulnerable—that some girls do not need
their selves saved by others. The multiplicity of experiences is important to remember. Although one discourse about girlhood may dominate at a given time, girls'
actual lived experiences are a multiplicity of girlhoods—a range of experiences.
While some girls may have been psychologically crippled by their socialization, not
every girl was. For various reasons, some were able to withstand the toxic aspects
of our culture, emerging as strong women with intact self-esteem and powerful voices. The feminist perspective of the riot grrrls seemed to facilitate this.

Ultimately, the riot grrrls turned away from the media's glare, focusing instead
on their grassroots work meant to subvert the status quo: performing their music,
producing zines, organizing chapters and holding conferences. Although people
continue to identify as riot grrrls today, the riot grrrl movement eventually fell off

the media radar. The mainstream had tasted riot grrrl, however. Though often mis-understood, girl power and other components of riot grrrl, like angry lyrics, sex-ually provocative posturing, and the appropriation of little girls' clothing, dangled like low fruit—ripe for the picking.

Notes

*   In riot grrrl literature, "grrrl" is sometimes also written as "grrl," with two rs instead of three

1.   The report was also cited in other articles related to girls' issues and follow-up stories about schools' attempts to close the gender gap (e.g., Van Tassel, 1992; Lombardi, 1993).

2.   Take Our Daughters to Work Day was the object of some antifeminist backlash, which charged that the program practiced reverse sexism by giving girls an opportunity not afforded to boys. The expansion to include boys addressed this concern, but the backlash continues.

3.   Zines—independently produced, self-published magazines or fanzines—typically take the form of a small pamphlet—often 1/4 or 1/2 the size of a full sheet of letter-sized paper—that has been inexpensively photocopied. Zine-writers often trade their zines with other zine writers, or give them away to their friends and acquaintances, or sell them for a nominal fee. In the riot grrrl scene, zines also may be sold at concerts or conventions, by mail subscription, or on consign-ment at independent shops (Kearney, 2006, p. 71–2). The internet—giving people the ability to blog on any number of platforms, sometimes within communities like LiveJournal—has cut into the production of zines; but at the same time, it has found a larger audience for printed zines, for they are now sold online in various internet shops, including Etsy.com.

4.   Examples are the May 1991 Washington, D.C. Riot in the Mount Pleasant neighborhood (a response to the police shooting of a Salvadorean man during a Cinco de Mayo celebration) and the 1992 Los Angeles riots (in the aftermath of the brutal police beating of Rodney King, an African-American man).

5.   Nirvana, Pearl Jam, and other once-indie bands from the Pacific Northwest had recently become mainstream megastars, so the region's vibrant music scene seemed worth watching.

6.   Tobi Vail (2010, Sept. 28) has recently reminded the readers of her blog that in the early 1990s, riot grrrls like herself thought their zines were ephemeral. For all intents and purposes, the inter-net did not yet exist in 1992, and zine writers never imagined their words would circulate and live forever online. At that time, zines felt more like private conversations between friends. For example, Vail printed only 35 copies of issue five of her *Jigsaw* zine. "Even though that fanzine seems like it may have been written for a lot of people to read," she explained, "I tried to keep it a secret." (Vail, 2010, Sept. 28). Negotiating the line between private and public—private zines, public band performances—proved complex for many in the movement.

2

Girl Power Goes Pop
The Spice Girls and Marketed Empowerment

"I being of sound mind and new Wonderbra do solemnly promise to cheer and dance and zigazig-ah. Ariba! Girl Power!"
—*The Spice Girls' "Power Oath" (1997)* [1]

"It's probably a fair assumption to say that 'zigazig-ha' is not Spice short-hand for 'subvert the dominant paradigm.'"
—*Jennifer L. Pozner, Soujourner: The Women's Forum (1998)*

According to the AAUW, the Ms. Foundation, and authors like Orenstein and Pipher, girls in the 1990s were hurting—the victims of systematically sexist cultural norms. As girls approached adolescence, society expected them to change their behaviors, attitudes, and appearances. The world told them to be submissive, meek, silent and weak, while looking conventionally pretty and watching their weight, to be heteronormatively attractive without being too sexual or provocative.

The riot grrrls devised their own solution to this problem: opting out of the mainstream culture to create their own counterculture. The young women of the movement rebelliously defied cultural expectations. They were loud, assertive, and strong, and they often refused to look conventionally pretty—instead drawing from a punk rock vocabulary as they created a new style. They mixed and matched girlish things, like knee-high stockings, baby barrettes, and pigtails, with elements that culturally signified masculinity, such as combat boots, tattoos, and piercings.

They dyed their hair unnatural colors and used their bodies as canvases for words of protest. With a relish for disrupting gender norms and the male gaze, some riot grrrls displayed sexually charged behavior for subversive and ironic reasons. Being shockingly provocative in protest was their calling card.

As a result, mainstream U.S. society often failed to comprehend the riot grrrls and their discourse on girlhood. Though adults worried about adolescent girls, the riot grrrls' solution—protesting and disrupting the status quo with an in-your-face, "don't need you" attitude—was so extraordinary that it was difficult for outsiders to parse. Their displays of aggression and sexual agency shocked and titillated the mainstream media. The riot grrrls' protests, steeped in irony and sarcasm, often were misunderstood as cries for help from wounded girls in crisis. Fixated upon these visuals, outsiders could not see the forest for the trees: the riot grrrls were bucking the problematic, prohibitive cultural norms for girls' behavior, attitude and appearance, and trying to save themselves in the process.

The British perspective on riot grrrl apparently differed. British riot grrrl bands, such as Huggy Bear—with whom Bikini Kill toured Britain and released a joint album, *Yeah Yeah Yeah Yeah*, in 1993—allegedly fascinated their nation. *Rolling Stone* characterized it as an obsession:

> By last fall [Huggy Bear] was attracting constant attention from Britain's two week-ly music newspapers, *Melody Maker* and *New Musical Express*. While the American riot-grrrl phenomenon was treated as a curiosity in the press, England ate it up, and to riot or not became a cultural preoccupation. (France, 1993, p. 24)

To riot or not: this debate offered choice, making the British mediated discussion of riot grrrl different from that in the U.S. Some critics loved the riot grrrls; others despised them. Whereas American media almost uniformly implied that rioting was disordered behavior to avoid, in England—home to a long-thriving punk scene—some British media presented riot grrrl as more than a form of deviance. It was worthy of discussion.

Shortly thereafter, a female British pop duo, Shampoo, co-opted the girl power slogan from the British riot grrrls. In 1994, Shampoo became a hit in England and, especially, in Japan. Several Shampoo singles reached positions in the top 25 in both countries that year. These included a popular song called "Girl Power," which peaked at #25 in the U.K. charts and #22 in Japan and helped bring the concept of "Girl Power" to prominence. As articulated in their angry lyrics, Shampoo's version of girl power was about girls doing what they want with their own lives—whether that meant behaving childishly, or toying with weapons, or being violent, or just dropping out—and chiding those who might suggest they were trying to be boys. In other words, their girl power called for a multifaceted expansion of the behaviors available to girls, and as their song ironically emphasized negative behaviors, girl power meant having a bad attitude for a good reason.

When the Spice Girls adopted girl power, however, their use of the slogan became the shot heard around the world. The Spice Girls had formed in 1994, created in reaction to the popularity of boy bands in the pop music world (Sinclair, 2004). Once together, the Spice Girls spent two years honing their act, shopping for management, securing a contract with a major label (EMI subsidiary Virgin Records), and producing their first album, *Spice* (1996). In the U.S., *Spice* would become the highest-selling album of 1997. It would ultimately sell 23 million copies globally, a record still unrivaled by any other all-female group.

As the Spice Girls' popularity skyrocketed throughout 1997, so did girl power's. The Spice Girls used the phrase "girl power" in countless related ventures and merchandise. One of the official Spice Girls t-shirts was a baby-doll-style (slim-fitting) tee, featuring "GIRL POWER" across the front in enormous block lettering. Keychains, pins, and scores of other official Spice Girls items followed suit—including a line of dolls released by toy manufacturer Galoob, which prominently featured "Girl Power" on the front of the box. The official Spice Girls magazine, *Spice*, frequently used "girl power" in teasers on the cover; for example the third issue in fall of 1997 featured in large type, "Girl Power to the MAX." The Spice Girls also created a one-hour television special, later released to VHS, called *One Hour of Girl Power*, and a bestselling book, simply called *Girl Power*. *Girl Power* sold 200,000 copies the day of its release and would go on to sell over a million copies, with translations into more than twenty languages.

As a result, with the Spice Girls' unparalleled global popularity, the concept of girl power shifted from a subcultural, don't-need-you rallying cry to a mainstream catchphrase that became popular among the Spice Girls' primary audience of 6- to 13-year old girls. Furthermore, the band attempted to make itself synonymous with girl power. They were so successful in this effort that their entire body of work informed girl power's conceptual evolution. Therefore, after the Spice Girls went on hiatus in 2001, effectively splitting up until their reunion tour began in 2007, new girl power products and texts derived more from the Spice Girls than from the riot grrrls. For this reason, it is useful to analyze the Spice Girls' contributions to mainstream girl power discourse. Their reign was a pivotal moment in the continuing evolution of cultural discourses on girlhood. Focusing primarily on the Spice Girls' products that featured the phrase "girl power," I explore girl power's meaning according to the Spice Girls. I then briefly discuss girl power's further evolution—its life after the Spice Girls.

The Spice Girls and Girl Power

Five female singer/dancers comprised the Spice Girls (see Figure 2.1). Each band member had a pithy, tongue-in-cheek nickname: Victoria Adams (now Beckham) was nicknamed Posh Spice; Melanie Brown, or Mel B, was nicknamed Scary Spice; Emma Bunton was called Baby Spice; Melanie Chisholm, aka Mel C, was called Sporty Spice; and Geri Halliwell went by Ginger Spice. As the nicknames suggested, each band member embraced a differentiated identity, rather than the uniform look of girl groups of the 1960s, such as the Shangri-Las and the Angels (Douglas, 1995). Reinforced by each member's unique style of dress, hair and make-up, and reported interests, each Spice Girl was easily identifiable to and memorable for members of the band's pre-teen audience.

Figure 2.1: The Spice Girls. Left to right: Emma Bunton, Melanie Brown, Geri Halliwell, Victoria Adams, and Melanie Chisholm ©Columbia Pictures Corporation. Photographer: Christophe Gstadler. Courtesy of PhotoFest.

The Spice Girls carefully positioned themselves as role models for their audience; they (and their ghostwriter)[2] stated this desire openly in their bestselling book *Girl Power*, writing: "We want young girls at school to relate to us, to be one of us. Kids can smell bullshit. We want to be positive role models for young girls and women" (The Spice Girls, 1997, p. 57). Therefore, they frequently sought to inspire their fans. For example, in *Spiceworld*—the Spice Girls' (1997) second book, based on their movie of the same name—Mel C, aka Sporty Spice, said, "The thing with Spice Girls is that all our dreams have come true. We think that if there's anything in the world that you can imagine you want to do, if you really want to do it, you can. We wanted to be pop stars and we were, so we thought, all right then, let's be movie stars as well! If you don't have a go, then you never know" (p. 94). Embracing the idea that they are role models is counter to how many superstars have handled their celebrity status; many have not wanted the responsibility that stating "I consider myself a role model" would entail.

As role models, the Spice Girls were particularly interested in demonstrating how to embody girl power. For example, on the packaging for Galoob's "Girl Power" line of Spice Girls dolls, the back side of each doll's box featured her corresponding Spice Girl's answer to the question, "What is girl power?" On her doll's box, Geri stated, "Projecting a positive attitude and energy. Believing in yourself and supporting each other—that's Girl Power and it works for me!" In this manner, from the release of their first album, *Spice*, the Spice Girls' promotions were as much about girl power as music. Consider the television commercial *Spice*. The song "Say you'll be there" played in the background, while the various Spice Girls took turns appearing in front of the camera. Emma said, "She who dares wins." Mel B said, "Watch out, lads! The girls are here." Geri asked, "What you looking at, boy? Girl power's coming at ya." The girls' statements were largely drawn from pithy, upbeat, pro-girl phrases found in the liner notes to *Spice*. Along with the ideas expressed in the Spice Girls' songs and by the Spice Girls themselves, these phrases can be read as the bundle of concepts Geri referred to in the commercial when she said, "Girl power's coming at ya." The liner notes' pro-girl phrases read as follows:

- WONDERWOMAN
- THIS VIBE IS CONTAGIOUS, FEEL IT, CATCH IT
- IT'S A GIRL'S WORLD
- SHE WHO DARES WINS
- IT'S A GIRL THANG
- COME ON BABY

- THE SPICE SQUAD ARE HERE
- WHAT YOU LOOKING AT BOY?
- CAN YOU HANDLE A SPICE GIRL?
- SILENCE IS GOLDEN BUT SHOUTING IS FUN
- FREEDOM FIGHTERS
- FUTURE IS FEMALE
- SPICE REVOLUTION

As signifiers of the Spice Girls' version of girl power, these phrases suggested that if a fan embraced girl power, then she could be like the Spice Girls: a person both strong and fun, looking to disrupt the status quo in a sassy, attractive way.

In the liner notes of *Spice*, "girl power" appeared only once, in the signature beneath Geri's photo. Her autograph read, "Girl power! Love, Geri xx" (Spice Girls, 1996). Geri has been credited as the group's chief proponent of girl power; she used the phrase most often. Robert Sandall, who was head of press at Virgin Records while the Spice Girls were popular, reflected: "[The Spice Girls] were a sounding board for a change that came over young girls at that time. Girl Power—it sounds like a dumb slogan. But it did actually contain a hard kernel of truth. There was this emergent sense that youngish girls were a newly empowered group. There was a sociopolitical message built into their appeal. And you have to give Geri credit for identifying that" (qtd. in Sinclair, 2004, p. 76).

The Spice Girls' debut single, "Wannabe," contained one facet of the Spice Girls' sociopolitical message. It was an upbeat, catchy anthem to the primacy of girls' friendships over romantic relationships. The Spice Girls sang that "friendship never ends"—so if someone wanted to date one of them, he needed to be friends with all of them. The concept spoke to a problematic and real pattern in girl culture, which feminists have often critiqued: through popular culture texts such as teen magazines, girls are often encouraged to compete for boys, rather than maintain friendships with each other (McRobbie, 2000). This divide-and-conquer strategy hinders attempts at female solidarity, thereby maintaining the status quo.

"Wannabe's" cheerful tone and sense of camaraderie resonated with pre-teen girls around the world. According to Sandall, "Whether it was Bangkok, Tokyo, Paris, or Buenos Aires, you got the same gaggle of girls, roughly the same age, all absolutely obsessed with that song" (qtd. in Sinclair, 2004, p. 76). These girls pushed "Wannabe" up the charts, making it an instant hit: Upon its release as a single in the U.S. in January 2007, it debuted on the *Billboard* Hot Chart at #11. This was a major accomplishment, beating the previous record for a U.S. debut by a foreign act, set in 1964 by the Beatles' "I Want to Hold Your Hand" (which debuted at number #18). "Wannabe" then held the number one spot for four weeks, helping to promote record-topping sales of the *Spice* album.

The video for "Wannabe," played in heavy rotation on MTV, laid important groundwork in establishing the band's identity. The video featured the Spice Girls being playfully disruptive, overrunning a building full of stuffy older people. In the video, it was clear from the Spice Girls' behavior that although they were a group of friends, they were unconcerned with being just like one another; they were individuals. The aloofness and pose-striking of Posh Spice, who wore a sophisticated little black dress and styled her dark brown hair in a bob, juxtaposed the sweetness of Baby Spice, whose girlish white dress and white-blonde hair in pigtails winked at innocence. Posh and Baby's dresses were countered by the casual styles of Sporty and Scary Spice: With her curly hair loose and full, Scary Spice wore a tank top and loose-fit pants that allowed her to spread her legs and gyrate while dancing—moves that would have been indecent in a tiny dress. Likewise, Sporty Spice's athletic tank top, track pants, and tight ponytail for her light brown hair afforded her room for displays of athleticism, which included backflips on a table. Finally, in contrast to everyone else, redhead Ginger Spice's sequined leotard, sheer black tights, and platform heels resembled nothing a girl would wear in everyday life. Her outfit evoked the idea of a circus ringmaster—dovetailing cleverly with her persona as unofficial leader of the Spice Girls.

In interviews and official Spice Girls materials, the band members positioned themselves as truly embodying the song: as a group of five friends who stuck together, no matter what, and who recognized the value of friendship. In their *Girl Power* book (1997), several of the Spice Girls reinforced the idea that the song was about their lived experiences as friends. Victoria wrote, "I was engaged, but broke away and found myself and my friends when I realised he wasn't right for me" (p. 7). Emma stated, "I also had a boyfriend and they helped me get rid of him," and Mel C continued, "I was in a pretty bad relationship as well, and he went out the window. We helped each other out to get what we wanted and we gave each other strength" (p. 40). Biographer Sinclair (2004) has marveled that the Spice Girls never deviated from this early path, projecting an image of solidarity to the world even while the band was developing deep rifts.

Although the phrase "girl power" did not appear in the song or video for "Wannabe," the Spice Girls and their management/marketing team began using the phrase "girl power" early on. To understand what the Spice Girls meant by "girl power" requires closely examining their products, which often implied that the Spice Girls and girl power were synonymous. For example, consider the front covers of the Spice Girls' official magazine, *Spice*. Each issue featured the statement

"The only official girl power magazine" across the top of the front cover, right above the title, boldly claiming that the Spice Girls were the only authentic purveyors of girl power in the marketplace. It would have been more accurate to call the magazine the only official Spice Girls magazine—understandable, given the number of unofficial magazines dedicated to the Spice Girls that proliferated during this period. (In fact, the statement was rephrased in exactly that way in Spring 1998, when Geri left the band.) But calling *Spice* the only official girl power magazine was a clever inaccuracy: it implied that the Spice Girls were the only ones who truly embodied girl power. This was reinforced by the U.S. promotional materials for *Spice: The Official Video Volume 1* (which had aired in UK on television as *One Hour of Girl Power*). One ad beckoned to fans: "They don't only talk about girl power, they live it. Just watch!" In interviews, the band's label took these claims a step further. For example, in an interview with *Spin* magazine, Ray Cooper—Virgin U.K.'s co-managing director—asserted the Spice Girls had invented girl power. He said, "They coined it. It's their theme" (qtd. in Goetz, 1997, p. 90). According to such logic, anything the Spice Girls said or did could be construed as signifying girl power—like the friendship ideal communicated in "Wannabe" and the Spice Girls' differentiated identities.

While arguing (rather dishonestly) that the Spice Girls were the creators and sole authentic source of girl power, the Spice Girls' materials additionally suggested that fans of the Spice Girls could embody girl power, too. This was implied by a teaser on the front of *Spice's* second issue from the summer of 1997, which read, "GIRL POWER! Trust it—Use it—Prove it—Groove it!" This teaser was adapted from the lyrics of their hit song "Who Do You Think You Are," which had debuted on the British charts at #1 that spring and subsequently became a commercial success throughout Europe. (Note that the lyrics did not feature the phrase "girl power.") As a magazine teaser, its meaning can be unpacked and interpreted as follows: "Girl power, which we Spice Girls (and our magazine) embody, is something you can trust. It's for real. If you follow in our footsteps, you can use girl power, too. You'll prove to yourself and others that girl power is valuable and empowering—and you'll have fun while doing so!"

Just what defined this form of "girl power," however, was not overtly clear. "Girl power" as part of a magazine teaser or as a slogan on a keychain offered little insight about the phrase's meaning. To learn what the Spice Girls meant by girl power, fans could turn to the Spice Girls' *Girl Power* book, published in 1997. The back cover promised to tell girls "how to get what you really really want," with "all you could ever want to know about growing up, having a laugh, making sense of life." The book opened with a list defining girl power:

GIRL POWER IS WHEN . . .

You help a guy with his bag
You and your mates reply to wolf whistles by shouting 'get your arse out!'
You wear high heels *and* think on your feet
You know you can do it and nothing's going to stop you
You don't wait around for him to call
You stick with your mates and they stick with you
You're loud and proud even when you've broken out in spots
You believe in yourself and control your own life (The Spice Girls, 1997, p. 6)

This list is reminiscent of the riot grrrl manifesto published by Bikini Kill in their eponymous zine (see Figure 1.2 in Chapter 1), despite the comparative brevity of the Spice Girls' list. While Riordan (2001) has cautioned that comparisons between the Spice Girls and the riot grrrls are often made "to condemn one of them" (p. 179), their stylistic similarities beg a comparison—not to condemn, but to illuminate the shifting discourses about girl power and girlhood. What were the Spice Girls saying about girl power, and how did this compare with Bikini Kill's vision for riot grrrl and girl power? Both shared an independent, girls-can-do-anything attitude, stating that girls can be capable, self-directed, and empowered. Both also foregrounded female solidarity. They spoke to the importance of bonds between girls—among friends for the Spice Girls, and within a community for the riot grrrls. Furthermore, both suggested the importance of girls' self-esteem—of having a voice and feeling empowered to use it. Though these ideas were couched in different terms in the two documents, the similarities between them indicated that the Spice Girls' girl power derived from the riot grrrl movement.

Despite these similarities, their differences made clear that in adopting girl power, the Spice Girls were no purists. The band members may not have had more than a passing familiarity with the riot grrrls. Nevertheless, the Spice Girls' adoption of "girl power" and the revisions they made to its meaning can be understood in relation to the riot grrrls who first created the term. The riot grrrls had a countercultural, antisocial bent; they claimed to desire a real revolution against the hegemony of capitalist society. The Spice Girls, however, were a product of the very capitalist system the riot grrrls were critiquing. The band members had been pursuing celebrity within that system for years—in some cases, for much longer than the band had existed. Therefore, the Spice Girls' vision of girl power was virtually unthreatening to the status quo, with nary a hint of a critique of capitalism.

Viewed with a cynical eye, perhaps it is for this reason that the Spice Girls also did not make statements that girls needed to be cultural producers. In the Spice Girls' world, it was just as good—and much more profitable—for girls to buy into the Spice Girls and let the band produce culture on girls' behalf.

Significantly, the Spice Girls' girl power also lacked anger. While the riot grrrls were angry at society for belittling girls as weak, dumb, and insignificant, and whereas Shampoo seemed on the verge of violence when they championed girl power in 1994, the Spice Girls made no suggestions that girls should be angrily disruptive—just playfully so. The Spice Girls' materials did not articulate a clear cultural critique of girls' systematic shortchanging, so what was there to be angry about? In the Spice Girls' version of girl power, politically driven anger was replaced with attitude—a sassy sense of self-assurance, and an assumption that girls had easy access to power. As Pozner (1998) noted, "There's no need for social awareness or activism when woman-centered politics come neatly with a UPC code—membership in the 'Spice Girl Squad,' the liner notes coax, grants 'instant girl power'" (p. 47). Furthermore, as media coverage of the riot grrrls had proven, female displays of anger could be alienating and misunderstood, feeding into long-standing stereotypes that women who show more emotion than is culturally acceptable are either hysterical or bitches (or both). Having a sassy attitude seemed a safer option, one that could even be fun—especially when it not only appealed to girls but also turned on men.

In short, the changes to the construction of girl power seem rooted in two interrelated factors: the Spice Girls' target audience, and their wish for mainstream success. The Spice Girls and their marketing/management team knew their fan base was young. Focused, less abstract, happier statements made these concepts easier for pre-teen girls to comprehend, and perhaps even to embrace a can-do attitude in their own lives. Importantly, they also made the concept of "girl power" less likely to cause parental concern than it did in the hands of the riot grrrls. The U.S. media had shown that anger and provocatively "unfeminine" visual displays would alienate and offend many in the mainstream. The Spice Girls walked a fine line: they appropriated the facets of the riot grrrl movement that were easily intelligible, discarding anything that might hinder their pursuit and maintenance of celebrity—the politics, the criticisms, the masculine stylings, the misunderstood behaviors and displays of angry aggression. The major cultural criticism the Spice Girls shared with the riot grrrls was the most socially acceptable: the need for girls to feel empowered, as evidenced by the AAUW reports, the work of the Ms. Foundation, and the plethora of books about the girl crisis.

Criticisms and Mixed-Message Feminism

Despite the fact that the Spice Girls' discourse featured empowerment rhetoric without much grounding in feminist critique, the band and their management team used their *Girl Power* book to construct the Spice Girls as feminist revolutionaries. *Girl Power* featured dozens of quotes randomly scattered across its pages, whose layout was vaguely evocative of a glossy zine. Among the many quotes, one statement attributed to Geri read, "We're about unity and solidarity between female friends" (p. 34). Another Geri quote read, "I'm an expressive person, very outspoken, I feel like a freedom-fighter trying to give girls the right to express themselves" (p. 69). A quote attributed to Emma read, "I expect an equal relationship" (p. 7), and another unattributed quote stated, "It's looking at yourself in the mirror and saying, 'This is me . . . I'm not going to be dominated by anyone, especially not men'" (p. 37). These concepts—solidarity, freedom-fighting, equality, male domination—are all feminist vocabulary terms that constructed the Spice Girls as a feminist cultural product for girls. Additionally, drawing upon the idea of a feminist revolution, the Spice Girls used the term "revolution" in their liner notes and to promote their feature film, *Spiceworld: The Movie.* [3] The film's theatrical posters featured the tagline, "You say you want a revolution?"—implying that *Spiceworld* and the band were the answer to that desire.

Yet when the word "feminism" appears in *Girl Power*, their relationship with it is tenuous at best. For example, the book's centerfold—a poster of the five Spice Girls lying provocatively on a bed, eyes closed with their hands near their crotches—featured this unattributed quote: "Feminism has become a dirty word. Girl Power is just a Nineties way of saying it. We can give feminism a kick up the arse. Women can be so powerful when they show solidarity" (The Spice Girls, 1997, n.p.). An article in *The Independent* found it problematic that these words were ghostwritten by a man and chosen to accompany a seductive photo taken by a man (Padel, 1997, p. 19). The sentiment is confusing: Does it argue that feminism is good or bad? In another rare instance in which the word "feminist" appears, the following quote is attributed to Emma: "Of course I'm a feminist. But I could never burn my wonderbra. I'm nothing without it!" (The Spice Girls, 1997, p. 15). Attempting to unpack either quote is problematic, for they are presented as acontextual stand-alone items in *Girl Power*, devoid of explanation. Consider the latter quote, assuming—for argument's sake—that the words originated with Emma, rather than a ghost writer or manager. Does Emma's self-esteem really disappear when her breasts aren't padded, or is she using hyperbole? Are we to read her statement as ironic? Tongue-in-cheek? Earnest? (And does she really believe the myth that second-wave feminists burned their bras?) Perhaps the lack of context is exact-

ly the point. It makes the rhetoric polysemic, easily open to a few different interpretations, depending on the reader's position. Commercially, this is a valuable strategy, for it is inclusive of a broader potential audience. But it offended many
feminists, including Pozner (1998), who sniped, "The revolution, when it comes,
will not be sparked by a Wonderbra" (p. 48). Moreover, in considering the Spice
Girls' target audience, polysemy is dangerous territory. Pre-adolescent children
developmentally have a difficult time comprehending irony—and if taken at face
value, Emma's sentiment reads like an imperative, rooted in societal expectations
and intertwined with underlying self-esteem issues.

This relates to another source of mixed messages: the Spice Girls' self-
presentation. In their version of girl power, the production of normative femininity was considered a means to empowerment. Playing against the stereotype that
feminists are unattractive by conventional standards—frizzy-haired, hairy-legged,
bra-burning hags—the Spice Girls suggested that playing with a feminine appearance can be empowering, for girls' pleasure only. *Girl Power* quoted Victoria, the
poshest Spice Girl, as saying, "If I want to wear a tiny skirt and a bikini top then
I'm doing it for me, not for any men who are watching" (The Spice Girls, 2007,
p. 56). Furthermore, with liner-note phrases like "What you looking at boy?" and
"Get your arse out!" directed at imagined male onlookers, the Spice Girls attempted to disrupt the male privilege that assumed girls were there for men to look at.
Yet despite this intention, the Spice Girls appealed to a male gaze. Photographs and
videos of the Spice Girls neatly minimized the impact of their feminism. When situated among glossy photos of Spice Girls posing attractively for the camera, the girl
power "revolution" looked like the status quo. It was not calculated to provoke negative attention; it would not feature, say, hulking, hairy-legged, tattooed and
pierced girls beating up scrawny boys during concerts.

For girls in the audience, the Spice Girls did not really represent new choices
in physical appearance. Despite the obvious differences of each band member's personal style, the Spice Girls were all conventionally pretty, with similarly slender body
types. Mel B's race offered a differentiation in skin color (she is of mixed heritage),
but she was "othered" by her status as "Scary" Spice, so called because of her hair
texture and her preference for "ethnic" prints and styles. Despite the band members' overall similarities, the different styles they wore allowed them to be presented as five distinct identities with which girls could choose to identify (Lemish,
2003). Meltzer (2010) noted, "Whether the Spice Girls were a nefarious attempt
to box up multifaceted women or just easily relatable shorthand for their young
audience, they were, at the least, very memorable. Each moniker was also a stereotype that could be seen as a product of the male gaze" (p. 79). Because the band

presented stereotypically feminine appearances as a new choice for girls, many scholars and feminists critiqued the band. Their basic argument was that true choice does not involve the reinscription of traditional beauty norms (see, for example, Lemish, 2003; Riordan, 2001; Durham, 2008). In a capitalist context, however, the question of whether such an act would possibly sell is legitimate; consider the brouhaha when Susan Boyle swept *Britain's Got Talent* in 2009. [4]

The Spice Girls also offered mixed messages regarding equality. Emma stated in *Girl Power* that she expected an "equal relationship" (p. 7), and in the Spice Girls' 1997 *Spiceworld* movie, Geri was shown explaining her perspective to an uncomfortable man at a party. She said, "I mean, it's not as if we want to be threatening to a man's masculinity or anything. Or, you know, be dominating." Elsewhere in the film, Geri—in disguise as a man—makes a peace sign and says, "Girl power! Equality between the sexes!"—as though the one incorporated the other. But in other places, the Spice Girls were quick to suggest that girls had supremacy over boys. This often came across as a "girls rule, boys drool" mentality—as part of an unhealthy zero-sum game in which one sex has to dominate, objectify, or demean the other. For example, in one scene of *Spiceworld*, the Spice Girls attend a party. There, they engage in a chauvinistic conversation about men:

Mel B: The thing about men is, right, they should be wheeled in whenever you want one.

Emma: You should be able to order them—like a pizza.

Victoria: Yes, right—(miming telephone:) "Can you send round a deep-dish Brad Pitt, twelve-inch diameter."

Mel B: No cheese.

From the mouths of the Spice Girls, the exchange is sassy and humorous; it can be read as a critique exposing the absurdity of male chauvinism's acceptance as normal, boys-will-be-boys behavior. But later in the film, the joking escalates. The Spice Girls find themselves on a set with a horde of hunky, scantily-clad men. They and their manager do not want the men there, and the men do little more than serve as eye candy and the butts of jokes: Although the men are never shown speaking, the girls speak constantly, dissing the men. As one man flexes his pectoral muscles, Geri jokes to her bandmates, "I mean, come on. Look at his muscles. He looks like he's got ferrets burrowing under there or something." Then, gazing down at another man's tight-fitting shorts, she asks her friends, "Think that's real down there?" Mel C dismisses the idea: "Looks like he's got a pair of rolled-up socks to me." By turning the tables on the male gaze, the Spice Girls objectify the men and subject their bodies to scrutiny. While this could be considered a form of equality—girls giving as good as they get—a world without demeaning objectification would be preferable. At what point does such humor go too far, especially considering the pre-teen audience for which it was intended?

In many ways, discourse surrounding the Spice Girls and their claim to girl power boiled down to debates over their authenticity (Driscoll, 2002). If they were really feminist, then why, when auditioning to join the group that would become the Spice Girls, did Geri allegedly tell the men running auditions, "I'm as old or as young as you want me to be. I can be a ten-year-old with big tits if you want"? Why did the band claim to have coined the phrase "girl power" when, clearly, they did not? Why, in *Girl Power*, did Victoria claim that the other four Spice Girls are "no good at maths" (1997, p. 37), when feminists were fighting to boost girls' interest and confidence in mathematics? Why had Geri, the band's strongest proponent of girl power, previously been a nude model, whose pre-Spice-Girls nude photos appeared in *Playboy*, *Hustler*, and *Penthouse* upon their rediscovery in 1998? Why, when asked by *Cosmopolitan* in 2002 if she would call herself a feminist, did Victoria Beckham say, "No, I wouldn't. We all admire strong, independent women, but I'm a romantic. [. . .] I like men to treat women like women"? And why, five years later, did Geri balk when a reporter from *The Guardian* asked if she were a feminist—claiming that feminism is "bra-burning lesbianism" that is "very unglamorous" and that emasculates men (Moorhead, 2007, p. 14)? Their feminism may have been a matter of convenience—useful as long as it would sell Spice Girls albums and products to their young fans. These post-Spice-Girl quotes in particular cast doubts about their claims to being role models, revolutionaries, freedom fighters, and all the other grandiose terms with which they described themselves during the band's heyday.

No wonder that when the Spice Girls announced a reunion tour, *The Daily Mail* published an article accusing the Spice Girls of killing feminism (Weldon, 2007). Though the accusation was overblown—feminism is alive and well, thank you—it crystallized the extent to which Spice Girls critics have focused on the band's dubious feminism. Had Geri never waved the girl power banner, the Spice Girls would have been just another sexy pop act, subject to critique in more commonplace ways.

Girl Power as a Lifestyle Brand

Despite long-standing doubts about the Spice Girls' authenticity, one thing is certain: the secret behind the Spice Girls' success was not simply their music. They were selling a brand image and a lifestyle—and its name was girl power. Maybe at the time, the band members really believed in it with all their hearts; maybe they did not. But either way, the Spice Girls became a lifestyle brand in short order, and girl power was at the heart of it. Although their management never, to my knowledge, openly called the Spice Girls a lifestyle brand, let us consider what lifestyle branding means, for it will help illuminate the Spice Girls' discourse on girl power and girlhood. *The Brand Glossary* offered this definition of the lifestyle brand:

> This is a brand targeted at an audience based on how they live, and it identifies itself with their interests and activities, wants and needs, likes and dislikes, attitudes, consumption, and usage patterns. The attributes of a lifestyle brand are tailored to specific audiences in order to achieve early adoption and sustained use. (Swystun, 2007, p. 72)

Writing for *Bloomberg Businessweek*, David Kiley (2005) noted, "Not every brand is a lifestyle brand. Those that seem obviously lifestyle brands to me include: Harley Davidson, Ralph Lauren, Martha Stewart, Ikea, RocaWear, Porsche, MINI, Zara, Old Navy. I tag these brands as 'lifestyle' brands because they are ones people want to wear and be identified with" (par. 4). Lifestyle brands provide identities, conferring their meaning onto the people who consume them.

Examples of lifestyle brands from the marketing literature help to further clarify the concept. For example, in marketing handbooks, Ralph Lauren is often held up as the original lifestyle brand. According to *World Famous: How to Give Your Business a Kick-ass Brand Identity*,

> The great American fashion designer Ralph Lauren invented the lifestyle brand and is considered the godfather of lifestyle branding, which is a brand that embodies the psychographic of its customers. The Polo Ralph Lauren brand is not about one product, but about a more refined, sophisticated, luxury lifestyle. It appeals to a very specific echelon of people. The brand suggests a lifestyle of considerable means and heritage. If there is such a thing as American royalty, it is encapsulated in the Polo Ralph Lauren brand. Capturing the essential features of a rare breed of refinement, excellence, and prestige, the brand suggests a renowned family name, a top-notch education, and all the trappings of culture and class. Polo Ralph Lauren is for those who live this life and for those who *aspire* to live this life. (Tyreman, 2009, p. 51).

In other words, the Ralph Lauren brand is so well known as being refined, excellent, and prestigious that wearing Polo Ralph Lauren clothing transfers these properties onto their owners, both in the wearers' minds and the minds of others who encounter them. A Polo Ralph Lauren wearer will be perceived as a different category of person than, say, an Old Navy wearer. Personal experience easily demonstrates how this plays out on a daily basis; people constantly make snap judgments about others on the basis of their appearances, including contextual cues, and first impressions can be very difficult to dislodge (e.g., see Goffman, 1959; Koji and Fernandes, 2010; Willis and Todorov, 2005; Zebrowitz, 1997). Therefore, in constructing identities, people purchase the support of established brands—whether upscale and prestigious, outdoorsy and organic, or hip and youth-oriented—to help construct a public image of the person they are and the life they lead.

Other famously successful lifestyle brands include MTV (Paoletta, 2006), L.L. Bean (Aaker, 2004), Playboy (Gunelius, 2009), and Virgin (Aaker and Joachimsthaler, 2000; Ellwood, 2002; Klein, 2000; Tyreman, 2009). In *Brand Leadership*, Aaker and Joachimsthaler praised Virgin's reach:

> Virgin is a remarkable example of how a brand can be successfully stretched far beyond what would be considered reasonable by any standard. The Virgin brand has been extended from record stores to airlines to colas to condoms to dozens of other categories. The Virgin Group comprises some 100 companies in 22 countries and includes a discount airline (Virgin Express), financial services (Virgin Direct), a cosmetics retail chain and direct sales operation (Virgin Vie), several media companies (Virgin Radio, Virgin TV), a rail service (Virgin Rail), soft drinks and other beverages (Virgin Cola, Virgin Energy, Virgin Vodka), a line of casual clothing (Virgin Clothing, Virgin Jeans), a new record label (V2 Records), and even a bridal store (Virgin Bride). [. . .] The elements of the Virgin brand identity—quality, innovation, fun/entertainment, value, the underdog image, a strong brand personality, and Branson—work for a large set of products and services. It has become a lifestyle brand with an attitude whose powerful relationship with customers is not based solely on functional benefits. (pp. 37–38)

Likewise, in *The Essential Brand Book*, Ellwood offered this synopsis of Virgin's status as a lifestyle brand:

> Virgin [. . .] sells everything from records, to airline travel, to cola drinks, to wedding parties, to clothing, to cosmetics and computers. This brand has the ability to connect directly with the consumer to convey a set of values. If consumers buy into those values then the logic is that they will appreciate any or all of the Virgin brand products. Virgin has become a true lifestyle brand, with people adopting its values as a convenient way of reflecting their own aspirations. (pp. 37–38)

In short, Virgin is an enormous company with a well-known expertise in lifestyle branding. Among people who are brand conscious, Virgin has made an impact; for example, flying Virgin signifies something quite different about a traveller than does flying AirTran.

Significantly, Virgin was also the Spice Girls' record label. Although the band members influenced many of the group's marketing decisions, Virgin played a significant role in marketing the Spice Girls (Sinclair, 2004). In one interview, the co-managing director of Virgin U.K. bragged that girl power was "a potent slogan to use for merchandise" (qtd. in Goetz, 1997, p. 90). If lifestyle branding entails "a concerted effort to market aspirations, images, and lifestyles"—"to establish a brand and to sell a lifestyle" (Michman, Mazze, and Greco, 2003, p. 68)—the Spice Girls' marketing team accomplished this in spades. In a 1997 *Spin* article titled "For the Spice Girls, Girl Power = Selling Power," author Thomas Goetz (1997) identified girl power as a "combination lifestyle/brand name," and questioned whether the Spice Girls were really a "girl group or marketing strategy" (p. 90). The strategies used to market the Spice Girls fit perfectly within a lifestyle branding framework.

Consider that the Spice Girls used girl power as shorthand for an empowered, can-do attitude that takes pleasure in disrupting male privilege, is supported by confidence in one's own body, embraces solidarity with one's friends, and boasts certainty that girls need not have male approval or relationships to be happy. Despite the shortcomings of and contradictions in the Spice Girls' approach to this message, many girls wanted this identity—with its set of values, ideals, and attitudes—for themselves. The Spice Girls knew that friendship, fun, and sassiness resonated with girls in the target audience. The Spice Girls further understood that pre-teen girls, who were generally too young to be interested in romantic relationships with boys, would embrace the attitude that girls rule and are equal or superior to males. Alongside the idea that girl power could fulfill girls' desire for control over their own lives, these ideas made a winning combination. Girls could easily embrace girl power and organize their own projected identities around it.

Purchasing Spice Girls products therefore was more than a way for girls to show their love of the Spice Girls' music; it was a way to demonstrate their personal belief in girl power. Additionally, parents aware of the girl crisis could offer positive reinforcement for their daughters' embrace of girl power by purchasing Spice Girls products for them. The products were plentiful, for lifestyle brands offer products across categories to extend the brand's values into all aspects of life: "all objects and services people use every day—what they wear, eat, drink, and smoke, but also their sedentary or traveling environment—furniture, bedding, wallpaper, decorator items, draperies, floor tiles, paint, tableware, luggage, and so on" (Chevalier and Mazzalovo, 2004, p. 151). Thus, the official Spice Girls products and sponsored goods included all of the following: lamps, mirrors, wallpaper, picture frames, posters, bedding (duvet covers), clocks, umbrellas, lunchboxes, china mugs, plates, handkerchiefs, wallets, money tins, wrapping paper, gift bags, calendars, diaries, organizers, mouse pads, watercolors, colored pencils, stickers, jigsaw puzzles, comb-brush-mirror sets, Polaroid cameras, body spray, shower gel, video games, make-up sets, temporary tattoos, toy mobile phones, FM radios, cassette players, microphones, amplifiers, shirts, sneakers, magnets, backpacks, tote bags, baseball caps, rings, necklaces, charm bracelets, toy nail salons, party sets (matching hats, decorations, party favors, napkins, plates and cups), candy (Cadbury's, Push Pops), potato chips (Walker's Crisps), soda (Pepsi), and scooters (Aprilla brand, made in Italy and exported to the UK) (West, n.d.).

This range of products would have made it possible for a girl's day to be completely filled with Spice Girls products, if her family had the means to purchase them for her. She could wake up beneath her Spice Girls bedding, turn off her Spice Girls alarm clock, and turn on her Spice Girls lamp to gaze upon the Spice Girls wallpaper, posters, picture frames, and dolls adorning her room. She could open her Spice Girls calendar to review her schedule before deciding which Spice Girls shirt, jewelry, and sneakers to wear. She could shower and shampoo with Spice Girls body wash and shampoo, brush her hair with her Spice Girls brush, put on Spice Girls makeup (if she was allowed to wear makeup), and check her overall look in her Spice Girls mirror. Then she could go down to breakfast, where she could eat and drink from her ceramic Spice Girls plates and cups. She could pick up her Spice Girls backpack, make sure her Spice Girls wallet is inside, and go out for the day. At school, she could take notes in her Spice Girls notebooks with her Spice Girls pens and pencils; or on the weekend, she could bring her Spice Girls Polaroid camera to a friend's house, where they could enjoy a Spice Girls-themed birthday party—eating a Spice Girls cake off of Spice Girls paper plates. If the attendees were asked to dress as their favorite Spice Girl (as one of my college students fondly recalls doing in first grade), she might ask her parents to buy her an official Spice Girls costume. Later, upon returning home, she could choose from any number of Spice Girls-branded activities to fill her free time—ranging from listening to their music, to playing their video game, to working on one of their jigsaw puzzles, to creating a painting with their watercolor paints. She could do these activities while snacking on Spice Girls chocolates and drinking Pepsi from a can that featured the Spice Girls . . . and then go to bed beneath her Spice Girls covers once more, satisfied with all the reminders of her empowered identity that her Spice Girls products afforded her that day.

Although this hypothetical 1997 pre-teen dream scenario is nightmarish in its extremity, and although the typical fan would have had far fewer Spice Girls products than this, it illustrates the extent to which the Spice Girls pursued commodification. In addressing their fans, the band was vehement about the importance of buying official Spice Girls products only. *Girl Power* (1997) concluded by imploring fans: "Remember, if it doesn't say OFFICIAL on the front, then it's nothing to do with us—and that goes for all those crappy excuses for magazines you see on the shelves, too. Don't buy them!" (p. 77). Official products were available in nearly every possible product category (including motor vehicles, thanks to Aprilla scooters); and in those categories in which the Spice Girls did not release products, unofficial products, pirating the Spice Girls' names and images, were often available. Most successful media texts and icons are heavily merchandized nowadays (think of Star Wars, for example), so this range of products is not entirely unusual. What *is* unusual is for a bestselling pop music act to so definitively communicate a set of values and a lifestyle that has little to do with the music, and so much to do with a cultural critique promoting girls' empowerment (tempered though it was). As mentioned earlier, Virgin Records head of press once admitted that girl power sounded like a "dumb slogan," but said that "it did actually contain a hard kernel of truth" (qtd. in Sinclair, 2004, p. 76). Milked for all it was worth, that kernel of truth imbued the Spice Girls' merchandise with deeper meaning, making them what *Spin* magazine recognized as "a combination lifestyle/brand name" (Goetz, 1997, p. 90).

Taken altogether, the marketing efforts and products created on the Spice Girls' behalf helped build the Spice Girls into a lifestyle brand. They were selling empowerment and self-esteem in the form of girl power, a term with which the Spice Girls claimed to be synonymous. By suggesting that the Spice Girls were the physical embodiment of girl power, all of their actions, products, and ideas could be seen as encompassed by the concept. If a fan wished, she could transfer girl power unto herself by purchasing and wearing Spice Girls products. Like a talisman, these objects would communicate that the wearer was not just an ordinary girl—she had girl power.

Girl Power in a Post-Spice World

The Spice Girls' embrace of girl power served well in promoting the band—but symbiotically, the band's promotions had also worked in service of the concept of girl power. Although the Spice Girls' mainstream version of girl power differed from the countercultural version that preceded it, they made the phrase better known than ever before. The Spice Girls and their marketing team accomplished this feat within the global marketplace in less than a year, starting with their major world-wide successes at the beginning of 1997. Geri, the unofficial leader of the Spice Girls and their chief girl power proponent, left the band to pursue a solo career in the spring of 1998; the band as a whole went on hiatus in 2001. Although the Spice Girls had tried to make girl power their own, the concept of girl power continued going strong after the band's reign ended. In 1997, the U.S. Department of Health and Human Services launched a national public education campaign called Girl Power! (Zaslow, 2009, p. 20). The campaign's official web site explained that it sought to "help encourage and motivate 9- to 14- year-old girls to make the most of their lives. Girls at 8 or 9 typically have very strong attitudes about their health, so Girl Power! seeks to reinforce and sustain these positive values among girls ages 9–14 by targeting health messages to the unique needs, interests, and challenges of girls" (U.S. Department of Health and Human Services, 2001). Zaslow (2009) noted that this governmental campaign legitimized both the idea of the girl crisis and that girl power held validity as a solution (p. 20). Girl power was even added to the *Oxford English Dictionary* in 2001, defined as "a self-reliant attitude among girls and young women manifested in ambition, assertiveness and individualism" (qtd. in Meltzer, 2010, p. 71).

In pop music, girl power manifested in various ways. Its influences could be seen to differing extents in the music and identities of various pop celebrities, including Britney Spears, Cristina Aguilera, Alanis Morissette, Hillary Duff, and Hannah Montana (Meltzer, 2010; Lamb and Brown, 2006). The use of girl power rhetoric to sell pop music has led Lamb and Brown (2006) to caution parents that they must help their daughters develop a critical eye and focus on all parts of a pop music act—not just the hype. For example, they suggest that parents help their daughters "focus on why a girl is up front singing. Is this girl power? Hillary Duff is a musical pop star not because she created a sound or wrote an original song but because she was a blond and pretty TV star who had a pleasant singing voice and young girls wanted to see more of her. When she's not singing, she's selling Barbie fashions" (p. 141). Girl power also featured prominently in many films, including *Legally Blonde* (2001), the remake of *Charlie's Angels* (2000), *Bend It Like Beckham* (2002), *13 Going on 30* (2004), *Mean Girls* (2004), and *The Sisterhood of the Traveling Pants* (2005). In 2003, girl power was declared an official new genre for films by *MovieMaker Magazine* (Smith, 2003)—characterized by a female character gaining acceptance and redefining the world around her in the process. Girl power became an important part of television's landscape, too, as we will see in Chapter Four—and Currie, Kelly, and Pomerantz (2009) have carefully explored all the variant meanings girl power has taken on as it has charted its course across popular culture (pp. 27–52).

Offscreen, girl power held up as an independent lifestyle brand long after the Spice Girls went on hiatus. Toys such as MGA Entertainment's Bratz dolls, racially diverse fashion dolls that successfully competed in the marketplace against Barbie, fell under the girl power banner; they offered opportunities for fashionable identity play similar to the Spice Girls. The American Girl dolls also fell under the girl power banner, but at a much higher cost than Spice Girls. These dolls cost $100 without any accessories (and accessories are calculated to have major appeal), justified by their apparent higher quality and the historical backstories offered for each doll.

Nearly any product imaginable could be sold if it had the term "girl power" or "girls rule" emblazoned upon it. Additionally, anything that claimed to empower girls could claim to be part of the girl power lifestyle brand, as many products did through their promotional copy. As girl power products spread, the Spice Girls' influence on girl power as a fun, feminine form of marketplace empowerment was widely evident. Stores sold countless t-shirts that said "Girl Power" and "Girls Rule!"; most came in the dainty "babydoll" style that favored by thin females, and many were in pink or purple, with the words in sparkly glitter lettering. Pins, keychains, and stickers also featured the phrase. Butterflies, flowers, peace signs, smiley faces, and other cheerful symbols frequently appeared on these products, suggesting that girl power was meant to support femininity. Many of the girl power products available in the post-Spice-Girls marketplace were relatively meaningless kitsch, with tenuous claims to girls' empowerment at best. Indeed, when one considers girl power's anticapitalist, grassroots feminist beginnings, the idea that products ranging from aprons to nail polish to elephant-shaped picture frames were sold under the girl power umbrella is mind-boggling (Hains, 2009).

To make sense of this requires reconsidering girl power's relation to the girl crisis. As discussed in detail in Chapter One, by the mid-1990s, many prominent organizations and authors had convinced parents and educators that adolescence was a difficult time for girls. Concerned adults knew that adolescent girls felt culturally devalued, with serious consequences on girls' self-esteem. So in the late 1990s, many a parent, aunt, and family friend purchased girl power products for girls—a friendly, fun way to show their support for girls' culture—even though this culture emerged not from girls, but as the creations of other adults, just like the products for sale. Girls' interest in products that offered empowerment rhetoric to girls was met with general approval.

Despite the positive intentions of friends and family, girl power may have been more a panacea for marketers than for girls. Riordan (2001) has argued that through girl power's commodification, "the original meaning of girl empowerment became watered-down so that it means something to everyone" (p. 290); Guthrie (2005) noted, "While Riot Grrrl offered girls something to do, Girl Power can only offer something to buy" (p. 237). The phrase has even been used to sell pornography (Hains, 2009), and it has been the key to the success of many brands targeting girls (Munk, 1997). This mindset was embodied by retailer Club Libby Lu's use of "girl power." Launched in 2001 by Saks Incorporated, Club Libby Lu was a shop that sold fantasy makeovers to five- to twelve-year-old girls. Until Club Libby Lu closed due to the financial downturn in 2009, the company made economic decisions with a proprietary "Girl Power Index Rating," developed by market research firm Forum Analytics. According to Club Libby Lu President Mary Drolet, the Girl Power Index Rating helped the company understand the "market potential of every major mall in the country" (Forum Analytics, n.d.). Girl power was thus not about empowering girls; it was about enticing them and their parents to spend money. The Girl Power Index Rating worked for nearly a decade, during which Club Libby Lu was incredibly popular, the site of countless girls' special days out and birthday parties. (Numerous parents posted YouTube videos documenting the experience; many are still online today.) But as a 2008 *Washington Post* article complained, the experience for sale at Club Libby Lu was anything but empowering:

> the club's version of dress-up involved hooking girls as young as 3 on glittery tube tops, tight pants, boas, nail polish, lip gloss, tiaras and runway modeling. Princesses and pop stars—hence sex—were in. So, dress-up was cool and fun, if it was sexy. No pilots or doctors or astronauts or firefighters to dress as in this place.

Reframing empowerment as sexiness has been in vogue since the Spice Girls were popular. As Douglas Rushkoff argued in *Frontline: The Merchants of Cool* (2001), in targeting teen girls, marketers have relied on "a collection of the same old sexual cliches, but repackaged as a new kind of female empowerment." It says, "I *am* a sexual object, but I'm proud of it." In *Packaging Girlhood: Rescuing Our Daughters from Marketers' Schemes,* Lamb and Brown (2006) described girl power as becoming a bait-and-switch in service of this message:

> Almost as soon as the phrase was coined, girl power was snapped up by the media and just about everyone else trying to sell your daughter something. What it sells is an image of being empowered. Once girls buy into that desire and go

after that image, they're told that the way to get that power is through makeup, clothes, and boyfriends. (p. 205)

Lamb and Brown therefore cautioned parents, "Be aware that every time the phrase 'girl power' is used, it means the power to make choices while shopping!" (pp. 2–3). In other words, in a marketplace filled with commodities, girl power has only one consistent meaning: "Buy this!"

Russell and Tyler (2002) studied a U.K. retail outlet chain called "Girl Heaven" that, like Club Libby Lu, focused on girls' makeovers. It was directly inspired by girl power and the success of the Spice Girls. In their fieldwork there with girls in the 8- to 11-year-old target audience, the authors concluded that although girls' experiences at Girl Heaven could be pleasurable, their experiences also emphasized that "the social construction of femininity within Girl Heaven renders bodily dissatisfaction and the stifling of aesthetic imagination and creativity in the process of becoming a woman virtually unavoidable" (p. 631). In encouraging its young consumers to buy into a heightened performance of femininity, Girl Heaven positioned girls as able to make individual identity choices, but in reality, these choices were repetitive and monotonous, and made consumption an imperative—something that must happen constantly. This scenario makes the production of femininity encouraged by mainstream girl power seems more obligatory than empowering.

In Zaslow's (2009) scholarly analysis of girl power media culture, she offered another take on why girl power has repackaged femininity and sexiness as empowerment. She observed that girl power has served to retain the feminine traditions of "beauty, care, and sexiness" while rejecting those encompassing "passivity, weakness, and dependence" to instead position girls as "active, choice-making agents" (p. 158). To make these new ideals work with the old, girl power recodes the performance of femininity as an empowering choice:

> one can 'own her sexuality' and use it as a tool or weapon to gain economic or social capital, or she can simply enjoy her own desire (which is coded as a sign of her connection to herself and her resistance to the denial of female sexual longing), and her own desirability (which is coded as a choice to be a sexual subject and to be appreciated by the female and male gaze). (p. 158)

This is an insightful explanation. The production of normative feminine beauty and sexiness requires the consumption of countless products, from the right clothing to the right makeup and skin care items. However, in recent years, feminist critics have understood the production of femininity as a heteronormative societal dictate that makes women's value and self-esteem dependent on their desirability to men. For girl power to be commercially successful, it must retain the norms of feminine attractiveness; the mainstream reaction to riot grrrls made that clear. But for girl power to be positioned as encompassing both strength and independence *and* normative femininity, the consumption of beauty commodities in pursuit of sexiness *must* be reframed as personally empowering. Otherwise, girl power collapses as an invalidated concept.

Zaslow (2009) further notes that in reframing the performance of normative femininity as a means to empowerment and in its emphasis on style and independence from men as a healthy individualism, mainstream girl power is a neoliberalist pursuit. Rather than seeking structural changes to the system through collective action, it "places an emphasis on self-improvement, self-correction, and individual empowerment over social change or state support" (p. 159). In other words, girl power shares much with power feminism as conceptualized by Naomi Wolf (1993), which was individualistic to a fault (Hains, 2009).

In less than a decade, then, girl power was reduced from a means of feminist empowerment to a new form of commodity feminism—the appropriation of feminist discourse to support the interests of the marketplace rather than of women or girls (Hains, 2009; see also Goldman, Heath, and Smith, 1991). Girl power's devolution into commodity feminism was problematic: it could too easily be stripped of its meaning, appropriated and reworked as a vehicle to reinforce dominant ideology.

Though many feminists have expressed concerns about this pattern, an intriguing question remains. What did the girls think?

Notes

1. qtd. in Sinclair, 2004, p. 60.
2. *Girl Power* was ghostwritten by Howard Johnson, a music writer, at the behest of the band's manager, Simon Fuller (Padel, 1997).
3. *Spiceworld* was a commercial success: Despite being panned by critics, it earned $77 million at the box office alone and an additional $25 million in DVD sales.
4. Boyle, a Scottish woman with a gorgeous singing voice, was the subject of intense discussion because her appearance does not conform to mainstream beauty ideals. One blogger summarized the unflattering conversations about Boyle thus: "A hideously ugly woman that looks like a mop mauled by a chimpanzee picks up the mic and sings a song from Les Misérablé [sic] on British Idol. And it's really good. And then everyone is amazed. [. . .] What is the assumption here, that ugly people can't sing?" (Goldenberg, 2009)

3

Did the Spice Girls Kill Feminism?

Young Feminists Speak

"Those little girls who first listened to the Spice Girls ten years ago are the ones who are now running up vast credit card bills on designer shopping they can't afford. They are the ones who are anorexic or bulimic (just like Geri was). They are the ones who are fuelling a rise in sexual diseases the like of which we haven't seen for generations."
—Weldon (2007), "How the Spice Girls Have Killed Feminism, subverted morality and embarrassed us all," The Daily Mail

Were the Spice Girls bad for girls? Critics have argued that the Spice Girls' used girl power to bolster sales, not self-esteem. Fay Weldon, quoted in the epigraph, went a step further, accusing the Spice Girls of leading U.K. girls to sexualize themselves, overindulge in alcohol, and subordinate themselves to men. "I'm embarrassed for the feminists," she wrote, "clinging on to the dream of a proud, equal, serious society, where justice ruled and lasses didn't throw away their hard-won equality in the pubs and clubs, puking up their resentments on the shoes of paramedics trying to help them out of the gutter" (para. 51). In the aftermath of Spice Girls fandom, were girls inoculated against feminism—brainwashed for life?

Weldon's allegations position the Spice Girls as powerful; their fans, weak and victimized. Fortunately, academic analyses of the Spice Girls have been more nuanced than those *The Daily Mail* (which some call *The Daily Hate Mail* for its frequent inflammatory rhetoric). When Lemish (1998) examined adolescent girls' use of the Spice Girls in their gendered adolescent identities, she carefully articulated differences between cohorts of Spice Girls fans (e.g., younger vs. older girls), noting both positive and negative findings. For example, she saw that girls played with femininity via the Spice Girls productively but only accepted identities as legitimate when "offered by a beautiful model" (p. 155). By exploring the tensions and contradictions of girls' Spice Girls experiences, Lemish brought their perspectives to the fore with nuance, respecting the variability of girls' interpretations of the Spice Girls' girl power.

Unfortunately, studies of girl audience members are rarer than studies of girls' media texts. The result is an imbalance in the literature: Academics' and critics' interpretations have been privileged over female youths' (Kearney, 2011).[1] Scholars who focus on texts risk misrepresenting girls or failing to account for their agency, and the epigraph is an extreme version of this: Weldon asserted that grown-up Spice Girls fans were overspending, suffering from disordered eating, and spreading STDs. But how did she know any of this correlated with their long-ago Spice Girls devotion? Her sweeping condemnation echoed the 1990s media condemnation of the riot grrrls. When girls are spoken *for*, instead of *with*, only a partial, flawed story can emerge.

Having considered the Spice Girls' strengths and weaknesses from a feminist perspective, and noting their overarching use of "girl power" to sell products, I wished to learn what it was like to grow up with the Spice Girls. In hindsight, did the Spice Girls have a positive influence on girls' feminist consciousness, a negative one, or something in between? To what degree did the Spice Girls' girl power empower girls, despite prioritizing profitability and reinforcing strict feminine beauty norms? Some young feminist authors have written on issues directly related to this question. For example, in *Manifesta: Young Women, Feminism, and the Future*, Baumgardner and Richards (2000)—both affiliated with *Ms.* Magazine—sang the praises of "Girlie," or mainstream girl power, as a legitimate feminist mode. They explained:

> "Girlie" says we're not broken, and our desires aren't simply booby traps set by the patriarchy. Girlie encompasses the tabooed symbols of women's feminine enculturation—Barbie dolls, makeup, fashion magazines, high heels—and says using them isn't shorthand for "we've been duped." Using makeup isn't a sign of our sway to the marketplace and the male gaze; it can be sexy, campy, ironic, or simply decorating ourselves without the loaded issues (a la dye your hair with Jell-O!). Also, what we loved as girls was good and, because of feminism, we know how to make girl stuff work for us. (p. 136)

From this perspective, mainstream girl power was a route to empowerment. It privileged women's personal experiences and ways of knowing. Just as men can continue enjoying their boyhood pursuits into manhood—sports, video games, trains, and so on—women, too, can recognize that what they "loved as girls was good" and need not cast them aside upon maturity.

Despite such rationales, mainstream girl power has proven divisive among feminists. Scholars such as Russell and Tyler (2002) have noted that girl power consumer culture contains both "pressures and pleasures" (p. 623) that some understand as a "controlling mechanism" but others view as a "creative space" (p. 623). Although we all create or perform gender through our daily interactions, our agency is constrained and/or enabled by the contexts in which they occur (Messner, 2000). Mainstream girl power thus could have enabled pleasurable performances of girlhood while also constraining girls within a circumscribed set of options.

Methodology

Though the Spice Girls' take on feminism was problematic, surely millions of girls were not mere cultural dupes, victimized by their purchase of Spice Girls merchandise and destined to become crisis-ridden adults. Kearney (2011) has argued that interviewing girls can "debunk the die-hard stereotype of girls as passive consumers, if not victims, of media" (p. 11). To explore the Spice Girls' roles in real girls' lives, I interviewed young women born between 1982 and 1992. In the Spice Girls' heyday, they were between five and 15 years old. I selected feminist-identified women to explore whether mainstream girl power has feminist potential, despite its known problems. Who better to address whether the Spice Girls had feminist meaning than Spice Girls fans who grew up to become feminists? These young women presumably approach popular culture with a skill set similar to the Spice Girls' feminist critics—but they also know, first-hand, what it was like to *be* a girl in the Age of Spice. They recall what it meant to say "Girls rule!", to participate in a global celebration of girlhood, to be part of a collective that propelled the Spice Girls to international stardom. Their insider knowledge is an asset.

Finding young women who identify as feminist can be difficult. Many say, "I'm not a feminist, but . . ." (Douglas, 1995, pp. 269–294; Evans, 2004, p. 7, p. 186). Douglas has noted that given the "baggage" of feminist stereotypes, prefacing feminist ideas with "I'm not a feminist, but . . ." lets young women espouse feminism with minimal risk of backlash. To recruit participants in this harder-to-reach population, I relied on snowball sampling: asking friends and acquaintances to recommend potential feminist interviewees and then asking those interviewees to recommend others. This yielded twenty interviewees, interviewed between December 2009 and April 2011:

- seven from a small liberal arts college (enrollment: 300), located in a rural town of fewer than 1000 residents in New England;
- three from the Feminist Majority Foundation's National Young Feminist Leadership Conference, held in Washington, DC in March 2010;
- four referred by members of the first two clusters (but who neither attended the college nor the FMF conference); and
- six located by my research assistant, Jenna Austin, a 26-year-old feminist-identified undergraduate.

After Jenna trained in qualitative interviewing techniques, she interviewed the six respondents she recruited as well as four of the respondents I recruited—half of the interviewees in all. I am grateful for her excellent work.

Each young feminist participated in an individual interview lasting approximately one hour—via telephone or in person—following a semi-structured interview guide. Every interview was transcribed, then analyzed for emergent themes.

The interviewees grew up in the U.S, recalled the Spice Girls' domination of the musical charts, and could speak in detail about their memories. All but three had been fans of the Spice Girls, reflecting the fact that most, but not all, girls were Spice Girls fans. About two-thirds were of Euro-American descent, while about a third had other family heritages. I hoped to learn whether these interviewees felt the Spice Girls were feminist, and whether the Spice Girls had played any role—positive, detrimental, or in between—in their feminist journeys.

A list of interviewees (note: all names are pseudonyms) and their demographic variables follows:

Abby, 19: Euro-American; middle class; raised in Springfield, VT

Adeleke, 21: African-American; working class; raised in Decatur, GA

Alyssa, 21: Euro-American; lower middle class or possibly working class; raised in Tyrone, PA

Calista, 21: African-American; middle-class; raised in Paterson, NJ

Chloe; 21: Euro-American; lower-middle-class until recently; raised in Clinton, NJ

Clair, 20: Euro-American; middle/upper-middle class; raised in the Silicon Valley, CA

Grace, 18: Euro-American (western European descent); middle class until high school, then upper-middle class; raised in suburban Philadelphia, PA

Hannah, 20: Euro-American; upper middle class; raised in Hamilton, NY

Isabella, 21: Euro-American (Jewish and Italian); upper middle class; raised in Princeton, NJ

Jia-Li, 22; Taiwanese-American (first-generation; both her parents immigrated from Taiwan); upper middle class; raised in Port Jefferson, NY

Kallie, 23: Caucasian—half Indian-American, half Euro-American (Irish, Scottish, German); middle class; raised in Bloomington, IL

Madeline, 20: Euro-American (English and French); middle class; raised in Concord, MA

Meredith, 22: Euro-American (Irish and Italian); middle class; raised in Billerica, MA

Miraya, 21: Asian-American (Indian); upper-middle-class; raised in Bergen County, NJ

Morgan, 26: Latina-American (Chilean), raised by an adoptive family; upper-middle-class; raised in Ann Arbor, MI

Natalie, 21: Euro-American ("general European mix"); middle class; raised in Pittsburgh, PA

Rose, 19: Euro-American; middle class; raised in Manhattan, NY and South Salem, NY.

Samantha, 24: Euro-American; upper middle class; raised in Hoffman Estates, IL

Tamika, 29; African-American (first-generation; both her parents immigrated from Nigeria); lower middle class; New York, NY

Tori, 26: Euro-American (Serbian and German/Scots-Irish descent); upper-middle class; raised in Concord, MA

Inspired by Fisherkeller's (2002) practice of inviting interviewees to read their interview transcripts and her preliminary analysis of their interviews (p. 161), I invited our interviewees to read and comment upon a draft of this chapter. I asked them to keep the following questions in mind as they read:

1. Is there anything you think I've presented inaccurately?
2. Is there anything you'd like to add or clarify?
3. Overall, how closely do you think what I've written actually reflects your experiences?

Of the twenty interviewees, ten responded to share their feedback on the chapter draft. Adeleke, Calista, Samantha, Hannah, Isabella, Miraya, Morgan, Natalie, and Tori confirmed they felt accurately represented by what they read. Miraya and Natalie shared some additional details about themselves; Morgan and Tori asked me to make small revisions to better assure their anonymity; and Tori and Calista each offered a clarifying comment. Alyssa felt well-represented except for one point, so I made a revision that satisfactorily addressed her concern. I hope that on the whole, this chapter accurately reflects the experiences of the women who so generously shared their thoughts with me.

Young Feminisms

Much ink has been devoted to analyses of feminism's meaning to young women, detailing a "third wave" that began as Generation X came of age (Baumgardner & Richards, 2000; Dicker & Piepmeier, 2003; Gills, Howie, & Munford, 2007; Henry, 2004; Heywood & Drake, 1997). The third wave has been criticized as an unnecessarily divisive label (Jervis, 2004), given that the agenda of the second wave remains a work in progress. Interestingly, most women in this study, who would be considered members of "Generation Y" rather than Generation X, did not claim membership in the third wave. The feminisms they espoused varied. Only a few spoke in terms of wave theory: two claimed to be aligned with the second wave; one articulated a perspective between the second and third waves; and one spoke of being a fourth-wave feminist. All, however, spoke with confidence about their feminist identities and perspectives.

A majority articulated feminism as a fight for equality. Some focused on equality in everyday life—women as men's social equals—while others strongly emphasized the need for equal pay in the workplace. Some tensions emerged regarding whether women and men are different but equal, with different strengths, or essentially the same, able to achieve the same things. A few took a broader view of equality not just between the sexes, but rather among all people. Many spoke to the importance of activism; several were currently or previously engaged in activist campaigns, and others spoke of a desire to engage in activism in the future. In some cases, through activism they had come to better understand other women's experiences—and also faced some backlash. This led them to renegotiate their own feminist perspectives.

Eight of the twenty interviewees credited their parents—often their mothers—for raising them in feminist environments. Raised to believe that women are men's equals, they learned to never let themselves become dependent on a man, and several remembered their mothers were their childhood role models. Some had also learned at an early age to critique media culture and its representations of women. Their feminist upbringings served as context for their recollected relationships to the Spice Girls as children as well as their adult perspectives on the Spice Girls, girl power, and feminism.

Negotiating The Spice Girls

How did these young feminists recall their childhood consumption of the Spice Girls and girl power? In my analysis, several themes emerged. The first set involved the pleasures and problems of Spice Girls consumption. Many spoke of their girl-hood enjoyment of Spice Girls' products and their make-believe play with friends. For some, consuming the Spice Girls offered important identity support. For example, for girls who were "girly" or "tomboys," the validation of their identities by popular music icons was meaningful and valuable—echoing Lemish's (1998) findings. For other girls, the Spice Girls' limited personalities and appearances created problems. Conflicts emerged between friends during Spice Girls play, often rooted in biases regarding physical appearance and/or race.

The second set of themes involved the interviewees' feminist conscience development. The Spice Girls' brand of girl power was sometimes interpreted as a pathway to feminism or a deeper feminist consciousness. However, while some girls embraced girl power's meaning, others—particularly two interviewees raised by feminist parents—experienced it as a meaningless catchphrase. Despite feeling the Spice Girls' feminism lacked authenticity, these girls were Spice Girls fans nevertheless. They had both criticized and embraced the band; it was not an either/or proposition.

The Pleasures of Consuming the Spice Girls

For most interviewees, consuming Spice Girls products was a pleasurable childhood activity recalled with fondness. Seventeen of the twenty interviewees had been Spice Girls fans. The exceptions were Adeleke , Jia-Li, and Tori. Adeleke (age 21; African-American; raised in Decatur, GA) recalled the Spice Girls were simply not popular at her predominantly black school. She reflected:

> ADELEKE: I don't really want to be like, "Oh, it's a race thing!" 'cause all the schools I've ever been to were predominantly black. But that could have been it, 'cause that was in the 90s, and I was way more into R&B. I was like, "Yeah, they're all right," but they couldn't really

sing. I think I was way more into groups who could actually sing, and they were just dancing around, like, "Ohhh, let me sing this song." But they weren't really singers.

Unlike Adeleke, Jia-Li's (age 22; Taiwanese-American; raised in Port Jefferson, NY) disinterest in the Spice Girls made her an anomaly at her predominantly white elementary school in Long Island. In fact, she didn't know much about the Spice Girls because a) she loved the Backstreet Boys and b) her parents were strict regarding popular culture. Once she realized the Spice Girls were "huge," she was "way behind." As the only Chinese girl at school, she recalled this as part of a broader struggle to fit in:

> JIA-LI: I had to work really, really hard to fit in. Throughout my elementary school childhood, I was constantly fighting against my parents—not yelling and door-slamming, but saying, "Well, they get to do that; why can't I do this?" or "They get to go to slumber parties; *I* want to go to slumber parties! Why can't I do that?" "They get to play sports and not just practice music"; I played violin and piano ever since I was four or five. [. . .] So I rebelled against that type of thing. I *would* wanna listen to the Spice Girls, but I wasn't allowed to.

Like Adeleke and Jia-Li, Tori (age 26; Euro-American; raised in Concord, MA) preferred other music to the Spice Girls. However, she took a much more active and emphatic dislike for the Spice Girls. A high school freshman when the Spice Girls gained international fame, she had previously become a riot grrrls fan, entirely abandoning any prior interest in pop music.

> TORI: No, no. I was never into the Spice Girls. By the time they were really big, I had stopped being into the poppy music, and I was into alternative music. So I was like, "Spice Girls—they are crappy!" So, yeah, I was never so into them.

Because Tori's older sister also found the Spice Girls so obnoxious, she recalled, "That really annoying song—that 'Wannabe' song—my sister and I used to sing it at each other, specifically to annoy each other." She felt the Spice Girls' version of empowerment was "shallow."

In contrast, the other interviewees recalled being Spice Girls fans. Morgan (age 26; Chilean-American; raised in Ann Arbor, MI) was such a fan of the Spice Girls that she has continued listening to their music to this day. "I know it sounds kind of silly," she said, "but there are some songs there that are classics. They weren't a band for very long, and they left an impression—at least for me, since I was younger." The Spice Girls' music was also important to Tamika (age 29; African-American; raised in New York, NY), who recalled that she and her friends really enjoyed the Spice Girls and admired them for their style.

> TAMIKA: They were hot, and they used to dress real nice. They had those plat-
> form shoes everybody wanted. And they were really sexy, and they
> were all about—like, the thing I liked about the Spice Girls was the
> fact that they weren't really tomboyish, but they were still ladies.
> They were feminine. At the same time it was interesting for me
> because remember they were from London and their style was a lot
> different from ours, and I just liked the music a lot, and the words.

As the other interviewees reminisced about the Spice Girls, few focused on the band's music in this way. They instead focused on play and consumption: pretend-ing that they were the Spice Girls during games with friends and deriving enjoy-ment from various Spice products. Meredith (age 22; Euro-American; raised in Billerica, MA) enthused, "I loved them." Her extensive Spice Girls collection included concert tee shirts; all the dolls, except Scary Spice (who Lemish (1998) noted was the band member least favored by her focus group participants); pillows; stickers; folders; and pencils—with which, she said, "I'd always write 'girl power.'" Enjoying the act of reminiscing, she said with apparent nostalgia, "I even had the lollipops."

Kallie (age 23; half Indian-American and half Euro-American; raised in Bloomington, IL) similarly had a room full of Spice Girls paraphernalia:

> KALLIE: I decorated my whole room with pictures of the Spice Girls I even pho-
> tocopied pictures of them from magazines to put them on my
> wall. I had the dolls; I spent my life savings on them. [. . .] I def-
> initely had a Spice Girls watch; I had two of their T-shirts; I went
> to Clarie's [a mall retail chain] and got a bunch of their stuff. That's
> a pre-teen for you.

While Madeline (age 20; Euro-American; raised in Concord, MA) did not own Spice Girls products, she said, "I took their CD envelope and taped it on my wall." She recalls that she "was really into them, probably more than other girls. Like, I would put on the CD and rock out to 'Spice up Your Life'—and I had a friend, and we would play Spice Girls." Her friend liked to pretend that she was Ginger Spice, while Charlotte was partial to playing Sporty Spice.

JENNA: Can you explain that a little more to me?

MADELINE: Yeah. I'd say it was probably more of our own personas trying to be in their situation. I would try to be the Sporty Spice character, and she would be the Ginger Spice character. But it was kind of hard to know exactly just what that is from the songs and, you know, the pictures. So I think we would probably project ourselves into it a lot, and mostly we would come up with weird situations and try to work it into singing the songs—or playing the songs on the CD and singing them.

JENNA: Can you remember anything specific instance or a specific thing?

MADELINE: I think we would do it almost like TV episodes. Like, today something was trying to cause the band to break up, and we were in a fight, and we would have to go somewhere and go on weird missions and have to work it out. That sort of thing. [. . .]

JENNA: Anything come to mind that you remember that you would make her say?

MADELINE: I would definitely chew out my friend pretending to be Ginger Spice, for whatever reason—although we sometimes had our own conflicts. If she was pretending that we were in a fight and she didn't want to sing any more, then I would just kind of come up to her and tell her she was totally sucking, and she had to suck it up, and we needed to sing.

Asked whether she favored Sporty Spice because of a personal interest in sports, Madeline replied, "I wasn't really into sports, but I wasn't that girly, you know, and I liked that she didn't want to be girly, either. And she didn't let people make her girly."

Like Madeline, Grace (age 18; Euro-American; raised in suburban Philadelphia, PA) also identified with Sporty Spice. Although Sporty Spice was "over the top sometimes," Grace liked that she was "very genuine. That's what I related to." On the other hand, Morgan favored Sporty Spice specifically because she enjoyed sports.

MORGAN: I think primarily, on the surface, it was her presence. Her demeanor, everything. She wasn't anorexic; she was healthy, and she was sporty. And there is a difference between being sporty and healthy. And at the time, the ideal of what every woman should look like—because of the media influences—was too anorexic and sickly. I was doing

Tae Kwon Do at the time; I was swimming. So I was doing all those sporty activities. Actually, at the time, I tried track and field and failed miserably, and that was when I realized I was much happier in the water. And she was someone I one-hundred-percent connected to because I do all these sports and I'm healthy. I'm happy, and I can 110% relate to her. I was confident at the time because before that, I tried to "fit in" with all these other "popular" girls. It was 8th grade when we did this project, and it was the same year I told myself, "I don't care what anybody else thinks. I'm tired of trying to fit in with everybody else. I'm just going to be how I am and dress how I wanna dress, and you can just accept me for who I am and what I do or not." It changed the entire view, perspective of me that everyone else had.

Unaware of Sporty Spice's behind-the-scenes battles with eating disorders, Morgan believed in her performance of athleticism and physical fitness, and this belief bolstered her own identity as an athletic, healthy, individualistic girl.

Although Sporty Spice was the Spice Girl most often cited by interviewees as being a useful support to their young identities, Clair (age 20; Euro-American; raised in the Silicon Valley, CA) recalled being "girly" and identifying with Baby Spice. She explained how her embrace of the Spice Girls' empowerment discourse led to her Spice Girls play and product consumption and also how it supported her girly identity.

CLAIR: There were a few things, like "When 2 Become 1" [the Spice Girls' ballad about safe sex] that I probably didn't get at that age. But most of it, the "girl power" and the "gotta get with my friends" parts, I *really* identified with. And at that point, I remember latching on to the empowering part and thinking it was cool, and dressing up as the Spice Girls—and doing their dances, and getting together with my friends, and getting all their collectables from the dolls to the magazines. Did you get the gum?

JENNA: Oh, the gum? Oh, no, but someone told me they had lollipops, and I didn't know that they had lollipops *or* gum.

CLAIR: They had gum with the little Spice Girls stickers in each pack of gum, and I'd collect the stickers. I had the T-shirts for sure and probably had pens. I probably had a subscription to the magazine. I got tall shoes and long socks and tried to do my hair like Baby Spice. I wore a "Baby" necklace.

JENNA: And what was it about Baby Spice that you could identify with the most?

CLAIR: I think it felt right. I didn't feel like I was any of the other ones. And some of the cute stuff she said, I think I'd say, and I liked the way that she dressed and the way that she looked. I was going for the blond-hair-and-girly part of it. It was during a time I was pretty girly.

Alyssa (age 21; Euro-American; raised in Tyrone, Pennsylvania) recalled being a tomboy in grade school, "wearing big baggy shirts and cut-off jeans." Girl power products like the "girls rule, boys drool" tee-shirts "didn't quite appeal to me," she said; "everything pink and purple and all the traditional girly stuff, I wasn't really into." Overall, she reflected, "I think I probably enjoyed it less than other girls because I do remember the other girls would have their folders with the [girl power] stickers and stuff."

Because Alyssa identified as a tomboy, Sporty Spice would have seemed a logical choice for her favorite Spice Girl; however, she preferred Baby Spice—at least until she learned that "Ginger had my same birthday, so she became my favorite," highlighting the whimsy behind some children's preferences. Unlike many other interviewees, she had never engaged in Spice Girls play with her friends. Although the Spice Girls were her entrée into popular music, Alyssa's peer group was not especially devoted to the Spice Girls—and many of her friends were boys. Between "not having very many friends who were obsessed with Spice Girls, not having a lot of extra family income and not feeling the need to own more than their CDs to feel like a real fan," she did not participate in the Spice Girls' consumer culture.

The only interviewee who favored Scary Spice was Calista (age 21; African-American; raised in Paterson, NJ). She liked Scary Spice and Sporty Spice best, appreciating that Sporty Spice was the strongest singer and got the best vocal lines—but personality-wise, Scary Spice felt inspiring. "Scary was the complete antithesis of me. I was quiet as a child, and she was loud and out there. It was fun to pretend to be her," Calista explained. Although Calista did not have many Spice Girls products beyond the cassette tapes, she loved the movie, and she remembered that she and her friends loved the lollipops.

CALISTA: That was a big thing in school. The lollipop came with a sticker, so everyone was trying to collect as many stickers as possible.

REBECCA: Oh, did you trade with your friends?

CALISTA: No, I kept mine! I don't think anyone really wanted to trade them. We just looked at each other's stickers.

REBECCA: Did you keep them in an album or anything?

CALISTA: No! I wish I had!

Of the interviewees who had been Spice Girls fans, only Kallie and Tamika recalled not having a favorite Spice. Kallie said she enjoyed the range of personalities presented by the Spice Girls. She explained, "The thing about the Spice Girls is they had this notion where it was just like they were like a bunch of different flavors, I feel like. I didn't identify with one; I'd have a different favorite every week back in that day."

Despite their limitations, the Spice Girls represented enough identity types to resonate with many girls. This is unsurprising, given the Spice Girls' global success; arguably, their successful marketing of girl types to young girls fueled their fame. For example, Morgan really believed in Sporty Spice's presentation as healthy and fit; she never knew she had struggled with an eating disorder (Sinclair, 2004). Likewise, Sporty Spice was Madeline's touchstone as she resisted pressures to become more feminine; and because the Spice Girls dolls had more variety in their appearances than Barbies at the time, Isabella (age 21; Caucasian/Jewish and Italian; raised in Princeton, NJ) took pleasure in using her Posh Spice doll as a regular Barbie doll, whom she asserted was prettier than the rest *because* she was a brunette. This defied the idea, promoted by Barbie and other Western culture discourses, that blonde hair is the most beautiful. At the same time, there was still a Spice Girl for blonde girly girls like Clair. Consuming and playing Spice Girls gave many girls a sense of cultural support and joy. This was not universal, however; some girls (like Alyssa) were not drawn to this type of play, and others actually recalled frustrations.

The Problems with Consuming the Spice Girls

For the women interviewed, frustrations involving the Spice Girls often involved roadblocks to their desired identity work. For example, Chloe (age 21; Caucasian; raised in Clinton, NJ) felt frustration from owning the wrong Spice Girl doll. She wanted Ginger Spice, but received Sporty Spice, instead—the Spice Girl who was about as different from Ginger Spice as possible.

CHLOE: There was all this consumer merchandise that went along with the Spice Girls, that I was really into.

REBECCA: Oh, did you have a lot of that stuff?

CHLOE: I had Sporty Spice the doll, which I didn't really—I was like, "Ugh." I was mad that my mom got me Sporty Spice, because I didn't really like her.

REBECCA: Which Spice Girls did you like?

CHLOE: Uh—I liked Ginger (laughing).

REBECCA: Was she your favorite?

CHLOE (laughing): Yeah, I think so. It was just like Sporty Spice didn't fit the sexy doll paradigm that I wanted, I think. And I was like, "What?" (laughing more.) It was just fun, you know?

REBECCA: Did you and your friends play Spice Girls?

CHLOE: No, we would just listen to the music, and dance, and watch the film.

REBECCA: So why do you think this sort of sexy doll type of Ginger was appealing to you?

CHLOE: Probably because I wanted to relate to it in that way, or like, I don't know—use the doll as sort of this fantasy mirror or something? And if the doll didn't represent what was in mind for me, in terms of that fantasy, it was like sort of a road block.

In other words, her mother's purchase of Sporty Spice hindered her fantasy/identity play and was recalled as a source of frustration.

Other girls' frustrations also centered on fantasy play. Natalie (age 21; Euro-American; raised in Pittsburgh, PA) and her friends typically pretended to be the Spice Girls during slumber parties, which—unlike play during school recess—involved dressing up.

NATALIE: I don't remember playing it in school. I remember at slumber parties, you would get all dressed up like them, and then we would watch the Spice Girls movie and act out the scenes while it was on the TV. And that's the kind of stuff I remember. I do remember the ritual of getting dressed up as being very important.

REBECCA: And did you and your friends have specific Spice Girls you would always dress up as?

NATALIE: Well, we all had favorites. My favorite was Baby Spice, but I wasn't allowed to buy Baby Spice because she had blonde hair and I have brown hair.

REBECCA: So who did they make you be?

NATALIE: They made me be Posh Spice.

REBECCA: She was very different from Baby Spice; she always walked around with like the serious like "I'm too good for this" look, right?

NATALIE: Yeah! She did, and we always made my little sister be Scary Spice!

REBECCA: Did she *want* to be Scary Spice?

NATALIE: No, it was because she had curly hair. It was very, very silly how we decided who was going to be who and what. It was very funny, very interesting.

REBECCA: So, it was based on look?

NATALIE: Yeah, it was based on look. It didn't matter who you liked. It mattered what you looked like, and, um, whether you had dresses, or, you know—My one tomboy friend was always Sporty Spice, and she didn't look anything like Sporty Spice. She just didn't have any dresses.

REBECCA: And so when you guys dressed up as the Spice Girls, besides having Sporty Spice in, like, tomboy clothes, what did dressing up as the Spice Girls mean at that age? 'Cause surely you didn't have a bunch of high heels and push-up bras.

NATALIE: No, we didn't have push-up bras, but we did have platform shoes, which were a really big deal then. Yeah, and so, like, we all kind of— I know I had platform sandals. So, I had those, and we all had— we were all young enough to have dress up clothes, which we modified to be Spice-Girl-like. I remember this red dress—it was this weird, silky red dress. One of my neighbors was getting rid of a bunch of clothes, and she gave it to me. She was in graduate school for Performing Arts or something, and so she had all sorts of hilarious ridiculous costumes. Um, that was really just to play Spice Girls with.

REBECCA: That must have been so much fun for dressing up.

NATALIE: Oh, yeah, I *loved* it. My mother also—mom had been married before my father, so she had this old wedding dress that my sister and I got to play dress up in. We totally destroyed it. But that dress, I *loved* it.

Natalie also noted that the girl who played Sporty Spice and didn't have many dress up clothes was, interestingly, usually in charge of the game. "She was the one who decided that I couldn't be Baby and my sister had to be Scary," she explained. In Natalie's peer group, then, those who did not fit their favorite Spice Girl's type—either physically or in clothing style—were pressured into playing a less-preferred Spice. Natalie still derived pleasure from this play, recalling her delight in having interesting dress-up outfits. Resources were important as her friends negotiated who would portray which Spice Girl: "The pecking order was certainly established or confirmed according to who got to be the desirable Spice Girls," she confirmed. Overall, Natalie's access to high-quality dress-up clothes satisfied and enthralled her during play, despite the other frustrating limitations she faced.

On the other hand, Jia-Li only tolerated Spice Girls play to be included at recess. She did not remember fights within the group over who would play which Spice Girl, because her friends would generally agree that whoever was *most* like a specific Spice Girl had the right to play that character. However, as she was not a Spice Girls fan, she was given the leftover role: Baby Spice, "which is not me at all. I'm not young, and I'm not blonde, and I'm not ditzy."

JIA-LI: There were five of us, and everyone picked one. They'd be like, "Oh, well, I *call* this one." And so then the only one *left* was Baby Spice, because everyone had already identified with a different Spice Girl. So, since I was part of that friend group, I just went along. Like, whatever. It's just another game. I just played along. It was just funny because they had to teach me what Baby Spice did. "Oh, well she puts hair like *this*." Or "She eats her lollipop like *this*." I was kind of like, "Whatever." [. . .] When they told me about Baby Spice, I was like, "That's not me at all [laughing], but I'll just play along."

REBECCA: Did it ever bother you to be coerced into being this Baby Spice who seemed nothing like you, or did it not matter because you didn't particularly like any of the Spice Girls?

JIA-LI: I remember being kind of annoyed that I was Baby Spice, just because it didn't fit me. But then again, I was trying to think, "Well, which of the Spice Girls would I really fit in with? So, I'm not Posh Spice; that's not my M.O. I'm not Sporty; I'm not Scary Spice either, I'm not fierce like that; and Ginger Spice, she's just a Ginger; what is there to that?" Yeah, I didn't fit in with any of them, so I was just like, "Whatever. Whatever. We're just going to play this game, and I'll just be Baby Spice."

For Jia-Li, then, an overarching issue with the Spice Girls was that none offered her a viable option to identify with, so during group play, she acquiesced; she didn't enjoy it.

Isabella recalled disputes during Spice Girls play with her friends, especially over who would play Ginger, "because she was the main Spice Girl." She recalled there being little to no flexibility in how roles were assigned between her friends, and even as a child, this bothered her:

ISABELLA: Looking back, I remember being like, "Ok, I'll be Posh Spice, but I have some issues with this." Mostly I *had* to be Posh Spice because I wasn't, like, a tomboy, but I wasn't, like, super girly. And I thought that Baby Spice was silly. Even at that time, I was like, "Why is she looking like an 8 year old?" I was not into it. I definitely was not a Baby Spice person. Part of it was that she [Posh Spice] had dark hair, and so if you are the friend with dark hair, you are automatically Posh Spice. I think she was probably the most sophisticated looking one, which I liked. I can still remember who was what Spice Girl, and it was always according to what style they were. I remember it always bugged me that all my black friends would immediately be Scary Spice. At the time, I was like, ok—I never had a problem if they *wanted* to be—I had a problem if they felt like they *had* to be.

Thus, although like Jia-Li Isabella didn't feel well suited to any particular Spice Girl, she found it problematic that some of her friends were shoehorned into playing certain Spice Girls on the basis of their appearances and racial heritage. She added,

ISABELLA: I remember these two girls fighting over who was going to be Scary Space. At the time, guys were just fighting over who's going to be what Spice Girl—but it was like, of *course* you are going to fight over who's going to be the only black Spice Girl. There was always this awkward conversation if one of them was, like, "I guess I'll be Baby Spice," but it didn't make any sense. Why is there only one? Why is there this tokenized, stereotypical image? Each of them were just, like, kind of an archetype of a certain type of girl. I think that created drama if there was two kinds of those kinds of girls in one space. If there were two sporty friends present, there would be an issue. That's why I think those characters got so powerful with that age group. People pick up characteristics that match them.

According to Isabella's recollections, then, Spice Girls play was a source of struggle among friends, as the Spice Girls' identities—bundled by intertwined appearances and personalities—did not allow for much flexibility in Spice Girls identity play among her friends. They adhered strictly to the limited range presented by the Spice Girls, with friends rarely permitting each other the fantasy of a Spice Girls identity unlike their own.

Calista could only recall playing Spice Girls once with her friends, at school; it was not a major pastime for her and her peers like it was for some of the other interviewees. Her experience reinforced some of the racialized overtones of Spice Girls play, however. Playing in a group of two white girls, one Hispanic girl, and another black girl, she explained that a "Baby Spice controversy came up."

CALISTA: We wanted to recreate the [laughing] military training scene from the movie. And so people would try to decide who would be who, and there was a girl, they wanted her to be Scary—but she didn't want to do it. She wanted to be Baby Spice, so I volunteered to be Scary.

REBECCA: And why did they want her to be Scary Spice?

CALISTA: [deep breath] This is gonna sound bad, but I didn't come up with this idea: She was Jamaican, and so she was dark-skinned. For some reason, they wanted her to be Scary. I never knew why.

REBECCA: So was she darker skinned than you?

CALISTA: Yeah. I guess that's why they thought she should be Scary by default.

REBECCA: So when you stepped in, did they let her be Baby?

CALISTA: Yeah, they let her be Baby. There weren't other overlaps or disagreements. In fact, someone thanked me for being Scary so we could just play Spice Girls without conflict. I think it was the girl who played Ginger.

Overall, these reflections offer some useful insights. Although many girls derived pleasure from pretending to be their favorite Spice Girl, other girls were prevented from doing so by their playmates (or, in independent play, by parents who did not cooperate by purchasing them their doll of choice—in many ways the same principle). The Spice Girls at times empowered girls through the range of personalities they offered. However, as the realities of the girls' recollected play illustrates, this did not always occur easily. Much Spice Girls play occurred in groups. This makes sense: there were five Spice Girls; what fun would it be to pretend to be a Spice Girl on your own, when the whole concept was that the band were friends forever—an unbreakable force of girl power solidarity?

The nature of Spice Girls play lead to recollections of contentious moments, however. Though the Spice Girls presented a range of identities, there were only five Spice "flavors"—each one-dimensional, lacking complexity. Merely a few salient characteristics defined each Spice. When children divvied up the roles, it wasn't about potential; none took turns experimenting with being the cute Spice Girl, or the athletic Spice Girl, and so on. Instead, two basic characteristics factored into their play assignments: personality traits and physical appearance (sometimes including mode of dress). The girls who matched on both counts, and who didn't have a peer who also matched, could succeed in negotiating to play their chosen Spice Girl. And if a girl like Jia-Li didn't match any of the Spice Girls, she was not invited to take her pick or alternate roles in an exploratory way; she was given the leftover.

As I heard from Natalie and Isabella, if a conflict arose within a peer group during role selection, physical appearance easily trumped personality. This had potentially racist overtones: In Isabella's mixed-race peer group, black girls did not receive group approval to play Baby Spice, because they were neither white nor blonde. Therefore, the peers asserted, the black girls couldn't possibly take Baby's role, even if they identified as girly: Girls with black skin were taught that they did not fit the girlishly feminine mold. While they were the only two interviewees who shared such experiences, it sounded like Calista's Jamaican-American friend narrowly avoided such a fate, thanks to Calista's intervention. Additionally, in dress-up play, personal resources—such as what kind of dress-up clothes a girl owned—served as yet another form of gatekeeping. Those with wardrobe choices had the upper hand, privileging a materialistic perspective. It is likely that other girls in the broader population experienced similar struggles.

Although Spice Girls play was imaginative, the children did not always have enough imagination to transcend cultural stereotypes of the sort reinforced—inadvertently or not—by the Spice Girls. Children are taught that what's inside counts, but in some peer groups, the outside took precedence. These manifest variables, being easier to see, seemed logical for the pre-adolescent girls to base their assignments on. For some, this mitigated the empowering potential of identity work during Spice Girls play: rather than exploring what they could be, they learned hard lessons about what society said they could *not* be. One might hope that in the end, this made some girls stronger, ensuring that they knew what prejudices and stereotypes they were up against. This, however, is hard to tell.

Girl Power Pathways

While our interviewees' experiences with Spice Girls play were sometimes sites of struggle, which may or may not have been productive, critics such as Weldon had at least a few things wrong. Far from being a feminist anathema, several indicated the Spice Girls' mode of girl power had positive benefits, serving as a pathway to feminism or deeper feminism. These connections bear exploring, for they suggest the popular black-and-white perspective of a media phenomenon being feminist or not is often overstated. As scholars conducting textual analyses have often asserted, the truth is frequently more complex: a media text can be simultaneously progressive and regressive.

Samantha (age 24; Euro-American; raised in Hoffman Estates, IL) grew up in a town with a "conservative mindset," with a conservative family of Republican Roman Catholics. Raised with limited access to television, she spent her leisure time reading, instead. She also loved popular music—"terrible music," she laughed. She argued, however, that her first encounters with feminist ideas came via the Spice Girls and other pop culture phenomena, such as the Power Rangers and the American Girls franchise, as well as her involvement with the Girl Scouts. "Given my family and my circumstances," she explained, "that was the way feminism reached me." She credits these girlhood experiences as a foundation for her "a-ha moment" regarding feminism, which came when she was in high school:

> SAMANTHA: Being raised Catholic—I mean, I must have been 9 years old or something when my dad and I wrote letters through our church for our representative, basically pro-life. Action letters. Then in high school, we were actually learning about legislation in history class and then thinking, "oh, I think I'm pro-choice" because it sounds more my side. And it was as simple as that. It wasn't a huge revelation on "how could I be so wrong"; it was more of "oh, yeah, that makes sense."

While other interviewees did not posit as direct a line from the Spice Girls to feminism, some said the band set them on a pathway towards more empowering music. For example, prior to listening to the Spice Girls, Kallie had only listened to Disney music; the Spice Girls broadened her tastes and horizons, priming her for subsequent pop musicians like Janet Jackson and Edie Brickell. She found their music empowering and fully credits the Spice Girls with helping her find music that wasn't "shallow."

Rose (age 19; Euro-American; raised in Manhattan and South Salem, NY) similarly believed Spice Girls led her to more empowering music—in her case, to the riot grrrls. "It's really funny that I went from being really into Spice Girls to, like, riot grrrl," she said, "because that's a very logical sequence, actually."

REBECCA: What's logical to you about it?

ROSE: It's just the whole feminism-but-also-wearing-pink, and, like, being girly. Riot grrrl is kind of the generation that comes from girl power, but it's also subverting it.

In other words, although the Spice Girls chronologically debuted after the riot grrrls, Rose's personal chronology was the inverse—and she believed the riot grrrls were responding to the Spice Girls. She continued by explaining the way she perceived the riot grrrls as subverting girl power:

ROSE: When I think about my pink phone, for example: I got it to be ironic— like, "Oh my God, isn't it hysterical that I'm getting this pink phone. How stupid is that!" And that's kind of what I think about, like, riot grrrl fashion. I had this, like, pink leopard skirt and I loved this pink leopard skirt! But at the same time, I was like, yeah, it's badass, it's pink. Pink can be badass. So that's why it's girl-power-esque.

Although Rose still enjoyed Bikini Kill, Babes in Toyland, Sleater Kinney, Le Tigre, Heavens to Betsy, and other riot grrrl bands, she said she had outgrown the forms of angry feminism they represented. She channeled her energy into volunteer work, instead. "[Riot grrrl is] very angry, and I don't think it's very productive," she said. Recollecting her early experiences with anger at women's status in society, she added, "But I think it doesn't necessarily have to *be* productive. It's empowering in a way." Citing a Babes in Toyland song in which the singer screams, "You're dead meat, motherfucker!" she noted, "If you feel that way—and you probably will, if that's happened to you—you should express it, and you should be able to express it without being silenced."

In short, although the Spice Girls debuted several years after the riot grrrls movement began, Rose and some of the other interviewees (including Calista, Samantha, Kallie, Alyssa, and Natalie, who also were or had previously been riot grrrl fans) experienced them in the reverse order—a sort of reverse engineering of girl power. This pattern offers an interesting theoretical consideration: Although the Spice Girls co-opted girl power from the riot grrrls, the Spice Girls' co-optation may have ultimately led some listeners back to girl power's originators. They may have watered down the riot grrrls' feminist impact, but by the same token, this may also have made them a viable form of beginners' feminism—bringing empowerment rhetoric to girls in a gentle, easily digestible way, priming them for more difficult, angrier, less mainstream feminist discourse later on. With digital music available online for instant download, or instant viewing and listening on YouTube, countercultural music is more accessible for today's listeners than it was just a few years ago. (For example, Calista found Bikini Kill online after hearing them on a movie soundtrack and liking their music.) The long tail of internet retailing allows people to find things online that they would likely never find in a local brick-and-mortar store or on MTV, and to interpret older music in dialogue with newer music—disrupting their true chronology.

Girl Power's Meaning—or Lack Thereof

Given these varied experiences, what did girl power mean to the young feminists I interviewed? Although critics have problematized the Spice Girls, many young feminists offered positive descriptions of girl power's meaning. Their readings often aligned with the Spice Girls' discourse. Asked what girl power meant to her as a girl, Calista responded, "At the time, I guess I thought it meant having fun with your friends. I didn't really think too much about it. I just remember repeating it. Like, 'Girl power!' But I don't think I knew what it meant." Reflecting with hindsight on whether girl power and feminism might be related to one another, she replied:

> CALISTA: Girl power is about doing your own thing, and being independent, and friendship between women. And, you know, those are feminist ideals. One of the main problems between women is self-internalized misogyny, and girl power is the antithesis of that.

As one of the youngest of the interviewees (she was only in second grade when the Spice Girls debuted), Calista thus related to the Spice Girls' messages about female solidarity via friendship. Isabella—the same age as Calista—also recalled girl power as a powerful promotion of girls' friendships. "It wasn't like I was like '*Yeah*, girl power!', but I definitely said it all the time. Thinking back on it, the movies didn't have any boys in them. They didn't have any—it wasn't about relationships or falling in love. It was about being with your friends that are girls, and having a good time, and doing what you want, and—you know—being there for each other."

In contrast, Morgan—a junior high student when the Spice Girls became popular—had broader feelings about Spice Girls' discourse on girl power. Asked what girl power meant to her as a girl, she replied:

> MORGAN: There is nothing you can't do. That is the biggest thing that I can 100% say without even a doubt. When I heard that, I thought, "I can go out and conquer the world. I can pull in all the stars, and they can come and live in my house. I will have night in my house all the time and all those beautiful stars."

For Morgan, then, girl power offered a beautiful vision of being capable of anything—even the impossible. Kallie had a similar perspective: She recalled girl power as an anthem of fierce independence.

> KALLIE: It just meant you could be anything and you don't have to care, and I feel like growing up is just, like, a girl is supposed to do this and that, and *isn't* supposed to do this and that. Girl power just kind of means, "Put all those guards down and fuck whatever anybody says"—sorry for using explicit language. They [the Spice Girls] seemed so carefree and living for the moment—I don't know, maybe in the movie, the messages seemed to be, "We're going to do what we want, we're going to say what we want to say. There's not going to be a filter. We're not going to act 'feminine.' We're not going to be lady like. We're going to do what we want and still be sexy, still be cool and still be real."

Kallie added that the Spice Girls' mode of girl power struck a good balance between moral messages and the idea that it's okay to have "fun being a girl, even if that's being a little promiscuous."

Although Jia-Li had not been a Spice Girls fan and never bought any of their products, she did remember loving the idea of girl power. She was allowed to purchase a few girl power products: t-shirts with smiley faces and flowers on them, peace-sign necklaces, mood rings, and the other accessories that she viewed as part of girl power. She remembered that people said "girl power" a lot, and she liked it when her peers said, "Oh, girls rule, boys drool" when "boys did something stupid." The attitude of girl power was most appealing to her.

REBECCA: So back then, what do you think you thought it meant?

JIA-LI: I think what I associated it with was how *awesome* girls are, but in a very attitude, active way. It's not necessarily how *nice* girls are, right? It's more just like, girls rock. They have attitude. They are fierce and cool and pretty, but not pretty in a passive sense—but like BOOM! Pretty! Just very punchy. Everything's got punch to it. I really liked that.

Chloe had a complex relationship to girl power because she experienced both the Spice Girls' version and a middle school support group called "girl power time." These were very different:

CHLOE: I used to go to my counselor all the time for counseling. I ended up seeing her and telling her about my life, and I think from a conversation that we had with each other, we needed this space for girls to talk about shit that was going on. I remember it being great because it was like group therapy.

REBECCA: And so what did girl power mean to you then?

CHLOE: It felt like a caring space I think, like a place where I was being listened too and like a place where I could resolve that I was having with my female peers. There was a lot of drama with this one girl who was always like very jealous of me. We had this sort of competitive relationship, and she would steal things from my house and then accuse me of stealing all her friends.

In contrast to the "girl power time" support group, Chloe understood the Spice Girls' version of girl power as about the marketplace:

CHLOE: I still view girl power as this commodity, like the Spice Girl lollipops and the dolls. It was this whole package, which I don't think is bad if you're trying to get little kids to get into it. Of course little kids like packages. I don't know if putting it into little kids hands nec-

essarily means that they are *getting* it. I don't know—it's sort of ironic because these women are media commodities. I still wonder
who is behind girl power, and I don't think it's the Spice Girls.

Grace had experienced girl power as empowering, specifically in relation to athleticism. "Because I did sports, I usually measure things based on like physical capac-
ity; so [when I heard 'girl power'] I would think of some girl putting her fist in the
air, and beating a guy or something." Grace's take-away from the Spice Girls was
a message about being true to oneself. "'I don't want anyone to change you.' 'Stick
with your friends.' 'Don't backstab.' That's pretty much what I got out of it: Just
be a good person in general."

Samantha also thought girl power evoked athleticism—specifically related to
the gains of Title IX. Asked whether she thought girl power and feminism are related to one another, Samantha reflected:

SAMANTHA: I think one begets the other. Before you're old enough to really
understand the history and the political action behind feminism,
girl power is just a really fun lighthearted way to celebrate being a
girl and that there is nothing wrong with being a girl. I never felt
that growing up. I don't know if my mom and her generation did,
but there was definitely a difference, you know, when gym classes
were segregated by boys and girls. I don't know if my mom even
had—I just don't know how life was, but I feel like I had more experiences and opportunity.

Abby (age 19; Euro-American; raised in Springfield, VT), who was raised by
her mother (she noted, "my parents haven't been together since I was 4"), felt that
being strong but girlish in men's absence was significant to her understanding of
girl power:

ABBY: Girl power is really interesting for me because, looking after my mom it's,
like, the absence of men. "Kicking butt" comes to mind—kinda like
being tougher than the boys, but still being girlie. For me, it just
meant being in my own sphere, and being, I guess, girlie, but also
being cool about it? [pause] I guess the resonating message for me
was girls can be cool, too. Like, girls can break the mold and, um.
. . . I don't know. Like, I was watching *Spice World* last night, and
they're out doing this military thing, and one of the lines from the
movie is, "strength and courage in a Wonderbra," and I guess that's
what Girl Power was to me. It was just, like, kicking butt and
being tough but not breaking a nail while doing that.

Not all of the young feminists recalled feeling girl power had a clear, strong meaning, however. Isabella experienced girl power as more of a catchphrase. She recalled, "I probably saw it more as kind of, like, elementary school 'Girls rule, boys drool.' Almost this empty 'Yah.'" Meredith also initially received "girl power" as a catchphrase:

MEREDITH: It did take me a little while to figure out that it wasn't just a saying to them—like, they actually had more of a meaning, you know,
'girl power,' like they were trying to make it known that that's
what they were about. So it did take a little while; but I think I took
it as just being comfortable with yourself, just owning who you are,
like being proud to be a girl, just being proud to you know to be
who you are and be comfortable.

On the other hand, some interviewees had understood what "girl power" meant to signify but did not find it personally meaningful because it seemed redundant; it had never occurred to them that girls were anything *but* empowered. Miraya (age 21; Asian-American; raised in Bergen County, New Jersey) explained:

MIRAYA: Looking back, I don't think that I ever thought it was seriously empowering, because I was told I could do anything by other adult figures.
I don't feel like those pop icons really made me feel that way.
Although, it was maybe a small part of it—but there were a lot of
boy bands that were around when I was in the 4th grade, and the
Spice Girls was the only popular girl band at the time. I remember
liking them because of that, partly.

Similarly, asked if she remembered how people used "girl power" when she was young, Alyssa replied:

ALYSSA: I remember it from the Spice Girls' movie. Oh, what's her name—
Ginger? They were all doing their superpowers that they had, and
Ginger could change her identity, and she came out of the phone
booth all, like, "Girl power!" and I remember being like "Whaaat"?
Like, even then, I knew that talking about girl power was stigmatized in a way. I guess it wasn't something that you thought about
as a little kid; it was just something you would do.

REBECCA: Hmm, right. So, can you elaborate on that more? Like, what do you
mean by all that?

ALYSSA: Well, like, I don't feel like I actively sought out like girly things or girl power things. I just was hanging around with the boys, and I never felt like there was something I couldn't do. If I wanted to do something, I was going to do it. No one really told me growing up, "You have to be like this or do this." I was already anti-pink. I don't think I ever really wore pink when I was little. I mean, I had Barbies, but I would make them have sex or something. I know I wasn't a very traditional, feminine kind of girl. I was a like-to-run-around-outside-and-play-video-games kind of girl. It wasn't something I needed to say. I didn't need to be told about girl power; I was already doing my thing.

Likewise, Madeline recalled:

MADELINE: It was a little bit redundant. Like, women had their liberation, and we didn't still need to be talking about it. [. . .] It was kind of, before I grew up and I realized there were differences in how men and women were treated, I believed we were all equal, and probably the same about my ideas about race. I thought it had all been solved, you know—it was the '90s.

Because of this feeling, when the Spice Girls proclaimed girl power, Madeline thought it was an "unnecessary reinforcement. But I understood why it was there, because, you know, when you're growing up people are always reinforcing the morals that they want you to have. So I kind of took it as a part of that." In other words, the concept of girl power fit in so well with what she already believed that it was nothing new to her; it was more of the same. As a girl, she only realized that girl power might be culturally necessary after learning how rare all-girl bands were.

MADELINE: I remember watching a Spice Girls documentary after they ended and they were reflecting on it, and they said that they were so 'girl power' because there were a lot of guy groups and there weren't many girl groups like them. And I thought there were always the Spice Girls so I hadn't thought about it like that. So I kind of knew where they were coming from more after I heard that. That's important, to have girls present in different genres of things, and not leave something all to the boys because then it will just be a boy thing.

Having grown up thinking the Spice Girls had "always" existed, their documentary led Madeline to think about a world without successful girl bands. In this way, ultimately, the Spice Girls did serve to raise her consciousness about unequal representation in the media.

In contrast to this sense of redundancy, Hannah and Natalie—both raised by feminist parents who were college professors—recalled believing girl power to be empty rhetoric. Prior to Hannah's punk days in high school, she recalled often wanting to fit better into the community. When the Spice Girls became popular, she latched onto them as a route to normalcy among her peers. Although she did not buy into the Spice Girls' claims to feminism, she recognized these claims might provide leverage with her parents, who carefully restricted her media use. Although her campaign to win access to the Spice Girls failed, she remembered her efforts well.

HANNAH: I was in third grade when the Spice Girls came out, and I was like, "They are so cool!" I couldn't understand why my parents weren't, like, buying me everything.

REBECCA: What do you remember liking about the Spice Girls? Why were they so cool?

HANNAH: They were just—I don't know. I mean, I think for me, it was not really anything about girl power or feeling empowerment. It was just being, like, "Oh yeah, I'm *cool.* I can do this. I can fit in." Which I didn't do very successfully, but, um, I don't know—it was just more of a popularity thing. But I could defend to my parents that the Spice Girls were talking about feminism. "Look at them— they can sing and be feminist!"

REBECCA: So did you consciously know they were feminist at that time?

HANNAH: Yeah, my parents had sort of given me some rough guidelines—like, they always used to tell me about the Barbie Liberation Front.

REBECCA: But your parents didn't end up getting you all kinds of Spice Girl stuff.

HANNAH: Oh, no—they didn't buy into the spirit. And I was like, "Shut up! Geez, I don't want to listen to you guys. I want to be cool now." Which was my first mistake. But I also remember just being like, "Ok, well, here are some grown ups that are really cool and really sexy and really popular. They get all these attention and people like them, so . . ."

When her efforts to win her parents' approval of her Spice Girls fandom failed, Hannah resorted to "sneak[ing] little peeks" at the Spice Girls on her friends' televisions (her family did not have a TV). She also borrowed her friend's Spice Girls tape, "which was a big deal"—but she didn't make a copy of it, "because my parents made me return it." Her access to the Spice Girls' music was extremely limited.

Coming to the Spice Girls with a critical apparatus and a sense of feminism, Natalie—like Hannah—also disbelieved the Spice Girls' message of empowerment.

REBECCA: What do you remember about "girl power" from back then?

NATALIE: Looking back, I remember it being really superficial. And, well, it was just something that you said or you did, and it didn't really have any translation into actions. It was just a phrase. It didn't have any deeper meaning. It was just something written on my t-shirt, and that's it. And there was no connection between "girl power" and how I was living my life, and, you know, the later actions I took.

In pursuing permission to listen to the Spice Girls from her feminist parents, Natalie—like Hannah—was inspired by her peers' interest in the band. "I remember that my friends really liked them," she reflected," so I kind of hopped on and decided that I really liked them, too." Unlike Hannah, however, Natalie ultimately received parental support for her fandom, making experience quite different. Natalie's mother struck a balance between criticism and support of her interest in the Spice Girls:

NATALIE: My parents—my mother especially is just one of those really outspoken feminists, and she was always like, "Wow, they're kind of, um—" the way they used their sexuality and their skimpy clothes and the fact that they're all really thin. That kind of stuff really bothered her, but she was really kind of excited that they were somebody. She really liked buying me all of the girl power stuff. [. . .]It was a place for her to connect, and it made her feel really good about putting her money, and, you know, she wanted me to have that background. [. . .] My mom came from a really conservative family, and I think she has a lot of stuff, a lot of pain left over from that she didn't want me to have. And she wanted me to feel empowered. It's very sweet, my parents are great!

Natalie was thereby permitted to share her friends' interest in the Spice Girls while becoming familiar with her mothers' concerns about the Spice Girls' visual presentation. Natalie also recalled receiving unexpected support from a lesbian couple at church who brought her Spice Girls kitsch week after week. "The women in my life were really excited about girl power," she recalled. "I think they were just excited that there was something that was focused on women." Natalie's mother purchased a lot of generic girl power items for her, as well. She reflected:

Asked whether, in hindsight, she thought that girl power and feminism were related, Natalie expressed ambivalence. This seemed largely rooted in the fact that as a girl, despite her ownership of so many girl power products, she could not personally embrace girl power as a mode of empowerment.

> NATALIE: Hm . . . I don't know! That's interesting. I have absolutely no idea. My kind of initial reaction is yes. I do have this feeling that "girl power" was a good thing, just because even if I didn't take it to heart, I think hearing that and having that as something I could say was meaningful, was important. I really think that girls are told that they are not powerful, or that their power lies entirely in their sexuality. So, I want to say that it is a feminist thing, but at the same time I really didn't take it to heart. It really wasn't meaningful, and that is distressing to think about. I'm not sure.

Any analysis of the Spice Girls as feminist (or not) must account for the varied, complex positionalities of their fans. The Spice Girls served a range of purposes in their fans' lives. For some, the Spice Girls were a site of pleasure, while for others, they were a source of struggle—surely with more variance, even, than that reflected in the sample of this study.

Did the Spice Girls co-opt feminism? Yes. But did the Spice Girls kill feminism? No. While co-optation is problematic, some girls who grew up with the Spice Girls fully embrace a feminist identity. Some look back and recall the Spice Girls using "girl power" as catchphrase, while others remember feeling empowered by their discourse. Some even traced a line from the Spice Girls' rhetoric to other sites of feminist engagement, suggesting that when feminism is watered down—used to sell products—it can also lead some consumers to more feminist texts at a later date.

As the Spice Girls receded from fame, the girl power banner unfurled on television. Here, once more, feminist discourse was co-opted for commercial interests, but in a new format. As a pop music act, the Spice Girls, whose personalities were depicted primarily through music videos, books, and their movie. On television, girl power was much more directly about narrative. Television programs within the girl power umbrella featured lesson after lesson about feeling empowered, being strong, and having self-confidence—in other words, offering weekly or daily opportunities for social learning among its viewers. But given the history of female representation on children's television, how did girl power prompt the greenlighting of so many stories about girls?

Note

1. There are several reasons for this imbalance. One is the challenge in reaching child audience members, requiring layers of approvals and consent from institutions and individuals. Another is that interviewing audience members is time- and labor-intensive: It takes many hours to conduct useful qualitative interviews, and many more to transcribe them.

4

Girl Power on Screen

The Rise of the Girl Hero

"It's normal for *this* girl to save *everybody*!"
—Jenny, "Return of the Raggedy Android," *My Life as a Teenage Robot*
(2003)

"Who else wants some?!!?"
—Bubbles, "Bubblevicious," *The Powerpuff Girls (1999)*

"I can*not* afford this jacket."
—Kim, "Bueno Nacho," *Kim Possible (2002)*

As the 1990s dawned, television's landscape was bleak for girls. Few children's programs depicted girls in interesting roles because the networks warred perpetually over ratings, and executives claimed stories featuring girls would yield fewer viewers than the traditional boy-dominated fare (Carter, 1991). When the Spice Girls became international superstars in 1997, and girl power proved capable of selling anything, their tune quickly changed. At decade's end, pre-teen girls abruptly became a viable, desirable commercial audience—a paradigm shift that gave them unprecedented attention from the networks.

The marketing industry had been speculating about how best to appeal to pre-teen audiences—boys and girls alike—for several years prior. In 1992, marketing professor James McNeal published *Kids as Customers: A Handbook of Marketing to Children* (1992), a follow-up to his influential *Children as Consumers* (1987). *Kids as Customers* presented marketers with data demonstrating that children influenced $130 billion in annual U.S. purchases—20% of all consumer spending. A group of children he called "tweens" were especially influential. "Tween" was a marketing concept that had emerged quietly in the 1980s (Siegel, Coffey & Livingston, 2004, p. x; Coulter, 2005, p. 332), derived from an abbreviation of the word "between" that resembles the word teen.[1] Definitionally, "tween" refers to a pre-teen conceptualized by marketers as older than a child but younger than a teen, with one foot in childhood pursuits and one foot in the teenage world. The age group encompasses children approximately 8 to 12 years old.

Through the 1980s, pre-teen children's buying power had increased significantly—in part due to the proliferation of single-parent families and two-career households (Coulter, 2005). Linn (2004) explained that in these families, many children were home alone from the end of the school day until their parents arrived home from work. Often called "latchkey kids"[2] in media reports at the time (Linn, 2004), their parents gave them significant responsibilities in the household, such as grocery shopping (Coulter, 2005); one study revealed that 50% of teens were "heavily involved" in shopping for family groceries (Sellers, 1989). Their latchkey situation made them readily accessible to advertisers, for their parents—concerned about their children's physical safety in their absence—often encouraged them to stay in the house until their arrival. Television viewing therefore became the activity of choice among many children from 3 to 5 p.m. (Linn, 2004, p. 131), allowing networks to deliver a substantial child audience to advertisers for 10 or more hours a week.

By decade's end, with the networks vying for tween viewers, children's programming had necessarily become more diverse—"both appealing and inclusive" (Banet-Weiser, 2007, p. 34). Informed by the discourse on the girl crisis and the success of the Spice Girls, new representations of girls constituted a significant amount of that diversity—not just in terms of their gender, but also their races and ethnicities, a strategy that led to tremendous success for the Disney Channel (Valdivia, 2008, 2011). No longer invisible, passive, or dumb, girls were everywhere. Girls were the title characters of new shows in which they acted smart, sassy, and savvy— fun viewing for boys and girls alike. Programs like *The Proud Family* (2001–2005, The Disney Channel), *Sister, Sister* (1994–1995, ABC; 1995–1999, The WB), and *That's So Raven* (2003–2007, The Disney Channel) centered on appealing depictions of smart African-American girls and their families. Soon afterwards, appealing shows debuted about Asian girls—such as *The Life and Times of Juniper Lee* (2005–2007, Cartoon Network), *Hi Hi Puffy Ami Yumi Show* (2004–2007, Cartoon Network), and *Na Hao, Kai-Lan* (2008–present, Nick Jr.)—and about

Latinas, such as *Dora the Explorer* (2000–present, Nick Jr.) and *The Wizards of Waverly Place* (2007–present, The Disney Channel). Smart girls with an interest in nature and animal behavior were depicted in *The Wild Thornberrys* (1998–2004, Nickelodeon) and *Naturally, Sadie* (2005–2007, The Disney Channel). *The Cheetah Girls* (2003, 2006, 2008) musical comedy movie series was also noteworthy. Produced by and aired on Disney Channel, *The Cheetah Girls* was about an eponymous all-girl band whose members were portrayed by Raven-Symoné and Kiely Williams, both African-American; Adrienne Bailon, a Latina (of Puerto Rican and Ecuadorean descent); and Sabrina Bryan, who is of mixed heritage (her mother is Caucasian and her father is Hispanic). And a host of animated shows were dedicated to the virtually unprecedented portrayal of little girls as the subjects of action-adventure programs: as intelligent, strong superheroes in their own right.

Figure 4.1: *The Powerpuff Girls* Left to right: Bubbles, Blossom, and Buttercup. THE POWERPUFF GIRLS and all related characters and elements are trademarks of ©Cartoon Network. Used by permission.

The Powerpuff Girls: The First Girl Heroes

Cartoons about little girls as superheroes debuted on television in 1998, when Cartoon Network launched *The Powerpuff Girls* (1998–2005). The show's 5-year-old heroines were Blossom, Buttercup, and Bubbles, born of a laboratory experiment gone awry. Seeking to create the perfect little girl, Professor Utonium devised a formula that called for eight cups of sugar, a pinch of spice, and a tablespoon of everything nice ("The Rowdyruff Boys," 1998). However, a drop of "Chemical X" fell into the mixture, creating an explosion from which the Powerpuff Girls were born—with "ultra-superpowers." In addition to the powers of flight and super strength, Blossom had ice breath and microscopic vision; Bubbles boasted a sonic scream and could talk with animals; and Buttercup had energy fists and the ability to create a torpedo spin. Unflaggingly civic-minded, they gladly dedicated these abilities to fighting any villains who threatened the City of Townsville—in between kindergarten and bedtime, of course.

Craig McCracken created *The Powerpuff Girls* when he was a 20-year-old sophomore studying character animation at the California Institute for the Arts. The year was 1992. Networks were airing virtually no programs for girls; girl superhero characters simply did not exist. So when the young McCracken devised an entertainingly implausible premise—cute little girls whose superheroic capabilities rival those of any macho superman—he ran with it.[3] McCracken would later recall that in creating the show, "I wanted the heroes to be strong, tough and cool. The juxtaposition of their being really cute and really strong seemed more interesting than if they had been muscley guys" (qtd. in Corliss, 2001, par. 9). Although girls were on the national radar because of the AAUW reports, McCracken did not develop the show with girl viewers in mind or with feminist intent. He was just a 20-year-old undergraduate creating something he felt that he and other young adults would enjoy. "I thought [the show] would get on Cartoon Network and college kids would watch it and there would be a few random T-shirts out there in the rave scene or in record shops," he mused. "But I had no idea that it would take off to this extent" (qtd. in DeMott, 2000, p. 1). As he told Weinkauf (2002): "I just thought it was cool to see these cute little girls being really tough and really hardcore" (para. 2).

Once *The Powerpuff Girls* joined the Cartoon Network lineup in 1998, audience response made clear that millions of viewers agreed with him. After debuting as the highest rated premiere in Cartoon Network history, it generated audiences greater than 2 million[4]—nearly a quarter of whom were adults (Hager, 2002, p. 2), many watching during regular prime-time screenings. By 2001, the series ranked first among 9- to 14-year-old children on Cartoon Network (McAlister, 2002). The cartoon received nominations for five Emmy awards and nine Annie awards (the animation industry's equivalent to the Emmy Awards), winning two of each (Advertiser Staff, 2000; imdb.com). Owing to all these successes, in 2002, *The Powerpuff Girls* became a full-length animated movie, a prequel to the cartoon series—to this day remaining the only Cartoon Network property to be released as a feature film in theaters. In other words, by playing with stereotypes about "cute little girls," McCracken inadvertently created a show that became so popular, it would help to transform mediated discourse about girls.

Children in the program's daytime viewing audience were split evenly between boys and girls, disproving the industry canard that boys will not watch television shows featuring female lead characters. This generated positive forecasts for sales of licensed products, through which top media brands often generate more income than via box office sales or advertising income. Networks therefore have increasingly wanted toys based on children's shows to be marketable to both boys and girls (Selig, 2010). As Brian Weinstock, vice president of boys creative at toy-licensee Trendmasters, enthused, "We've always been really excited about the boy aspect of the show. [. . .] They watch the [*Powerpuff Girls*] show and tell us, 'These girls kick butt!'" (Ebenkamp, 2001, para. 26). Although *Powerpuff* licenses were predominantly girl-oriented, t-shirts and action figures for boys, especially featuring villains like mutant monkey Mojo Jojo, fared well. Licensing companies' strong interest in *The Powerpuff Girls* and the subsequent success of *Powerpuff* merchandise set an important industry precedent.

During its heyday, *The Powerpuff Girls* boasted a merchandizing empire worth nearly $1 billion (McAlister, 2002, p. C-1), ultimately exceeding that number in total sales (Simpson, 2009). In 2000 alone, Cartoon Network's character marketing and merchandising strategy for *The Powerpuff Girls* yielded $350 million in retail sales. Timing was everything: the Powerpuffs' star rose as the Spice Girls' star set, partially facilitating the success of *Powerpuff Girls* products. The *Powerpuff* product lines were similar to those of the Spice Girls, cutting across all categories, from band-aids to bedroom sets. Filling the void left by the Spice Girls in the marketplace, *The Powerpuff Girls* served as a continuation of the girl power lifestyle brand established by the pop divas. Just as grade school and pre-teen girls were devoted consumers of all things Spice during the "Spicemania" of 1997–1998, grade schoolers and pre-teens devoured everything offered by Powerpuff licensees from 1999 to 2001. Fans of the show could purchase countless products, many of which were tailored to the interests of the "tween" demographic; a comprehensive list of *Powerpuff* merchandise would be at least as long as a list of Spice Girls products, if not longer.[5] Better yet, *The Powerpuff Girls* were so cute that their products were also purchased for pre-schoolers *and* by adult women for their own enjoyment—the same demographic to whom the hyper-cute Hello Kitty merchandise appeals (DeMott, 2000, p. 3).[6] Demand was so high that McCracken could not keep up with the frantic pace at which new licenses for his characters were granted. He told one interviewer, "The way I find out about a lot of products is looking on eBay actually. I'll go check it out and say, 'Oh, I've never seen that shirt or I didn't know they made erasers'" (qtd. in DeMott, 2000, p. 3).[7]

Meanwhile, critics loved *The Powerpuff Girls*, with *TV Guide* naming it one of the top 10 new kids' shows ("Briefs," 2000). As a whole, *The Powerpuff Girls*' success generated a tremendous amount of media attention. A subset of the *Powerpuff* coverage enthused about the cartoon's feminist promise. Perhaps this was creditable to widespread awareness of the girl crisis: many critics were quick to praise *The Powerpuff Girls* for redressing the way television represented girls, dubbing it "a kind of feminism for pre-schoolers" (*The Sentinel*, 2002, p. 27). Likewise, Hopkins (2002) wrote, "After decades of feminist critique, media images of weak girls are finally losing currency" (p. 11). She cheered the heroic, aggressive Powerpuff Girls as feminist heroes who reflected positive changes for girls onscreen and "in real life, too." (p 11). With this overlap between what was cool in McCracken's eyes and what was cool in young feminists' eyes, Cartoon Network and McCracken found themselves basking in unexpected feminist praise (McAlister, 2002, p. C-1).

When *The Powerpuff Girls Movie* was released in 2002, McCracken encouraged this assessment in interviews promoting the film. By that point, his theoretical consciousness had evolved; he recounted that his girlfriend, *Powerpuff* storyboard artist Lauren Faust, had encouraged his awareness of the show's feminist potential. He said that she had told him, "I really wish I had a show like this when I was growing up. This would have helped me to have these kinds of powerful role models" (McCracken, qtd. in Weinkauf, 2002, para. 9). He often characterized *The Powerpuff Girls* as part of a "new feminism"—albeit a heavily commodified one that "isn't about denouncing things that are girlish. It's about embracing going shopping and buying shoes and wanting to be cute. You can embrace all that at the same time and still be really powerful. [. . .] I think the [Powerpuff] girls are a symbol of that new strength" (para. 7). As he liked to tell interviewers such as Havrilesky (2002), "My girlfriend basically taught me a lot of that" (para. 7).

Havrilesky (2002) conceded, "It's tough to dislike a guy who humbly credits his girlfriend for his feminist sensibilities" (para. 8), but the implications of packaging female strength in cute, girlish packages were not lost upon her. "Given a recent Gallup poll that found that only 25 percent of women today consider

themselves feminists, the Powerpuff Girls may reflect a shift from embracing political and social labels to choosing between carefully packaged products that have ideologies encoded deep within their shiny exteriors," she wrote. "Why take on a
political label when you can wear a cool-looking t-shirt that says the same thing,
but without any of the negative associations? Is she a feminist? Oh, no! She just loves
those Powerpuff Girls" (para. 21). Her assessment hearkened back to the Spice Girls'
cooptation of girl power: by stripping girl power of its more serious feminist
underpinnings and saying that feminism was a dirty word that needed to be
"kick[ed] up the arse," the Spice Girls steered girl power from a critically conscious,
countercultural form of activism into a mode of pro-girl rhetoric unbacked by
action but easy to purchase and adopt as a lifestyle brand. It seemed *The Powerpuff
Girls* used a similar playbook.

Holden's (2002) *New York Times* review of the *Powerpuff* film concluded that
feminism was simply not central to the cartoon or the characters' appeal. He
wrote, "It would be easy to make lofty claims for the Powerpuff Girls as representing a strain of feminism filtered down to the post-Britney generation that recon-
ciles the disparities of being cute and ultra-feminine (the squeaky voices and big,
round ready-to-bat eyes) and of feisty self-determination. But what's really so
appealing about the characters is their resemblance to everyday children" (p. E3).
In other words, their authentic childlike behavior—complex, rather than overly sim-
plified like so many previous depictions of boringly perfect little girls—was what
Holden felt was truly noteworthy about the brand.

Sailer's (2002) review of the *Powerpuff* film went further. Noting the hoards
of journalists who had built up the film for "furnishing girls with strong, empowered feminist role models" (para. 1), he chastised the media for "never notic[ing]
that 'Powerpuff Girls' is an action show by guys" (para. 2). This charge was not
unlike Padel's (1997) criticism of the Spice Girls' production by a team of men, and
it is a reasonable thing to question regarding any popular text purporting to be feminist. As my interviewee Chloe mentioned in Chapter Three regarding mainstream commercial girl power: "I still wonder who is behind girl power, and I don't
think it is the Spice Girls." Recognizing the political economy in which media texts
are produced is important in any critical analysis. As such, Sailer called *The
Powerpuff Girls* "another example of a broad trend in current culture: pseudo-
feminist male fantasies about violent females, as in 'Lara Croft: Tomb Raider' and
'Charlie's Angels.' The nerdier the fellow, the bigger the charge he seems to get from
watching girls whomp guys" (para. 3).

In Sailer's assessment of *The Powerpuff Girls*, he was thinking along the same
lines as Havrilesky (2002), who asked, "Tough heroines are certainly the flavor of

the month, as evidenced by shows like *Alias* and *She Spies*, but do these shows echo real changes in our culture's concept of gender, or are they just a passing trend? Can female power truly be respected if it's consistently packaged as supernaturally sexy or freakishly cute?" (para. 6) In grappling with these questions, she raised another. "The more salient question for budding feminists may not be whether it's acceptable to be powerful and pretty at the same time, but whether being powerful without being pretty is even an option," Havrilesky wrote. Echoing the feminist critiques of the Spice Girls' emphasis on appearance such as Lemish's (1998) finding that girls only accepted the Spice Girls' identity choices insomuch as they were presented by normatively pretty women, Havrilesky argued, "When Janet Reno's appearance garners more sniping than her policies, and Britney Spears' looks get more glowing reviews than her songs, it's difficult to see how real power in the absence of beauty could ever be enticing to a new generation of girls, even with the help of the Powerpuffs. Power that depends on beauty may remain forever in the eye—and in the hands—of the beholder" (para. 24). The concerns with girl power inherent in the Spice Girls' version persisted: Though normative femininity had been criticized by the riot grrrls and the discourse of the girl crisis, girl power discourse on television continued raising red flags by presenting normative femininity as an implicit societal mandate. In short, Havrilesky (2002) and Sailer (2002) suggested that *The Powerpuff Girls'* feminist potential needed to be considered in the broader context of women's representations and their audience members' perceptions—a charge this book seeks to answer.

Girl Heroes Galore

Though the Powerpuff Girls were pioneers—blazing a trail on children's television, where they were not to be joined by other girl superheroes until three years after their Cartoon Network debut—they could be read in discourse with female heroes on prime-time television who were their contemporaries. These included *Xena: Warrior Princess* (1995–2001); *Buffy the Vampire Slayer* (1997–2003), based on a much campier 1992 film of the same name; *La Femme Nikita* (1997–2001); and *Charmed* (1998–2006). These tough characters fought crime, boasted supernatural powers, and appeared normatively feminine—just like their kindergarten contemporaries, *The Powerpuff Girls*. All of these texts could be interpreted as reflecting shifting cultural discourses regarding women and power—representing worlds in which female strength and agency prevailed. However, because of their collective emphasis on appearance, Goodale (1999) argued that "the beautiful babe as superhero [. . .] didn't model empowerment so much as sexuality" (p. 13). Many pre-teen and teenage girls enjoyed these shows, with *Buffy* and *Charmed* especially enjoying the dedication of younger audiences. They generated substantial income from sales of dolls, notebooks, jewelry, books for pre-teen and teen readers, trading cards, games, and other toys and collectables. In addition to inspiring audiences with their daring acts of bravery, most of the leading characters had physical appearances calculated to appeal not only to male viewers but also to female audience members invested in performing normative femininity. (See Figures 4.2 and 4.3.) Hence, Sarah Michelle Gellar secured a high-profile four-year contract with Maybelline cosmetics while portraying Buffy. The success of the tough-and-pretty formula gave rise to a proliferation of prime-time shows about beautiful heroic women, like *Cleopatra 2525* (2000–2001), *Alias* (2001–2006), and *Tru Calling* (2003–2005).

Figure 4.2: Sarah Michelle Gellar as Buffy in *Buffy the Vampire Slayer.* © WB.
Courtesy of PhotoFest.

Figure 4.3: *Charmed.* From left to right: Holly Marie Combs,
Alyssa Milano, Rose McGowan. © Warner Bros. Television. Courtesy of PhotoFest.

Alongside this latter set of "tough girl" shows, five new children's cartoons about girl heroes emerged in rapid succession, one per year: *Totally Spies* (2001–2007), *Kim Possible* (2002–2007), *My Life as a Teenage Robot* (2003–2009), *Atomic Betty* (2004–2008), and *W.I.T.C.H.* (2005–2006). Their creators hoped to garner great ratings on screen from boys and girls and to make great profits on merchandise as interviews in many industry magazines revealed. However, the creation and green-lighting of the post-*Powerpuff* girl hero cartoons were influenced not only by the successes of *The Powerpuff Girls* and The Spice Girls but also of shows such as *Buffy the Vampire Slayer* and *Charmed.* For example, *Totally Spies* creator Vincent Chalvon-Demersay has cited the Spice Girls and the film *Clueless* as his show's inspiration (James, 2002); and Rob Renzetti, who had worked as a director for *The Powerpuff Girls*, took inspiration from his favorite television show, *Buffy the Vampire Slayer*, in creating *Teenage Robot* (Goodman, 2005).

With these various influences, the newer girl heroes differed from the Powerpuffs on a major point. They were not "essentially sexless" kindergarteners (DeRogatis, 2002, p. 43) whose 1992 origins as a college project predated the Spice Girls and Buffy's debut on television. Instead, with the exception of the middle-school-aged Atomic Betty, these new girl heroes were attractive teenage high school students. The upshot was that in all of the new girl hero cartoons, a watered-down sexiness linked characters across shows and networks. If a girl was a hero, she was more likely to wear revealing clothing than her onscreen counterparts who did not engage in superheroics, establishing key visual aspects of the genre. As Ostrow (2003) stated critically in a *Kim Possible* review, "The animated heroine's competence is always equated to a sexy look. Kim Possible performs her superhero feats with her navel showing" (p. F-01). Despite such criticisms, the formula proved successful; for example, *Totally Spies* became an international hit, airing up to three times a day and boasting one million viewers daily in the U.S. alone, consistently ranking in Cartoon Network's top four children's shows (James, 2006, p. 6).

In fact, the formula seemed calculated to boost the shows' appeal to boys, as a way to secure the largest audiences possible. Even though networks had never been concerned about alienating girls by programming boy-centered shows, they were determined to make girl-centered programming inclusive of boys. As many people involved with the various shows told interviewers, they kept boy viewers in mind from the start. In this regard, the mix of action-packed fighting and visually appealing girls was a calculated move that allowed shows like *Totally Spies* to rank first. It was also worlds away from the girl power of the riot grrrls, who promoted female-only spaces and adopted a devil-may-care attitude when accused of reverse sexism. The networks' determination to invite boys into girl power discourse therefore marked another significant change in girl power. The riot grrrls had separatist tendencies and were quick to express anger at males and the system of patriarchy. The Spice Girls performed for girl audiences and called for equality of the sexes, but they playfully welcomed male attention as long as the men played by the Spice Girls' rules. Girl power cartoons—created and produced by men for a medium that had long privileged the interests of male viewers—took a different tack: in depicting fictional girls, they not only appealed to girl viewers but also actively courted boys. They wanted as many tweens as possible to view these cartoons, and the higher the percentage of boys watching alongside girls, the better.

Reading the Girl Heroes

This brief history begs the question: Were *The Powerpuff Girls* and other shows about pretty-but-tough females feminist, effecting change for girls in real life, as Hopkins (2002) argued? Or, as Havrilesky (2002) asked, could such representations successfully command respect from viewers? Durham's (2003) analysis of girl power television shows indicated that although the young women in *Buffy the Vampire Slayer* and *Sabrina the Teenage Witch* used their bodies in ways that reflect the mastery of power, they were so trim that their bodies did not look strong. This made them less threatening to viewers who, accustomed to being in the voyeur position in relation to their television viewing, would feel uncomfortable with girls whose bodies have traditionally masculine-coded attributes, such as bulging muscles. By latching onto the "new feminism" to promote the interpretation of *The Powerpuff Girls* as a true feminist text, McCracken—perhaps unwittingly—situated himself within a contentious debate between feminists that involved not only gender but also race and a critique of the capitalist ideology (e.g., Baumgardner & Richards, 2000).

Despite these debates, in the popular press, critics asserting that girl heroes were good for girls proliferated. Consider the praise that Hopkins (2002) heaped upon *The Powerpuff Girls* in her article for *The Sydney Morning Herald*, a major Australian daily newspaper:

> To behave aggressively is no longer considered unfeminine and unattractive. [. . .] For better or worse, girl heroes are now aggressors; they have laid claim to a masculine alliance with action. In pop culture representation and in real life, too, girls are releasing their anger, frustration and aggressive impulses.
>
> Today, "fighting like a girl" is something to be proud of. Girls are fighting back, not just against male violence but also restrictive stereotypes of feminine passivity. Today's girls don't just want the tough action hero; they want to *be* the tough action hero. They might play at being "girly," but they have become all that they ever wanted in a man. (p. 11)

In the aftermath of the concerns raised about the girl crisis in the early- to mid-1990s, such arguments were persuasive and hopeful. However, just as Weldon (2007) offered no support for her claim that the Spice Girls had been detrimental to a generation of young women, Hopkins (2002) offered no support for her claims that *The Powerpuff Girls* and their ilk were great for girls. In fact, Hopkins seemed to conflate real girls with fictional girls in both her article and her book, *Girl Heroes: The New Force in Popular Culture* (2002). Did shows like *The Powerpuff*

Girls and *Kim Possible*, with their strong, empowered girl heroes, represent material change beyond the screen? Was there any evidence for positive effects on real girls?

Cognizant of these perspectives on girl power and the girl heroes—cartoon and prime-time—I set out to learn what no one else seemed to be asking. What did real girls take away from mediated girl power? Were girl heroes good for girls? Unconvinced the answers were so simple or dichotomous as "Yes, girl heroes are good for girls" or "No, they are not," I determined to learn how girls interpreted heroic girl characters—their behaviors, their physical strength, their feminine appearances. Girl hero cartoons were the ideal avenue for this inquiry, and to answer these questions, I wished to speak with actual pre-adolescent girls. The process would be lengthy: unlike the interviews about the Spice Girls that I would later conduct with adult feminists in their late teens and early twenties—involving 20 one-hour-long interviews—I would spend over a year building relationships with groups of girls, screening and discussing girl power cartoons with them. In this way, I would experience the cartoons at the same time that they were experiencing them—rather than relying on interviews after the fact—and, in the process, gather rich details about their lives and perspectives. (I will discuss the methodology of my fieldwork in Chapter Five.)

Before embarking on this field research, however, I needed to conduct a thorough textual analysis of the cartoons. The major themes that emerged across the texts would inform my research with pre-adolescent girls, suggesting to me which episodes I might screen for them and what topics I might closely listen for in our conversations. In other words, the textual analysis would help me develop a framework for the interview process. I therefore recorded episodes of the following programs as they aired on television:

- *The Powerpuff Girls* (November 1998–March 2005; Cartoon Network)
- *Totally Spies* (November 2001–March 2007; Cartoon Network)
- *Kim Possible* (June 2002–June 2007; the Disney Channel)
- *My Life as a Teenage Robot* (August 2003–May 2009; Nickelodeon)
- *Atomic Betty* (September 2004–January 2008; Cartoon Network)
- *W.I.T.C.H.* (January 2005–December 2006; Toon Disney)

These six cartoons were current when I began my fieldwork with pre-adolescent girls in February 2005. I aimed to watch the cartoons as obsessively as their true fans would. Therefore, from 2003 through 2006, I viewed a fairly comprehensive sample of nearly 300 episodes. Fan-written transcripts, collected online from rowdyruff.net, offered me a strong understanding of the few *Powerpuff Girls* episodes that I did not view. Online episode guides provided a general sense of what little I missed in the other five shows.

Figure 4.4: A scene from *Kim Possible*. Kim Possible (right) with her sidekick and best friend, Ron Stoppable (left) and his naked mole rat, Rufus. © Disney. Courtesy of PhotoFest.

Figure 4.5: *My Life as a Teenage Robot.* Jenny (center), a six-foot-tall blue and white robot, is bullied by the mean girls at her high school. ©2010 Viacom International Inc. All Rights Reserved. Nickelodeon, My Life as a Teenage Robot and all related titles, logos and characters are trademarks of Viacom International Inc. Courtesy of PhotoFest.

Figure 4.6: *Atomic Betty.* Atomic Betty (left), a Galactic Guardian and defender of the cosmos, with Robot X-5, a member of her crew. © Atomic Cartoons.

As I viewed these 300 episodes and read additional episodes' transcripts and summaries, I noted the themes communicated within them and sought to develop a holistic appreciation of each show. Grounded in the literature on the girl crisis, girl power, and feminism, I asked myself what these cartoons suggested about girl power's current meaning in the marketplace and for viewers. I wished to learn how, if at all, their discourse addressed concerns raised by the AAUW, the Ms. Foundation, and authors such as Mann, Orenstein, Pipher, and the Sadkers, and whether they dovetailed at all with the ideas of the riot grrrls and the Spice Girls. After my preliminary viewing of and notetaking on each episode, I analyzed the major themes within and across the six cartoons using grounded theory. For this task, I drew upon discourse analysis (Casey et al., 2002), which, as Duke and Kreshel (1998) have argued, is an appropriate method for analyzing gender constructions in the media.

Figure 4.7: *W.I.T.C.H.* Top row, left to right: Irma, Cornelia, Will, Hay Lin, and
Taranee transformed as the Guardians of the Veil. Bottom row, left to right: Irma,
Taranee, Will, Cornelia, and Hay Lin in their everyday clothes. © Jetix Concept
Animation. Courtesy of PhotoFest.

Using dialogic theory (Newcomb, 1991), I considered how themes from the six shows were in discourse with one another—an important point, as many of the girls in the viewing audience were fans of several of these shows at once. While some of the key themes that emerged in my research were found across the various programs, others were emphasized within only one or two of the shows. This meant that different viewers may have left these shows with different ideas about girlhood and empowerment, depending on which programs and episodes they watched, which storylines they attended to, and how they interpreted the stories they encountered. Like all television programming, these cartoons were multivocal and polysemic (Ceccarelli, 1998). Therefore, the themes that emerged from my analysis were complex—both positive and negative from a feminist perspective, and sometimes, contradictorily, both at once. (Also, because of the medium and the sheer quantity of episodes. there were more themes to consider in girl hero cartoons than in the Spice Girls' oeuvre.)

What follows is a sampling of the emergent themes that I felt would be useful focal points as I conducted fieldwork with pre-adolescent girls. Although more themes than these existed—for example, acts of violence, which have been a source of criticism but are beyond the scope of this book—these are the themes that seemed most suited to my inquiry regarding the empowering potential of girl hero cartoons.

Representing Girls: Strong in Numbers, Weak in Diversity

From the outset, it was clear that these cartoons' very existence addressed one critical concern: they had a positive impact on the representation of girls on television. No longer a victim of symbolic annihilation, girls could be seen on screen in great numbers, in leading roles and engaging in a range of unstereotypical behaviors. They were active and agentic, rather than passive, weak objects. From a critical feminist perspective, however, some problems also became immediately visible to me as a viewer. The girls had very little variance in body type; they were either tiny little girls or svelte teenagers. They offered very little racial diversity; only *W.I.T.C.H.*, the last of the six to be introduced, clearly incorporated girls of varying races, as detailed in Chapter Nine. This overall uniformity in body type and race meant that although girls were finally represented on screen in new, empowering ways, their physical appearances reflected the values of the privileged white middle class, which could potentially limit which girls in the viewing audience would feel empowered by these new story lines.

Breaking the Binary: Femininity and Strength

In every case, from *The Powerpuff Girls* to *W.I.T.C.H.*, the girls' feminine appearances were juxtaposed with their superhero status. This occurred both visually and in the verbal discourse of these media properties. For example, a *Kim Possible* poster available for purchase stated that Kim was a "cheerleader by day, crime fighter by night," and her theme song lyrics explained, "I'm your basic average girl, and I'm here to save the world." The term "powerpuff" made this juxtaposition explicit, grafting together the seemingly dissimilar term "power"—with its connotations of masculinity and strength—together with "puff," which evokes thoughts of the powderpuffs used to apply makeup and similarly "lightweight" things. In other instances—for example, in *Totally Spies*, where the girls' identities as crime fighters are a secret—the girls are able to complete their missions in part because their foes do not think they could possibly be a threat, as they are only girls. This juxtapositon was important, for it made the case that femininity and strength are not binarily opposed to one another. Strength and power are not inherently masculine, these shows argued; strength and power can be embodied in a feminine individual. Discourse on the deessentialization of femininity and strength was peppered across the girl hero genre, lightly echoing the crime-fighting sequences in the *Spice World* film and prime-time girl hero programs like *Buffy* and *Charmed*.

Overall, in girl hero cartoons, the characters' compliance with normative femininity was part of the point. The girl heroes demonstrated that femininity and strength are not mutually exclusive, and they easily defeated the macho male villains who serve as antagonists. This suggested that although femininity normally denotes passivity, girls could synthesize both sides of the masculine/feminine duality. They could be girlish and strong, small and powerful—denaturalizing the idea that masculinity is superior to femininity. Furthermore, they disproved the active/passive binary, demonstrating that passivity was not an undeniable female trait—even on television. An inherent challenge, however, is that regardless of one's reasons or desired outcomes for engaging with normative femininity, it still involves conforming to an object position and a consumer position—strength or no strength.

Solidarity and Collective Action

The six girl hero cartoons' discourse on solidarity and collective action was not uniform across the programs. Rather, it differed depending on how the cartoons were constructed. The cartoons featuring groups of girl heroes who worked together—*The Powerpuff Girls*, *Totally Spies*, and *W.I.T.C.H.*—offered positive messages about female solidarity. The individual girl heroes depicted in these shows often demonstrated that they were able to solve crimes and fight their foes individually, but working as a group, they had the unconditional support and understanding of close allies. They were not isolated from other girls, like solo girl heroes Betty of *Atomic Betty* and Jenny of *My Life as a Teenage Robot*. The girl heroes whose superhero identities were openly known to those around them— *The Powerpuff Girls, Kim Possible, My Life as a Teenage Robot*—also differed significantly from traditional superheroes, because they were part of society. They did not live a double life featuring secret superhero identities in a Clark Kent/Superman fashion: Everyone knew who they were, and they behaved the same in daily life as when fighting crime. These qualities combined to construct these girls as superheroes who break the mold.

The girl heroes depicted in *The Powerpuff Girls* and *W.I.T.C.H.* further differed from classic superheroes because rather than wielding power in a hierarchal manner that would place them above everyone else, they empowered their communities by actually sharing power with them. Unlike traditional superheroes, who "stand above and beyond their fellow men [. . .] inimitable, and therefore disempowering to more ordinary men" (Aisenberg, 1994, p. 12), most girl heroes in these cartoons did not mitigate the power of others. Instead, their toughness often inspired collective action by "normal" people in their cartoon worlds, showing that they are, in fact, imitable. *The Powerpuff Girls* and *W.I.T.C.H.* offered many instances of solidarity and collective action being extended out beyond the core group of girl heroes. In fact, across the entire story arc of *W.I.T.C.H.*'s first season, the team of guardians worked with rebels on the planet Meridian to overthrow an evil prince. Through their example, the girls inspired more people to join the revolution, and they were ultimately victorious. Likewise, on many occasions, Blossom, Bubbles, and Buttercup effectively inspired the citizens of Townsville to take action and fight on their own behalf—even "normal little girls" who an enemy, Mojo Jojo, described as "weak, helpless, and scared." As a result, in the episode "Slumbering with the Enemy," Mojo Jojo was shocked when the normal little girls defeated him—a victory for normal little girls everywhere (Hains, 2008a).

Female Strength as Anomalous

Of the six shows examined in this chapter, *The Powerpuff Girls* was the only one that *explicitly* stated that normal girls can be powerful. In the other shows, the heroes were the exception to the rule, the only strong females in their worlds. *W.I.T.C.H.* also featured collective action, as mentioned earlier but featured revolutionary work as largely men's domain. The men of Meridian were at the core of the rebellion to overthrow a cruel prince, and women were mainly depicted as worried mothers, on the sidelines of the action. Therefore, in many ways, various girl hero cartoons implied that female strength was anomalous—a legacy of shows such as *Charlie's Angels* and *The Bionic Woman* (Inness, 1999). The Spies on *Totally Spies* were the only girls who engaged in bravery; when their rival from school, Mandy, accidentally found herself on a mission with them, her helplessness and histrionics hindered the mission. On *Atomic Betty*, Betty's otherworldly adventures in outer space offered no room for the assistance of normal girls, and the organization of extraterrestrial Galactic Guardians within which she worked was nearly uniformly male. Although Kim Possible had a trusted female friend, Monique, she showed little aptitude for or interest in Kim's line of work (except for in a special made-for-TV *Kim Possible* movie, *A Sitch in Time*, set in a bleak alternate future that future never becomes reality). The people who did help Kim were all male.

My Life as a Teenage Robot took the idea that the girl heroes are anomalous one step further. The show made a clear statement to this effect in "Return of the Raggedy Android," which offered discourse stating that strength in girls was not "normal"—that strength and femininity do not mix (Hains, 2007a). In this episode, Jenny wore an "exoskin" that turned her appearance from that of a blue-and-white metallic robot into a normatively pretty girl—caucasian, with red hair, freckles, big doe eyes, and a cute outfit. But while wearing the exoskin, it was impossible for her to fight crime: the exoskin refused to cooperate, insisting that pretty girls don't fight—they let boys take care of things. The only way Jenny could resume her superheroics was by discarding the exoskin. Thus, to an even greater extent than the girls on *Kim Possible, Totally Spies, Atomic Betty*, and *W.I.T.C.H.*, Jenny's atypical strength also underscored the presumed weakness of other females. This contradicted the progressive message offered by *The Powerpuff Girls* about the strength of normal girls by reinscribing female strength as anomalous (Hains, 2007a).

Girl Power: Exclusively for Pretty Girls

Alongside *My Life as a Teenage Robot's* troubling suggestion that feminine girls could not actually be physically strong, the other shows offered another problematic suggestion: that only feminine girls could be empowered through girl power (Hains, 2004). The principal characters of *The Powerpuff Girls, Totally Spies, Kim Possible, and Atomic Betty* nearly uniformly embraced normative femininity, with relatively little variation, as a review of Figures 4.1 and 4.4 through 4.7 demonstrate. My analysis suggests that this served two functions. On the positive side, it suggested that females could embrace femininity without being disrespected for it. This would be empowering to those who wished to engage in normative femininity and found pleasure in it. However, the negative inverse of this was an inscription of power—and therefore girl power—as not in the domain of all girls, but only those who could meet normative feminine standards. Leaving the underlying ideology of normative femininity intact and unproblematized, the shows' uncritical embrace of normative femininity excluded girls who could not or would not conform (Hains, 2004).

The idea that only conventionally pretty girls could be part of the girl power movement was communicated in *Powerpuff* episodes such as "Twisted Sister," an Emmy-winning episode, and "Knock It Off." These episodes featured "misfit" Powerpuff Girls who were not only poor superheroes but also unsightly and deformed. Although the Powerpuff Girls were kind to their homely sisters, a disconcerting reading of these texts was that girl power precludes those who fail to conform to certain expectations of feminine beauty. The misfits' deformity, while not the main point of the episodes, posited a link between ineffectual deployment of power and feminine shortcomings. These episodes suggested that their version of girl power did not encompass girls who could not or chose not to succeed at feminine performativity. The visual lesson was that ugly girls cannot effectively embrace girl power. Empowerment eludes them (Hains, 2004).

This message was reinforced in episodes of various girl hero cartoons, in which the girl heroes themselves became unable to fight crime because they looked "ugly" in some way. For example, Jenny in *My Life as a Teenage Robot* occasionally received modifications that inadvertently made her look ugly—like new eyes that were too googly, or external ears that were too large, or a "virus" that caused her to sprout "pimples" made of nuts and bolts. In every case, her altered appearance interfered with her ability to battle alien foes. On *Totally Spies*, Alex could no longer fight crime when she accidentally became muscular after consuming energy bars; somehow, her unfeminine muscularity made her a worse hero, not a better one. Even the Powerpuffs were temporarily incapacitated when bad luck befell their appearances, as when Blossom received a terrible hair cut ("The Mane Event") or when Bubbles was fitted with eyeglasses ("Bubblevision").

Making Girls' Intelligence Palatable

In the girl hero cartoons, the protagonists' intelligence stood in contrast to the unintelligence surrounding them; they routinely beat oafish, dunderheaded foils. This was significant, for as numerous portrayals of spinster librarians and bespectacled wallflowers suggest, female intelligence is often depicted as an undesirable trait in popular culture. Lyn Mikel Brown (1998) has noted, "Girls are supposed to be smart and appear dumb" (p. 159). Perhaps it was because of the discourse on the crisis of female adolescence, which revealed that as girls approach adolescence they lose confidence in their academic abilities, that the cartoon girl heroes made such clear displays of their intelligence.

The stigma against smart girls is strong, however. Smart girls are perceived as socially awkward, or uppity, or threatening, in ways that smart boys never are. Therefore, these cartoons rendered the girls' intelligence palatable by making them exceedingly nice (Hains, 2007b). In fact, in the shows featuring multi-girl crime-fighting teams, the smartest girl on the team was always the nicest girl—the red-headed leader. Thus, while all the girl heroes were portrayed as being intelligent in contrast to various foils, Blossom, Kim, and Sam were a step above the rest—book-ish, interested in school, earning superior grades, excelling in math and science, and aiming to please their teacher—certainly positive representations in consideration of the concerns about girls' academic performances raised throughout the 1990s. They were too humble about their gifts, however. Instead of replying to compliments about their intelligence by saying "thank you," the girls constantly deflect-ed them. For example, when a boy admired Sam's science abilities, she replied, "I just read it and then it's, like, stuck in my mind forever. Kinda dorky, huh?" ("Brain Drain"). Such tactics unfortunately made the girls' intelligence seem less significant to their superheroics than they really were. While girls in the viewing audience could not aspire to be superhumanly strong or acquire amazing crime-fighting gadgets, they could be studious and embrace their intellectual abilities—which doesn't seem too tall an order for shows presenting role models. Instead, the smartest girls' humility was part of a broader patten in which the smartest girl heroes were also unfalteringly nice. Unlike their teammates—and unlike real girls who alternate between being mean and nice to those around them (Brown, 1998, p. 109)—they were unflaggingly, perfectly pleasant. They were also the most norma-tively feminine in appearance, with the longest hair (consider Blossom and Sam in comparison to their teammates, as well as Kim Possible's enviable locks). While it was positive to suggest that smart girls can be liked by their peers, their flawlessly nice behavior and nice appearance meant that the smart girls were absolutely con-formist in behavior and appearance outside the real of crime-fighting. As a strate-gy to allow these girls to be visibly smart, it problematically reinscribed white, middle-class expectations of girls (Hains, 2007b).

Nice Girls and Mean Girls

The girl hero cartoons often positioned the "nice" cartoon girl heroes against other girls who were mean. Many of the mean girls were located at school—girls of the stereotypical nasty cheerleader variety, not presumed to be very bright but still a thorn in the heroes' sides. When a strong female other than the lead characters appeared on one of these shows, she was almost always a villain—such as Shego in *Kim Possible*, Sedusa on *The Powerpuff Girls*, Nerissa on *W.I.T.C.H.*, and Queen Vexus on *My Life as a Teenage Robot*. While such villains balanced the depictions of wrong-doings so that they were not exclusive to male characters, they also had implications for appropriate female behavior and use of strength (Hains, 2007b). A key example of this was Shego, a highly intelligent supervillain on *Kim Possible* and one of Kim's major nemeses. Shego's story suggested that if intelligent girls were not nice, they risked becoming mean, socially outcast girls. Shego looked very similar to Kim, but with dark hair, and their personalities were opposites, for Shego was incessantly sarcastic, outspoken, and rude. Her backstory was that she and her four brothers once composed a superheroic crime-fighting team, but she found herself drawn to the idea of using her superpowers for evil. Shego's older brother revealed to Kim that Shego was always a "smartmouth," implying that her verbal assaults were the root of her outcast status.

In other words, a cautionary tale emerged from the girl hero cartoons: If a girl is nice, she might become a well-loved and admired leader—but if she is antisocial and objects to the status quo with sarcastic, angry barbs (not unlike the riot grrrls), she might become perceived as a villain or as failing at femininity. Thus, while the smart cartoon girls' strategic niceness allowed them to display their intelligence and power openly, this strategy was also compared with negative consequences for being "smartmouthed." The cartoons never presented a middle ground—only the two extremes, which is rather discouraging (Hains, 2007b).

Discussion

By depicting strong, intelligent, and empowered girl leaders, girl hero cartoons reacted against the idea that girls were victims of an unhealthy culture. Shows like *The Powerpuff Girls, Totally Spies, Kim Possible, My Life as a Teenage Robot, Atomic Betty,* and *W.I.T.C.H.* offered pre-teen girls role models that some girls would plausibly find useful as they approached adolescence. Read against the context of the early- to mid-1990s fears about adolescent girls' declining self-esteem and academic performances, girl power cartoons may be considered to have been a valuable source of cultural support for girls. In line with some recommendations of the

American Association of University Women's report, they suggested that society values girls' lives and culture. The representation of so many powerful girls on television was itself important progress. It helped rectify the symbolic annihilation of girls. No longer marginalized, girls—and girl power—were front and center in the cultural environment of the early- to mid-2000s.[8]

Despite this progress, the themes that emerged in my analysis of *The Powerpuff Girls, Totally Spies, Kim Possible, My Life as a Teenage Robot, Atomic Betty*, and *W.I.T.C.H.* were complicated and contradictory, progressive and regressive—much like the Spice Girls' discourse, but to an even greater extent, as the discourse of girl hero cartoons had multiple sources. To recap, the progressive themes centered upon girls' strength and intelligence. I found that the cartoons promoted the idea that girls can do anything, disputing the idea that power is masculine, for boys only. They made the case that femininity and strength are not dichotomous but can instead be embodied in the same individual. Story lines sometimes even depicted femininity itself as being a source of strength or emphasized the power of collective action through depictions of community empowerment. At the same time, numerous problematic themes were present in the cartoons. The girl heroes fit within narrowly defined standards for girls' appearance and behavior: The majority were of a privileged race, class, and/or body type (primarily white, middle- to upper-middle-class, slim, and able-bodied), very pretty, and—except during crime-fighting scenes—behaving in ways that aligned with cultural expectations of girls. Furthermore, in the cartoons' narratives, "pretty" and "ugly" girls, and "nice" and "mean" girls, were often pitted against one another—placing additional emphasis on physical appearance and normative behavior and undermining the concept of female solidarity. Many of these shows further implied that although girls can be physically strong, female strength is anomalous; in their cartoon universes, only the lead characters could be heroic girls. This contradicted the empowering message that girls can do anything.

Adolescent girls grapple with the overwhelming societal message that—unlike boys—they need to change their looks and behaviors. Inadvertently or not, girl hero cartoons seem to have been sending many of the same signals, potentially undercutting the cartoons' ability to effect real change. But as I asked regarding the Spice Girls, would the alternative have sold in the marketplace? What would cartoon heroes modeling a less commercial, less normatively feminine version of girl power even have looked like? In the aftermath of the Spice Girls' success, the concept is almost unthinkable. Likewise, these cartoons sometimes positioned female strength as abnormal, unusual—yet they were heralded as role models by the press and parents. Could fictional girl heroes really have served effectively as role models when their abilities were beyond the grasp of real people? Of course, unusual characters make for good storytelling, and these stories would have been less compelling if the girl heroes dwelled in worlds in which everybody was like them. In this light, their anomalous status made sense. However, it also underscored that girls deserve more than on-screen visions of empowerment. They need to feel empowered by what occurs in their everyday life as well.

These questions are difficult to grapple with in the abstract. They are best addressed in conversation with real girls from the viewing audience—the focus of the remainder of this book.

Notes

1. Like tween, the teenager was also a marketing category before it became a mainstream term, originating with the success of *Seventeen* magazine in the 1940s (Schrum, 1998, p. 144).
2. Linn (2004) cynically notes the industry created the word "tween" as a replacement for the phrase "latchkey kids" because the latter had depressing connotations (p. 131).
3. McCracken's cartoon was originally called "Whoopass Stew," with the accidental ingredient instrumental in the girls' creation being a "can of whoopass"—sassy '90s slang used to pseudo-threaten someone. (E.g., "I'm gonna open a can of whoopass on you, boy!") "Whoopass Stew" debuted as part of Spike and Mike's Sick and Twisted Festival of Animation, which annually tours North America. Soon thereafter, Cartoon Network aired two episodes of "Whoopass Stew" under its new, network-approved *Powerpuff Girls* title as part of its World Premiere Toons project—airing "Meat Fuzzy Lumpkins" in February 1995 and "Crime 101" in January 1996. Cartoon Network used the World Premiere Toons project to select shows to greenlight shows for their own runs as series, and because these *Powerpuff* episodes were consistently ranked top with viewers, the show became a Cartoon Network series (Cartoon Network, 1998).
4. On Sept. 8, 2000, an episode of The Powerpuff Girls broke another Cartoon Network record: it "posted a 3.4 rating, or 2.2 million households, making it the most-watched program in Cartoon's history" (Moss, 2000, para. 6).
5. *Powerpuff Girls* products still available on ebay.com and Amazon.com as of 2011 include shirts, sneakers, jeans, shoes, dolls, paperback books, Little Golden books, chapter books, coloring books, stickers, videos, wristwatches, wall clocks, handbags, special edition Monopoly, lunch bags, toothbrushes, cookie jars, trading cards, perfumes, beach towels, wooden scrunchie holders, address books, notebooks, pens and pencils, toy cars, balloons, magnets, cake pans, jewelry, curtains, shower curtains, pins, piggy banks, puzzles, Lite Brite sets, bedding (up to King size), rugs, wallpaper border, mugs, "Girl Power Games" for Windows 98/XP, a "Power Kit" boxed set (featuring a Little Golden Book, stickers, a coloring book, posters, and glitter glue sticks), a

Powerpuff Girl edition Barbie (dressed in a *Powerpuff Girls* t-shirt and carrying a packet of *Powerpuff* stickers), backpacks, keychains, candy, beverages, video games (for the Gameboy), and band-aids.

6. Because *The Powerpuff Girls*' popularity far outlasted the Spice Girls' (the cartoon had an seven-year run, from 1998–2005), many *Powerpuff* products are still available for purchase via online retailers such as Amazon.com.

7. The Licensing Industry Merchandisers Association recognized the property's tremendous success with two awards in June 2001: "Entertainment License of the Year" and "License of the Year" (Center for Communication, July, 2005).

8. In fact, this type of representation and awareness of girls' having been shortchanged resulted in a backlash that began in the late 1990s and continues today. Some call the claim that girls are shortchanged a "noble lie" that is "not so noble," for it allegedly causes harm to boys and casts girls as victims when they are not (Kleinfeld, 1998, p. 31).

5

Methodology

Reasearching Girl Power with Girls

"What are you doing here, anyway?"

—*Tanya, age 10, Euro-American*

Interviews with girls were the logical corollary to my analysis of the various discourses on girls, from the girl crisis to girl power. Because of the numerous girl-centered television shows rooted in girl power, I wished to learn how pre-adolescent girls interpreted girl hero cartoons and negotiated girl power, on screen and in everyday life. What did girls of 8, 9, 10, and 11 years old—mere infants and toddlers when the Spice Girls mainstreamed girl power—think of being a girl? Having never known a world without girl power, what did girlhood mean to them? I wished to learn their thoughts about key girl power ideas—strength, intelligence, behavior, appearance, femininity, and equality between the sexes.

To this end, I conducted field research in 2005 and 2006, with three groups of 8- to 11-year-old girls. I engaged with and observed the girls and their peers during their regular activities, and we screened and discussed girl hero cartoons together. Later, I individually interviewed some girls in their homes. The primary cartoons we screened together were *The Powerpuff Girls, Totally Spies, Kim Possible, My Life as a Teenage Robot, Atomic Betty,* and *W.I.T.C.H.*, though we later branched out into other programs per their requests. I discuss these studies in greater detail later in this chapter.

In my research, I drew in part upon Claudia Mitchell and Jacqueline Reid-Walsh's methodological work in girl culture and children's popular culture. They have articulated the usefulness of a "girl-method" in exploring relationships between age, gender, and the social value of media texts in girls' lives. Girl-method refers to the following:

1. Working *with* girls (participatory), *for* girls (advocacy), and *about* girls
2. Taking into account who the researchers are (and what their relationship to girlhood is)
3. Including the girls themselves as participants (so that they are agents and not subjects)
4. Addressing the cultural contexts of the girls in terms of race and class: *whose* girlhood? (Mitchell and Reid-Walsh, 2008, p. 17)

Components of this girl-method characterize a number of recent works in the interdisciplinary (and usually feminist) field of girlhood studies (p. 23). This book is intended as a contribution to this field. Therefore, I drew upon girl-method and related methodological approaches that constitute a "background to girl-method" (p. 17). *Researching Children's Popular Culture: The Cultural Spaces of Childhood* (Mitchell and Reid-Walsh, 2002) provided a useful reference point as it discussed many ways to study popular culture with children. As I planned to shift between screening programs for girls, observing them during their day-to-day activities, and interviewing them individually, I needed a multi-method approach, and the practices and perspectives articulated in this book were helpful. For example, the authors argued children should be respected by researchers as experts on the popular culture they consume (p. 9), but noted that children are used to adults denigrating their popular culture interests. "Moral panics" about popular dolls, toys, and programs are widespread and recurring (p. 26).[1] Bearing this in mind as a barrier to good research with children, I sought to engage with girls in a supportive manner, wishing to hear whatever they had to share about girl hero cartoons and other popular culture texts they felt were important—even though, as mentioned in Chapter Four, I had some concerns about the messages within these programs.

In designing my studies, I attended to decisions articulated by a few other researchers. For example, in *"Good Guys Don't Wear Hats": Children's Talk about the Media*, media literacy researcher Joseph Tobin (2000) investigated how children talk about movies, emphasizing "media representations of violence, gender, race, colonialism, and class" (p. 3). He screened movie excerpts for small groups of children, then asked them to discuss video clips they had just viewed. Tobin reasoned this strategy would allow the children to offer him rich, concrete responses (p. 7). He therefore selected clips suiting his research interests, screened them for his participants, and asked them questions.

Based on the success of Tobin's system, I selected episodes of television programs that suited my research interests and screened them for the participating girls. Girl hero cartoons dealt with a range of topics, but because of my interest in girl power's discourse on strength, femininity, and girls' empowerment, I decided to screen episodes that dwelled upon these issues.

- From *My Life as a Teenage Robot*, I screened "Raggedy Android," "Return of the Raggedy Android," and "Hostile Makeover." The first two depicted Jenny's desire for and struggles with the pursuit of a normatively feminine appearance, and the third showed Jenny's appearance changing for the worse—resulting in "self esteem issues"—because of an enemy plot.
- From *The Powerpuff Girls*, I screened "The Mane Event," in which Blossom's bad haircut got in the way of her crime fighting; "Members Only," in which the Powerpuff Girls are discriminated against by the Association of World Super Men; and "Twisted Sister," in which the Powerpuff Girls create a fourth sister who is an unsightly and ineffective superhero.
- From *Kim Possible*, I screened "Blush," in which a villain makes Kim self-conscious and therefore a less effective superhero; "Go Team Go," which depicted the "smartmouth" female character Shego's descent into supervillainy; and "Kimitation Nation," in which Kim feels her uniqueness is threatened when everyone copies her sartorial style.
- From *Atomic Betty*, I screened "The Great Race," in which Betty attempts to balance dating a boy with saving the world, without revealing her secret identity; and "The Ghost Ship of Aberdeffia," in which at a Halloween campfire Betty tells some of her peers—including the mean girl, Penelope—a tale about her outer-space bravery, but which none of them believe could be true.
- From *W.I.T.C.H.*, I screened "It Begins" and "It Resumes," the first two episodes of the series—chosen not for any particular themes, but because the program was serial in nature and new to television, making our screenings many girls' introduction to the series.

When we screened these episodes together, the groups operated like a book club—not unlike the "after-school book club" research methodology Napoli (2003, 2004) used to study pre-adolescent girls' readings of the Mary-Kate and Ashley

Olsen book series. Our "video club" proved an effective way to explore these texts: Because the meaning of television content is often constructed socially, produced as people discuss on-screen stories, focus group-style research on media content often approximates people's interpretative processes in other everyday contexts (Buckingham, 2009). Further to this, groups facilitate the study of gender construction—a major concern of this study—for gender, too, is constructed socially, through "the collective practices through which children and adults create and recreate gender in their daily interactions" (Thorne, 1993, p. 4). This underscores the validity of group conversations as a method for my study.

I also found David Buckingham's media literacy research useful to my study design. For example, in *Children Talking Television: The Making of Television Literacy* (1993) and *Moving Images: Understanding Children's Emotional Responses to Television* (1996), Buckingham made a case for *not* bringing specific television programs to the children in his studies. Rather, he asked them talk about the television that they had been viewing in everyday life. This loaned the study much ecological validity. Given my specific goals of learning about how girls read girl power media, however, I needed to discuss specific media texts with children, like Tobin (2000) and Napoli (2003, 2004). However, I appreciated the breadth of learning made possible by Buckingham's approach, so I decided to welcome conversations diverging from the television shows we watched together. This included conversations about other programs the girls enjoyed and whatever other topics my participants wished to discuss. Buckingham (1996) also conducted additional, in-home interviews with about one quarter of the children in his study (20 out of 72) to further contextualize his findings. In this vein, I interviewed as many children as possible in their homes.

The Studies

My fieldwork began with studies in two locations, from February through June of 2005, at after-school day care programs in adjacent towns. At the Nonprofit Aftercare Program in Waterhaven², the following fourteen girls signed up to participate—five of whom were not in the eight-to-eleven-year-old age range I sought for the study due to an error when the program directors sent paperwork home to the parents.

> Bailey, 9; African-American (key interviewee)
> Brianna, 8; African-American
> Cheri, 11; African-American

Corine, 12; Euro-American

Desirée, 8; African-American (key interviewee)

Francelle, 6; African-American

Gia, 7; African-American (key interviewee)

Kiara, 9; African-American

Madison, 8; African-American (key interviewee)

Rhea, 9; African-American (key interviewee)

Roshanda, 6; African-American; sister of Desirée

Shantel, 6; Indian-American

Simone, 7; African-American (key interviewee)

Tiana, 6; African-American

From this initial group, six served as key interviewees: They met with our group most regularly, and I got to know them better than the other girls. We had 22 meetings in total, at which various configurations of girls attended.

Simultaneously, at the Suburban Elementary Aftercare Program in Claret Park, ten girls in the following list signed up to participate in my study.

Angela, 8; Euro-American (key interviewee)

Audrey, 9; Euro-American (key interviewee)

Bobbi, 10; Euro-American (key interviewee)

Cynthia, 11; African-American

Kelly, 9; Euro-American (key interviewee)

Kylie, 9; Euro-American (key interviewee)

Lauren, 9; Euro-American

Maria, 8; Euro-American (key interviewee)

Megan, 9; Euro-American

Zoë, 8; Euro-American (key interviewee)

Seven remained with the group, serving as key interviewees. We had 25 meetings in total, with various girls attending each meeting.

Our meeting dates varied according to each site's availability, but I spent approximately two afternoons a week at each location. Most visits were about two hours long, wrapping up by about 5 p.m. as the girls' parents arrived. An hour to an hour and a half of each meeting was dedicated to screening a girl hero cartoon video, then conversing about it in an open-ended way. The theme of the video tended to direct our conversations in specific ways, which I encouraged. Because these groups ran concurrently, I screened the episodes listed above in the same order at parallel meetings. I began most conversations by asking the open-ended question, "What did you think of this episode?" At other times, the girls were so excited to discuss something about the episode that they jumped right into conversation before I had a chance to ask them anything. I followed their lead.

Following this, I additionally organized a group at the Township Public Library, which served several adjacent towns including Claret Park. This group ran from October 2005 to May 2006, with a winter break.

Abby, 10; Euro-American
Chrissie, 9; Euro-American
Chyna, 11; African-American
Crystal, 10; African-American
Darcey, 10; African-American
Elizabeth, 10; Euro-American
Ellie, 10; Euro-American
Franceska, 11; African-American
Jewel, 11; Indian-American
Kylie, 9; Euro-American (from the Suburban Elementary group)
Zoë, 9; Euro-American (from the Suburban Elementary group)

Unlike the Suburban Elementary and Nonprofit Aftercare groups, where the participants already knew one another and regularly spent time together outside of our group meetings, these 11 girls came together specifically to participate in the group, which the library advertised as a special program. Its characteristic was therefore that of an ongoing focus group. We met roughly every other Saturday for three to four hours—the entire morning—typically watching more than one video during a session. As it featured a few girls from the Suburban Elementary group, we watched different episodes than did the prior two groups—mostly focusing on episodes that the girls requested. Episodes screened included *Teenage Robot* episode "Grid Iron Glory," in which alien villains infect Jenny with nanobots that make her hulkingly masculine (culminating in her joining her school's all-male football team); *Powerpuff Girls* episode "Monkey See, Doggy Do"—a special request of the girls, who loved the episode's depiction of the Powerpuff Girls as puppies; and several issues of other shows that the girls videotaped and brought in for discussion, such as *Bratz, That's So Raven, Lizzie Maguire*, and *Full House*.

I videotaped, transcribed, and analyzed all meetings by theme in a multi-stage coding process using grounded theory.

To triangulate and incorporate more ethnographic research into my study, I also observed eleven lunch recess and library sessions at Suburban Elementary during February and March of 2006. During this time, I followed up with as many of my original participants as possible, talked casually with many additional children, and wrote field notes immediately afterwards. I also interviewed the principal, librarian, and two aftercare program staff members. I would have liked to hold additional video club meetings at this time, but due to budget cuts, the aftercare program could not have me back. (To meet state regulations, a staff member had to be in the room with me at all times, and they had no one to spare.)

At Waterhaven Elementary School, I wished to visit the Nonprofit Aftercare Program video club participants during their lunch recesses, but I was not able to secure institutional permission. I was, however, able to return to the Nonprofit Aftercare Program for a series of six additional video club meetings in February and March of 2006. Several girls who had been part of our group the previous year no longer attended the Nonprofit Aftercare Program; one (Simone) had transferred to a private school, while others had withdrawn from aftercare for reasons I did not know. To the remaining group, at Rochelle's request, I added Zayonna, who had joined the Nonprofit Aftercare Program that fall. She was a close friend to the other girls, and Rochelle did not want her to be excluded, so she sent an invitation to Zayonna's parents on my behalf. In total, then, five girls participated at this time.

Bailey, 10; African-American
Desirée, 9; African-American
Madison, 9; African-American
Rhea, 10; African-American
Zayonna, 10; African-American

They seemed to take pride in it: Judging by comments they made to other children when we would leave the main room to speak privately together in the school library upstairs, their participation in this small group made them feel special.

Following these video club meetings, I also visited the girls on site about once every week or two in April and May, with Rochelle's permission. We would chat on the playground together during their aftercare routines, and occasionally, I helped them with their homework. To further triangulate about life at the Nonprofit Aftercare Program, I interviewed the program site director, an aftercare program staff member, and a Waterhaven Elementary custodian.

Finally, I asked the parents of all participants from each location whether I could individually interview their daughters in their homes at their convenience.

None of the families from Nonprofit Aftercare expressed interest. From the Township Library program, the families of Elizabeth and Jewel agreed. From Suburban Elementary, the families of Angela, Kylie, Maria, and Zoë agreed. I also interviewed Maura, who was not in any of the video groups but whom I knew from my fieldwork at the Suburban Elementary, at this time. She had heard I was interviewing some of her classmates and asked if I could please come interview her. "It sounds interesting," she said.

Whose Girlhoods?

As the preceding lists show, the girls at Suburban were primarily Euro-American, while the girls at Nonprofit Aftercare were primarily African-American. At the Library group, six girls were Euro-American, three were African-American, and one was Indian-American. These racial breakdowns reflected differences in the communities. According to the 2000 Census, the programs' towns had comparable average incomes, with respective median household incomes of $49,000 and $47,000. However, their populations differed racially: The residents of Suburban Elementary's town, Claret Park, were 93% white and 2% black, whereas residents of Waterhaven, the Nonprofit Aftercare Program's town, were 75% white and 19% black. (For comparison, the 2000 U.S. Census found that whites comprised 75.1% and blacks comprised 12.3% of the total U.S. population.) In Waterhaven, a strong majority of the children who attended the public elementary school (73%) were African-American; most of the Euro-American families in town were concerned about the school district's quality (it was in the bottom 15% statewide), so they sent their children to private (usually parochial) schools. (Suburban Elementary had no analogous problems, being ranked in the top 25% statewide.) These contexts are relevant to the participants' discussions of girl power and the girl hero cartoons we viewed.

The backgrounds of the children attending the aftercare programs where I conducted fieldwork accentuated the groups' differences. At the Nonprofit Aftercare Program, the majority of the children and employees were black, while at Suburban Elementary, the majority of the children and employees were white. I recognized that as a white woman, I was an outsider in the predominantly black community at the Nonprofit Aftercare Program. It was thus understandable to me that the Nonprofit Aftercare families declined to let me interview their daughters in their homes, as mentioned earlier. I recalled Jiwani's (2005) insight that when researchers wish to study preteen children from populations that have been "marginalized, criminalized, and stigmatized" (p. 173), gaining access can be impossible. In the U.S., Euro-Americans frequently construe African-Americans in negative ways, fearing they are criminals and supporting policies that further marginalize African-

American individuals and communities. This was the case in the communities surrounding the Nonprofit Aftercare Program, as we will see in Chapter Nine. While some of the families may simply have been too busy to invite me to their homes, I suspect that at some level, Jiwani's explanation that marginalized communities use a "code of silence" to eschew "potential public scrutiny" and to "protect themselves from negative societal sanctions" was salient (p. 174).

Respecting their decisions, I worked to adopt a "white anti-racist standpoint," a concept Tolman (2002) attributes to Ruth Frankenberg (p. 215), and consulted with African-American women at the Nonprofit Aftercare Program—a long-time employee and the program director—about my interviews with the girls. As part of this standpoint, I also invited two African-American scholars to review a draft of Chapter Nine of this book, which most directly addresses the issues of race and racism in the African-American girls' lives. Throughout the analysis in this book, I also strive to avoid describing either my white participants or my black participants in "monolithic" terms (see Tolman, 2002, p. 215). (The reader will note that I interchangeably use the terms "Euro-American"/"white"/"caucasian" and the terms "African-American"/"black." I also sometimes use the term "people of color" to inclusively describe people who are not white, as an anti-racist strategy to clarify that race must be understood in a more complex way than a binary of black and white.)

It also bears mentioning that my work at the Nonprofit Aftercare Program in Waterhaven was not my first experience in a black community. For over a year, I lived in an apartment complex in a town I'll call "Chesterford." Chesterford was also primarily African-American and of a similar socioeconomic demographic to Waterhaven. The overall layout of the Chesterford apartment complex—which had hundreds of units—was in two large, sprawling circles, one nested within the other. The outer circle was well maintained, cost a little more to rent, and was inhabited primarily by white families. As a graduate student with minimal income, I could not qualify for an apartment there. My apartment, in the inside circle, was not visible to the surrounding community. As it was not part of the "public face" of the sprawling apartment complex, by comparison it was poorly maintained. The rent was lower, and a majority of the residents were African-American. I enjoyed the open spaces between building clusters, which featured stunning grassy fields and large, hundred-year-old trees; my next-door neighbor said she did, too. She had two children, and she told me she had moved there from the city because it was the kind of place she always dreamed her children would grow up. Although some of my friends and acquaintances suggested I was living in a "dangerous" area, I felt safe; I believed they were conflating issues of race, class, and criminality.

Waterhaven, home of the Nonprofit Aftercare Program, reminded me of Chesterford, but many residents were property owners, rather than renters. It was a town to which many upwardly mobile African-American families had moved, escaping the major urban city nearby.[3] Beautiful single-family homes and duplexes on generously sized urban lots, with good-sized driveways and garages, were available for reasonable prices; the property values there were depressed in comparison with the nearby suburbs, such as Claret Park, where Suburban Elementary School was located. This made it possible for many former city dwellers to become first-time homeowners, and public transportation into the city was available, making a commute to good city jobs reasonable. On the downside, because of the relatively low tax base, Waterford's school district was underfunded, as I will detail in Chapter Nine.

About the Researcher

To help readers situate me within this study, I would like to offer some additional personal background. I am a white woman of Italian-American and French-Canadian descent who grew up in suburban Methuen, Massachusetts, north of Boston on the New Hampshire border. I have pale olive skin, dark brown hair, and dark brown eyes.[4] I am of the middle class (but have not always been). I grew up in the 1980s, and when I was the age of my study's participants, I enjoyed numerous children's television programs based on toys: *Care Bears, My Little Pony, Popples, Pound Puppies, Rainbow Brite*, and *Strawberry Shortcake* were all favorites. I owned multiple toys from each of these properties (especially the My Little Ponies). Like many children who grew up in that era, my after-school, after-homework hours were filled with television viewing—typically Nickelodeon programming or reruns of shows like *The Brady Bunch* and *Bewitched*. At times during my study, "moments of remembering" my girlhood interests and activities seemed to enrich my perceptions of the girls in my study (Thorne, 1993, p. 26). I was also on guard for the ways memories can distort perceptions of the present, however, and therefore tried never to assume that what might have been true for me would be true for these girls, twenty years later. Thorne's (1993) reflections on these processes were helpful methodologically.

When I began my study in 2005, I was a 28-year-old doctoral student. My hair was long, reaching the middle of my back, and although I am 5'8" tall, I was routinely mistaken for a teenager—not just by the study's participants, but by people in the community, ranging from cashiers to waiters to faculty members. (As one of my doctoral program's professors noted, "You know, when you don't wear makeup, you look about twelve.") I wished to be accepted as a near-peer by the girls in my study, differentiated from the authority figures at school and day care (Thorne, 1993, p. 16)—striving to be the "least-adult" of the adults they knew (Mandell, 1988). To this end, I dressed casually for our meetings, often in clothing from the Gap or Old Navy, and behaved in as casual and friendly a manner as possible. I avoided speaking authoritatively to the girls unless they were putting themselves or others in danger (e.g., by roughhousing) or doing something that could risk our group's ability to continue meeting (e.g., sneaking food into the library during our meeting, which was against the rules and which, after the first incident, the janitors reported to school authorities).

About a month into my study, I realized this strategy was working too well: The girls believed I was a teenager. Consider this conversation from March 2005, in which I mentioned to the girls at Suburban Elementary that I was originally from Massachusetts.

KYLIE: Massachusetts?

REBECCA: Mm-hmm.

BOBBI: So did your whole family move down here?

REBECCA: No, just me and my husband.

KYLIE: Husband?

REBECCA: Yeah. I'm married. [Angela sits up, mouth agape.] Did you know that?

ANGELA: No! Never!

Some of the girls in each group could not believe I was old enough to be married, so I settled the matter by asking my husband to make a guest appearance at each location. This attempt at clarity introduced a new issue: Some began referring to me as a teacher, even though that was not my role. It was difficult for them to situate me; compared with the roles of other adults in their lives—parents, teachers, caretakers—my status was anomalous. However, we developed a strong rapport, and the aftercare employees who overheard our conversations (due to child care regulations, one employee was obliged to be in the room during all our meetings) would remark afterwards that they were "amazed" or "surprised" by how freely the girls shared with me, and by how much they had to say. ("I can't believe they talked so much," one employee said after attending an early group meeting at Suburban Elementary. "I've never heard Maria say so much in one sitting.")

Although my study's participants constituted a qualitative, non-representative sample of girls, the richness of my data supports the results I report. I gathered far more data than can be included in this book: dozens of video and audiotapes, 1,981 pages of single-spaced transcribed interviews, two notebooks of hand-written field notes, and five binders of collected field materials. I have done my best to select quotes and examples that do justice to my participants, who were so generous in sharing with me both their viewpoints and their personal lives. In the chapters that follow, I use strong representative examples from our conversations to illustrate the themes that emerged across groups in my qualitative analysis (particularly across the Nonprofit Aftercare and the Suburban Elementary groups, as these groups watched the same cartoons in the same order). At other times, especially in Chapter Nine, I rely upon "magnified moments" (Hochschild, 1994) that did not occur across groups, but rather were unique incidents of "heightened importance" (p. 4). By their metaphorical richness, elaborateness, and resonance, these magnified moments offered "window[s] into the social construction of reality" (Messner, 2000, p. 766).

The girls in my study were interesting and bright. Their behavior ran the gamut from people-pleasing to disruptive, with some as eager to answer my questions as others were to sit upside-down in their chairs and kick the music stands of the band room we met in. Whenever we hit upon a topic that interested them, however, they had quite a lot to say. I learned how the girls watched television—who had sets in their rooms and who watched with their families; who had TiVo and who watched cable. I learned that many slept with their stuffed animals, liked riding bikes in the summer and building snow forts in the winter, and worried about problems with their friends. I learned who watched *Lost* with their parents (but clutched the couch cushions to hide during the scary parts) and who had the *Mr. Hankey's Christmas Classics* CD (an age-inappropriate *South Park* recording given to one girl by her father during a custody visit). They enjoyed telling me about events in their lives: their birthday parties, first communions, chorus and band concerts, new puppies, and ice skating accidents. Most of all, I learned firsthand that if an adult is willing to listen—non-judgmentally, with sincere a interest in whatever interests them—pre-adolescent girls have a lot to say.

Notes

1. Mainstream criticisms of the riot grrrls, detailed in Chapter One, are an example of a mainstream moral panic; the allegation that the Spice Girls killed feminism, used to frame the interviews I conducted in Chapter Three, are an example of another.
2. Note: All individual and place names have been changed to assure my participants' anonymity.

3. Note that this upward mobility is by comparison to their origins. They were often working- to lower-middle-class, but they had improved their families' economic situations.

4. I have sometimes been mistaken for being Latina or Jewish, or for having Indian or Middle East heritage. I have no reason to believe the girls in my study assumed I was anything but Euro-American, but I previously have been made aware of my apparent ethnic ambiguity.

6

Girls Rule!

Sexism, Strength, and Intelligence

"Girls can do as many things as boys can do."
—Desirée, age 8 (African-American)

"Girls can be strong, too."
—Brianna, age 8 (African-American)

"Girls are smarter than boys in every way!"
—Kylie, age 8 (Euro-American)

Boys are strong; girls are weak. This stereotype has been used countless times to insult boys ("You throw like a girl!") and constrain girls ("Sweetie, don't; you'll get hurt"). As Dowling (2000) has explained, it seems "culturally inevitable" and "natural" (p. 56) that women are weaker and have less power than men—but this is simply a "frailty myth" (p. 3) Most differences in physical strength between the sexes result from socialization, not nature. Social norms lead parents, teachers, and other caretakers to subconsciously gender-train children beginning in infancy: they coddle and overhelp toddler girls, stifle girls' interests in athletics, and encourage adolescent girls to be as small as possible—and being small virtually guarantees being weak (Dowling, 2000). This socialization does more than diminish women's physical potential; it also intertwines with the subordination and disempowerment of women (p. 195).

In the late 1990s, the Powerpuff Girls smashed these gendered boundaries with superhuman strength. Although their strength and power were of fictitious, fantastic form, their superior strength disrupted the dominant discourse of girlhood as inherently weak. More girl hero cartoons followed, such as *Totally Spies*. Taking a page from the Spice Girls' playbook, their protagonists were strong teenagers who were also smart, or athletic, or sassy. Fast, tough, and brilliant, these girls were not just as good as boys; they were *better*—stronger and more intelligent. A "girls rule" ethos permeated the genre.

Within a few years, however, the message that girls are unfailingly strong and smart fragmented. New girl hero episodes and series contradicted themselves and each other. The genre offered a range of mixed messages about girls' strength and intelligence, as we saw in Chapter Four: In some instances, all girls could be strong; in others, female strength was anomalous, or available only to pretty girls, or acceptable only if mitigated by flawlessly "nice" behavior.

How did real girls read these conflicting messages? Did they accept girl power's basic position that girls are physically and intellectually strong—even boys' superiors? This chapter explores how preadolescent girls drew upon "girls rule" discourse in their understandings of girls' and boys' comparative strengths, both physical and intellectual, and displays of sexism against girls.

Girls Rule: Negotiating Male and Female Strength

In 1998, Lemish found many young girls believed in the Spice Girls' "girl power" slogan "as an expression of independence, strength, success, and sense of self-worth. 'It means,' explained one twelve year old, 'equality . . . that girls are strong, each one in her own way.' Her friend added, 'And the songs, they are the kind that think that we need equality and that girls need strength'" (p. 153). Cartoons such as *The Powerpuff Girls* carried this torch, presenting girls as strong and equal to boys. The episode "Members Only" exemplified this: Because the Powerpuff Girls idolized the televised superheroics of the Association of World Super Men[1] (AWSM, or "awesome"), they applied for membership in AWSM—beating the men at every test of strength and speed. When the girls triumph, however, the men balked.

Major Glory: Membership denied.

Blossom: What?!

Buttercup: But we passed all the tests!

Bubbles: I thought our powers were good enough.

Major Glory: (*baby talk, leaning down to her*) Aww . . . baby Powerpuff no-no goo-goo noof? (*normal voice, back at podium*) Look, kids, you're missing the point. This is the Association of World Super Men! You're little girls. We are the men! The protectors, the hunters, the fighters, and the show-offs—(*pounding podium*)—and the noisemakers! You are little girls. You should be at home with your mommy, learning how to cook and clean, and . . . blah-blah-blah-blah-blah, whatever women stuff.

In the end, the supermen got their comeuppance: A villain attacked AWSM, and no one but the Powerpuff Girls was strong enough to defeat him. Once AWSM owed the Powerpuff Girls their lives, the tables turned. Adulating their new heroes, the men asked to become "The Society of Associated Puffketeers." When the Powerpuff Girls agreed, the men disbanded AWSM and donned attire like the Powerpuff Girls': short dresses, white knee-high socks, and black Mary Jane shoes. They beamed with pride in the episode's closing shot, while the Powerpuff Girls floated above them with expressions of amusement and laughter.

From a viewer's perspective, this cross-dressing conclusion to *Members Only* was unexpected and humorous because in Western culture, it is considered debasing for men to wear or use items marked as feminine. Some men try to avoid association with pink-hued products, whether a necktie or a toothbrush, since pink is considered a feminine color, and some men even disdain foods such as salads, which have been associated with dieting and therefore women. (Advertisements and other popular culture items, including television shows and tee-shirts, proclaim, "Real men eat meat"; salads are constructed as somehow being the opposite of meat. The foolishness of this idea helps reveal the unnaturalness of the social construct that men and women, too, are opposites.) Within this cultural context, when the men of AWSM became Puffketeers who wore dresses with pride, they rejected the idea that femininity is debasing. "Members Only" thereby offered a complex message: While it may seem funny for men to dress like females, it does not have to be degrading or demeaning. The men's pride in their new attire made it clear they did not feel like the butts of a joke. Many viewers may have laughed or just smiled at the episode's closing sequence, but the conclusion was polysemic, open to interpretation. One valid reading of the conclusion was that girl power is about more than girls' strength and importance. Girl power also means girlhood is valuable; sexist attitudes about femininity are wrong.

How did real girls understand the cartoon's narrative of male chauvinism undone—of gendered power differentials inverted? After girls at Suburban Elementary and the Nonprofit Aftercare Program viewed "Members Only," I asked them to share their likes and dislikes about it.[2] The girls were quick to criticize the displays of misogyny that dominated the story. At Suburban Elementary, Angela (age 8; Euro-American, Maria (age 8; Euro-American), and Audrey (age 9; Euro-American) commented:

> ANGELA: I didn't like when the AWSM Club or something—I didn't like that the Powerpuff Girls couldn't join the club.
>
> MARIA: I also didn't like it whenever, after the people who did something and then when they lost, whenever everyone started, like, saying, "You lost to a girl" and started making fun of 'em.
>
> AUDREY: I disliked it when the AWSM superheroes were being mean to the Powerpuff Girls when they passed all their tests. I thought that was mean.

Audrey suggested the supermen were mean to the Powerpuffs "because they're bigger."

Likewise, at Nonprofit Aftercare, Madison (age 8; African-American) and Gia (age 7; African-American) responded:

> MADISON: They were being disrespectful.
>
> GIA [agreeing]: They were being disrespectful.
>
> MADISON: They say, "You're all just little, tiny, little girls."

I asked why they thought the men were being "disrespectful." Madison recalled Aesop's fable of the lion and the mouse, in which "the mouse is tiny, and the lion is big." She believed the men had to learn that small people are not unimportant. The group then wondered whether jealousy was to blame for the men's bad behavior.

> MADISON: The men—just because they, they passed all the tests, they—I was thinking they [were] jealous.
>
> REBECCA: You think so?
>
> DESIRÉE: I don't think they're jealous.
>
> REBECCA: What would make them jealous?
>
> MADISON: Because they took—they're better than them. [Laughing] Broke the man's back. [She is referring to a hero whose back was thrown out during a lifting contest with the Powerpuff Girls. As a result, he lost to Buttercup.]

GIA: The, um, person who had broke his back, he was jealous because, um, Buttercup is stronger, she had—she could pick up the school buses and whales and she picked up the person with the building, and she picked up a building that was so high that, um, no one else could pick it up.

BRIANNA: And they were jealous that, um, that they were good, so that's why they [kept trying] to test them in something else.

Brianna (age 8; African-American) agreed jealousy was to blame; only Desirée (age 8; African-American) dissented from this growing consensus. When I asked why, she replied:

DESIRÉE: They think that, um, not all women, they think that men is, like, better than girls, like, they not the same, or they stronger than girls or something.

REBECCA: Uh-huh.

BRIANNA: Girls can be strong, too!

Desirée's answer suggested she had a still-inchoate sense of sexism: She could tell it existed, but she had little vocabulary to express what she sensed. Clearly, however, she felt male chauvinism was why the supermen refused the girls' membership. Her reading was in line with the producers' apparent intended lesson that sexism is wrong. This message was not received by all viewers, however: Some girls drew from experiences other than sexism—such as jealousy, and the fable of the lion and the mouse—to inform alternate readings of the story's moral.

In other girl hero cartoons, the stereotype that men are strong and women are weak was often taken as a given. Only a few story lines directly contested cultural norms as "Members Only" did; others reinscribed sex role biases. Consider *W.I.T.C.H.*, the Toon Disney story of five girls who learn they are Guardians of the Veil, defenders of the barrier between Earth and another world, Meridian. When the girls at Suburban Elementary watched the debut episode of *W.I.T.C.H.* together, I asked them to share their likes and dislikes. Angela singled out one line of dialogue:

ANGELA: I dislike the part where, um, that guy, um, he said to the other guy, um, "Tell the men to stay strong and tell the women to not get worried" or something.

She was referring to the conversation in which Caleb, leader of the rebellion in Meridian, told a compatriot he was leaving for Earth. Clasping the other man's shoulders, he said, "Tell the men to stay strong, and the women not to worry. I hope to see you soon." In context, the line was a throwaway—an uncontested, unproblematized piece of the narrative, followed almost immediately by a major action sequence in which Caleb was intercepted by the show's major villain and transported to Earth.

> REBECCA: So what did you think of that part?
>
> ANGELA: I wish they'd get to know that, like, not all women are afraid of every-
> thing, they're not gonna freak out. Some boys freak out or
> something.
>
> REBECCA: So what did you think of that comment, then?
>
> ANGELA: I didn't like it. He just doesn't know what he's talking about. That's
> why he's a boy. [shaking her head]

When I asked if anyone else had noticed the comment, Kylie (age 8; Euro-American) replied first, saying, "No, I didn't really care about it." Bobbi (age 10; Euro-American), who had not noticed it either, asked, "What was the comment again?" Angela offered, "Like, uh, telling the men stay strong, and tell the women to—" "not worry," concluded Kylie. Bobbi pondered this and offered the following thoughts:

> BOBBI: So, that kinda means that, um, women are weak and men are strong.
> Well, the thing is, I don't agree with that—
>
> ANGELA: Of course *I* don"t.
>
> BOBBI: But, I mean, it is true. I have played baseball the same exact time as my
> neighbor. We're both ten years old; he's a month younger than me—
> but the thing is, he always beats me.
>
> REBECCA: He does?
>
> BOBBI: I can never win.
>
> REBECCA: How come?
>
> BOBBI: But—I don't know, he's just better. But we're the same exact age, we start-
> ed baseball at the same exact time, and we both played t-ball, we
> played two years of pitching machine, and we both are doing our
> second year in minors this year. So it doesn't make sense that he
> always beats me and I can never win.
>
> REBECCA: So how do you relate that to what we were just talking about, about
> that comment on the TV?

BOBBI: Well, the comment was that, well, it meant really that men are stronger than women, so women shouldn't try. But, I mean, I guess I don't, like, believe in that, but I guess it seems true because, I mean, he always beats me. We're the same age, we've been playing baseball the same amount of time, and we, like, both started the same time and everything. So it doesn't makes sense, like, why does he always beat me?

During this conversation, Bobbi struggled to reconcile her lived experiences with her sense that this directive was wrong. Like the girls who could not discern sexism as the source of conflict in "Members Only," Bobbi did not yet have access to contextual clues that might help her make sense of her experience. Although she and her neighbor joined the baseball team at the same time, perhaps he had been encouraged his whole life to be physically engaged because he was a boy. Perhaps his father had played ball with him for years; perhaps he had received more opportunities to develop and practice his skills at recess and during gym class.

This points to an important difference between the discourses of the girl crisis and the riot grrrls, and the discourses of mainstream girl power. The latter offered no explanations for structural and societal inequalities, even though it should be possible for programs that claim to be feminist to do so in an age-appropriate way. Therefore, although Bobbi knew something seemed wrong, and although she loved girl power media, she did not understand the social construction of gender, how the everyday sexism critiqued by the AAUW functioned or how it could limit girls.

When Bobbi asked, "Why does he always beat me?", I turned to the other girls in the group.

REBECCA: What do the rest of you think?

KYLIE: Cause they're boys.

REBECCA: What do you mean by "cause they're boys"?

KYLIE: Because boys are boys and girls are girls.

REBECCA: And what does that mean?

KYLIE: I don't know. [Laughing] I got it off the TV.

Kylie's response—that "boys are boys and girls are girls," a comment she got "off the TV"—may have been a half joke. However, it made an excellent point. If Kylie looked at the world of media to learn whether boys and girls are different or the same, she would have been told repeatedly that boys and girls are different (and unequal). A "boys are boys and girls are girls" mentality reinforces the status quo. As Barthes (1972) has famously noted, toys have long functioned in support of this gender construct. Children learn about future roles and work options through toys available in rigidly gendered packaging (p. 52). Television programs and other media texts have also served the same function. As dialogic theory suggests (Newcomb, 1988, 1991), viewers understand television episodes based not just on the individual program's content but in relation to the content of other programs they consume. This means audiences are active participants in the meaning-making process, rather than passive recipients of producers' intended meanings. Therefore, though television producers and some critics claimed girl power could empower girls and change the way they saw girlhood, this was a tall order. Read in context with other aspects of children's culture, the girl hero cartoon genre did not present enough new story lines to change girls' perspective.

In fact, girl hero cartoons mirrored television's prevalent "boys are boys and girls are girls" discourse in how they visually signified girls' strength. Cartoon girl heroes never looked as strong as they should have—there was nary a muscle to be seen. As discussed in Chapter Four, the girl heroes' physiques were slight and svelte, fitting the standard look for female heroes in action-adventure and sci-fi shows including *Buffy the Vampire Slayer, Alias,* and *Charlie's Angels.* Even a slightly muscular appearance would better signify physical strength, but musculature generally is considered masculine; if a girl looks too strong, too large and imposing, she is undesirable and unattractive. This assessment, rooted in chauvinism, coerces females into accepting the falsehood that they are inherently weak (Dowling, 2000).

On rare instances, some cartoon girl heroes temporarily gained a muscular physique. These girls became instantly unattractive to boy characters. E.g., in *Totally Spies'* "The Incredible Bulk," Alex accidentally ate energy bars laced to make those who consume them grow enormous, hulk-like muscles. When Alex's giant muscles emerged and her voice lowered, she instantly becomes a misfit. Contrary to the logical result of her heightened strength—that she might be better at attacking villains—she became unable to control her body. In short order, her boyfriend Raymond dumped her. He was a gym instructor and competitive bodybuilder who never knew of her double life as a crime-fighting spy, and faced with her new muscles, he simply backed away from her, hands outstretched and smiling: "I'm not sure it's going to work out between us. It's just, I've got this thing about seeing girls who are more ripped than I am. Sorry!" Although Alex reacted by lunging towards him in fury, her teammates Sam and Clover accepted this in a matter-of-fact way. They just laughed and restrained Alex, saying, "Easy, girl!"

The girls I interviewed believed that Alex looked bad with muscles. As Kylie said, "Her muscles made her ugly and her voice made her sound ugly." Despite this, the girls disagreed with Raymond's decision to break up with her. At Suburban Elementary, Audrey and Megan (age 9, Euro-American) speculated that Alex's muscular form was not the real reason Raymond broke up with her but rather an excuse.

AUDREY: I thought that was mean [when he dumped her], because I think he knew that she really really liked him a lot, and I think that got him mad, real mad.

REBECCA: Megan, what did you think?

MEGAN: Um, I thought they were kind of mean and maybe didn't mean it. And I think he kind of had that face that, um, he didn't, that he had another girlfriend, and he didn't like her anymore.

REBECCA: Oh, so you thought he had another girlfriend.

When I asked if Alex's boyfriend was correct in saying that girls should not be as strong as boys, they were adamant in their answers:

AUDREY: No.

MEGAN: No!

BOBBI: We can be as strong as we want.

REBECCA: Yeah?

ALL: Yeah!

REBECCA: What were you going to say, Kylie?

MEGAN: That's how boys are mean.

KYLIE: I just do this! [making 90-degree muscle gesture]

The girls at Nonprofit Aftercare also disliked the episode's conclusion. Desirée said, "I liked the whole thing except for the end." The other girls agreed. I asked how she would have preferred for the episode to end, and she said, "For her not to get dumped." When I asked whether it is "okay or not okay for girls to get stronger than guys," the girls were adamant that it is okay. Desirée said, "Girls can do as many things as boys can do." Desirée's sister Roshanda (age 6; African-American) said, "It doesn't matter what the boys think!" Rhea (age 9, African-American) declared, "It's not the boys' opinion to tell the girls what they can do!"

In other words, many girls believed it wrong for boys to limit or judge girls. They were unwilling to accept the idea that surpassing the strength of boys was socially unacceptable. If men disliked girls' displays of strength, they could not believe it was because the girls were subverting gendered norms; thus, if a boy dumped his newly muscular girlfriend, it was not because his masculinity was threatened. The males were just being jealous, mean, or *stupid*.

Boys Are Dumb: Negotiating Male and Female Intelligence

The girls in my study were unaware of structural inequalities or the concepts of sexism or chauvinism. This was understandable; the concepts are rarely taught in elementary school, and U.S. children's television programming is ill equipped to address such issues. Owing to this knowledge gap, the girls in my study usually attributed sexist incidents to a simpler cause: boys' stupidity.

The unfair idea that boys, as a group, are inherently stupid was promoted in part by girl power's "girls rule" discourse—an oppositional discourse that pitted girls against boys and presented girls as superior. In her study of young Spice Girls fans, Lemish (1998) noted that many of her study's participants interpreted girl power in just this way. When asked what the Spice Girls' girl power meant to them, Lemish's nine- to eleven-year-old interviewees replied: "That girls are better"; "there are boys that think that they are better than girls, so the Spice Girls try to prove that it is not so"; and "they want to show that girls are important, too" (p. 154). In this way, Lemish explained, "the Spice Girls were recruited as ideological support in everyday experiences of gender inequality and prejudice" (p. 154).

In the years following Lemish's study, girl power's "girls rule" discourse increasingly fixated upon the charge that boys are stupid. The popular "Girls rule, boys drool" catchphrase inspired other anti-boy slogans, like "Boys are stupid, throw rocks at them" and "Boys eat boogers when nobody's watching." The popular David & Goliath company drew protests when it mass-produced t-shirts with these slogans and others, including "Boys lie, make them cry" and "Boys are dumb" (illustrated with a boy thinking "2 + 2 = 5") (Boettcher, 2004). Such slogans played into the ingroup/outgroup bias that developmental psychologists have found is a common characteristic of children's gender identity development: Children typically have positive feelings about their own sex, favoring it over the opposite sex. The developmental psychology studies have not determined whether favoring the ingroup correlates with actual hostility or animosity towards the opposite sex, however (Martin & Ruble, 2009). In fact, in their comprehensive review of the gender development literature, Martin and Ruble (2009) noted that "some researchers may have misinterpreted children's positive ingroup feelings in structured interviews as overt rejections of the other group" (p. 357)—an important point.

Girl hero television cartoons frequently were in dialogue with this problematic boys-are-dumb concept and the developmentally typical ingroup/outgroup bias. On most shows, the girl heroes were not just stronger than the males in their worlds. They were smarter, too; their intelligence contrasted sharply with the rank stupidity of male villains. E.g., *The Powerpuff Girls* featured the Amoeba Boys, incredibly stupid gigantic one-cell organisms who always caused trouble but presented no challenge to the Powerpuffs; similarly, the Gangrene Gang and Rowdyruff Boys showed few signs of intelligence as they caused trouble. Likewise, in *Kim Possible*, Dr. Drakken was an ineffective villain because he wasn't as smart as he thought he was. He lacked the intelligence to execute his grand schemes, and his female sidekick, Shego, was clearly smarter than him, though he did not recognize it. Meanwhile, Kim's sidekick, Ron Stoppable, liked to goof off and had a hard time being serious. Kim was a model student; Ron was the class clown.

It was in this context that, when discussing "Members Only," Megan reflected that the boys she knew were like the members of AWSM: They were "mean," quick to assert superior strength, and lacking intelligence.

MEGAN: The boys down the street, they chase me and my two friends around. Like when the weather is warm, or not too cold, we like to chase the boys everywhere, and they have these little plastic swords and say they can hurt us with plastic swords.

REBECCA: And what do you think of that when they say that?

MEGAN: I think that they're not smart. I don't think that they know anything about plastic.

REBECCA: Yeah. Why, if they knew something about plastic, what would they say instead of that?

MEGAN: They would say that they're stronger and that they can beat us with four people against three; then sometimes we have more than three people, cause there's other people and friends.

Megan, thinking logically about strength in numbers, took pleasure in turning the boys' comments around on them. The boys could pretend they could hurt the girls with their swords. As far as Megan was concerned, the swords were irrelevant—and their sex was, too. The groups' comparative sizes would determine the outcome of any threatened altercation.

The claim that girls are smarter than boys arose in other conversations with Caucasian girls as well. For example, when I asked the girls at Suburban Elementary whether it was okay for girls to be strong, the girls agreed. Kelly (age 9; Euro-American) and Kylie noted:

KELLY: We're smarter than the boys, anyway, cuz they never pay attention in school.

REBECCA: They don't?!

KELLY: No.

KYLIE: I know boys don't pay attention; girls do!

REBECCA: Really!

KYLIE: Girls rule!

Asked why they thought the boys don't pay attention, the girls replied excitedly, nearly talking over one another:

[Kylie has been lying on her stomach across two chairs; she straightens up at this point, fully engaged.]

KYLIE: I sit next to a boy named Jimmy in school. He always tries to talk to me.

REBECCA: He does?

KYLIE: No, and every time I try—I walk up to the whiteboard, he's, like, right in front of me, and he's like, "Are you looking at me?" and I'm, like, "Eww, no!" [*Rebecca chuckles*] cuz he always thinks I'm looking at him!

AUDREY: This kid in my class, Tim, he doesn't pay—he wouldn't pay attention at all [. . .], and then after we have snack, later on in the day, like two o'clock, three, he's still eating his snack.

REBECCA: Wow.

KYLIE: Oh, and Billy, he doesn't even pay attention at all.

In many similar conversations, the Caucasian girls I spoke with told me—with great passion—that girls are boys' superiors. Girls are smart, attentive, and behave well in class; they rule. Boys, lazy, hungry, goofy, and inattentive, drool. Kylie's use of the phrase "girls rule" to summarize this ingroup-favoring argument exemplified the girls' ready use of girl power rhetoric, which had been around since she was a baby; as discussed in Chapter Two, the Spice Girls introduced a heavy-handed "girls rule, boys drool" mentality into the mainstream in 1997, when Kylie was just a year old.

Note, however, that the traits these Caucasian interviewees praised regarding female students were the behaviors expected of girls like themselves. Girl hero cartoons often depicted their most intelligent female characters as studious, attentive, obedient, polite good students. This is worth critiquing because what the girls at Suburban Elementary claimed made them better than boys was that they did what was expected of them as young, white, middle-class females: presenting themselves "as helpful, as smart and capable, as responsible, as productive" (Cherland, 2005, p. 101). As Cherland explained in her analysis of her memory-work with her own daughter, "In positioning herself as capable, helpful, and productive, Elisabeth was reading cultural discourses that told her how she was inscribed by the dominant culture and responding by demonstrating her position as a white, middle-class girl. This was not a choice. She did it because it was necessary for her psychic survival [. . .]. She had internalized the disciplining codes for whiteness and the social expectations for living out those codes, and she did not resist them, because enacting them gave her pleasure" (p. 101). Perhaps for similar reasons, the girls in my study took pride in how much better they fulfilled these expectations than they believed their male peers did. In many cases, they excelled at being white, middle-class girls, while being understandably unaware that cultural expectations for boys and girls, and for individuals of varying races and classes, differ. In many contexts, including education, Kylie's summation is the dominant mindset: Boys are boys and girls are girls. Girls are expected to behave well and therefore, by virtue of behaving like girls should, are better students for it; but boys will be boys, and they will be more readily forgiven for fighting, having short attention spans, or joking around (especially if they are white, as scholars such as Banks (2005) have documented).

At the same time, the perception that girls have been doing better than boys in school has led to mainstream concern about boys' welfare. At the end of the 1990s, landmark books on boys' emotional well-being were published: *Raising Cain: Protecting the Emotional Life of Boys* (Kindlon & Thompson, 1999) and *Real Boys: Rescuing Our Sons from the Myths of Boyhood* (Pollack, 1999). These were heralded as boys' answer to *Reviving Ophelia*. A few years later, reminiscent of the discourse on the girl crisis and the AAUW reports, much ink was devoted to the subject of boys' underachievement. Books on the subject included *The Minds of Boys: Saving Our Sons from Falling Behind in School and Life* (Gurian & Stevens, 2005), *Helping Boys Succeed in School: A Practical Guide for Parents and Teachers* (Neu and Weinfeld, 2007), *Boys Adrift: The Five Factors Driving the Growing Epidemic of Unmotivated*

Boys and Underachieving Young Men (Sax, 2007), and *The Trouble with Boys: A Surprising Report Card on Our Sons, Their Problems at School, and What Parents and Educators Must Do* (Tyre, 2008). The latter followed up on Tyre's 2006 *Newsweek* cover story on the same subject. The cover read, "The Boy Crisis. At Every Level of Education, They're Falling Behind. What to Do?" The article raised alarm, noting:

> By almost every benchmark, boys across the nation and in every demographic group are falling behind. In elementary school, boys are two times more likely than girls to be diagnosed with learning disabilities and twice as likely to be placed in special-education classes. High-school boys are losing ground to girls on standardized writing tests. The number of boys who said they didn't like school rose 71 percent between 1980 and 2001, according to a University of Michigan study. Nowhere is the shift more evident than on college campuses. Thirty years ago men represented 58 percent of the undergraduate student body. Now they're a minority at 44 percent. This widening achievement gap, says Margaret Spellings, U.S. secretary of Education, "has profound implications for the economy, society, families and democracy." (Par. 3)

Such statistics make literal belief in the boast that "girls rule" more problematic. While the devotion with which real girls embraced the idea that girls can do anything—that they're smart, strong, and valuable—constituted progress, the open disdain for boys' intellectual capabilities that often accompanied the idea was unfortunate. The developmental psychology literature suggests girls may have made such claims as a reflection of "stereotypes about boys getting into trouble," rather than actual hostility (Martin & Ruble, 2009). Nevertheless, as I mentioned regarding *Spice World's* over-the-top objectification of men, life ought not be a zero-sum game in which the sexes compete to dominate and belittle each other. Equality between the sexes is a worthy goal, but declaring that "girls rule, boys drool" is useless reverse sexism. It does nothing to address the persistent structural inequalities girls continue to face, and it may even distract from the ways in which girls' lives and situations do *not* "rule."

The Reality: Girls Rule?

Although my Caucasian interviewees seemed to enjoy discussing how girls "rule"—proclaiming girls were smarter than boys and just as strong (at least potentially so)—from my standpoint as an observer, their lived experiences differed from this rhetoric. These girls often complained to me about how boys mistreated them, taunting them, calling them names, and disrupting their games. I witnessed some incidents firsthand while conducting field observations during lunch recess at Suburban Elementary. As noted in Chapter Five, I could not secure comparable access to Waterhaven Elementary School, where Nonprofit Aftercare was located. Their principal would not meet with me or grant me permission to visit the campus during school hours; my access to the children was only through the aftercare program. Therefore, this section focuses on my observations in the field at Suburban Elementary, which had a primarily white, middle-class population. Although playground behavior is not everything, play is important work in children's lives, and patterns during designated play times are telling.

On many of my visits to lunch recess at Suburban Elementary, I observed the following pattern. A group of girls would finish eating lunch before the boys and congregate outside to jump rope in the middle of the schoolyard. A few boys charged into their game at top speed, pulling the jump rope out of the girls' hands, ruining whatever jumping record the girls had been trying to break. The boys attacked repeatedly until the girls took their jump rope to a side corner of the school yard, yielding the center of the yard to the boys. The boys then started a sports game (often football), taking up significantly more space than the girls, though their numbers were about equal. While football requires more space than a jump rope game, the boys' means of claiming playground space seemed unjust. (My own girlhood memories resonated somewhat with this situation: I was reminded of my grade school, where the "boys' side" and "girls' side" of the schoolyard were clearly delineated by school authorities. The boys' side was substantially larger, giving them ample room for football, while the girls' side was too small for the girls to engage in many recess sports.) My field notes captured one recess jump rope game, its sudden interruption, and the girls' reaction with this description:

> Kerri caught my eye and beckoned me over. She, Bailey, Christine, and a few other girls were playing jump rope and asked me to watch. They were singing:
>
> Teddy bear, teddy bear
> Turn around
> Teddy bear, teddy bear
> Touch the ground
> One, two, three, four . . . [etc.]
>
> One girl said she had gotten up to 24 earlier, and that's what everyone was trying to beat.

The girls were jumping in the middle of a rectangle often used for football, etc. by the boys. [Suddenly], three boys literally ran into their game, jumping into the rope and running away. I asked the girls why that happened, and they said the boys always bother them that way.

Eventually, the girls moved to another part of the schoolyard. It was the only way they could enjoy their game in peace.

On a later occasion, when another group of girls encountered the same harassment, I asked why they did not complain, either. They said they had complained many times, but it never made any difference. They were always forced away from the nice, sunny, paved area on which they wanted to play and off into a corner. Sometimes the boys would go out of their way to run through their jump rope games there, as well, which made it clear the boys' actions were not just about clearing room to play sports—it was about power. And the girls had given up. They no longer fought back.

Problems with the boys harassing the girls while they played jump rope was a lengthy topic of conversation during some of the home interviews I conducted: It really bothered some of the girls. For example, Kylie—who said that during recess, "All I mainly do is jump rope. That's what all the girls do"—had received a rope burn to the neck two days before our home interview when a boy deliberately ran into the rope while she was jumping "for no reason." "I had to go to the nurse," she said. The school's response to the boys' harassing behavior was not to modify the boys' behavior but to make the girls move: "We tell the safeties, and, um, they made us move over where they were, so the boys wouldn't jump in," Kylie explained. "So we were safe for the rest of recess."

During my home interview with Angela, she made a connection between the boys' bullying the girls during jumprope and other problems on the playground that the school had not yet dealt with. After Angela complained that it was annoying when the boys disrupted the jump rope games, we had this exchange:

REBECCA: So what's up with the boys being annoying on the playground?

ANGELA: Well, they just want to, like, get into things, and they're trying to be all funny, but they're really not. Like, today, there's this really gross, like, drawing thing inside the tube in the gym–you know that— there's two—like, you know that jungle gym that was fenced in?

REBECCA: Mm-hmm.

ANGELA: And that—and it had, like, these little—whatchacallits—they're, like, those big—it's like a clock, except for it's not really a clock, it's like a tube kinda—it's not a tube—it's like a sphere kinda—it's half a sphere. And inside people, like, say bad words. And there's this gross thing. And, you know the—I'm not gonna say it.

REBECCA: You can say it if you want. I won't be upset.

ANGELA: Like, it's not a curse word. But it's really gross.

REBECCA: Oh.

ANGELA: It said, "Insert"—um–"something here." [Angela trails off.]

REBECCA: [whispers] What?

ANGELA: Um, the P word. [silence]

REBECCA: Hmmm.

ANGELA: I told my mom.

REBECCA: What?

ANGELA: The P word—p-e- [Angela pauses]. Yeah, that one.

REBECCA: Okay.

ANGELA: And–and it had a drawing—a picture of a girl—[Angela gestures]

REBECCA [reacting to the gesture]: Ew!

ANGELA: —opening her mouth.

REBECCA [sympathetically]: Oh, that's disgusting.

ANGELA: I know. Um, and—me and Rosa was, like, "Ew! Can't we just, like, paint this whole jungle gym, like, red?"

REBECCA: Yeah.

ANGELA: So nobody could draw on it, and then we could overpaint it. That was a good idea, though.

REBECCA: So, did they paint over it? Or is it still that way?

ANGELA: It's still that way.

REBECCA: How long has it been that way?

ANGELA: Long time.

In other words, the girls who enjoyed playing on the playground equipment had to face vulgar graffiti (which Angela's mom assumed was teenagers' handiwork) about male sexual aggression and female sexual subordination during their playtime. Some children made this area even worse for others to play in by saying "bad words." As Banks (2005) has noted, "there are spaces at school like the school yard that adults cannot control and students must negotiate" (p. 186), presenting opportunities for some students to experiment with taboo behaviors—to the possible entertainment, discomfort, or indifference of some of their peers. Although Angela did not specify what the bad words were, I had witnessed some goings-on during recess and library periods. Scatological insults were common (one boy wanted everyone to call another boy "the poop king"), and gay bashing was a too-common preoccupation. Accusations flew about certain boys being gay, of certain girls being lesbians, and, perplexingly, of certain boys being "half-lesbians." Angela and Kylie independently noted that Rasheed, a boy who regularly ran through the jump rope games in a manner likely to cause harm, had beaten up another boy called James, saying he was "gay." Another girl, Tanya, confided that a boy named Justin had caused her a lot of trouble, finally getting in trouble with the principal when he called her "a homosexual and gay"—a case we will discuss further in Chapter Seven.

The combination of sexually themed graffiti, the "bad words" spoken at recess, and the homophobia perpetuated by children like Rasheed and Justin arguably constituted a climate of sexual harassment at Suburban Elementary. At first blush, this may seem odd, given that we are discussing third, fourth, and fifth graders. However, the literature suggests sexual harassment begins in primary school (e.g., American Association of University Women, 1993, 2001; Murnen & Smolak, 2000; Trigg & Wittenstrom, 1996) but typically is not recognized or addressed early on (Lichty, and Torres, Valenti, and Buchanan, 2008). Gonick (2006) has noted that by high school, harassment frequently becomes a threat of violence; girls who do not conform to expectations for gender norms (such as queer or trans girls) may be threatened with or experience physical assault, including rape. Adults too often react to girls' harassment with "a 'boys will be boys' type of argument, downplaying the harassment as merely an expression of desire rather than as a threat of violence" (p. 125). For all these reasons, it is important for schools officials to work with students who harass their peers, trying to help them understand—as the Suburban Elementary principal did with Justin—that these behaviors cannot continue.

In the reality of playground struggles and schoolyard sexism, most of which occurred in places where adult eyes could not bear witness and where adult intervention was uncommon, what was the idea that "girls rule" and "girls are strong" besides empty rhetoric? The girls arrived outside first and were driven aside when the boys finished their lunch. When the boys' behavior caused girls physical injury, the school responded by having the girls move for their own safety. This implied that girls needed to be protected and that boys had the right to take all the space they desired, through any means. Furthermore, the graffiti on the playground was not retouched or removed. Perhaps school officials actually had not been informed, but Angela believed that they knew about it. This may have signaled to some children that that school officials either did not recognize the playground was fostering a negative climate or that they did not find it pressing enough to address. Altogether, although Suburban Elementary was regionally recognized as an excellent suburban public school, it seemed unofficially to endorse male privilege as the status quo.

In short, my study of Suburban Elementary suggested that while girl power rhetoric may have helped the Euro-American girls in my study think better about girls' position as class of people, this perception had little to do with reality—except, perhaps, that the girls' behavior was "better" than the boys.

Five years later, when I conducted follow-up interviews with some of the girls from my study (see the Epilogue for more details), I asked what they recalled about the playground dynamics between the boys and girls. At thirteen years old, Angela remembered that when the boys would take over the playground, "I would always be alone. I wouldn't really have anybody to play with, so I wouldn't complain to much, 'cause I wouldn't really have anything to do anyway. I think that if it happened now [i.e., in eighth grade], we would probably talk to them about it and say that they're wrong." She felt that everybody got their fair share now that they were in middle school. Fifteen-year-old Bobbi recalled that in hindsight, she never had a problem with the boys taking over the Suburban Elementary playground—in part because, as a tomboy, she usually played with the boys. "It does kinda make sense that the girls can move over," she argued, "as long as they have room. Don't double dutch in the middle of a football field. There were a lot of ignorant people who were like, 'I'm-a be double dutchin', right here!' And it was like [pause], 'Chill.' Like, you would just look at them and be like, 'Are you serious?' I definitely know there was room off on the side, where they had room to double dutch, and the boys could play football and kickball. If you have twenty people who want to play kickball and four people who want to double dutch, then the kickball people should get the kickball field."

Fourteen-year-old Kylie disagreed. As one of the girls whose jump roping was regularly interrupted and shunted aside by aggressive boys, she recalled pointedly that there was not room to jump rope off to the side, "It was the *hill* part," she said, "so you *couldn't* jump rope." Thirteen-year-old Maria agreed that the boys' actions had been a problem, and she indicated that the inequities continued; as a seventh-grade student athlete, she felt the boys' athletic teams often received preferential treatment, just like the boys did during elementary school recess. She explained,

MARIA: In sports, they get more priority over the girls sometimes.

REBECCA: Like what? Like, at gym? Or . . .

MARIA: For the sports you have to try out for and everything? Like, they get new stuff more than the girls. And like, yesterday, how it was raining? The boys got the gym, even though they were supposed to have practice outside. Like, the boys got the gym instead of dividing it [with the girls].

These recollections add another layer of complexity to the situation. While some girls like Angela and Kylie felt the playground dynamics had been a problem, others—like Bobbi—sided with the boys. And while Angela suspected such issues would no longer be an issue at the middle school level, Maria—who unlike Angela was a student athlete—attested that the problems continued. In her view, the boys continued to enjoy unfair preference in accessing resources, such as the physical space needed to practice and play their sports.

While the girls were still in elementary school, where else did they turn for ideas about girls and strength? In talking with my participants about girls' strength and intelligence, the girls often cited another important source: their mothers. This resembled the young feminists' comments in Chapter Three, crediting their mothers and other caretakers with raising them to believe in girls innate worth and equality. For example, after watching *Atomic Betty* episode "The Great Race," which featured some "mean girl" behavior (see Chapter Four), the girls at Suburban Elementary discussed the differing ways in which girls and boys act mean. Abruptly, Kylie asked:

KYLIE: Did you know girls are smarter than boys in every way?

REBECCA: They are? [Kylie nods.] Where did you learn that?

KYLIE: My mom.

REBECCA: Hmm. And what do you think of that?

KYLIE: I think she's right!

REBECCA: [laughs] What makes you think that she's right?

KYLIE: Cuz, um, boys are, like, kinda stupid!

Angela also cited her mother:

ANGELA: Like, I remember my mom said that, um, boys thought that girls, like, weren't that important, and they didn't know how smart they could be. Like, boys think that it's not really, like, it's not every day that girls show them they're strong, but girls are real strong like me. Like, I picked up, like, a thirty- or twenty-pound weight lift thing, and it was, like, at my friend's house, and then there's, like, boys there, and they're, like, "I thought boys were stronger than girls" and we're, like, "Well, you're in first grade, he should be wrong!" [Rebecca laughs.] And then, um, the boys didn't let girls vote, and then Susan B. Anthony changed that.

REBECCA: Yeah, that's true, they did change that! Cool!

ANGELA: I think that was good.

The detail about Susan B. Anthony suggested that Angela's mother had gone beyond platitudes, instead giving her daughter concrete examples of women's fight for equality in history. Angela was applying what she learned from her mother to both her interactions with boys and to what she viewed on screen. This offers some insight as to why Angela may have been attuned to noticing small instances of sexism on screen, such as Caleb's throwaway comment on *W.I.T.C.H.*, discussed earlier in this chapter.

I revisited some of these comments made during visits to key participants' homes a year after the group discussions took place. I reminded Kylie that she told me her mother said that "girls are smarter than boys in every way," which Kylie did not remember. ("I didn't tell you that!" she exclaimed.) However, Kylie's mom confirmed that she had in fact told Kylie that girls are smarter than boys: "That's what I said. Boys don't grow up as fast as girls around this age, and they—they're not as mature, so they're still acting like little—little boys."

On the other hand, Angela did recall telling me girls are stronger than boys. Her mother Delia offered a lengthier explanation of what she had taught Angela on this subject.

DELIA: I tell her that—you know—girls can do anything that boys can do [Angela says, "girls can do anything that boys can" with her].

REBECCA: [to Angela] Wow, listen to you saying it—

JEANNINE [Angela's 7-year-old sister]: You jinx.

REBECCA: Jinxy.

DELIA: Physically, though, um—you know—we don't always like to admit it, but boys *are* stronger. Physic—biologically, they are. But—*but*—that doesn't mean that we can't do–play sports or do whatever that they do—

ANGELA: No! No! We're—they're not stronger biologically—like, they're not stronger in anything. Cuz girls—girls—

DELIA: Angela took it to the next level.

ANGELA: —girls just want to sit around and be fat, because—[Rebecca laughs]—because they think that we're not stronger so we can't do anything about it. Oh yes we can!

DELIA: That's right. And it's good that they believe that women are strong.

ANGELA: I do!

DELIA: Physically and mentally, too. It's important.

ANGELA: Yeah. But they really are—girls can be as strong—if they work really hard, they—it doesn't matter how their body's shaped, or if they have six packs—

REBECCA: If they have six-packs. [general laughter]

DELIA: They can work on their muscles. You're right, Angela. They can. They can.

I posit that girl power rhetoric, so popular in the media and therefore among children, helped Angela take her mother's wisdom "to the next level." However, the specificity of Delia's advice and the history she shared seemed to benefit Angela, enabling her to call out and critique glossed-over sexism. Perhaps the more parents share concrete ideas about girls' strength and equality with their daughters, the better their daughters may become at negotiating the conflicting messages about girlhood (and girl power) circulating in our cultural environment.

Discussion

In depicting girls' superheroic feats and exceptional intelligence, girl power cartoons promoted the idea of girls' superiority to boys. Overall, my participants' devotion to this "girls rule" rhetoric seemed to offer a few benefits. They perceived the category of "girl" as a positive thing; they felt smart and capable; and the idea that "girls rule" may have bolstered their academic self-confidence.

At the same time, "girls rule" rhetoric failed to offer a meaningful critique of concepts such as gender roles, sexism, and socialization. Girl hero cartoons occasionally attempted to do so, as in *The Powerpuff Girls'* "Members Only," but for many young viewers, these efforts went over their heads. The issue may be that unlike cartoons for preschoolers, girl hero cartoons lacked a formal curriculum. They were created to be cool, not instructive. As such, they did not offer viewers

age-appropriate explanations of concepts related to girl power and empowerment—a great opportunity missed, considering the pedagogical functions that television can serve. This meant that when faced with inequalities and differences
between boys and girl—on screen, as in "Members Only," or off-screen, in neighborhood sports—most participants had a hard time understanding and interpret-
ing these issues.

Among the participants who did understand on-screen depictions of sexism,
parental guidance seemed a key variable. The interviewee whose mother had spoken in detail about girls' equality and feminist progress demonstrated the keenest
ability to criticize the regressive depictions she saw on screen. Research on parents'
roles in critical media literacy may lend insight into best practices for helping children negotiate media texts and the complexities of cultural gender expectations.

Unfortunately, the "girls rule" rhetoric seemed disconnected from realities of
the schoolyard relationships between the Euro-American boys and girls in my
study. During my observations of lunch recess, the boys pushed the girls around
regularly, and the girls did not stand up for themselves. The girls were too nice to
yell at the boys, and as the schoolyard monitors had not sided with the girls in past
infringements, the girls believed change was impossible. In that context, at least,
they were disempowered. Such squabbles may seem trivial from an adult standpoint,
but they constitute a part of girls' socialization nonetheless. The additional problems of sexually explicit graffiti on the playground equipment and homophobia
among the children made things even worse.

While I was unable to make observations of my African-American participants
during their recess periods, it bears mentioning that when I asked if they ever had
problems at recess with the boys at school, they claimed that they did not.
According to my field notes, one afternoon when the girls at Nonprofit Aftercare
pointed out the area on the playground they preferred at recess, "I asked if the boys
ever take over the playground. Zayonna [age 10; African-American] laughed and
said that when the boys are trying to play, the girls deliberately walk around and
get in their way." It is important to remember that both social class and race play
significant roles in how identity is constructed and what behaviors various people
feel appropriate for themselves. If Zayonna's boast reflected the reality of their recess
experiences, perhaps for this reason she and her friends did not feel as constrained
by the "tyranny of nice and kind" (Brown and Gilligan, 1992, p. 88) as their Euro-
American counterparts at Suburban Elementary. They felt comfortable taking
their share of the playground.

Overall, I would suggest that when girls in my study used the phrase "girls rule,"
they referred less to real girls like themselves than to a conceptual set of "girls," pop-

ularized via mediated texts. In the minds of pre-adolescents, what are the characteristics of these mediated conceptions of girls, and how do real girls relate the conceptual girls to their own lives and identities? Chapter Seven offers some answers to this question.

Notes

1. The Association of World Super Men included characters from *The Justice Friends*, part of Cartoon Network's *Dexter's Laboratory* (1996–2003) cartoon, for which Craig McCracken was a writer.
2. This was my usual first question about any show we screened together.

7

Girl Heroes and Identity

The Limited Typology of Girl Power

Tomboys say: "Come on, let's fight"
—from a drawing by Madison, age 8 (African-American)

Girly girls say: "Need to get my nails done"
—from a drawing by Desirée, age 8 (African-American)

Divas say: "Come on, let's go to the mall"
—from a drawing by Madison

In previous decades, critics lamented the passive, helpless female characters found on children's television. These representations reflected a broader cultural mindset that "girl" equaled "dumb," "bad," and "weak" (Bikini Kill, 1991), in which many girls felt their opinions did not matter (Carter, 1991). Children's television has frequently cast girls in one of two narrative clichés: princesses in peril or token females. Stories about princesses, from Cinderella to Snow White to Princess Peach, have underscored the presumed weakness of females and implied that helplessness is romantically desirable. These tales have reflected broader cultural norms in which girls are encouraged to learn dependency and helplessness, believing that a man will someday take care of them—a mindset called the Cinderella complex that is psychologically unhealthy and limiting and can be economically detrimental to women (Dowling, 1981). Orenstein (2011) unpacked the role such stories are currently playing in the lives of girls in *Cinderella Ate My Daughter*, the problem is ongoing.

The other trope: a token female surrounded by a cast of males. Citing examples from children's television including Smurfette on *The Smurfs*, Miss Piggy on *The Muppets*, and Kanga in *Winnie the Pooh*, Katha Pollitt (1981) famously called this pattern "the Smurfette Principle." Meanwhile, in texts targeting teens and adults, representations of the token female have been even worse, as these characters have frequently been reduced to sex objects "for the boys" (Lamb and Brown, 2006). Jessica Rabbit in *Who Framed Roger Rabbit*, Angela in *American Beauty*, pop stars like Christina Aguilera and Britney Spears, and girls in countless horror films and prime-time television programs have all capitulated to the male gaze.

In each of these clichés, the males depicted are varied and interesting, whereas the girls are shoehorned into one of a few limited tropes, defined primarily by their sex. Their identity: *the girl*.

When girl power programs like *The Wild Thornberrys* (Nickelodeon, 1998–2004) and *As Told by Ginger* (Nickelodeon, 2000–2009) debuted, they represented progress. *The Wild Thornberrys* featured a smart, spunky, red-headed animated girl named Eliza who could talk with animals. While she and her family traveled the world to film documentaries, Eliza frequently saved animals from trouble—in many ways a precursor to Nick Jr's hit preschool shows, *Dora the Explorer* (2000–present) and *Go, Diego, Go!* (2005–present). *As Told by Ginger* was a cartoon about a smart, thoughtful red-headed junior high student, depicting her challenges and successes navigating her school's social strata. She worked to maintain her friends from grade school even as the "popular" girls in junior high became friends with her, placing her in conflicting situations. Banet-Weiser (2004) argued that despite the commercial, apolitical nature of shows like *Thornberrys* and *Ginger*, they offered a "different cultural script" that "challenge[d] conventional narratives and images about what girls are and who they should be" (pp.135–136). Their stories were not about passivity or weakness; they were more centered on forms of strength and courage. They did not emphasize physical beauty or sexualize their lead characters; the cartoons' animation styles presented the girls as multi-faceted individuals. (Both were produced by Klasky-Csupo and featured a similar aesthetic as their hit cartoon, *Rugrats*—squiggly and kind of misshapen.) Not just girls, they were people.

Concurrently, girl hero cartoons presented a bolder challenge to dominant girlhood discourses, depicting groups of girls working towards a common cause. Some girl heroes had superhuman strength (like the Powerpuff Girls and Jenny, the teenage robot), while others skillfully channeled human strength into martial arts (like the Spies and Kim Possible). Although these shows drew criticism for depicting violence, the fight scenes and their outcomes charted new ground. The girls were not damsels in distress; they were heroes in their own right. Unlike numerous precedents in media targeting adults—such as *The Avengers* (ITV/ABC, 1961–1969) and *Charlie's Angels* (ABC, 1976–1981), in which the female heroes would get out of their depth and need to be rescued (Inness, 1999)—girl heroes were self-sufficient. Furthermore, they were not tokenized within larger groups of males; they were strong in number. Finally, their *raison d'être* was never to look good for the boys. Though some parents and critics complained about Kim Possible's midriff-revealing top, girl heroes were infrequently depicted seeking romance. After all, they were superheroes dealing with more urgent matters. When they did flirt with romance, their behavior was mild, often awkward—never sexy.

Like their contemporary girl power shows, girl hero cartoons thus contested the media's practice of defining girl characters by their *girl*-ness. Each girl hero had a distinct personality, intelligible without reference to male characters. Their identities suggested a spectrum of possible girlhoods: the cute one, or the athletic one, or the smart one, or the fashionable one, or the sassy one. As we saw in Chapter Three, for at least some pre-adolescent girls, this range offered welcome support—constituting an improvement over simply being the (weak, passive, token, and/or sexual) *girl*.

Simultaneously, cartoon girl heroes' identities lacked complexity. Girls, it seemed, could not be cute *and* sassy, or athletic *and* smart. Though a few exceptions existed (for example, Taranee in *W.I.T.C.H.* was both intelligent and athletic), girl heroes typically were one-dimensional. After all, they appeared in kids' action-adventure cartoons, not high drama. Still, as discussed in Chapter Four, girl hero cartoons claimed to offer girls positive role models and were received as such by some critics and parents. Given their one-dimensionality, could they live up to the hype? Meanwhile, cartoon girl heroes presumably were understood in the broader contexts of their young audience members' viewing, in which long-standing stereotypes prevailed. How, then, did real girls understand girl power's discourse on girls' identity possibilities, as represented by girl hero cartoons—and what meanings did they derive from these depictions?

Girly Girls and Tomboys: Girl Types in Opposition

One day at Nonprofit Aftercare, three girls and I sat together in the school library, conversing about girl hero cartoons. As the discussion meandered, Desirée commented that girly girls "care what other people think," while tomboys "don't really care and do what their minds say." When I asked if they could tell me more, Rhea and Desirée replied with enthusiasm, completing one another's thoughts:

DESIRÉE: [A girly girl] is like a girl that wears nails and does up her hair—

RHEA: They'll be like, "I broke a nail—"

DESIRÉE (in a sing-song voice): "I broke a na-ail!"

RHEA: —and like, if they're grounded off their cell phone, they'll like cry or something like that—

DESIRÉE (with a smile):—and if you're a tomboy, you really don't care.

Figure 7.1: A drawing by Gia, age 8. Gia's mother is a "girly girl."
(*Visit growingupwithgirlpower.com for a full-color version of this image.*)

The girls at Nonprofit Aftercare often described television characters, other people, and themselves as either girly girls or tomboys. In doing so, they clarified what each term meant to them. Girly girls enjoyed wearing stereotypically feminine accoutrements; Gia reported her mother is a girly girl, "cuz she likes to wear skirts and dresses all the time." She drew her mother as having brown skin, blonde hair, a red belly shirt (revealing her midriff), a long blue skirt, and high heels (see Figure 7.1). Brianna called Blossom of *The Powerpuff Girls* a girly girl, and Desirée said Sam of the *Totally Spies* team was "definitely a girly girl." The long-haired Blossom and Sam were both the de facto leaders of their teams, and they were also unfailingly nice, as described in Chapter Four. Desirée explained she and her sister were a tomboy and girly girl, respectively: she identified with Buttercup, the rough-and-tumble Powerpuff, while her sister was "more like, uh, Bubbles"—the blonde, cutesy one. "She's kind of soft," she explained. (Note that the girls in my study's aftercare locations all wore uniforms to school—at both schools, polo shirts in specific colors were required—so I couldn't see whether their styles reflected these identities.)

On the other hand, tomboys had interests the girls deemed boyish. Gia identified as a tomboy because she enjoyed "boys' sports, like soccer, and baseball, and basketball." Her drawing of herself and a friend playing football contains no markers of femininity; without her explanation, the drawing would easily be assumed to depict two males (see Figure 7.2). Using similar logic to Gia's, Brianna declared, "I'm a tomboy because I have all boy cousins," whose interests she shared. By suggesting tomboys' interests belonged primarily to boys, the girls construed tomboys' interests as neither gender neutral nor typical for girls. Tomboys were a nonnormative girl type who took an active disinterest in the girlish things that usually defined young female identity. Desirée thought of herself as a tomboy because "I don't do no makeup, no nail polish, no little curly stuff in my hair." At Suburban Elementary, Angela offered a similar rationale for being a tomboy: "[Being a tomboy] is just fun. You can run around, play, you don't have to care about your nails, 'cause I chew them." Likewise, when Kylie shared her interest in Bratz dolls and stickers, Angela replied, "I'm a tomboy. I don't like any of that stuff." In this way, self-described tomboys rejected normatively feminine girly girl accoutrements, expressing a resistant, oppositional identity. Studies have shown that young people often construct identities oppositionally (Allard, 2002; Brown, 1998; Eder et al., 1995; Lesko, 1988, p. 127), and this seemed true among my tomboy-identified participants. Their oppositional tomboy identities could even be understood as cultural criticisms—what Thorne (1993) described as "resist[ing] the constraints of stereotyped 'feminine' behavior" (p. 113).

Figure 7.2: A drawing by Gia, age 8.
Gia's drawing of herself and a friend, who like to play football for fun after school.
(*Visit growingupwithgirlpower.com for a full-color version of this image.*)

Although our groups' tomboys seemed proud of their identities, they were often ostracized by other girls. At Suburban Elementary, I witnessed that girly girls sometimes used "tomboy" as a put-down or a label with negative connotations—declarations of their superiority to tomboys. It also differed from how I witnessed tomboys handle girly girls' interests. Unlike the tomboys in Renold's (2006) study, who actively denigrated their "'girlie' peers' preoccupation with fashion and romance" (p. 503), the tomboys in my study did not seem to bundle into their rejection of the girlish any insults towards girly girls. Instead, they asserted that they were themselves tomboys and didn't like those kinds of things.

One afternoon at Suburban Elementary, some participants insisted girls are never as mean to boys as boys are to girls, because girls are more "polite" than boys. Audrey and Kelly stated tomboys were the only exception. Audrey explained:

> Some tomboys act like boys, and boys are mean. And then [the tomboys] always play with [the boys], mostly. So [the tomboys] get all [the boys'] tricks off of them, and the boys turn the girls into not-polite people.

Tricks that Audrey said tomboys learn from boys include "shutting the door in people's faces, tripping people, poking them hard, and calling them very bad names." These statements suggested that in a girl power context—which proclaimed "girls rule" and "boys drool"—girls who identified with the stereotypically "boyish," rather than the mainstream-sanctioned "girlish," were at risk of being perceived negatively by other girls. Tomboys might be perceived as undesirable "non-polite" troublemakers, assumed to be learning "tricks" from the boys—not admired for their feisty independence. Interestingly, Audrey's ideas about tomboys' behaviors differed from the literature on girls' relational aggression, which has typically focused on psychological—not physical—tactics. But as Aapola, Gonick, and Harris (2005) have noted, "It is still culturally more unacceptable for girls and women to express any type of aggression, particularly in public arenas, than for men" (p. 119).

The idea of tomboys' inferiority to other girls had implications for the everyday lives of girls like 10-year-old Tanya (Euro-American), whom I met on the Suburban Elementary playground during my fieldwork and who was not a member of my video club group. Tanya was playing by herself one winter day on the monkey bars while several girls including Kelly played nearby. Tanya had blunt-cut, chin-length blonde hair, a wiry build, and wore a winter jacket that was gender-neutral, sporty looking in a simple mid-tone blue. At first sight, I almost mistook her for a boy. We struck up a conversation, and she mentioned she usually didn't play on the monkey bars; she preferred playing sports with the boys. That day, she had arrived outside too late. The teams already chosen, she was on her own.

When I introduced myself, she asked, "What are you doing here, anyway?" I explained I was researching what girls watch on television and like to do for fun. In the field notes I wrote that afternoon, I summarized our conversation as follows:

> [When I explained that I was there to talk with girls about their interests], Tanya perked up and said she loves karate—that she's an orange belt, going soon for green. She said she'll be an "instructor" soon and "hold things." Without prompting, she also volunteered that she's "not a girly girl" and looked over at Kelly and

her friends—in pink, purple, and pale blue jackets. I said, "if you're not a girly girl, what kind of girl are you?" She said, "I'm a tomboy." Then she explained that she doesn't like playing the games *they* play; they play imagining games too much, which is why she plays with the boys.

Then she told me about a boy, Justin, who has a buzz cut and glasses, who lives near her and has harassed her at home and at school for a long time. [. . .] She said that in third grade, he made a mean drawing of her, making her fat and making her face all scary. She said he showed the picture to other kids and lots of kids were mean to her. [. . .]

[Then] she told me a vague story about how Justin did something bad to her, for which he got in trouble with the principal, and that then he harassed her more at home because he claimed the vice principal told him he could harass her "at home but not at school—which is *not true*." I asked what exactly got him in trouble, and she said, "He called me a homosexual and gay."

Judging from our conversation, as a tomboy, Tanya had trouble with some peers. She and the girls at her school didn't want to play together, as she didn't like the girls' fantasy-based make-believe games. One boy had drawn mean pictures of Tanya and suggested that she was a lesbian,[1] prompting trouble for her with children of both sexes, even at this early age. As Bhana (2005) has explained, "By the time young girls begin attending primary school they have already embarked on the lifelong process of constructing their gender and (hetero)sexual identities. Sexual and gendered cultures are pervasive in primary schools—even among seven- and eight-year-old-girls" (p. 163). Further, citing Judith Butler's work on gender and heteronormativity, Renold (2006) found that even among children, deviations from gendered norms can result in doubts about an individual's heterosexuality and result in "shaming and policing (or 'othering')" of the deviant individuals (p. 493). While most children in Renold's study endured some forms of gendered and/or sexualized teasing, children thus positioned as "other" were the most routinely teased and humiliated by their peers (p. 499). Likewise, Martin & Ruble (2009) found multiple examples of this behavior in the gender development literature. Given the contexts I described in Chapter Six—that gay-bashing seemed a bullying activity of choice at Suburban Elementary—Tanya's problems within the normatively sexual and gendered culture of her school were very real. For over two years, Tanya had been teased and ostracized, just not fitting in. The issue would be ongoing; despite the principal's intervention in Justin's bullying, her problems remained unresolved.

Although Audrey claimed tomboys are aggressive, "not-polite" people who antagonize girls, during recess, Tanya seemed to move in completely separate circles from the other girls. She so preferred playing sports with the boys that I was unable to talk with her at other recess sessions, as she was usually playing football. It did not seem that she wished to engage with the other girls in any way, antagonistic or otherwise; she just wanted to play with the boys.

Among the other third- and fourth-grade "tomboys" at Suburban Elementary, ostracization seemed a common problem. Though the other tomboy participants did not volunteer they had been harassed by homophobic peers, some had endured taunts for failing at femininity—implying that third- and fourth-grade children had been monitoring one another for heteronormative behavior and enforcing compulsory heteronormativity. Children begin negotiating gender, race, class and sexuality at an early age (Aapola, Gonick, and Harris, 2005, pp. 45–6), and as Gonick (2006) has noted in relation to the identities of queer girls, "There is no question there are severe consequences for those living outside normative gender/sex categories" (p. 121). Although tomboyishness was acceptable within girl power discourse, at Suburban Elementary "tomboy" seemed a difficult identity for white, middle-class girls to negotiate. Some girls stigmatized others for their perceived failure or nonconformity. Cherland (2005) found Foucault's panopticon useful in understanding this behavior—how females "gaze upon themselves and each other and come to internalize the strictures of femininity. Gender is (like race) a performance. [Certain performances are] culturally approved and culturally *required* for children [who are] white, middle class, and female" (p. 104).

For example, Maura (age 9; Euro-American) was a self-described tomboy who spent many lunch recess sessions with me, and whom I later interviewed in her home. Although not a member of my group in the Suburban Elementary Aftercare Program, she was a frequent topic of discussion because she was friends with Kelly, and some days, Maura would insist that Kelly skip our group to play with her. Maura would really badger her about it—sticking her head into the music room over and over again, until Kelly conceded. Witnessing this behavior, the other girls in the group would complain. Angela said Maura was "rude," and soft-spoken Maria commented, "Sometimes it's good if you're shy, cause you can tell Maura isn't shy." Kelly agreed that Maura was "bossy." I realized later that Maura's reason for badgering Kelly was simple: She had no one else to play with.

Maura loved animals of all kinds—including reptiles and bugs. She was proud of her collection of dead bugs and mummified snakes, courtesy of a family member employed at a zoo. Sometimes she shopped in the boys' clothing section, where she could find t-shirts featuring spiders and reptiles. (One day, she said she wore the same spider t-shirt as a boy she knew—but "I didn't care," she said.) During my fieldwork, she was teased and taunted regularly by other children, who called her names like "Gorilla Girl"—not because of her interest in zoo animals, she said, but because "I have more hair on my arms than other people, and that can sometimes make me seem different. They make fun of me." Although Durham (1999) has noted that in adolescence, for the average child, "'difference' is terrifying and abhorrent" (p. 202), Maura seemed confident and self-assured regarding her difference; at least, this was how she presented herself to me. If her otherness bothered her at times, during our conversations, she adopted a confident attitude. I never saw her play with other children at recess, either, underscoring her social isolation. In fact, I have pages of field notes from one disconcerting lunch recess session during which, no matter where Maura and I moved, a group of five popular girls circled us menacingly, giving Maura dirty looks. (Maura said that was how they always treated her when the teachers weren't looking. As mentioned in Chapter Five, the children at Suburban Elementary often mistook me for a teenager, and presumably this group did, as well—permitting me to witness their unmodified behavior.)

Many girls who sought my playground company were self-described tomboys who often spent recess alone, like Maura. (The lunch periods were divided by grade level, with a small period of overlap between adjacent periods. I typically attended two or three back-to-back lunch recesses, so during my visits, these tomboys spent time individually with me, as opposed to in a small group with me.) For example, Angela rarely had friends to play with at lunch, so she seemed happy whenever I arrived. During our conversations, she often looked longingly after the more socially integrated girls whom she said she wished would play with her—some of whom, like Maria, were members of our viewing and discussion group. These girls would give me a friendly hello on seeing me, then run off to play with their robust circle of friends. I felt sure that if Angela had the option, she would have spent lunch recess with them, not me. Interestingly, this differentiated my study from many other works rooted exclusively in ethnographic fieldwork: Thorne (1993) argued that much research on gender and children is skewed towards the most visible, dominant (i.e., popular) children encountered in the field, while others—the less popular children—are marginalized by researchers (p. 97). I suspect that because girls like Angela and Kylie knew me from the video club the previous year, an activity they had self-selected (perhaps because they did not have very many friends to spend time with during Aftercare), this helped skew at least some of my field research towards the girls on the margins.

One unclear point: Were Maura, Angela and Tanya ostracized for being tomboys, or did they adopt tomboy identities in response to ostracization? This is a question I cannot answer, as I only witnessed snapshots of their lives. Either way, however, they seemed isolated—unlike the tomboy-identified girls in Renold's (2006) study, for whom tomboyism was often a route to more social power (p. 502). This suggested that while some girls felt empowered to choose between girly girl and tomboy identities, the choices were not equally appealing to the girls in my study. Girly girls—the Baby Spices and Bubbles of the world—received social rewards for performing normative femininity. Meanwhile, as tomboys did not look or act feminine, the Sporty Spices and Buttercups risked harassment and social isolation. Although tomboy characters in girl hero cartoons were loved and accepted by their teammates, there seemed to be a hierarchy in my fieldwork settings. In my participants' elementary schools, girly girls were on top. In other words, despite girl power's progress, girls often viewed media and everyday life through the lens of stereotypes, in which the dominant narrative suggests femininity is valued above all else.

Evidence emerged in my participants' explanations of these girl types. Although they defined tomboys by contrasting tomboys' interests with those of girly girls, the inverse was not true. Self-proclaimed girly girls did not mention boys or boys' interests as a point of comparison. The simplicity with which girly girls could be defined—almost tautologically, i.e., girls who like to be girly—had a different quality than the process of defining tomboys according to their dislikes. This discourse of tomboys as a *different* type of girl suggested that the girly girl could be considered standard, the feminine norm against which all girls—girly girls and tomboys—measured themselves and each other.

Taken altogether, perhaps these factors indicate that girls who identified as tomboys were quite strong. Embracing this identity choice could be an assertive stance—an interpretation supported by some scholarly literature that has found tomboyism to be a mode of resistance against compulsory heterosexuality (Halberstam, 1998; Renold, 2006). Even if they were sometimes pained by the treatment they received from their peers, these girls did not try to change or conform. They insisted they were tomboys who didn't like girly stuff.

When I reinterviewed some of the "tomboys" from Suburban Elementary five years after my fieldwork took place, several still maintained nonconformist identities, even in adolescence—a time when the literature on the girl crisis would suggest they should have succumbed to the coercion I had witnessed them facing on a daily basis. At thirteen years old, Angela insisted that she was unconcerned with dressing to fit in with her eighth grade peers; "I just dress the way I like," she said.

"I don't want to be labeled, 'cause the people who want to be labeled are the people who can't find their place—so they just want to fit in." Likewise, fourteen-year-old Maura asserted an oppositional identity and style. "I don't really like a lot of the styles today. At all. I think they're kinda stupid," she explained. Ignoring what was considered fashionable, she said, "I love doing socks with weird colors, and— I don't really like to just stick to the basics. I like to kind of do quirky things that not many people would think of." In general, both expressed a continuing disinterest in what their peers thought about them. This continued nonconformity was in line with the gender development literature (see Martin and Ruble, 2009), which suggests that girls whose behavior is not gender-typical tend to be fairly stable in the degree of their gender typing over time (whereas children who are strongly gender-typed—e.g., girlie girls—tend to become even more gender-typical as they age).

Divas: Girly Girls with a Tomboy Attitude

Although the Nonprofit Aftercare participants initially suggested two types of girls existed—girly girls and tomboys—they soon introduced another type: the diva, who never came up at Suburban Elementary. The diva's first mention was after five girls and I viewed a *Kim Possible* episode. In the episode we screened, "Blush," the villain Dr. Drakken was tired of always being defeated by Kim and sought novel ideas to help him defeat her. He read some teen magazines and decided that as Kim was a teenager, embarrassment must be her Achilles' heel; so he sprayed her with a concoction that would cause her to evaporate completely if she becomes embarrassed enough. He then sent two "embarrassment ninjas" to follow her around and secretly force her into embarrassing situations (often involving physical mishaps that made her look clumsy). When a boy named Josh asked Kim on a date, she accepted—and her potential for embarrassment skyrocketed to dangerous levels.

When the girls and I discussed the major characters from that episode, Desirée said that she thought Kim was acting a little crazy in the episode; she didn't like the way Josh treated Kim. She also thought Josh was funny looking. However, Gia and Brianna thought Josh was cute, and they thought he treated her fine. They all said they could identify with Kim's embarrassment; Desirée recalled how embarrassing it was when she fell out of a bunk bed once, and Brianna was mortified when she slipped on an icy patch and hit her head in front of her whole family.

Then, I asked the girls what they thought of other *Kim Possible* characters, generally speaking. Rhea replied, "There was this other character named Monique, and I like her." Rhea said Monique was voiced by Raven Symoné, the star of Rhea's favorite television program, *That's So Raven*—another Disney Channel property. Rhea liked Monique and Raven because "Raven is kinda like a diva, sometimes—and she acts the same way as Monique." I asked for clarification. What was a diva? Rhea offered, "They're kinda, like, tomboy, kinda, but they're actually really girl-ish at the same time."

To facilitate further discussion, I gave the girls paper and asked them to illustrate the differences between divas, girly girls, and tomboys. I hoped this visual method would help them clarify their meanings and foreground any visual cues for differentiating the three girl types. After completing their drawings, I asked each girl to elaborate upon what she had drawn ("Please tell me about your drawing"). They responded in terms of the girl types' physical appearance and perceived behaviors and attitudes.

Madison (see Figure 7.3) illustrated the three girl types with the following drawings: an angry tomboy ready to start a fight, an aloof diva, a girly girl who wanted to go to the mall. She explained:

Figure 7.3: Drawing by Madison, age 10
(*Visit growingupwithgirlpower.com for a larger version of this image.*)

MADISON: The first one is a tomboy [on the left]. And, she has a bun [pointing to the top of the head], and she doesn't like to wear her hair out, but her mom has to brush it and stuff, and her belly button's not showing—ooh, she don't got no shirt on!

REBECCA: [chuckling] Oh, do you want to go put a shirt on her?

MADISON: Yes.

REBECCA: [still chuckling] Go quick. [Lots of giggling all around about the shirtless drawing.]

MADISON: Now she has a shirt. She has pants, long pants, Nikes on—and she says, "Come on, let's fight!"

REBECCA: Why does she want to fight somebody?

MADISON: Because—why does she want to fight some—She must be mad at somebody.

REBECCA: OK.

MADISON: And this [middle picture] is a diva. She has a shirt that says "Love." And her whole outfit is sparkling, if you see.

REBECCA: I can see that.

MADISON: And, she has high heels on.

REBECCA: Are they—I can't tell—are they shoes or are they boots?

MADISON: They're boots.

REBECCA: I thought so.

MADISON: And she has layers in her hair—see, like, it curls like that [tracing the horizontal lines midway down the figure's hair], and then it gets down like that. She has layers, and a little bang [tracing the forehead]. And her–she has a smile [tracing the smile]. And this [picture on the right] is a girly girl. She has twisties in her hair like I have [pointing to the figure's hair].

REBECCA: Twisties like–

MADISON: Like, the blue—like, see the gray right there? [pointing to the gray in the figure's hair] That's her hair just goin' like that [moves her finger from right to left across the figure's hair], and–

REBECCA: So they're not cornrows, they're not braids, they're just twists?

MADISON: The blue thing—yeah, the twist—the blue things are twisties.

REBECCA: OK.

MADISON: If you see.

REBECCA: I see.

MADISON: And it says, "Come on, let's go to the mall." [Rebecca chuckles.] And that's the girly girl—she has high heels on. And, this is her long hair [pointing to the far right picture and tracing with her finger the figure's hair—basically, it's the rectangle around the figure].

REBECCA: Wow.

MADISON: At first I was looking at it.

REBECCA: Her hair is longer than the diva's.

MADISON: Uh-huh. She's a girly girl, she likes her hair all the way out.

REBECCA: So, how can you tell the difference between a diva and a girly girl? Like, how are they different from each other?

MADISON: A diva, like, she's—she's, like—hmm—well, a diva, hmm—she, like, wears—fashion clothes every day. And the girly girl, she just might feel a little down and wear some jeans and a sock, like I always wear on the weekends. [then, softly] Except on Sundays, because I gotta go to church. [aloud] So, that's how you can tell. And, girly girls don't have to have long hair. And divas don't have to have short hair. Cuz I saw a diva on *America's Next Somethin' Idol*, and she had long hair, didn't she—that lady?

REBECCA: Well, this is fantastic. Thank you so much. Can I keep that?

MADISON: Sure.

Madison's depiction of the tomboy as angry and ready to fight someone was in discourse with Audrey's argument that tomboys are impolite, unlike other girls, and perhaps also with some young tomboys' isolation. Picking fights is socially unacceptable behavior for girls, so Madison's vision highlights that tomboys are not normative. On the other hand, Madison's girly girl is almost a self-portrait, as indicated by Madison's personal note about what girly girls wear on Sundays (and the clothing emblazoned with Madison's own initials). Her girly girl had a hairstyle like Madison's and a happy smile. The girly girl and the diva wear similar clothing—shirts and skirts that leave the midriff exposed—but the diva's outfit sparkled, while the girly girl's had ruffles. Contrasted with the tomboy, Madison's diva and girly girl had much more in common. According to Madison, the difference seemed to be the diva's heightened concern with fashion; she never takes a day off.

Other girls' drawings also contrasted behaviors. For example, Desirée's drawing (see Figure 7.4) featured a girly girl dressed entirely in pink, wearing a "belly shirt" that says "Cutie" on it, high heels, stockings, and "kinda a jungle skirt." The diva wore "flavor" clothes—clothing with "flair" that had a "flippy" cut to it, in two shades of purple—as well as lip gloss and high heels. Desirée said that the diva was on her way to an interview for a television modeling show and feeling nervous. The tomboy (which Desirée labeled "tom girl") dressed in yellow-orange and black and looked sad.

Figure 7.4: Drawing by Desirée, age 10
(*Visit growingupwithgirlpower.com for a full-color version of this image.*)

DESIRÉE: And this [far right picture] is a tomgirl. She got braids, cuz she don't
like havin' her hair in, like, out like this [pointing to the diva's hair,
which flips out]. And she–she got basketball, she got a basketball
shirt on, it says "Number 23," and she got, like, sneakers on cuz she
don't like wearin' her good sneakers so she got the circle kind.

This underscored a difference: while the girly girl and diva enjoy wearing
good clothing, the tomboy was so casual that she did not even like to wear her good
sneakers.

Desirée's girl type drawings had a lot in common with Madison's. Her diva and
girly girl were identifiable by their skirts, and they looked only slightly different
from each other. The girly girl wore pink and a skirt with a playful cut to it, while
the diva's flared sleeves and skirt looked elegant. As in Madison's drawing, only the
tomboy looked unhappy—which seemed related to Desirée defining the tomboy
according to her dislikes. My interviewees seemed to embrace the idea that performing femininity is fun and pleasurable, and it did not sound very fun to be a
tomboy—not even for self-identified tomboys like Desirée.

The Nonprofit Aftercare participants could easily identify these types in one
another's drawings, suggesting the visual cues presented by different girl types
were critical. For example, Simone (age 7; African-American) presented the drawings in Figure 7.5 without any captions (she added them later).

Figure 7.5: Drawing by Simone, age 8

SIMONE: OK. This is diva outfit [far left], cuz divas usually—like, when they're wearin' pants, their pants always go stickin' out like that. And the girly girl has a skirt goin' to the side. And, like, one of those shirts—

MADISON: Oh, like a bathing suit?

SIMONE: Yeah. And it has one little skirt—shirts that go like that [outlining her left side just inside her own shoulder], and then it's, like, a sprinkle—a top that's goin', like, wrinkle. And, um, the, um, tomboy I didn't write [i.e., she didn't label it on the page yet, but it's the far right drawing] has, um—what's those things called?—um, um, um, basketball shorts [pointing at them] with pockets. They're really, really dark green—like, trash can dark green. And they—and he has, um, a long—well, he has a jersey shirt [pointing to it], and a white shirt under it—well, a dark green shirt under it.

[Desirée wanders over and looks at Simone's drawing. She nods in approval and says, "Great!"]

REBECCA: Desirée, if you were looking at those, would you know which one was which, even though they are not labeled?

DESIRÉE: Um, let's see. [She looks at the drawings.] This one's [middle] definitely a girly girl; this one's [far right] definitely the diva cuz she got
those flava clothes.

REBECCA: Is "flava" a brand, or is that just, like, a saying?

DESIRÉE: A saying. And you can tell this [pointing to the tomboy outfit] is a
tomboy.

As a whole, the girl types' sartorial implications are significant. As Pomerantz
(2008) has explained, style is not just about fashion: "Style enables girls to signal
belonging, friendship, conformity, religious beliefs, politics, resistance, rebellion,
ambivalence, anger, desire, cultural and lifestyle affiliations, individuality, image,
and personal taste. [. . .] It is a tool for identity construction and negotiation [and]
a form of power" (p. 64). This lends insight into the linking of each girl type's clothing and attitudes: Personal style communicates identity. Thus, tomboys' clothing
is more utilitarian; their shirts feature numbers on them, like those on sports jer-
seys, and they wear shorts or pants and sneakers. Unconcerned with performing a
normatively feminine physical appearance, they are unconcerned with normative
behavior, too. They frown, scowl, and pick fights. In contrast, the smiling girly girls
and divas wear clothing in bright colors associated with girlishness (pink or purple), with sparkles, ruffles, "flava" flair, or a "jungle" cut. Their shirts may have say-
ings like "love" and "I love me" on them, and they favor high heels. Girly girls may
dress down on weekends, but divas always dress up. The latter set of priorities bring
to mind Malik's (2005) findings on beauty and fashion rituals' importance for fashionable tween girls: They serve as "a crucial aspect in the construction of a fun and
style-aware self," offering "opportunities for self-expression, nurturing, pampering,
and celebrating girlhood" (p. 271). Furthermore, divas' clothing choices seem
more exaggerated than girly girls', evoking Russell and Tyler's (2002) study of the
U.K. girl power/makeover retail outlet called "Girl Heaven." There, femininity was
an "exaggerated performance [. . .] in which a feminine artifice is supposed to be
able to celebrate itself" (p. 631).

During various meetings, the Nonprofit Aftercare participants offered examples of television divas: Dijonnay from *The Proud Family*, Clover from *Totally Spies*,
Lizzie on *Lizzie Maguire*, Cornelia from *W.I.T.C.H.*, and Bonnie and the villain
Shego from *Kim Possible*. With time, I developed a richer understanding of what
the girls meant when they called a person or character a diva. As Rhea indicated
in her initial definition ("They're kinda, like, tomboy, kinda, but they're actually
really girlish at the same time"), the girls' use of the term "diva" was in discourse
with girly girls and the tomboys. The girly girl is pleasant, pretty, and nice to every-

one, and the tomboy is more independent and less concerned with being nice and conforming. The diva is a girl who competently achieves a feminine look, like the girlies but has an I-don't-care attitude resembling tomboys' open dismissiveness of the girlish. The diva performs femininity but acts however she feels. Compared with the pretty princesses who behave in passive, uninspiring ways, the diva is actually interesting. She is outspoken, self-confident, assured, and stands up for herself— a cartoon reification of the Spice Girls' manifesto. For me, the diva also brings to mind Thompson's (1998) explanation that "the black cultural model for woman-hood is [. . .] not about being nice, or being a lady, or not upsetting people [. . .]. It's about being capable and competent. It's about being someone to reck-on with" (p. 536). The diva as introduced by the African-American girls at the Nonprofit Aftercare Program certainly fit this description (although not all the on-screen divas they identified were black). The diva also dovetails with the literature on African-American girls' verbal skills: Studies have shown them to be superior to white girls at initiating and handling direct verbal conflicts (Thorne, 1993, p. 102). The outspoken diva's representation by characters across girl hero texts as well as programs like *That's So Raven* suggested that as a girl power archetype, she had particular resonance for African-American girls, whether intentionally or not.

In a predominantly white elementary school context, girl hero divas' sassy inde-pendence was not always endearing. The Euro-American girls at Suburban Elementary felt dubiously about these outspoken characters. For example, after watching *W.I.T.C.H.* for the first time, they did not particularly like Cornelia, whom the Nonprofit Aftercare girls had identified as that show's diva. Zoë (age 8; Euro-American) disliked how Cornelia acted upon meeting Will, who was new to the school. She also disliked Cornelia's reaction upon learning from Hay Lin's grand-mother that she and her four friends are super-powered Guardians.

REBECCA: Zoë, what did you want to say?

ZOË: That girl with the long, blonde hair, Courtney–

REBECCA: Cornelia?

ZOË: Yeah, well, she was actin' like she didn't even care, and when she, when girl's grandma was talkin', it sounded like she didn't even care because even if, when it sounded like she didn't care about anything else, she shouldn't have had to been with them in that group, like to attack the earth.

(While Hay Lin's grandmother explained their destiny, Cornelia alternately looked disgusted, made sarcastic comments, and rolled her eyes. Later, she told her friends, "You know, I still don't believe *any* of this stuff. No offense to your grand-ma or anything, but she's, like, completely deluded. Probably not enough vitamin D.") Angela's reaction to Cornelia was similar to Zoë's; she commented, "If only they took her out." Clearly, the Caucasian girls in my study found this diva's atti-tude problematic.

The perception that divas had bad attitudes had some implications for girls' interactions with one another in real life—even for the African-American girls. For example, Gia—another self-identified tomboy—accused Rhea of being a diva one day on the playground, when she refused to push her on the swings. (Rhea's response to this accusation was to roll her eyes and refuse to engage.) Similarly, Brianna complained that her 10-year-old big sister was a diva: "she thinks she's *all that* and she flips her hair in my face, and that's what makes me mad at her." Unlike the girly girl who, like Kim Possible, claims that she is "no better than anybody else" in the interest of fitting in, the diva feels superior to those around her—and she shows it.

In other words, though on-screen divas appealed to many girls, girls display-ing diva characteristics in real life may not be accepted by their peers. The way Gia chastised Rhea, the way Brianna complained about her sister, and the way Zoë and Angela complained about Cornelia in *W.I.T.C.H.* suggest a hierarchy exists with-in girl power media and the broader culture. In this hierarchy, the girly girl is on top. She reproduces the culturally promoted idea of the normatively feminine girl, pretty and nice. As Aapola, Gonick, and Harris (2005) have summarized, "'Niceness' means controlling one's emotions and first and foremost one's aggres-sive feelings, being sweet and friendly, succeeding at school and obeying one's par-ents" (p. 118; see also Hey, 1997, pp. 55–65; Brown, 1998; and Lesko, 1988, pp. 131–3). With such behaviors, girly girls are therefore unobjectionable.[2] As Bettis, Jordan, and Montgomery (2005) have explained regarding girls' behavior in groups, "Being nice to everyone ensured popularity, and popularity bestowed status and power. The irony was that popular girls were not allowed to demonstrate that power publicly" (p. 73). Brown and Gilligan (1992) have called this "the tyranny of nice and kind, the power of the perfect (white, middle-class) girl" (p. 88): Such girls who follow traditional norms of femininity receive social rewards, but behavior break-ing with this norm—displays of anger or power, failure to self-silence, the adop-tion of any role untraditional for females—leaves them vulnerable to social rejection and ostracization. Even among African-American girls who loved divas on televi-sion, "diva" was used to criticize other girls' actions.

If the girly girl is at the top of the girlhood identity hierarchy, the tomboy is on the bottom. She breaks the mold in terms of both behavior and appearance. Although on-screen tomboys are loved and respected by their peers—*a la* Sporty Spice and Buttercup—this universal approval is not reflected in reality (at least, not among the girls in my study). Where does this leave the diva? She believes herself to be on top, but popular opinion makes her position more variable, depending on her particular context (possibly depending on whether she finds herself among African-American girls at Nonprofit Aftercare or Euro-American girls at Suburban Elementary, to offer one possible variation). Her physical appearance aligns with social norms, and it is not terribly different from the girly girl's; presumably, she reaps many of the same social rewards for this visual performance of femininity. The question mark is her attitude. With the right amount of attitude—like Monique on *Kim Possible*, or Ginger Spice—she could boast a social status equal with or superior to the girly girls. (Merten (1997) has explained that while niceness is an ideal among popular girls, it is often unrealized: Girls can sometimes be very popular without being nice.) But if a diva has too *much* of an attitude for her particular peer group, all bets are off. What happens when a diva crosses the line?

Divas and Mean Girls: A Fine Line

If a girl acts like too much of a diva, she runs the risk of being relabeled as a fourth type of girl: a mean girl. My participants frequently discussed television's depictions of popular mean girls. At the dawn of the new millennium, books about mean girls had become their own cottage industry, much like the Ophelia industry before them, contributing to yet another shift in cultural discourse about girls. While some girls were still understood as victims, others were understood to be waging psychological warfare on their peers through relational aggression—as damaging, or more so, than the physical aggression thought to characterize boys' disagreements. Books on the topic included *Odd Girl Out: The Hidden Culture of Aggression in Girls* (Simmons, 2002), *Queen Bees and Wannabees: Helping Your Daughter Survive Cliques, Gossip, Boyfriends, and Other Realities of Adolescence* (Wiseman, 2002), *The Secret Lives of Girls: What Good Girls Really Do—Sex Play, Aggression, and Their Guilt* (Lamb, 2002), *Fast Girls: Teenage Tribes and the Myth of the Slut* (White, 2002), and *Slut! Growing Up Female with a Bad Reputation* (Tanenbaum, 2000). Concerns about meanness among girls were widespread enough that Wiseman's book was optioned by Paramount and served as the basis for the 2004 Lindsey Lohan film *Mean Girls*, for which Tina Fey wrote the screenplay and appeared in a major role. In most of these texts, Aapola et al. (2005) noted that mean girls were represented as powerful but in crisis—in need of "adult intervention to bring her back on to a path for successful development" (p. 49). Much of this discourse trickled down into the girl hero cartoons, in which mean girls were common; as detailed in Chapter Four, discourse on girls' behaviors that contrasted "nice" (girly) girls with "mean" girls was prominent in the girl power cartoons I analyzed.

What, exactly, constituted meanness? Currie and Kelly (2005) defined "meanness" as encompassing "acts of ridicule, name-calling, backstabbing, gossip and social exclusion" (p. 163)—often done in a covert way. When Merten (1997) studied meanness among junior high girls, she found that when girls had worked hard to become popular, they sometimes used meanness as a strategy to put more distance between themselves and their unpopular peers—a way to maintain "a feeling of specialness" by deliberately alienating others (p. 188). Merten further noted that having a reputation as a *nice* popular girl required being flawlessly "supernice," which is almost impossible to maintain; meanness is an easier alternative (p. 188). Currie and Kelly (2005) noted that although the adolescent girls in their study of meanness attended various schools, the popular girls tended to be mean: One thirteen-year-old subject told them, "Whenever I think of the word 'popular' I think of people going, 'Oh my god, I don't like your clothes. Go away!'" (p. 163). In fact, Currie and Kelly (2005) worried the literature had focused on girls as "mean" or relationally aggressive with such consistency that it was shaping how adults perceived children's behavior. By presenting meanness as "uniquely female," identical behaviors in boys were being overlooked, and covert relational aggression among girls was naturalized—allowing adults to write off as "normal" girl behavior, rather than addressing it properly (p. 171).

In line with this trend, my participants easily discussed mean girls at length. For example, after screening the cartoon *Atomic Betty*, I asked what they thought of the episode ("The Great Race"). Although Angela's top-of-mind response was that she thought the alien feline villain, Maximus I.Q., was strange, she was concerned about the prevalence of mean, teasing characters found, she said, in "usually every cartoon."

> REBECCA: Angela, what did you want to say?
>
> ANGELA: I want to say that I think that some of it's kinda weird, and some of it's OK. The weird part is that the cat—he's, like, a villain, and, like, it's kinda weird.
>
> REBECCA: So, what do you mean about it being weird that the cat's a villain?
>
> ANGELA: Because cats can't really—cats don't stand on their two legs, and their cat, he could stand on his two legs. Like, if cats could stand on their

two legs, they could do a lot of things that they can't usually do. Like, if he was on four legs, I don't think he would come be a villain.

REBECCA: Ha! OK.

ANGELA: Cuz then they do a lot of other stuff.

REBECCA: What else did you think of *Atomic Betty?*

ANGELA: I think it was OK.

REBECCA: What was OK about it? What do you mean by that?

ANGELA: It's kinda, like, usually every cartoon, sometimes they have this person who's, like, mean, like, teasing them or something, and I think that's OK because some cartoons don't. But I think it's kinda like every cartoon except for, like, people don't go on to different galaxies and things like—they do, but she's not—it's kinda weird, that— I thought once I saw on another episode that she went outside into space without a helmet. People can't breathe.

REBECCA: Right. OK.

The other girls perked up when Angela discussed mean characters and began to offer their own contributions.

KELLY: I have an example what she means by there's someone who teasing them. In the show *Kim Possible*, Bonnie teases her.

REBECCA: Right.

ANGELA: On *Totally Spies*, Mandy teases all of them.

REBECCA: Huh.

KELLY: Who's Mandy?

ANGELA: There's this girl named Mandy.

KELLY: What other TV show has someone who teases?

KYLIE: On *Rugrats*, Angelica teases Tommy and the babies.

REBECCA: That's true.

KELLY: *Lizzie Maguire*—Kate; *Raven*, there's Andre—no, not Andre, I keep forgetting their name.

ANGELA: Yeah.

KYLIE: Alissa, I think it is.

KELLY: No, it isn't.

ANGELA: Alana!

KYLIE AND KELLY: Alana!

REBECCA: OK.

KELLY: And then there's this—what about the show *Fairly Oddparents?* There's somebody who teases him—

KYLIE: Uh, Vicki.

KELLY: Vicki teases him.

KYLIE: His babysitter.

KELLY: His babysitter tea—Vicki teases him. His teachers—

ANGELA: Jimmy!

KELLY: No, wait!

KYLIE: In *Jimmy Neutron*, uh, Cindy.

KELLY: Cindy and Libby.

KYLIE: Cindy and Libby.

In just a few minutes, the girls readily and independently devised a list of mean, teasing characters from children's popular culture landscape. They began by listing the mean popular girls featured on three of the girl power action-adventure cartoons we had been watching together: Penelope on *Atomic Betty*, Bonnie on *Kim Possible*, and Mandy on *Totally Spies*. They then branched out into other girl-centered programming—*That's So Raven* and *Lizzie Maguire*—and the universally popular *Rugrats*, *Fairly Oddparents*, and *Jimmy Neutron*. Although Angela said each show had a mean "person" and Kelly said each had "someone who's teasing them," every character mentioned was a girl. (The girls from the Nonprofit Aftercare Program later devised a similar list.)

My participants frequently commented that mean girl were "snobs" and positioned them in opposition to nice girls, with very little common ground. According to Bettis, Jordan, and Montgomery's (2005) research with pre-teen girls, the word "snob" is "one of the most reviled descriptors of girls at this age and a factor in losing popularity" (pp. 73–74), and according to Merten (1997), being seen as "stuck-up" is a pitfall that can be "corrosive" to a girl's popularity (p. 188). Consider this conversation with Bailey (age 9; African-American), Simone, and Madison, held after we screened the same *Atomic Betty* episode at Nonprofit Aftercare:

REBECCA: So, what do you think of Betty?

BAILEY: She's nice.

REBECCA: What makes her nice? What are the qualities of a nice girl? [Bailey shrugs.] Simone?

SIMONE: Like, you don't fight—well—[Simone cuts herself off abruptly—perhaps because she remembers that Betty does indeed fight.]

REBECCA: Hm!

MADISON: Ooh! I know!

REBECCA: What?

MADISON: You know what a snob is?

REBECCA: Yeah?

MADISON: Someone that, like, sticks up their head and think they're all that and stuff. Like the girl on *Atomic Betty* with the black hair—she wanted, she wanted the boy to notice her.

REBECCA: OK. So, what makes a girl a nice girl?

MADISON: That she's not a stick-up, a snob—

SIMONE: [correcting Madison] Stuck up.

REBECCA: She's not stuck up?

MADISON: Yeah. And she's not like this [head back, chin sticking out] with her chin up and all cool. And she's OK if a boy ask her out, I guess she'd just go with him, unless she doesn't like him.

I then asked why they thought mean girls appeared on so many shows. The girls I interviewed at the Nonprofit Aftercare Program and the Suburban Elementary School agreed that the mean girls are meant to teach a lesson. After screening the same episode of *Atomic Betty*, I had the following exchange with the girls at the Nonprofit Aftercare:

REBECCA: What do you think of the other characters besides Betty?

BAILEY: The girl with the black hair is kinda snobby.

MADISON: That's what I said!

REBECCA: Yeah—Penelope, right? I think that was her name. Why do you think there's a snobby character on the show?

SIMONE: Cuz, if they need, like, a mean egg like most shows do to teach a lesson—

MADISON: Like [on] *Kim Possible!*

BAILEY: Yeah!

SIMONE: —they will have to have a nice person that people know about to make, like, their self, like, nice and mean, and they're on the same show, and then if the person [was also nice], that would be kind of boring.

REBECCA: Right. Any other thoughts on Penelope and why there are snobby girls? Yeah?

BAILEY: To show that she shouldn't be mean to the people.

REBECCA: Hmm. How did they sh—how did they use her to show that?

BAILEY: Because, like, she isn't someone you want to be like.

REBECCA: That's true. So, it's better to be Betty than to be Penelope. [Bailey nods.] Are there any girls in the other cartoons that we've been watching, are there snobby girls?

BAILEY: Yeah. Bonnie—

MADISON: Yeah—*Kim Possible.*

BAILEY: There's this other girl with black hair—and there's these two girls in, um *Robot.*

REBECCA: OK. So there's Bonnie in *Kim Possible*, the two mean girls on *The Teenage Robot*—who's the other one you're thinking of?

BAILEY: I don't know her name, but–

REBECCA: Which cartoon?

BAILEY: *Totally Spies.*

REBECCA: In *Totally Spies.* Ohh!

SIMONE: Mandy, Mandy, Mandy—I don't know her.

MADISON: Oh! Mandy! [at the same time, SIMONE: Oh! I know her!]

REBECCA: So, that's a lot of snobby girls in the cartoons.

SIMONE: Pretty much.

In this way, the Nonprofit Aftercare participants read television's "snobby" mean girls as meant to teach a lesson about being nice to others, in part by making it clear which character viewers to identify with: the nice girl heroes, not their popular-but-mean classmates. The cartoons seemed to draw upon the mean girl literature to teach their viewers lessons about the perils of being mean.

The girls at Suburban Elementary offered a similar interpretation:

REBECCA: This is an interesting point that you girls brought up. What do you think's going on? Why are there so many teasing characters?

KELLY: I think they just don't like them at all. [. . .]

ANGELA: I was thinking—oh yeah—I think it's kinda normal that every cartoon has a person that, like, teases. I think they put a teasing character in the shows because they just want, like, to make–

KELLY: Tryin' to teach a lesson.

ANGELA: —or maybe sometimes they say if somebody does something funny to the main character or something, then maybe it can [be] funny, and maybe they could see how people—other people feel when they're getting pushed around.

REBECCA: That's interesting.

KELLY: Yeah, it proves a point in a story.

REBECCA: Like, what kind of point? And then it's Kylie's turn.

KELLY: Like, the, I don't know, it just proves a point, like—

ANGELA: I don't know which point.

KELLY: I know one—don't judge a book by its cover" and "don't judge a person [by] how they look."

These participants thereby pointed to the possibility that mean characters teach child viewers a lesson about not only being nice to others, but also about looking beyond appearance. Kelly noted that on *Fairly Oddparents*, Timmy is teased for having "teeth like mine. But they're called 'Kung Fu Overbite.'" Kylie and Angela pointed out that on the cartoon *Braceface*, a mean girl was always making fun of the lead character, Sharon, about her braces. Kelly pointed out that on *Phil of the Future*, Phil's younger sister Kim "annoys him." Kylie said that on *Drake and Josh*, Megan's little sister was "a torture" who played mean tricks on the main characters—some of which were related to physical appearance. Kylie explained one trick played on Josh as follows:

KYLIE: And on one show, um, they taped something about Josh when they did stuff to Josh. Like they put lipstick and stuff on him, like, makeup and lipstick. And then they just, um, did it, and then they had this little show on the Internet.

(In other words, Josh was emasculated by his sister, broadcast on the internet wearing women's makeup for all to see.)

As we discussed television's mean characters, my participants sometimes debated how girl heroes should interact with mean girls.

KYLIE: Um, I think to Penelope, she's just mean to her [Betty] cuz if you want to be treated, um, if you want to be treated right, you should treat the other person like that. But Penelope is not doing that, so, um, she should give—Betty should just do it right back at her.

AUDREY: No she shouldn't.

REBECCA: How come?

AUDREY: Because, um, she should be setting a good example for her—for Penelope because if she starts being nice to her and ignoring her, um, Penelope will get angry cuz she's not listening to her and then she'll just start being nice.

REBECCA: Hmm. That's possible.

KYLIE: I'm not finished!

REBECCA: OK. Go ahead.

KYLIE: And, um, unlike boys, she's, like, [shrugs]—she's, like, nice to them cuz she, like, hits on them.

ZOË: Like, I think she acts nice to everybody, but it seems Penelope is, like, just a snobby brat because she acts like she's all that to Betty, and then she acts—and then, I think Betty wasn't wrong when she said that thing to Penelope, like, when, after she batted her eyelashes [at the boy Betty liked], and then Betty said something—I can't remember what she said.

MARIA: Um, I think that she's nice because, like, whenever that girl's mean to her, she doesn't do anything mean back to her. Like, she won't say anything to her or do anything to her; she'll just kind of ignore her. Like, she won't say anything. Cuz then it gets into a whole situation because—wait—if it gets into a situation then a lot of people will know about it and then they can get in trouble from it. So she won't say anything, except maybe she'll just say, "Stop it."

The idea promoted by *Atomic Betty* and echoed by some participants seemed to be that the solo girl heroes—being nice girly girls—should treat their peers the way they wanted to be treated. If others were mean to them, they should ignore that behavior and hope that things will get better. However, as we saw earlier in this chapter and in Chapter Six, ignoring mean behavior does not always make things better. Sometimes, it is necessary to involve parents and school authorities. If girl power cartoon producers wished to empower girls, perhaps the girl heroes they depicted needed to do more. Beyond defending innocent people from villains, they could have modeled progressive behavior in the private sphere—bucking the tyranny of niceness by standing up for themselves, in ways relevant to real girls' lived experiences.

Discussion

Girl power presented a finite range of identities to girls. The personalities of the five Spice Girls were cartoonish, calculated to be easily read by mass audiences; as we learned in Chapter Three, some girls found these choices satisfactory, but others did not. The cartoon girl heroes' personalities were not far removed from these mainstream girl power originators. Girl hero cartoons featured either one, three, or five lead characters, making the available personalities limited to simple types. While the reality is complex, and while my participants' responses and descriptions were not necessarily uniform, the African-American girls I interviewed cited three basic types of acceptable identities for girls: girly girls, tomboys, and divas. The Euro-American girls also frequently discussed girly girls and tomboys as major girl types, but were more likely to discuss mean girls—an unacceptable identity type—than divas. By marketing such specific, clear-cut girl types across the girl power lifestyle brand, mainstream girl power discourse placed limits on the types of girlhood, and therefore on the behaviors, attitudes, and appearances, that fit within the girl power rubric.

Within that rubric, girly girls seemed to be at the top, particularly among my Euro-American interviewees. In the broader cultural environment, normatively feminine girls reaped the most social rewards, while tomboys and divas were ostracized for speaking their minds, failing to conform to the normative, white, middle-class expectation that girls should be nice. If divas believed they were above their peers, with their outspoken natures, they risked becoming categorized as the type of popular girl who is "mean." The dichotomy between mean popular girls and perfectly nice popular girls seemed devoid of substantive middle ground in girl hero discourse; so, too, was the dichotomy between girly girls and tomboys.

Some Euro-American girls in my study had difficulty appreciating the diva-type girls on screen. (They did not even have a word that they used to pinpoint that character type.) In contrast, the African-American girls I spoke with sometimes expressed admiration, indicating the "diva" attitude had a different reception among different demographics. African-American cultural ideals of womanhood (Thompson, 1998) may have influenced the girls at Nonprofit Aftercare to perceive divas more favorably, while the tyranny of niceness prevalent among Euro-Americans may have made it harder for the Suburban Elementary girls to see value in behaving as a power to reckon with. This has class considerations, as well: Walkerdine (1997) has argued that middle-class girls are assured that they are somebody, but working class girls learn they must struggle to become somebody (p. 154). If you already know you are somebody, and that being somebody in the norms of your community requires being nice, then performing the girly girl identity may valued. If you are fighting to prove you are somebody, then perhaps the tactics of the diva—the sassiness, being a force to be reckoned with—may become of more value.

Aapola et al. (2005) have also noted that oppositional identities adopted by children frequently relate to ideas about race, class, ethnicity, and/or gender. Niceness is a value at the intersection of being white, middle class, and female; therefore, culturally speaking, it is positioned as the norm. (Consider, for example, Cherland's (2005) examples of Elisabeth's adult recollections of how she *should* have behaved at the age of nine, in ways that speak to white middle-class ideals and white privilege.) The diva—which embodies outspoken independence as values—may thus be possible to read as an oppositional identity.

The identity types presented by girl hero cartoons therefore had some complexities from an audience reception perspective. The girl types presented by girl hero cartoons did little to dislodge or disrupt the broader pattern that rewards girls for producing normative femininity and penalizes those who do not. Judging from my participants' conversations, the range of girls depicted in girl hero cartoons often promoted conformity. Whether a girl perceives she has two identity choices (girly girl or tomboy) or three (diva), no matter the terminology she uses, her choices are needlessly limited. Numerous studies have replicated the idea that girls perceive specific types of girls. The terminology they use varies across time and place, but the trend is towards the categorization of girls according to types—much as the Spice Girls did. This categorization is both reflected by media culture and reinforced by it.

One day, after yet another conversation in which girl types (tomboys and girly girls) were mentioned, I asked the girls at Suburban Elementary a question. Could they think about different types of *people* for me? Instantly, they presented a creative, lengthy list. It included not only "girly girls" and "tomboys," but also "wacko kids," "teasers," "geeks" of many kinds (writing geeks, chess geeks, computer geeks, etc.—meant to describe serious interests that are focal points of identities), "dorks," "bullies," and "normal kids." This list's extensiveness suggested they perceived a greater range of identities and interests as available to "people" than to "girls." This underscored that though girl power media constituted an improvement over earlier depictions of girls, girl power's construction of girlhood was nevertheless constraining: when specifically discussing girl power heroes, my participants' lists were much more limited. Girl power offered progress on some counts, while simultaneously reinscribing the status quo on others.

At the same time, the impact of the cartoons' narratives regarding status quo reinforcement varied among different demographics. Among the girls I interviewed, the diva characters were most open to interpretation; perhaps among other communities of girls, other girl hero identity types presented additional sites of struggle and complex identity work. There was likely more variance among audience members than that I witnessed in my study.

For real girls, drawing upon one-dimensional identities presented many challenges. Perhaps this was why, when a year after our first set of meetings I followed up with my participants at the Nonprofit Aftercare Program for several months, they perceived more girl types than they had previously. When I asked them if they remembered talking about the types of girls with me, they said that did. They replied:

RHEA: There are all kind of girls. Tomgirls, there are girly-girl—

BAILEY: Tom.

MADISON: Girly-girls.

RHEA: Girly-girls, like, rough girls—sensitive girls, I swear.

MADISON: I'm sensitive.

RHEA: No, not like that. I mean—

BAILEY: Sensitive, sensitive, crying.

RHEA: Weird girls—who are really just weird. [Inaudible chatter between the girls] Bullies are girls.

MADISON: I hate bullies.

RHEA: Groups of girls—that bullies. Geek girls–smart but [inaudible]. Dumb girls.

BAILEY: Ugly girls, short girls, tall girls.

RHEA: Ugly girls, tall girls—

MADISON: You could go on and on about girls!

REBECCA: Yeah. Do you remember how—you might say something like, "Oh, you know, that Bonnie on *Kim Possible*, she's a mean girl, and she's such a diva"?

RHEA: She's a *jealous* girl.

In this conversation, then, the girls began with the two girl types they originally presented to me—tomgirls (tomboys) and girly girls—but followed these with many more girl types. Interestingly, although Rhea referenced bullies, no one included mean girls or divas in the conversation. When I mentioned Bonnie as a possible mean girl/diva, Rhea corrected me, categorizing Bonnie as *jealous*. It is hard to say what variables may have factored into their changed perspectives. It could have been developmental—growing older and seeing the world as a bit more complicated. Also, at this point, these girls had begun outgrowing the girl hero genre. As we will see in Chapter Nine, they had developed a strong preference for other programs, like *That's So Raven*, *Bratz*, *Sister, Sister,* and *Full House,* in which a wider range of girls are presented.

During my initial fieldwork, however, many girls seemed to view the types of girls as small in number. In addition to presenting challenges regarding identification, physical appearance was also an issue. While behavior did vary among the girl types presented by girl hero cartoons, they physically looked interchangeable. Although this chapter has dealt mainly with the behaviors and dress of the girl types my participants identified, it is crucial to note that whether a character was a girly girl, a tomboy, a diva, or a mean girl, she had one basic *slender* body type. Variance was virtually nonexistent. How did real girls negotiate the imperative of thinness endemic to Western culture, which permeates everything from the evening news to girl hero cartoons?

Notes

1. The scholarly literature has debated whether a link exists between tomboyism and adult lesbianism and/or transgenderism, though many adult women who identify as heterosexual recall having been tomboys when they were young (Gottschalk, 2003).
2. This may explain why the girl hero teams typically were led not by their group's tomboy or diva, but by the character identified by my participants as its girly girl: Blossom on *The Powerpuff Girls* and Sam on *Totally Spies.* According to a study of girls' leadership by Shinew and Jones (2005), when natural leaders emerged among girls, they were frequently recognized as leaders among their peers because of their niceness, their compassion, their altruism and caring.

8

Girl Heroes and Beauty[1]

The Visual Limits of Girl Power

"People call me fat all the time."

—*Bobbi, age 10 (Euro-American)*

"Mary Kate's anorexic. Mary Kate's anorexic."

—*Simone, age 7 (African-American)*

In the 1990s, concerns about girls' self-esteem fueled the girl crisis discourse. When adolescent girls fixate on unattainable beauty ideals, as is culturally expected of them, negative consequences can arise. The onset of female adolescence correlates with a preoccupation with physical appearance, a decline in self-esteem, and a decline in academic achievement, as explained in Chapter One. Ideally, if girl power were a solution to the girl crisis—and it has been presented as such (U.S. Department of Health and Human Services, 2001; Zaslow, 2009)—media texts targeting this demographic would display sensitivity to these problems, embracing girls of variant appearances and body types. Unfortunately, mainstream girl power's representations of female bodies have echoed other media texts. Aapola, Gonick, and Harris (2005) noted, "Media images of women tend to reify dominant cultural standards of beauty, rather than support the diversification of images of femininity" (p. 134); this has been true in girl power media, as well. Just as slim-fitting girl power baby-doll tee-shirts limited the body types within reach of girl power's lifestyle brand, girl power media pertains "exclusively to heterosexual women who have desires for men, makeup, and size zero bodies: basically, the marketed, unattainable perfection, which is produced by and for the gaze of the patriarchy" (Petrovic and Ballard, 2005, p. 197). This reification of culturally normative beauty ideals is a significant shortcoming of girl power.

Girl hero cartoons—a narrower girl power genre—also engaged in exclusionary depictions. The adolescent girl heroes were invariably tall, slender, and invested in producing a heavily normative consumer-based femininity. Further to this, a serious majority were white, as I will discuss in Chapter Nine. Besides failing to offer healthy portrayals of girls who were short, heavy, disabled, darker-skinned, and/or uninterested in the beauty myth, the girl hero cartoons negatively represented characters whose bodies deviated from the ideal. In consequence, girl hero cartoons perpetuated the unhealthy discourse that the feminine ideal is actually the norm, and that girls who deviate—for any range of hereditary, environmental, health, or deliberately resistant reasons—are inferior to girls who successfully perform femininity.

Girls learn from an early age to assess whether girls and women in real life and popular culture meet dominant beauty ideals. Despite being raised with girl power and in the aftermath of widespread girl crisis discourse, the young girls in my study were invested in these practices. Constantly scrutinizing the appearances of girl heroes and the girls and women they knew, they seemed to derive pleasure from this process. Their viewing was not limited to children's programs; some even watched appearance-centric shows like *The Swan*, *The Biggest Loser*, *Extreme Makeover*, and *America's Next Top Model*, which centered on criticizing and improving women's appearances. Many participants enjoyed showing their mastery of this knowledge. As their own bodies matured and developed, however, they turned that critical eye upon themselves—and the experience was anything but pleasurable. This chapter considers girls' reactions to on-screen characters' physical appearances and relates these practices to the girls' self-esteem.

Physical Appearance on Screen

Cartoon girl heroes had a fairly uniform look. The youngest heroes had small bodies and large heads: The kindergarten-aged Powerpuffs Girls' heads were roughly the same height as their bodies, and three times as wide, while middle-school-aged Atomic Betty had a body roughly a head-and-a-half high, and also three times as wide as her body. (See Figures 4.1 and 4.6 in Chapter Four.) The older cartoon girl heroes also had oversized heads, though somewhat less exaggerated; their heads were a little wider than their waists, rather than several times so. (See Figures 4.4, 4.5, and 4.7 in Chapter Four.) They were slender and long-legged, with slightly round-ed breasts (as opposed to the highly exaggerated buxomness of some female heroes in prime time and, especially, in comic books, which openly pander to a male gaze). Nearly all the cartoon girl heroes appeared of Euro-American descent.

The girls I interviewed often had little to say about these characters' looks. For example, at Suburban Elementary, Audrey described the Powerpuff Girls as "cool and pretty." Zoë and Kylie also described the Powerpuffs as "pretty," and Kylie elab-orated slightly, noting, "their hair, it's always, like, nice, and, um, I like their dress-es and shoes." Recalling an episode of *My Life as a Teenage Robot* in which Jenny receives a spray-paint makeover, Desirée at Nonprofit Aftercare described Jenny as looking "cute" and "pretty." "Pretty" was the default, it seemed.

Interestingly, perhaps because most girl heroes were usually depicted in the same outfits,[2] this pattern differed from that found by Lemish (1998) in her study of young Israeli Spice Girls fans. Her interviewees could be very specific about what they liked about the Spice Girls and why, offering many details about each Spice Girl's unique stylings and sartorial choices. Prettiness was nevertheless the overrid-ing theme; as Lemish explained, "What was striking [. . .] in the girls' talk about these multiple options, was their acceptance of them as legitimate as long as they were offered by a beautiful model. A girl could be anyone—as long as she was pret-ty" (p. 155).

In contrast to my participants' concision regarding the girl heroes' appealing appearances, they could specify many dislikes. For example, when Alex of *Totally Spies* became extremely muscular in "The Incredible Bulk," Kylie said, "She looked ugly. Her muscles made her ugly and her voice made her sound ugly." Audrey agreed, saying, "She sounds like a man!" After we screened *W.I.T.C.H.* for the first time, my participants at Suburban Elementary debated whether the five superhero girls looked "cool" or "weird."

ZOË: I think they looked weird because how small the wings were, and how high their socks were, and then, like, they had a green shirt and then they had a point in the front, but, like, all flat and straight in the back and then, like, they had a skirt, a purple skirt, that goes up right up to right there, to their waist.

ANGELA: Yeah, they could be rock stars like that—not.

REBECCA: [chuckles] Kylie, what did you think?

KYLIE: I think their outfit was cool because they have wings, and they got long, those long, um, big sleeves. And then they have this skirt that goes up like this and goes to their belly button–

ZOË: Like, at the bottom of—right here [pulling up her shirt and pointing to the bottom of her belly button]. [some chuckling]

KYLIE: And, um, I like their shoes and their wings. And I also liked their hair a little bit.

Although Kylie liked the *W.I.T.C.H.* girls' outfits, this conversation illustrated my participants' specificity when critiquing cartoon characters' appearances that seemed deviant. Angela and Zoë's excited tones suggested they took pleasure in this process—perhaps as a way to distance themselves from deviance constructing themselves as superior.

It also demonstrated how disagreement could lead to more fruitful conversation than agreement that characters are "pretty." Perhaps because "pretty" is a social norm, there is little to say about it. Deviance is easier to discuss—and girl hero cartoons depicted plenty of deviance but always in negative ways. For example, we watched several girl power cartoon episodes in which a main character's physical appearance suddenly deviated from the norm. In *Powerpuff* episode "The Mane Event," Blossom receives a terrible haircut from her sisters, and in "Twisted Sister," the sisters create a new Powerpuff who unsightly and an ineffectual superhero. In several *My Life as a Teenage Robot* episodes, the protagonist Jenny had appearance trouble—e.g., in "Hostile Makeover," a robot villain from outer space makes Jenny look ugly in an attempt to compel Jenny to join forces with her; and in the *Totally Spies* episode "Passion Patties," the Spies hunt a villain whose addictive cookies make people obese.

My participants were generally sympathetic when the main girl hero characters unwillingly deviated from normative femininity. For example, regarding Jenny, the Teenage Robot, and her constant quest to look more like a "normal girl":

TIANA: [Jenny] probably feels like she's an outcast from everybody because she probably doesn't get invited to a lot of social events [. . .]. Anyway, like, she'd be at parties and stuff, she probably couldn't get dressed up like the rest of the girls, like I'll go buy a new dress, and I got a new Gucci pocketbook, I got new jeans and sneakers. She can't, like, wear that kind of stuff, she's, like, blah. She can get, like, a paint job.

Regarding Blossom of *The Powerpuff Girls*, Bobbi expressed empathy:

BOBBI: [The episode] was OK, um, but the strange thing is, is that Blossom had perfect hair and Bubbles and Buttercup didn't, and when I sleep over at my friend's house, they wake up with perfect hair, and I wake up and my hair is real knotty and it's all over, and it's just strange, and I don't they should've made fun of Blossom because they should've thought of the consequences.

As girls in the viewing audience generally identify with characters they admire, my participants tended to see these situations from the characters' perspectives. In contrast, they found it funny when one-off characters unwittingly departed from prevailing feminine norms. For example, while Angela did not like it when Clover of *Totally Spies* was afflicted with the "Passion Patties" cookie addiction and grew obese, she and most other girls found it funny to see various non-recurring characters afflicted. When asked why, my participants focused on how the cartoon characters were rendered. Zoë replied that they just looked funny because their entire bodies were small, except for the stomach, "which is a big, humongous ball." Kelly agreed: she said they each looked like "a bouncing ball," and Maria said they looked like her hamster.

Angela concluded it was funny because real people can't get as fat as the characters in the cartoon. Because of the medium, the girls did not take "Passion Patties" too seriously. However, social learning theory suggests the divide between cartoon's fantasy worlds and real-world situations is not as wide as we might think. In a comment illustrating this point, Angela justified the humor of "Passion Patties" by blaming the obese characters for their own problems:

ANGELA: They shouldn't have opened their mouth so they wouldn't eat any cookies and they wouldn't get fat.

Children like my study's participants could easily apply this logic to real-world situations. It implies it is okay to make fun of people for failing to conform when conformity is within their control. However, obesity is a global epidemic (World Health Organization, 2007). It has serious health implications, and people do not willingly become obese. My participants' idea that obesity is preventable and funny was therefore a problem. However, the cartoon we watched does not bear responsibility for that; to the contrary, the cartoon's narrative depicted normal people becoming overweight because a villain's plot made self-control impossible. This suggests that as children's cartoon viewing is in discourse with ideas from the surrounding culture, it is sometimes difficult for them to grasp a story's moral— an important point, as girl power and girl hero cartoons often attempted to boost girls' self-esteem through positive lessons.

Another episode whose lessons my participants had trouble grasping was "Twisted Sister," in which the Powerpuff Girls sneak into their father's laboratory and create Bunny, a fourth Powerpuff who is ugly and unintelligent—unlike her smart, pretty sisters. The episode contains several positive lessons: that children should have a strong work ethic, that sneaking around can have dire consequences, and that one should not judge other people too quickly. However, I also worried the cartoon suggested the real problem with Bunny was not the sneaky, careless way she was made but rather with how she looked. Because of these concerns, I asked my participants what they thought the Powerpuff Girls learned in that episode. Angela's response was that the Powerpuff Girls did not learn a lesson "because," she said, "there's nothing to learn." A year later, when I visited her at home, Angela insisted that only programs for younger children teach lessons to their viewers.

> ANGELA: [The cartoons I watch] don't have a point to the show, they don't, like, have a goal, like, to be, um, like, they don't learn a lesson every day. But they don't, like, learn a lesson, like, like, on the *Teletubbies*—wait, not on the *Teletubby*—on *The Wiggles*—"time to share! Let's share! This is how we share! We take a toy, give it to somebody else, and play with it."

Among some girls, then, girl power cartoons' well-intended lessons may not have been consciously learned, partly because they perceived a difference between educational programs for preschoolers and the cartoons for pre-teens, which—though sometimes lesson-oriented—lack the formal curricula of their preschool counterparts. Preschool programs teach, but pre-teen cartoons entertain and are not to be taken seriously.

Other participants recognized girl hero cartoons' pedagogical functions though.

> KYLIE: The lesson is never to go into somebody else's lab and don't create something that's dumb.

> ZOË: The lesson is, you shouldn't go in someone's lab, without the person's permission, and [. . .] next time, ask Professor to help you make another one so she won't explode and she won't be stupid like Bunny. And she won't cry, like, every time they say she wasn't a good one, cuz she *would* be a good one if they didn't create her without Professor because she just had all these weird problems with her body—hump back, crooked teeth, feet spaced out, hairy ears, all this other stuff.

Kylie and Zoë seemed to have a basic grasp of the moral of "Twisted Sister." In addition to the producers' intended messages, Zoë also indicated Bunny would have turned out alright if the Powerpuffs' father had helped them, because she would neither have been "stupid" nor have "had all these weird problems with her body." Yet one of the episode's lessons was not to judge people by how they look, and it attempted to separate Bunny's behavior from her appearance. Her "weird problems" with her body were beside the point. Zoë's response conflated the real problem—the way the girls created Bunny and her resultant undesirable behavior— with Bunny's appearance.

Equally problematically, I would argue Bunny's physical appearance and behavior made her resemble a girl who has a disability. Ervelles and Mutua (2005) have noted that in mainstream girl power discourse, the "disabled girl" is invisible. They comment that "even in radical notions of Girl Power," the heteronormativity with which it is infused "rest[s] heavily on ableist ideologies of independence, assertiveness, and strength laced with patriarchal notions of beauty and attractiveness. Girl Power, thus defined, leaves neither material nor discursive spaces for a differentially constituted *disabled* girlhood" (p. 254). By failing to use this physically "other" Powerpuff Girl to critique normative femininity and ableism, *The Powerpuff Girls'* depiction of Bunny as indubitably inferior to her smart, ablebodied, pretty sisters—and my participants' reaction to this aspect of the cartoon—offer support for Ervelles and Mutua's argument. Girl power discourse is no more inclusive of disabled girls than it is of girls who are fat, visibly muscular, and so on.

Might the intended message of "Twisted Sister" have been received more clearly if Bunny looked as cute as her sisters—if the visual of a non-normative, arguably disabled girl had not been associated with all the other problems that arose in the episode? Among some girls, girl power cartoons' well-intended lessons may not be learned, because viewers sometimes conflate appearances with personality traits. This is a reason why so many scholars have criticized the stereotyping of women, minorities, foreigners, the elderly, the disabled, and other marginalized groups in the media (e.g., Gerbner and Signorielli, 1979; Gerbner, 1998; Tuchman, 1978). I fear that in many cases, the girl power cartoon characters' physical appearances compete with or negate other, more positive aspects of these shows.

Physical Appearance in Everyday Life

Conversations about the girl heroes' appearances often segued into conversations about my participants' own appearances. For example, after discussing how funny obesity seemed in "Passion Patties," Bobbi revealed she did not agree with the other girls' perception of its humor or even with Angela's assertion that real people cannot get that fat. The lone voice of dissent, she negotiated this storyline in a different, more personal way than did the other participants. She seemed to empathize with all of the characters—not just the girl heroes—in part because she was often teased about her weight. She read the cartoon as in discourse with her own painful experiences. As a result, my participants' conversation quickly turned from laughter to quiet reflection as Bobbi, an athletic girl, shared how her peers make fun of her for being "fat."

BOBBI: I'm big-boned, so a lot of people say that my thighs are really fat.

REBECCA: Oh!

BOBBI: But—it really annoys me. I'm jealous because all my friends, like, most people you look at them, their thighs are, like, this big [making a circle with her thumbs and forefingers]. I'm so jealous.

REBECCA: Yeah. I never had thighs that big. [Molly, the day care employee who is in the room with the group, starts to laugh a little.]

BOBBI: And then, there's other people that, like, have Livestrong bracelets, for example, when my friends got theirs, they fit in the size that was, like, for Build-a-Bears.

MARIA: I do.

ZOË: I do.

BOBBI: And, like, these people are in fourth grade, they're my age, they fit in the sizes for a teddy bear, and I was really jealous of that because I had to get a bigger size, but the size for a teddy bear was loose on them, and it was really tiny on me, so that annoyed me, too. But—

MOLLY: Are you talking about the bracelets?

REBECCA: Yeah. They make all kinds of name brand products for Build-a-Bear. Like, you can get Sketcher sneakers and Limited Too t-shirts for your Build-a-Bears.

BOBBI: And, you know what else? Like, if, like, there's this girl that lives down my street—sometimes she's my friend, sometimes she hates me, like, and sometimes she can be, like, really, really rude—and I gave her, like, two chances when I shouldn't have—I should only have given her one—but, um, she was being really rude, so I'm not her friend any more, but when, when she wants to play with the other people, who are *my* friends, it always causes a big fight, and she's, like, "Well, you're so fat!"

MOLLY: Well, that's rude.

REBECCA: That is really rude.

BOBBI: She calls everybody fat. And, um, people call me fat all the time—

REBECCA: I'm sorry they do that!

BOBBI: —and I hate it.

REBECCA: I think you girls all look very healthy. I don't think any of you are too skinny or too fat. I think you all look just right, don't you think so?

MOLLY: I think you're fine.

REBECCA: I think they're beautiful.

BOBBI: I think there's a—or, no, I don't think, I know—there's a commercial on TV for Wal-Mart, and then they were saying, "I'm not trying to be thin, I'm just trying to be healthy."

REBECCA: Right. And that's important.

This was the first extensive exchange I had with any participants about weight. I usually did not tell my participants what I thought about the issues we discussed to avoid leading them into giving answers they might think I wanted to hear. For example, when Desirée asked what I thought of Bratz dolls, I replied, "What do *I* think of Bratz dolls? I think that a lot of girls like Bratz dolls." In Bobbi's case, however, I needed to be supportive, build rapport, and avoid any sign of agreeing that she was "fat."

As time went on, the Suburban Elementary key interviewees often shared such stories with our group, confiding about the cruel things that other children had said to them. I regularly offered them support, affirming they were fine as they were.

Simultaneously, however, participants at both Suburban and Nonprofit Aftercare seemed quick to judge others' appearances. For example, Rhea once said, "No offense, but my principal wears her pants all the way right here, "pointing to a spot right above her navel and eliciting a laugh from her peers. They used appearance to judge material culture, too. While I was interviewing Angela in her kitchen, she stopped mid-conversation to point out a cereal box to me, because it promoted Millsberry.com on the side. Millsberry was a children's "advergaming" web site run by General Mills: it offers many child-friendly games alongside advertisements for General Mills' cereal products. Millsberry allows its users to create characters with diverse hair colors (natural and unnatural), hairstyles (a huge range, including pretty styles, punk styles, and bald heads), facial features (eyes and noses of all shapes, mouths in numerous expressions), and attire. Until General Mills ended the service on December 31, 2010, Millsberry was a safe place for children to play with appearance and identity. Pointing to a Lucky Charms box, Angela said:

ANGELA: I need to plays [sic] Millsberry. And, these are the people [pointing to the three characters on the side of the box]. Like, you can't even make them on—like, she's pretty. I want to make her [pointing to the blond girl in the middle of the picture] with brown hair. But you can't!

REBECCA: Wait. Wait. So, what makes her pretty?

ANGELA: Like, she has different kind of hair, different clothes, different smile, different eyes. They're all pretty. And the skin.

In other words, Angela wished she could create a character who looked like the one on the cereal box in her Millsberry game, but it was impossible within the parameters of Millsberry.com to do so. The girl she admired was pictured from the elbows up in a sleeveless red top with stars on it. She had fair skin, large, wide-set eyes, an almost invisible nose, a huge smile, pretty bangs, and two ponytails. She was a typical girly girl. It was possible to make girly girl characters in Millsberry, of course—just not ones that looked like this emblematic Millsberry girl. Angela expressed frustration that she could not make her Millsberry character as pretty as the blonde, feminine cartoon character depicted in Millsberry advertisements. Despite being an avowed tomboy, and despite the fact that Millsberry did allow users to create characters that subverted some mainstream norms (e.g., female characters could have mohawks and buzz cuts, and wear things like combat boots), Angela wanted her own feminine online identity. She believed that the appearance of this character she wished to recreate was "different," when it was really very similar to how mediated girls commonly look.

My participants also enjoyed discussing Bratz dolls—fashion dolls of diverse racial identities. Unlike the do-it-yourself characters children could create on Millsberry.com, Bratz fashion dolls uniformly met the dominant standards of feminine beauty to which so many girls aspire: long hair, long legs, and ultra-feminine, sexualized clothing in trendy styles. (See Figure 8.1.) During my fieldwork, Bratz dolls had become incredibly popular with pre-teen girls, cutting significantly into the profits of Mattel, which once had a monopoly on the fashion doll market with Barbie. Although Rhea disliked Bratz on the grounds that they look "creepy"—she said she felt like their big eyes were watching her at night, so she refused to own or play with them anymore—other participants loved everything about their Bratz dolls, especially the way they looked. Bailey enthused that Bratz were "so cute" because "they have nice hair." Desirée added, "When I think of the Bratz, it's because they're so cool because I like their clothes. And their hair is so cool because you can do it in style." (Note the difference in this language versus the language the girls previously used to describe the girl heroes: the girl heroes were "pretty," and the Bratz were "cool"—suggesting that they were possibly understood as girly girls and divas, respectively).

**Figure 8.1: Bratz Forever Diamondz Doll: Yasmin
Courtesy of Getty Images.**

"Forever Diamondz" is one of many Bratz lines. Each line is categorized by clothing style. The "Forever Diamondz" dolls' clothes are heavily embellished with diamond-style sparkles. They wear belly shirts and jean, fur shrugs, and glittering accessories. Yasmin's shirt says "Girly" and her hair is heavily highlighted. The other dolls' shirts say "Lucky," "Glam," "Sugar," and "Babe."

My participants volunteered that they not only wanted to play with Bratz dolls; they also wanted to look like them.

MADISON: Let me ask you a question. Um—Desirée, what do you like— would you like an outfit like the Brat dolls?

DESIRÉE: Yes, I would, but just in, like, a longer skirt this size–

BAILEY: A smaller shirt.

MADISON: I would get a short skirt.

DESIRÉE: —and just—

BAILEY: A smaller shirt.

DESIRÉE: I want a shirt kinda—

BAILEY: Covering the top.

DESIRÉE: Yeah.

My participants often made comments like these when Bratz arose in conversation: They thought Bratz were cool and wished they could dress just like them— in revealing halter tops or belly shirts, in short skirts or tight pants, and with "bling-bling" accessories. Unlike Barbie, who at least came in astronaut and teacher editions, dressing up in revealing clothing appeared to be the only pastime Bratz modeled for young girls. As stated in the manufacturers' promotional copy for the "Funk N Glow" line of Bratz dolls, recommended for children ages 6 to 11, "Bratz know how important it is to be seen!" (see Lamb & Brown, 2006, pp. 218–219).

My participants frequently judged celebrities' appearances as well. For example, during my visit to Zoë's home, she showed me her CD collection. I noticed her Britney Spears CD, *Baby One More Time*, but she said she no longer liked Britney Spears.

REBECCA: Oh—when *did* you like Britney Spears?

ZOË: When she didn't smoke and when she wasn't chubby.

As is often the case, for Zoë, a pop star's behavior and physical appearance were key to her likeability. Pop stars don't just perform music; they perform identities, too. Thus, while perusing teen magazines together at the Nonprofit Aftercare center, my participants were quick to assess pop stars' photographs. As Pomerantz (2008) has noted, when girls' police other girls' appearances, this indicates they have internalized the male gaze. They use the same criteria boys would use to assess one another and feel their surveillance is "normal" (p. 69).

KIARA: Oh, here's Beyoncé and Gwen Stefani! This is Gwen Stefani [pointing to a picture of her]–

REBECCA: OK.

BAILEY: That's Beyoncé.

KIARA: And that's Beyoncé.

REBECCA: What do you think of Gwen Stefani and Beyoncé?

KIARA: [pointing to a column of pictures of Gwen Stefani] Gwen Stefani, Gwen Stefani, Gwen Stefani–

BAILEY: Oh, she's pretty in that picture!

MADISON: [pointing to the top picture in the column] I hate that picture! [pointing down the column] I like this picture, and this picture, and that—

REBECCA: [pointing to the top picture] Why do you hate that picture?

MADISON: Yuck!

REBECCA: Why do you hate that picture?

MADISON: Because her hair!

KIARA: It looks pretty—she looks like a normal person there.

MADISON: She looks like a ugly person there.

Asked what they think of Gwen Stefani and Beyoncé—by which I meant their music—the girls fixated on the stars' appearance. Hairstyle again emerged as an important characteristic for assessing a female's appearance. When Madison and Kiara disagreed on Gwen Stefani's appearance, her hairstyle was the key variable. The girls were not making up these criteria; they learned them from the broader culture. The girls' discourse was in dialogue with mainstream femininity discourse. Even the magazine served pedagogically in this regard: Another Gwen Stefani photograph captured her with pink hair and braces, with the caption, "Yuck!" On spotting it, Madison said loudly, "Yuck! That's right! That's yuck!"

Given my participants' concerns with their appearances, as well as their focus on the appearances of cartoon girls, dolls, and celebrities, it follows that some were aware of dieting and weight loss strategies. When Bobbi shared a diet strategy she heard about on the news, the other girls listened with apparent interest:

BOBBI: They said that there's a diet that you have to eat more. If you reset your metabolism every three hours, something happens and you don't get fat, or something like that, and it's a diet.

Some girls had a basic understanding of eating disorders, as well, thanks to tween idol Mary Kate Olsen's well-publicized battle with anorexia.

BAILEY: [Looking at an advertisement for *Teen People* magazine:] There's Ashley.

REBECCA: Oh, who's that?

MADISON: Hey! She dyed her hair?!

BAILEY: Yeah! She dyed her hair black!

KIARA: Who? Who did?

REBECCA: Oh, is that one of the Olsen twins?

BAILEY: Yeah, that's Mary Kate and Ashley.

REBECCA: Which one is which?

MADISON: This is Ashley [pointing to the brunette on the right], this is Mary Kate.

REBECCA: How do you know?

MADISON: Because, one, one of them—

BAILEY: They dyed their hair different.

SIMONE: Mary Kate's anorexic. Mary Kate's anorexic.

REBECCA: What's "anorexic" mean?

SIMONE: Like, when you're, um, like, really skinny, like this [she holds her hands vertically parallel a few inches apart].

BAILEY: Ask Mary Kate.

MADISON: [playfully] Hi, I'm Mary Kate.—

REBECCA: Hey, let's–let's stop for a minute. What—how does—how do people get anorexic?

KIARA: They lose—

BAILEY: Mary Kate—

MADISON: I'll tell you what happened to her.

REBECCA: Tell me Mary Kate's story. Let's stop for a minute so we can talk about Mary Kate. Cuz we got plenty of time.

MADISON: There's so many different reasons with other people. But Mary Kate, she—she's been on a dangerous one. She hasn't been eating for days; exercising every single minute, hour, second; never eating. She did not eat—anything. Not even drinking anything.

SIMONE: [when Madison says, "never eating"] And she had an eating disorder.

REBECCA: Why? [in response to what Madison has been saying]

MADISON: That was dangerous.

REBECCA: Why'd she do that to herself?

MADISON: She wanted to lose weight.

BAILEY: She was on a diet. She wanted to get skinny.

REBECCA: But—I bet she was already skinny.

BAILEY: She was!

SIMONE: She was!

MADISON: She looked just like her sister, but now she—

REBECCA: So wait—which one is the anorexic one? Mary Kate, or—

KIARA: Mary Kate.

BAILEY: That's Mary Kate and that's Ashley.

REBECCA: This is Mary Kate, and that's Ashley. [blonde and brunette, respec-
tively] And she's [pointing to Mary Kate] too skinny.

KIARA: Mmm [indicating indecision]

REBECCA: Why do you think these girls want to be so skinny?

KIARA: To show off their boobs.

Although Kiara commented that celebrity girls want to be skinny "to show off
their boobs," not all girls expressed comfort with this aspect of female development.
For example, when Angela gave her younger sister Jeannine and me a tour of her
Millsberry web site, Angela showed us the character her friend Gracie had designed
for her: a Caucasian girl with short brown hair and a nice smile, wearing a light blue
Millsberry cap (with a gold M on the front), a light blue short-sleeve shirt with a
Millsberry M on the front, blue jeans with a brown belt, and dark shoes.

ANGELA: I don't know why they have those [moving the cursor on the character's chest].

REBECCA: Why they have what?

ANGELA: Um, these. [She puts the cursor on one side of the character's chest,
then the other.]

REBECCA: Oh, her breasts?

ANGELA: Yeah. [chuckles] I don't know why they have them. [Rebecca chuckles.] I don't know why they have them.

JEANNINE: Angie, don't they have bras?

ANGELA: No.

REBECCA: No, Jeannine, I don't think they have bras.

ANGELA: Yeah. I don't think, yeah.

REBECCA: Why, do you wish they did? [Jeannine nods.] Why?

JEANNINE: Because when you put the bra on, and then you put the shirt on,
you look hotter.

REBECCA: You look hotter? What does that mean? [Angela is being silly, giving the camera a close-up of her right eye.]

JEANNINE: Um, it kinda means, like, hot means, like, you're cute. [Angela doing an eye close-up: "Hi, peeps!]

REBECCA: "Hot" means "cute"?

JEANNINE: Yeah.

Although childhood is constructed as a time of innocence, and "the presumption of childhood innocence sustains the perceived immunity to sexual knowledge: young children are innocent and play is innocent" (Bhana, 2005, p. 164), children's play is not always innocent. Bhana found that girls' play culture "is invested in heterosexuality and offers a strategic space through which girls resist, contribute, and contest their sexual and gendered identities" (p. 164). Thus, while Jeannine seemed interested in using Millsberry to explore a normatively gendered sexual identity— a safe place to play with being "hot"—Angela did not. In fact, she expressed discomfort with the small breasts visible under her Millsberry character's sporty t-shirt—first by questioning why her character had breasts in the first place, and then by acting silly while Jeannine talked about bras and hotness. This is an ongoing tension in girls' media culture: As Wertheimer (2006) has argued, the North American construction of the child "is fraught with contradictions whereby the child is perceived as embodying asexual innocence while simultaneously finding herself eroticized in countless cultural texts" (p. 210)—which seems to be the case here.

In wishing that she could put a bra on a Millsberry character to make her "hotter," then saying that "hot means, like, you're cute," seven-year-old Jeannine illustrated an important point. Girls are taught at an early age that they need to look "cute," but in today's marketplace, "cute" and "hot" have become conflated (Lamb and Brown, 2006, pp. 52–54). In fact, the mother of a participant from the Township Library group confided that she and her husband were horrified to realize that their daughter was playing an "adult" video game one day: Sexy Dress Up. This popular, free online game is available on many web sites, such as Game2000.com, which features ample non-adult content, too. Sexy Dress Up features a scantily clad cartoon woman, standing on a beach with an array of outfits and accessories. Gamers can dress her however they like: in belly shirts and short skirts, a sailor outfit, a French Maid uniform, pirate clothing, or a body-sized condom, among other options. The Sexy Dress Up woman does not look that different from "Bling Bling" Barbie, though she is more muscular. It is easy to see how a child would mistake the game for an age-appropriate one.

During my study, Sexy Dress Up was highly ranked in search engines, so a child searching for variations on "dress up games" or "dress up dolls" could encounter it with ease. (As of 2011, it is no longer as highly ranked under these searches, but it still appears under "most popular games" on dress-up game aggregators.) My participant told her mother she could not tell that it was adult content, and her mother admitted that even though she and her husband were in the room when their daughter began playing, they did not comprehend the game's nature until their daughter had removed an outfit, leaving the "doll" graphically naked and moaning.

In a previous study, Willett (2005) noted online dress-up dolls meant for girls tend to be exaggeratedly sexy, with provocative clothing choices like thongs frequently included. After observing girls playing with online dress-up dolls, she noted, "One could speculate that users are playing with power and fantasizing about their future bodies" (p. 284). She concluded that online dress-up games deliberately present exaggeratedly sexual, "overwhelmingly curvaceous" digital versions of Barbie or paper dolls, encouraging girls to fulfill their interest in "play with sexy images" through "a powerful medium—the sexy female body" (p. 284).

With mainstream and digital children's commodities resembling sexy images that are intended for adult consumption, girls' beauty ideals are less and less compatible with a healthy body image. Their "cool" clothing often implies a sexiness that girls are not ready for, and girls' fashions cause problems in schools. In fact, the principal of Suburban Elementary told me that his school district had implemented a uniform for the first time only three years earlier, in part because girls kept wearing what the principal called "midriff tops" (my participants called these "belly shirts") and other revealing clothing to school.

REBECCA: Even at the elementary level?

PRINCIPAL: They all did, throughout the whole district.

Selling sexiness to children is a disconcerting practice that the American Psychological Association (APA) has criticized. The APA (2007) reported that the sexualization of girlhood is rampant in U.S. society, and that it is detrimental to girls. In the long term, it may lead to sexual exploitation, and it affects girls' cognitive development, self-esteem, sexuality, attitudes, and beliefs. Mainstream girl power cannot be understood outside this context; as Durham (2008) has lamented, "Girls are bombarded with the myth that semi-nudity constitutes 'girl power'" (p. 80).

Physical Aspirations: Personal Appearance in Girls' Drawings

As mentioned earlier, my participants often shared the hurtful comments other children made about their appearances. In my group of Euro-American girls at Suburban Elementary, our conversations often segued from what other people said into self-criticisms. These participants assessed their own bodies with the same eye they cast upon celebrities, Bratz dolls, and Millsberry characters. For example, shortly after Bobbi told us how people would tease her by calling her fat, Angela said, "I think I am kinda chubby." She commented, "I want to be like my dad, because he's skinny, but he eats so much—I don't ever see him eat any fruit—or vegetables. But he's so skinny." My participants spoke easily about how they wished they could look, and their wishes aligned with the ideals of normative femininity. Sometimes, expressions of desire for thin appearances arose unexpectedly. For example, at some meetings, I would give the girls art supplies and ask them to draw whatever they'd like. On one occasion, Kylie drew a picture of herself; in this image (Figure 8.2), the proportions of her figure and her stylistic choices resembled those of Bratz dolls, girl power heroes, and other media icons.

Figure 8.2: A drawing by Kylie, age 9
(*Visit growingupwithgirlpower.com for a full-color version of this image.*)

REBECCA: All right. Come tell me about your picture.

KYLIE: Um, that's what I want to look like.

REBECCA: It is?

KYLIE: Yes.

REBECCA: Like, what you want to look like when?

KYLIE: I don't know—when I'm a teen.

REBECCA: Yeah? Tell me about what this picture looks like.

KYLIE: Um, well it's just me in a tank—I'm in a belly shirt and I'm in a skirt, and there are flowers around me.

REBECCA: Uh-huh. And, so what is exactly, like, if you could describe it, what would you want to look like when you get older?

KYLIE: Mostly like this.

REBECCA: Like, so what adjectives would be used to describe that girl?

KYLIE: Pretty, beautiful, um, [long pause], um, thin—I don't know.

The desire to be thin ran strong among my participants. This pattern emerged again after three girls and I screened the *Teenage Robot* episode "Hostile Makeover" together. In that episode, Jenny has an acne-like break out of nuts and bolts on class photo day, and she does not want to have her picture taken. The photographer says Jenny is having "body image issues," but in an open-ended discussion after screening the episode, this point never came up. Since so many parents, educators, and psychologists share concerns about girls' body images, I wanted to find out what my participants thought about this content. Therefore, as our discussion seemed to be winding down, I initiated a conversation about it.

REBECCA: So, the next thing I have is more of a comment, and I just want to see what you girls say. So, the lady who was taking the school photos, she said to Jenny something about Jenny having body image issues.

KELLY: What does that mean?

REBECCA: What do you think it means?

ANGELA: I think it means, um, like—like, she's getting bigger and she's growin' or something. And I know what else—I think I know what else it means—it means—

KYLIE: Should we show you on the camera? I mean, on the TV.

REBECCA: If you want to, you can find it.

Kylie finds the spot. There is some chatter by the girls while they watch it. It lasts about one minute.

> REBECCA: OK, so talk to me about what the camera lady meant about the body image issues.

The girls didn't immediately respond; Kylie and Kelly had started goofing around. I prodded:

> REBECCA: OK, so talk to me. Tell me what she was saying.
>
> ANGELA: Who's saying?
>
> REBECCA: What the camera lady was saying.
>
> ANGELA: "Watch the birdie."
>
> REBECCA: What was she saying after that?
>
> KELLY: "Smile." That's what Lexus said when she was, like—
>
> ANGELA: Yeah! She's, like, "Work it!"

The girls chattered unintelligibly for a few moments. To help them to focus, I decided to offer them a definition.

> REBECCA: Well, do you want to know what I think "body image issues" means? I think what they mean is, sometimes people, like boys and girls, will think that they look a certain way—like, worse than they really look, so they're really self-conscious about their bodies and their appearances. That can actually be a problem with people, especially with girls—you know, they might think that they're fat when they're not, or that they're ugly and they're not.
>
> KYLIE: I do!
>
> ALL: I do!
>
> REBECCA: What do you mean?
>
> KELLY: I do.
>
> REBECCA: Why do you think that?
>
> KELLY: I don't know.
>
> KYLIE: I think I am.
>
> REBECCA: I think you're all beautiful.
>
> ANGELA: I eat too much!

At this point, the conversation became quite animated, and the girls started talking over each other. My definition of "body image issues" resonated with them; this new vocabulary led them to share an avalanche of appearance concerns.

KELLY: And people make fun of my teeth.

ANGELA: How can you eat so much and then get skinny?

KELLY: I hate it! I get annoyed whenever people say, "Your teeth are too big."

REBECCA: I think your teeth are fine.

ANGELA: People say my teeth are big.

KELLY: [to Rebecca:] No, they're not.

ANGELA: Mine are huge. [pointing to her front top teeth]

KELLY: Mine are, too. They overlap my other teeth.

REBECCA: So, do you think that most of the girls that you know have, like, concerns about the way they look?

ANGELA: My friend Gracie thinks she's fat.

KELLY: My mom told me that if my teeth weren't that way, there would be something else people would worry about. Like my hair color. Even though people like it, people say I have orange hair, when I have something else.

REBECCA: Hmm. I think you have beautiful hair.

KELLY: I heard on TV my hair is called mahogany red.

REBECCA: It's beautiful.

KELLY: I know! And I don't like it, though. I want it more blonde, more brown.

ANGELA: [She says a good bit of this while Kelly is still talking] I don't like the style of my hair. I like it straight. I went to a hairdresser, and she made my hair straight, and it was good!

REBECCA: But there are those who want curly hair, so they go to the hairdresser to have it made curly.

ANGELA: Yeah, that's the thing. Curly-hair people want straight hair, and straight-hair people want curly hair. I'm not saying I like—I want straight hair.

By expressing their interests in having smaller teeth, being skinny, and changing their hair color and texture, the girls made it clear that despite their young ages, they had already begun thinking about body projects. In *The Body Project: An*

Intimate History of American Girls, Brumberg (1997) explains that the body "is a consuming project for contemporary girls because it provides an important means of self-definition, a way to visibly announce who you are to the world" (p. 97). She explained that the centrality of body projects in girls' lives is comparatively recent, rooted in the modern, twentieth-century femininity imperative requiring "some degree of exhibitionism" (p. 98). Harris (2005) noted this trend has been exacerbated by current popular culture, which presents celebrity glamour as ordinary or normative through reality television and makeover programming. She explained, "[C]urrent times emphasize self-invention and the importance of the project of working on the self for success for all girls. Middle-class status is no longer assured through marriage or inheritance but must be secured anew by anxious families and their daughters, who are negotiating a very different economic and social order from a generation ago" (p. 216). Looking the right way—that is, in line with celebrity culture—is considered a pathway to success. However, pursuing this target is not only very difficult, expensive, and time-consuming; as Aapola et al. (2005) note, the target itself shifts constantly. The beauty industries perpetually make small changes to the notions of beauty they promote, leading girls and women to feel their bodies "can never be quite right, and can always be improved. This improvement becomes an imperative of identity and happiness for young women due to the complex relationship between self and body" (Aapola et al., 2005, p. 137).

To better understand the girls' visions of their own body projects, I asked them to illustrate their ideas.

> REBECCA: OK, I've got a great question for you. Here's what I would like you to do. I would like you to draw a picture for me of what you think you look like, and put next to it what you *wish* you looked like. Because this is very hard for me to understand how such beautiful girls—
>
> MOLLY: [an Aftercare employee]: You guys are all great. I don't know why you'd want to change yourself.
>
> REBECCA: I know, but I've got to understand what it is they're saying, you know, because they're being very detailed. [To the girls:] So, make sure you label what they are. [To Molly:] Cuz, you know, I mean, I think we both agree that these are beautiful girls, and they're healthy girls, and they don't need to gain any weight or lose any weight. I think they're fine.

From my standpoint as a researcher, this was a complex situation. I had not planned to ask girls to draw their ideal selves; such an idea would never have occurred to me, because it seems risky—a way of introducing problems into the group. (For example, such an activity might some lead girls to consider which parts of their bodies they disliked for the first time.) These girls clearly had very specific ideas about their ideal bodies, however, and wished to share them, so illustrative drawing seemed reasonable to help them communicate their ideas.

Also note that Molly, the Aftercare employee, normally was silent during our meetings. Her presence was legally required, because I was not an employee of the Aftercare center; she typically sat in a corner and observed. She seemed shocked by the girls' disclosures, however, so as one of their regular caretakers, she spoke up. In response to my aside to her, she replied by addressing the girls directly:

MOLLY: You guys should be happy with yourselves—inside and out.

REBECCA: Yeah. I mean, cuz, you know, what I was thinking about this episode is they're saying Jenny has body image issues, but she really *is* having problems, you know, she really *does* look that way? You know, whereas you girls all look great. Don't you know what I mean?

MOLLY: They're great.

The girls did not react, but continued criticizing themselves as they eagerly rearranged their chairs so that they could draw. While drawing, they told me stories about their friends:

ANGELA: I had a friend—and she was real—she had real good hair, she was real skinny, and she eats a lot, and she doesn't go to a gym. She said–she says, "I'm"–she's, like, "I'm fat. I don't like my hair. I don't like its color." And I kept on saying to her, "Well, your hair—I wish I could have your kind of hair. You're, like, the only one I've met who could put your hair up in a ponytail and make it look like the way you do, like, every day."

KELLY: Well, I put my hairs up in a ponytail.

ANGELA: But she makes it look kinda prettier than a—than mine when I put mine in a ponytail. I just do it normal; she does her hairs, it's like, like you put a scrunchy in, but it's just a ponytail. And she says she doesn't like the color of her hair. And I said I wanted blonde hair like hers.

KYLIE: Who says she doesn't like it herself?

ANGELA: Gracie.

KYLIE: Gracie?!

ANGELA: Yeah.

KYLIE: I wanna get highlights.

KELLY: I wanna get highlights, too. I want it browner. My hair a little browner.

ANGELA: And she says she's fat, and I'm, like, "You're skinnier than me!" That's what I say. [She goes back to her drawing.]

REBECCA: [to Kelly:] Have you got examples of friends saying things to you about the way they look?

KELLY: No. Except one. They told me that our, um, gym teacher said that, um, most of–a lot of girls in our school have those problems, and people—I mean, a lot of people at our school have those problems, and all—like, most of them are girls.

REBECCA: Have what problems?

KELLY: They think they're too fat or something

As the girls completed their drawings, they explained them to me individually. Kylie described her drawing (see Figure 8.3) as follows:

Figure 8.3: Two drawings by Kylie, age 9

REBECCA: OK, so, Kylie, would you tell me about your picture?

KYLIE: That's what I look like now [girl on left], that's what I want to look like [girl on right].

REBECCA: Can you describe for me the qualities of those two people? Like, tell me about what they look like?

KYLIE: Right here [on left] I'm tubby, and right here I'm skinny.

REBECCA: OK. What else is different between you now and what you wanna look like?

KYLIE: I wanna have long hair.

REBECCA: Yeah? And your clothes would be different?

KYLIE: Yes.

REBECCA: How would your clothes be different?

KYLIE: Um, because I'm wearing a dress.

REBECCA: Now, is that part of how you want to look different?

KYLIE: Yes.

REBECCA: What's on your head?

KYLIE: A crown.

REBECCA: [chuckling] Why is there a crown on your head?

KYLIE: Cuz I wanna be a princess.

REBECCA: Ahhh. Well, I'd have to say I don't think you're chubby now. Just for the record. I think you're beautiful.

KYLIE: Thanks.

As was the case in Kylie's previous drawing depicting how she wanted to look as a teenager, her physical size and the style of her clothing were the key visual aspects she wished to use to construct her identity. Her comment about wanting to be a princess offers insight, as the pretty princess is one of the most prominent girly girl types circulating in popular culture. Disney has made a fortune by bringing together its heroines under the "Disney Princess" line (Orenstein, 2011); even *Dora the Explorer* released a fairy princess model, undercutting Dora's identity as an active, intelligent pre-school role model.

Kelly also focused on her body's size and clothing as she made her drawing (see Figure 8.4).

Figure 8.4: Two drawings by Kelly, age 10.

KELLY: This one's for what I look like now.

REBECCA: OK. So, tell me all about it.

KELLY: It's me!

REBECCA: OK. Can you describe it to me? Can you give me, like, adjectives and stuff?

KELLY: Nope. [She switches pictures.] This one is what I wanna look like. This [pointing to the shirt in the picture] is the new shirt we get this year at my dance class.

REBECCA: OK.

KELLY: It's pink. And I'm getting an adult small, so—now, I don't want one, an adult small.

REBECCA: What do you want?

KELLY: Medium.

REBECCA: An adult medium?

KELLY: No.

REBECCA: A kid's medium?

KELLY: Yep.

REBECCA: Why? What's the difference between an adult small and a kid's medium?

KELLY: They're in different places. They're, like, for different sizes of people.

REBECCA: Oh, OK.

KELLY: I like one better cuz I have shorter hair, and that's the hair I want.

REBECCA: Yeah, I need you to, like—you told me the other one is what you look like now, but can you to explain to me what the difference is?

KELLY: This one [showing the picture of what she looks like now] is a different shirt and shoes—

REBECCA: Right. So, how is—your face looks different between the two.

KELLY: I like this one a lot [referring to the picture of what she wants to look like].

REBECCA: Yeah? What is it that you like better about this one?

KELLY: She has shorter hair, this looks like she's in a medium size shirt, she has shorter pants and shorter shoes. And her eyes and mouth and I have eyebrows are different.

REBECCA: So you would rather your eyes be, like, bigger like that? [pointing to the eyes in the picture of what she wants to look like]

KELLY: Mm-hmm.

REBECCA: OK.

KELLY: And—I don't know what else I should say.

As with Kylie, physical size and clothing were key points Kelly wanted to change about herself. Kelly was less concerned with adopting a new style of clothing, however, than she was with the size of that clothing. She did not want to grow up to wear an adult medium. Instead, she wished she could decrease in size from her present adult small down to a kids' medium, which is actually several sizes smaller. Unlike Kylie, who wanted longer hair, Kelly wanted shorter hair, and she wished her facial features could change, too. Note that in her wishful drawing, her arms are alarmingly thin, and her head is disproportionate to her body—resembling the stylized look that appears across animated texts, from *Totally Spies* to Disney films.

Angela's before and after pictures share many of Kelly's traits. In explaining her drawing (see Figure 8.5), Angela's listed dislikes were especially lengthy.

Figure 8.5: Two drawings by Angela, age 8
(*Visit growingupwithgirlpower.com for a larger version of this image.*)

ANGELA: Um, this is what I think I look like [right side of the paper], and this is what I want to look like.

REBECCA: OK. So, can you explain to me the difference between these two Angelas?

ANGELA: Well, this one has curly, like, short hair [on the right], and my shoes are bigger, I'm chubby, and I can't wear the shirts I like, and I can't wear the pants I like—

REBECCA: How come?

ANGELA: —because the zippers come undone, because—and because today a lot of people were making fun of me because I had my zipper undone, because every time I try to zipper it, my pants, they always fall down. Isn't that amazing?

REBECCA: Oh, no!

ANGELA: And so that's why I think I'm fat. And—

REBECCA: Do you think you're fat because of your zippers?

ANGELA: Yeah, and—

REBECCA: Maybe it just means you're growing out of your clothes, not that you're fat.

ANGELA: No, I mean I got new clothes three days ago, and this is one of them—

REBECCA: Maybe it's not made well.

ANGELA: And they're the size.

REBECCA: Maybe it's not you—maybe it's the clothes. Anyway, just food for thought. OK, so, you're not wearing the clothes that you like, and your hair is short and curly. You look pretty—you have a very pretty face.

ANGELA: And my nose—I mean, my—

REBECCA: Oh, did you write the size of the shoe? [pointing to the left shoe in the picture]

ANGELA: Yep. Size two and a half. That's how big my shoes are.

REBECCA: So you think your shoes are *too* big?

ANGELA: Yes. And I have brown eyes.

REBECCA: OK. You have brown eyes in that picture.

ANGELA: Mm-hmm.

REBECCA: OK. Tell me about the what-you-wish-you-could-look-like picture.

ANGELA: I just needed to tell that my bangs—they're always, like, up, above my eyes kinda—and this one, I have bangs that are, like, near my eyes. I think I look pretty that way. And I like longer hair. And I can't draw blue—I wanted blue eyes, but I couldn't do that. [She switches to the other picture, showing what she wishes she could look like.] It says, "I am"—

REBECCA: What does it say? "I am ?"

ANGELA: It says "thin" right here [pointing to the girl's right leg].

REBECCA: It says, "thin" and "cool."

ANGELA: [pointing to the shoes] And this is size one. My shoes are size one there.

REBECCA: Does that say "one" or "one and a half"? I think it says "one and a half." I can't tell.

ANGELA: This says "one." [pointing to right shoe]

REBECCA: And what does it say on your shirt?

ANGELA: I just don't feel like saying that. But, I need to tell the difference. Like, my teeth—[pointing to the "now" picture] I have teeth that are, like, huge, and I didn't show that kinda. And this one [pointing to the "want-to-look-like" picture] I have OK teeth. I wanna have, like, teeth that aren't, like, the spacing or any big huge teeth or any small teeth or any crooked, and—that's all.

REBECCA: OK. Well, thank you very much for sharing this with me.

ANGELA: And I wanted blonde hair.

REBECCA: You wanted blonde hair.

ANGELA: I have—the only thing I like about me is because I like—is my skin. I never get a sunburn, even in the hottest weather.

What an overwhelming list. Refusing to consider that the fit of her clothes was more problematic than her body, Angela felt certain she was overweight. Her comment that her clothes were "the size" echoed Kelly's focus not on what would fit her well but whether she could squeeze herself into a smaller item. By wishing she could change everything about her appearance, except her skin, Angela—like many other participants—expressed a consuming worry that her body did not align with the exceptionally thin ideal, which they perceived as the norm. In Angela's drawing, she diminished all her physical attributes, except her hair—an obvious marker of normative femininity. She, Kylie, and Kelly said through their pictures that they wished their bodies would just shrink away.

Girls Growing up and Growing Self-Conscious

As aforementioned, Euro-American girls sketched all the drawings in the previous section. I never asked my African-American participants to draw such pictures for me, because in our conversations, they were not self-critical. Their lack of self-criticisms seemed to align with the psychological research, which indicated that adolescent African Americans are generally more satisfied with their bodies than are adolescent girls of other races. (E.g., see Mayville, Katz, Gipson, & Cabral, 1999; Neumark-Sztainer, Croll, Story, Hannan, French, & Perry, 2002.) As I mentioned earlier, I wished not to independently introduce an activity like drawing their ideal bodies to my participants; I felt it would be irresponsible to potentially imply that girls should wish to change themselves. Due to the nature of my fieldwork, in which I brought my participants girl power texts and then let them lead the conversation, there were many instances like this—in which I talked about a subject with one group but not another.

When I followed up with my key interviewees from Nonprofit Elementary a year after our initial meetings, they had all grown quite a bit. They didn't look like little girls anymore, and Bailey seemed to have grown a foot. I also noticed self-criticisms in casual comments they made to me on the playground—criticisms which had not occurred the previous year. For example, Bailey wished she were not so tall; Desirée and Zayonna worried about their weight; Bailey complained her voice was getting too deep; Rhea disliked her hair. Around the same time, they had become interested in boys: When we walked upstairs to the school library together, they would hang out of the stairwell window to call down to boys were playing in the schoolyard below. They also talked about which boys they liked, sometimes teasing one another about their crushes in front of me, and sometimes asking for advice. As I recorded in my field notes from March 10, 2006:

> Because it's a beautiful day today—the first really warm day of the season (in the 70s)—when I arrived, the girls asked if we could talk outside, in private without the other kids around. As we talked, they were quick to reproach other kids who entered the area, telling them to go away. Rhea addressed one boy's objections with, "We're with a *teacher*"—and I had to note that I'm *not* a teacher, of course. (They agreed—teachers are *old*, which apparently sets them off from me.) Anyway, when we got to "the worm" [a play area in a set-off part of the school playground], they asked what we should talk about, and I said anything they want. I think it was Bailey who proposed that we talk about boys, because "they're kind of cute." Each girl told me a little about a boy she liked—nothing too specific, but Desirée related a story about a boy who asked where she was the other day, and she said she was getting her hair done, and he complimented her on her hair. She wanted to know if that meant he wanted to be her friend, or if he *liked* her. I said "friends" sounds good, but you never know—boys don't usually notice hair, I said. They agreed.

I inquired about the girls' self-esteem and their new interest in boys when I interviewed Rochelle, Nonprofit Aftercare Program's site director, at her home. Rochelle was on site daily after school and attended to the children's goings-on. She had known many since they were toddlers, having worked at the Nonprofit Daycare Program a few years prior; children from the Nonprofit Daycare Program often transitioned into the Nonprofit Aftercare Program in first grade.

REBECCA: Are there particular issues that the girls face that maybe the boys don't? Or things in their interactions with the boys?

ROCHELLE: Yes. Right now, our girls—between, I guess, ten, eleven, nine—are going through this weight thing.

REBECCA: They're going through a weight thing?

ROCHELLE: A weight thing, yeah.

REBECCA: No.

ROCHELLE: Yeah. I'm hearing, you know, stories or that girls come, "He called"—you know, crying because Johnny has been teasing and saying, "You're fat."

REBECCA: When did this start? This hasn't been going on right along, has it?

ROCHELLE: I would say for this past year.

REBECCA: Was it this way last year? [I.e., during the time frame of my first set of group interviews.]

ROCHELLE: No. Just in the last year. A lot of times, you would find it more Caucasian girls would go through the problem with the weight thing—

REBECCA: Right.

ROCHELLE: —but our Black girls are now going through the problem with the weight thing. I mean, you're gonna look at how the women are dressing—you know, with the hipsters, and you want to be able to wear the hipsters, but your stomach out, and everything else—and, you know, and it's just, like, "I don't wanna look like that. I wanna look like Beyoncé." If you got this boy that's calling you fat, and you're coming of age, and you have a little bit of weight on you—or baby fat—you may not be big or anything like that. [But you] just start to think, you know, and look at yourself. Cuz you wanna be thin. They're watching these shows—*America's Next Top Model.* That's a—that's a—that's a—[struggling for the right word]

REBECCA: That's unrealistic, yeah.

ROCHELLE: Yeah. But that's what our girls are going through because that's what they're going home and watching. So, of course, they want to—and they're into it like it's a soap opera show! Yes! Not even just the kids—the adults are! You know, I'm hearing stories—young teenagers—"I gotta go home and watch *America's Next Top Model!*" It's like a soap—I'm like, "Oh my God." I mighta saw one episode of it, and maybe—might have only saw, like, two minutes of it. I was just not interested in it.

REBECCA: Oh no.

ROCHELLE: So we've had a couple of issues. A parent even came to me, [saying] that a little boy had called their child "fat." And they were upset about it. They are going through this stage.

REBECCA: Well, and I know that I was surprised when I was there, like, the last time [. . .] Bailey's getting all uncomfortable. She's like, "I'm too tall. And my voice is too deep."

ROCHELLE: Mm-hmm.

REBECCA: And I'm thinking, you know, she's—she's beautiful. She's tall for her age. She's almost as tall as me now.

ROCHELLE: She is very tall.

REBECCA: But, I didn't realize that there were more, like—

ROCHELLE: And she's lost a lotta weight. She was heavier than she was.

Triangulating in this way helped me make sense of my participants' self-criticisms. I already knew that during my absence in the previous year, they had become self-critical and developed an interest in boys. From Rochelle, I learned their self-criticisms went beyond what I had witnessed, and they were going through a "weight thing." Bailey had even lost weight. Rochelle suggested the appearance-focused television shows the girls favored were a contributing factor, and she felt the boys instigated some concerns with the comments they made to the girls. This makes sense as at least a partial explanation, considering that the girls were newly interested in gaining the attention of some boys. As Davison and McCabe (2006) found, girls' self-worth decreased when others made negative assessments of their appearances, suggesting girls' adolescent issues such as self-esteem and self-image may be highly contextual. It was sad to see a group of girls who seemed self-assured a year earlier becoming so hard on themselves.

Discussion

It is difficult to do justice to my participants' complex negotiations of physical appearance. However, in this chapter, several interconnected findings emerged. My participants had difficulty specifying what they liked about their girl power heroes' appearances, but they could easily critique non-normative characters' appearances. My participants seemed likely to empathize with heroes who unwillingly failed to conform but made fun of non-recurring characters similarly afflicted. Physical appearances contain their own semiotic messages, which compete with and contradict the narrative messages of some girl hero cartoons. As such, my participants had trouble grasping girl hero cartoons' intended narratives—lessons such as not judging people based on their appearance. This implies that visual stereotyping conflates appearance and personality for pre-teen viewers, teaching them the opposite: You *can* tell a book by its cover.

My interviewees were quick to critique the appearances of girls and women in popular culture if they did not align closely enough with normatively feminine ideals. Unfortunately, they were also frequently criticized in similar ways by their peers, and they attended to broader cultural messages about the pursuit of normative femininity, demonstrating a basic awareness of diet strategies and eating disorders. These facts had implications in the girls' everyday lives. Even the littlest girls in my study, such as Angela's younger sister, were aware that the mainstream culture calls for girls to be "hot," to flaunt their breasts and wear sexy clothing—an idea with which some participants were uncomfortable. Unfortunately, the boundaries between the vision of feminine beauty that is sold to little girls and to adult men are blurring, so the desire to be "hot" and to dress like Bratz dolls is tremendously problematic. Even parents cannot always tell the difference between online cartoon game content for children and the similar-looking adult content.

As a result of all of this, my participants were quite critical of their own appearances. They knew how to critique the appearances of girls and women in popular culture, and they had learned to turn these critical tools on themselves. Unfortunately, when they measured themselves against the ideal, they knew they fell short. In Angela's case (which is surely not unique), because she did not look like the unattainable ideal, when her clothing did not fit her properly, she assumed the problem was with her body—not the clothes.[3] As some participants grew older, boys' comments may have heightened the girls' insecurities about their changing bodies. Many girls I spoke with wished to become smaller in every way and modify their appearances through haircuts and highlights and "cool" clothing in a smaller size than what they currently wore. This was even an issue among tomboy-identified key interviewees, suggesting that embracing the tomboy identity alternative to the girly girl and diva discussed in Chapter Seven does not necessarily shield girls from internalizing cultural beauty ideals. At my participants' ages, they could do little to satisfy their appearance aspirations; they had little money to spend, and besides, their schools' uniform policies banned revealing girls' clothing. However, the cultural imperatives for what constitutes beauty is, within limits, constantly changing (Brumberg, 1997); these slight but elusive shifts lead to greater profits for the beauty industry as well as insecurities for girls and women, who can never get it right. By chasing elusive standards of fashion and beauty, females become trivialized; as Bordo (1995) noted, "If we are never happy with ourselves, it is implied, that is due to our female nature, not to be taken too seriously or made into a political question" (p. 253).

Given the broader cultural context, empowering girls through television content seems a Sisyphean task. Any progressive messages contained by girl power cartoons are drowned in the sea of normative femininity in which our society swims. It might have helped if girl power cartoons avoided capitulating to the norm and subverted it—not with inward intentionality but through outward action. The question is, what would such a cartoon have looked like, and could it succeed in the marketplace? Girls are indoctrinated into normative femininity from such an early age that girls may not even be willing to watch a program in which role model girls do not meet their high standards for physical appearance.

It might help if producers created more girl-centered cartoons with protagonists who are not teenagers but younger girls—more like the Powerpuffs. A study by Wardle and Watters (2004) revealed that going to school with older girls correlates with greater levels of body dissatisfaction in 9- to 11-year-old girls. They have higher incidences of body image issues, including having internalized a thinner female ideal body and perceiving themselves as more overweight than girls who attend schools with a smaller age range of students. If this is the case, the same social learning implications might apply to girls watching television programs and consuming other popular culture artifacts depicting girls older than themselves. There is no easy answer, however; aspirational viewing occurs across most segments of society, and tween girls are keen on getting a taste of teenage life—of glimpsing into their futures. However, I think this fire is largely fueled by the girl culture industry. Would girls be so eager to play at growing up if the marketplace weren't funded with countless dollars spent persuading girls to want to do so?

It seems girls negotiate girl power in the same way they negotiate the rest of our cultural environment. Dialogic theory helps make sense of this. Most problems with girl power are non-exclusive to girl power itself. For this reason, it is difficult to debate girl power cartoons' merits independently, for any girl who views them brings along biases and perspectives internalized from the broader cultural environment, with its laudatory views on the normative feminine beauty ideal. As a result, girl power cartoons' deliberate messages about not judging people based on appearance are sometimes overwhelmed by what girls bring to their viewing, making shows' progressive content misunderstood, misinterpreted, or unnoticed.

Perhaps for these reasons, my African-American participants reported the shows they preferred were not girl hero cartoons, but rather about African-American girls, typically situated in a supportive family environment. These shows featured a greater range of body types and were situated in a more realistic world than the superpower crime-fighting shows of the girl hero genre, and their racial diversity is very important.

Notes

1. A early version of part of this chapter was published in *Televizion,* as follows: Hains, R.C. (2008). Are super girls super for girls? *Televizion,* 21(E), 10–15. Published by the International Central Institute of Youth and Educational Television, Munich, Germany. It has been adapted for use here with permission.
2. The exception to this was *Totally Spies.* Unlike the other shows, its characters constantly wore new outfits. This was possible because its production company, Marathon, hired a French fashion agency to design extensive wardrobes for the characters Alex, Clover, and Sam—1,200 animated outfits in all (Burgess, 2002, p. 51). Early on, they planned to sell *Spies*-based fashion apparel to 7- to 11-year-old girls, calling it a "pivotal category" (Castleman, 2004, p. 27). Indeed, in April 2006, Kmart began selling an exclusive line of *Totally Spies* clothing for tweens and junior girls ("'Totally Spies!' line hits Kmart," 2006, p. 15).
3. Note that the mannequins in shopping malls are constructed to ridiculous proportions—e.g., 5'8" tall with 30"-23"-31" measurements, or 5' tall with 32"-23"-31" measurements, and thighs of 18" and upper arms of less than 10." Although these proportions were significantly smaller—yet taller—than the average size 14 woman in the U.S., the mannequins are said to be proportioned "so the clothes look right and fit they way they are supposed to"—suggesting that the fit is indeed more about the clothes than the wearers (Bentley, 1999, p. 210).

9

Beyond Girl Heroes[1]

Girl Power, Racism, and Power Relations

"Every single person right here is White."
—*Crystal, age 10 (African-American), referring to photographs in a cheerleading book*

"A Black man–he was Black–he was laying on the ground because he was poor. And I saw—I saw it, too—a Caucasian man, he went and *kicked* him."
—*Madison, age 9 (African-American), relating an incident she witnessed during her family's Baltimore vacation*

One sunny afternoon in May 2005, when I pulled up to Waterhaven Elementary School[2] to visit the predominantly African-American Nonprofit Aftercare Program, something was amiss. Two police cars were parked near the entrance, and the playground was deserted. Inside, all the program's children and staff were congregated in the cafeteria. Every seat was taken, so older children stood along the wall while younger ones sat on the floor. A line of African-American Aftercare employees and Euro-American police officers watched the group.

A harried-looking Aftercare employee approached me. I asked what was going on. She replied, "All the kids have to stay down here for a while. I'm sorry—you don't have to stay if you don't want to."

"I'll stay," I replied. I scanned the room and saw five girls in my group seated together in the corner near the stairs to the library. They were watching me. "Maybe I can interview them down here. Is it okay to use my camera?"

"Sure," she replied. "You can take them up to the library later, but it could be a while." Then she hurried off.

Uncertain what was happening, I approached Rhea (age 9; African-American), Bailey (age 9; African-American), Simone (age 7; African-American), Gia (age 7; African-American), Desirée (age 8; African-American) and Kiara (age 9; African-American), who seemed happy to see me. As I handed out some chocolates, Rhea said the police were there because one of the little boys had been beating up his parents—but that sounded like an unlikely rumor.

Figure 9.1: Bratz Dolls. Bratz are racially diverse, available in a range of skin tones and hair colors. Front row, left to right: Yasmin, Cloe, Jade, and Sasha. Back row: The same dolls in their original packaging. Photo by Michael Buckner/Getty Images for Distinctive Assets. Courtesy of Getty Images.
(*Full color image available at growingupwithgirlpower.com*)

Desirée's sister Roshanda (age 6; African-American), Shantel (age 7; Indian-American), and Francelle (age 6; African-American) soon asked to join us. They were originally part of our group but rarely met with us anymore: As they were the youngest girls who had signed up, our discussions tended to be over their heads.[3] I welcomed them anyway with some chocolate.

Francelle carried a pile of Bratz dolls with her. The racially diverse Bratz, created by MGA Entertainment, had overthrown Mattel's Barbie as the top-selling fashion doll. (MGA and Mattel have since engaged in multiple legal battles over alleged intellectual property theft on both sides.) Though Bratz were not girl heroes like *The Powerpuff Girls*, they fell under the girl power lifestyle brand, with their fashion-and-friends-centric Spice-Girls-style appeal. In fact, one of the many lines of Bratz dolls available was a band, the "Bratz Angelz," consisting like the Spice Girls of five members: Cloe, Jade, Sasha, Yasmin, and Roxxi.

When Francelle offered to show her dolls to everyone, I said sure and pulled out my camcorder.

> REBECCA: OK. So Francelle, today, has brought us some show-and-tell. She brought us Bratz dolls. But before she starts, some of you girls started commenting about Barbies. What did someone say—they colored their Barbie's hair? [Bailey raises her hand, indicating that it was her.] What did you do that for?
>
> BAILEY: [shrugs] I don't know. I just wanted to.
>
> RHEA: I don't like 'em. I don't like 'em. I just don't like 'em.
>
> KIARA: I hate Barbies!

The girls' reasons were many. Roshanda said Barbies "don't do enough movement." Rhea didn't like Barbies because they have a big gap "right there," in the crotch, that makes them walk funny. Gia complained Barbie's shoes come off, making them too easy to lose.

> RHEA: [sounding critical] Bratz, they take off their whole ankle and their toes and everything to take off their shoes.
>
> GIA: And they're fashionable!
>
> RHEA: They don't have Barbie kids either. They don't have Barbie kids, they don't have Barbie pillows, they don't have Barbie whatever. All those Bratz do.

At this point, our conversation was interrupted when Francelle's father, Marcus, arrived to take her home. However, she really wanted to share her Bratz dolls, so her father agreed to wait just a few minutes. When I asked her why she liked Bratz, she replied,

> FRANCELLE: I like them because you can do their hair and stuff. And you can change their outfits, like, if you want to be a fashion designer, it can help by picking out clothes and stuff.

As Francelle proceeded to explain which outfit came with which doll, Marcus interjected that she had "2,000" Bratz dolls in a large container. Francelle had many Barbies, too, but she really didn't like many of them anymore. "I may as well have a yard sale," she said, "and I'm gonna sell all the Barbies except the Barbies I like."

After Francelle and Marcus left, Gia organized an Uno game with the other girls. Then, abruptly, a policeman began addressing a large group of children, mostly young African-American boys. He spoke so that the entire room could hear, and the girls turned their attention to him. I followed their gaze. As I pointed my camera towards the officer, he said:

> POLICEMAN: . . . is mace. This is mace. [Inaudible comment.] When we deal with someone who's out of control, we are the last resort, which means we have no choice but defend. The police never lose. We can't lose. If we do, there's anarchy, and there's no [inaudible]. Now, [if] I can't grab him, then I'm gonna spray him. This stuff right here, if I spray you in the face with this, you will cry like a baby for at least a half hour. You cannot wash it off with water, you cannot wash it off with soap. The only thing that will make this stuff wear off is time. If I can't control you with this—

> UNKNOWN CHILD: A gun?

> POLICEMAN: No. Then I can control you with this [holding up a steel baton]. Now, this looks like nothing, right? [He snaps it downward; it makes a snapping noise and the baton expands in length.] But if I whack you with that—[The camera focuses back on the girls; Bailey was trying to tell me something about the reason for the police officers' visit.]

I was stunned. Here was a Caucasian police officer addressing a large group of primarily African-American children as though—to my ears—they were the future criminals of America. Some girls left our group to listen more closely. When Rhea returned, she was unsettled because the officer had shown the children his bullets. "I hope he doesn't pull out that gun, that's all I'm saying," she told me nervously.

When Kathleen, a staff member, walked by, I asked what was going on. She explained a five-year-old boy who was "out of control" had repeatedly run off of the premises, leaving Rochelle, the site director, to hold him down bodily for twenty minutes while the staff called everyone on the boy's contact list in an effort to send him home. Unable to reach his parents or other designated caretakers, they called the police.

REBECCA: Has something like this happened before?

KATHLEEN: Yeah.

REBECCA: With that boy?

KATHLEEN: No. There's other children. It's happened.

REBECCA: So, where is the boy now?

KATHLEEN: He is outside with the police.

REBECCA: They had to put him outside with—is he in, like, the cop car?

KATHLEEN [nodding]: Because Rochelle can't sit there for another twenty minutes with all the kids, you know?

REBECCA: Yeah, wow. I can't believe they had to call the cops. Are the parents gonna freak out about that?

KATHLEEN [confused]: Huh?

REBECCA: Are the parents gonna freak out?

KATHLEEN: I mean, he has problems in school here, kicking a teacher, punching boys and stuff.

Although I was surprised the Aftercare staff had called the police for a disciplinary issue, children of this age group are capable of inflicting harm on themselves and others. With the boy's parents unavailable, they had few alternatives.

In recent years, schools having police discipline children has repeatedly appeared in the news. For example, in Florida, an 8-year-old boy was arrested five times for assault. He threw a pipe at one teacher, bit another in the knee, and threw desks, chairs, and books at his peers (Holewa, 2011). His superintendent told the *Orlando Sentinel* that calling the police is a last resort: "When you have to protect the safety of children or staff and can't do so by any other means, you call for help" (Holewa, 2011, par. 11–12). Other arrests have been more controversial: In Idaho, an 8-year-old autistic girl was arrested after a "scuffle" when teachers refused to let her wear a special jacket during class (Netter, 2008), and in New York, a 12-year-old was arrested for writing "I love my friends Abby and Faith. Lex was here 2/1/10)" on a classroom desk with a green marker. CNN quoted the girl as saying, "They put the handcuffs on me, and I couldn't believe it. I didn't want [my classmates] to see me being handcuffed, thinking I'm a bad person" (Chen, 2010, para. 4). CNN also noted another child in New York had been arrested after writing "Okay" on a desk in 2007, and that in Chicago, 25 children as young as 11 were arrested during a middle school food fight.

The rise of arrests and police detentions of schoolchildren is a complex matter, with children's advocates decrying the practice (Chen, 2010, para. 7). Police intervention may sometimes be warranted, but as the pattern is relatively recent, no widely accepted guidelines exist outlining when to request police intervention. Furthermore, police officers frequently lack special training in handling children, leading to some mishandling of these cases. This seemed an issue in the officer's lecture at Nonprofit Aftercare: Were he trained in addressing children, would he have positioned them as criminals?

When I asked what prompted the officer's speech, Kathleen explained,

KATHLEEN: Nadine [another employee] was having problems [and wanted the kids to know] you've got to respect authority. You know, boys can be [inaudible] regardless of your age, and, you know, she was just talking. That's a policeman saying [inaudible] things to the kids.

REBECCA: The kids are really listening. I mean, they're rapt with attention. The girls seem kinda freaked out, though.

KATHLEEN: They think they can do whatever they want without consequences, you know?

REBECCA: Right . . .

KATHLEEN: She said, "If I was—" Nick [the boy in the police car] is five years old. Regardless of your age . . .

I wondered: Was it appropriate for Nadine to have made this request of the police? The Nonprofit Aftercare Program had its protocols for handling children endangering themselves or others. The last resort was calling the police. Changing the focus of the police officers' visit by asking for an unplanned lecture seemed ill advised. Advanced scheduling of a separate visit would have been preferable, allowing for a conversation about the lecture's desired focal points and outcomes. Instead, by independently asking the officer to address the children—while singling out the boys as troublemakers—Nadine arguably bore some responsibility for introducing the discourse of criminality into a daycare setting. In fact, although the words spoken were the officer's, not Nadine's, she stood nearby, supporting his words and authority with her stern body language and facial expressions.

While Kathleen and I spoke, Gia had abandoned the girls' Uno game to listen to the police officer speak. When she returned, she was acting strangely. As a complete non sequitur, she blurted out:

GIA: [bouncing a ball] You know me! I do the wrong thing.

REBECCA: [concerned] No, you're not wrong! You're a wonderful girl!

GIA: No, I'm not! I'm *wrong*! If you come to my house—you do not want to come with me because I'm terrible.

At the same time, Shantel began telling a detailed story about her pre-immigrant life as a little girl living in "the Indian place," where she said she helped make belts in a factory. In the factory, she said, "If you don't do the work, they whip us. They whipped big people, like, fifteen times, and they whipped me ten." One of the girls said in horror, "They should've whipped you zero times!" Shantel replied, "I was trying my best to get away, and the policemans were coming." After this, she said that she and her mom snuck on a boat and came to America, even though the police tried to stop them. Her story would have continued longer, but Kathleen, returning to earshot, was aghast. She reminded Shantel that she had cared for her since she was a toddler and that the story couldn't be true. (Later, Shantel would apologize at Kathleen's insistence, saying with embarrassment that she had been surprised to hear those words coming out of her own mouth.) Her story seemed sparked by the presence of the police officer, however, as evidenced by the role of the Indian policemen in her narrative. I interpret it as a symptom of extreme discomfort with the officer's presence and his words.

In short, on this afternoon, a group of white police officers came to Nonprofit Aftercare for a disciplinary issue. An African-American Aftercare employee who felt disrespected by her predominantly African-American young charges asked the Caucasian officers to speak to the mostly African-American children about how to "respect authority." Rochelle later told me that this year was one of her staff's most difficult in some time, for the simple reason that a majority of the children in the program were very young. They were used to dealing with a more balanced group of younger and older children.

Sadly, the officer may not have had training in this task, and although he was likely well intended, his racial biases showed through. Studies have shown that even trained police officers are influenced by a range of subconscious biases; when making split-second decisions on whether to shoot a potential criminal, they are significantly more likely to ascribe criminal intent to people of color than Caucasians (e.g., Correll, Park, Judd, and Wittenbrink, 2002; Payne 2006). Similarly, at Nonprofit Aftercare, the officer's words positioned the children as criminals. This rhetorical positioning occurred through his use of the second person in statements like "If I spray *you* in the face with this [mace], *you* will cry like a baby" and "I can control *you* with this [baton]" (emphasis added). Whether or not he meant to criminalize these children, his remarks leave one to question whether he would have addressed a group of white children in the same way.

In tandem with the officer's potential racial bias, unconscious internalized racism also may have been at play in Nadine's original request. African-American men are commonly perceived as "threatening, menacing, or overly aggressive" (Wingfield, 2007, p. 205) or as "loud and angry" (p. 206); a related stereotype is that African-American males are prone to criminal behavior (e.g., Oliver, 2003). The criminalization of black males is such a pervasive stereotype that it can easily be internalized. (For more on the nature of internalized, intra-minority group prejudice, see, for example, Perlmutter, 2002.) Unfortunately for the Nonprofit Aftercare children, there were some consequences—perhaps only short term but perhaps longer—to the discourse introduced by the police officer and, indirectly, Nadine. Gia began feeling badly about herself, declaring herself a girl who does "the wrong thing," for no good reason. Shantel, too, reacted noticeably, spinning a tall tale about enduring brutal violence, while others like Rhea just seemed uncomfortable and unsettled.

Race Relations in Social Context

The scholarly literature has documented white people's racism towards African-Americans, and indicators of racism were evident in Waterhaven, where Nonprofit Aftercare was located. Many relatively upwardly mobile African-American families had moved there in the past decade or two, escaping the major urban city nearby. Although many were not quite middle class, by comparison, their working- to lower-middle-class status was an improvement; many of their extended family still lived in the worst areas of the nearby major urban city. (During a follow-up interview in 2011, Madison reported that in the past year, her uncle and another man who was like an uncle to her—both African-American—had been shot dead in separate violent incidents in the city, where they and other family members had still resided.) Though the houses in Waterhaven were spacious and appealing, on generously sized lots, the town's property values were depressed. In 2006, single-family homes in Waterhaven started at approximately $90,000, but homes were more than twice that—$189,000—in adjacent Claret Park, where Suburban Elementary was located. Many former city dwellers could thus become first-time homeowners in Waterhaven, especially given the remarkably liberal mortgages available from the late 1990s until the housing bubble burst in approximately 2007. (Sadly, as of April of 2011, Waterhaven's county had one of the highest foreclosure rates in the entire state, with Waterhaven ranking third county-wide.)

The influx of urban African-Americans to Waterhaven prompted an exodus of white families fearful of this rapid minority population growth. (This contributed to the deflation of Waterhaven's property values.) As mentioned in Chapter Five, according to the 2000 U.S. Census, 75% of Waterhaven's residents were white and 19% were black. (For comparison, blacks comprise 12% of the total U.S. population—and at nearby Suburban Elementary School, the residents were 93% white and 2% black). Whites often view the racial segregation of their neighborhoods as "normal" and fail to perceive ways in which their isolation from racial minorities can be problematized (Bonilla-Silva and Embrick, 2007, pp. 330–331). Residential segregation usually inhibits the intermingling of whites and blacks—and the less contact they have with one another, the greater the differences they believe exist between their groups (Morris, 2005, p. 101; see also Bonilla-Silva and Embrick, 2007). When whites believe white practices and standards to be the norm, they believe any existing differences to be incorrect—circularly justifying racist and prejudiced beliefs (Bonilla-Silva, Goar, and Embrick, 2006, p. 247). Race and racial identity thereby contribute to how people organize their social experiences (Morris, 2005, p. 101)—where they are willing to live, shop, study, and so on.

Given that in predominantly white areas, the meaning of blackness to Caucasians is "lower class," "dangerous," "poor," and "exotic" (pp. 101–102)—and that many whites believe blacks to be "lazy," "welfare dependent," "receiving preferential treatment," and oversensitive to perceived racism (Bonilla-Silva and Embrick, 2007, p. 341)—the white exodus from Waterhaven can be read as a racist pursuit of continued segregation. White families also fled the public school system: Although 75% of Waterhaven's residents were Caucasian, 73% of students at Waterhaven Elementary School were African-American—a surprising inversion of the statistics. (For comparison, at Suburban Elementary, Caucasians constituted an 84% majority.) According to my study's participants, however, the faculty and principal were not African-American. Using a yearbook-style publication, I confirmed that Waterhaven's teachers, school librarian, and principal appeared to be Euro-American. The only people of color I saw employed there were janitors and lunch ladies. Therefore, the girls at Nonprofit Aftercare who attended Waterhaven Elementary (which was most, but not all of the participants) spent their days with a majority of African-American peers, taught by white women, and supervised by a white principal. African-American adults were found in lower-paying, low-prestige positions: cleaning, cooking, and child care. (An interview scheduled with the principal to discuss her perspective on the school and its place in the district was cancelled by the principal without cause.)

When staff members at Suburban Elementary learned I was also conducting research in Waterhaven, they expressed concern regarding my safety. For example, Minnie (age: mid-50s; Caucasian) had moved out of Waterhaven 34 years prior, as did many of her peers: "Everybody's moved out," she said. Her colleague Molly (age: mid-50s; Caucasian) still lived in Waterhaven, but she agreed: "Nobody wants to live around here. I wouldn't be living in Waterhaven if I had children—if my children weren't grown."

REBECCA: Why wouldn't you live in Waterhaven? Because of the schools?

MOLLY: Definitely because of the schools. And the area.

MINNIE: And that was the greatest place to grow up when I grew up there.

MOLLY: I am not a privileged person, but—

REBECCA: The houses are beautiful there.

MINNIE: Yeah. Big.

MOLLY: Until the Blacks moved in. Now, I'm not prejudiced, but it's the truth. Until they moved in and just—[she trails off]

REBECCA: What happened after they moved in? Is it that they didn't take care of the property? Or that people didn't want to live here?

MINNIE: Some do.

MOLLY: Yeah, I can't say all. That's not true. Like, the people next to me are very nice, and they're Black, and—[pause]—somebody just stole my license plate!

REBECCA: No!

MOLLY: Yes. [chuckling] Yeah, that's never happened to me before. You know what I mean?

MINNIE: But I think bad things can happen anywhere.

MOLLY: Yeah, that's true. Yeah. Yeah. [. . .]

MINNIE: I'm not afraid to go out and walk around the block at night in my neighborhood yet.

MOLLY: No, I don't. But, yeah.

REBECCA: You don't in your neighborhood? Too bad. I'm sorry to hear it's declined so much.

MOLLY: Well, yeah. I mean, you know. It's not afraid afraid, I just don't, you know—I feel like I am the minority. [chuckles] You know. And that's not a very comfortable feeling.

In this way, as the neighborhoods had changed from a predominantly white population to having a visible African-American population, some remaining white residents had become uncomfortable, including Molly and Minnie. They seemed threatened by Black people. Within particular neighborhoods, like Molly's, some remaining Caucasians had become the racial minority and presumed themselves unsafe, fearing the African-Americans could be criminals. Unfortunately, this belief has racist roots; when Molly asserted that she is "not prejudiced, but . . ." she was employing a strategy common among whites who wish to deflect potential charges of racism when they express racist beliefs (Bonilla-Silva, 2002, pp. 46–50). This sheds some light on Waterhaven's racial dynamics: People strive to act and speak in "color-blind" ways (p. 46), but racism is often just below the surface.

Molly's comment that she would not live in Waterford if her children were still young was reflected more broadly in Waterhaven. Because white families seemed to fear for their children's education and safety within the public schools, the private (especially parochial) schools in the area thrived. Meanwhile, Waterhaven's underfunded school district struggled (likely another factor in the town's lower property values, as families seeking a better-ranked school district would look elsewhere if they could afford to.) Waterhaven students scored well below average on statewide standardized tests; in 2001, Waterhaven was in the bottom 15th percentile of elementary schools statewide and in its county, where it was ranked 56th out of 66 elementary schools. (In contrast, Suburban Elementary was in the top 25% statewide and was ranked 23rd in the same county.)

Tayshaun (age 25, African-American), a Waterhaven Elementary janitor, and Hailey (age 26, African-American), a Nonprofit Aftercare employee, shared their insights about this pattern. They had grown up together in Waterhaven and were graduates of its public school system. Hailey felt the quality of education in the district, which encompassed several adjacent towns, varied, and both lamented the absence of financially comfortable families in the school system. They believed anyone who could afford to send their children elsewhere did so.

> TAYSHAUN: I would say even a lot of the Black families, like just because of the way this district is, like, they try and send their kids to private school, too. And it's just, it's unfortunate that a lot of them can't afford to do it, but the education—I mean, it's OK, it really fluctuates between schools. Like, it really depends on *what* school. This school [Waterhaven Elementary] is OK. Certain other schools aren't as good, education-wise.

> HAILEY: District's not a bad district, it just needs some help.

TAYSHAUN: The big problem's financial.

HAILEY: Yeah. I think if the parents who send their kids to private school sent their kids to this district, it would probably make a big difference, just because the parent-teacher interaction would be there. You know what I mean? People who actually—these people who send their kids to private school—they go to the school all the time.

In other words, middle-class families who might have worked to improve the public schools were instead supporting private schools. Scholars studying the social construction of race have critiqued the ways in which race is about "inclusion and exclusion," involving selective distributions of power that generate "particular patterns of stratification" (Lewis, 2003, p. 285). In Waterhaven, the power distributions and stratification patterns in children's schooling were clear: White families withdrew their children from public schools and redirected their resources to exclusive private schools. Paying tuition for these private educations, they would never vote to raise property taxes to benefit the school system. Despite these facts, white administrators and teachers remained in charge, perhaps reflecting a time when the student body had looked like them. Although Caucasian families wanted little to do with Waterhaven's school district, their very absence indicated their privilege and power.

Rochelle, director of the Nonprofit Aftercare, explained she often felt like Waterhaven was an inner-city school system. An African-American woman in her early 30s, Rochelle's family had moved to Waterhaven from the nearby major urban city. (She and her sister jointly owned a Waterhaven home.) Enrolled in college to become a K-12 teacher, she was student-teaching in the city. This informed her perspective on Waterhaven:

ROCHELLE: This school district [in Waterhaven] is like the inner city, because most of the kids, or most of the families, have come out of the city. And even the parents of the new kids that started the program, a lot of them have moved from the [major urban city] area. You know, I'm dealing with educated parents here and everything else. But if you came from the inner city, it's still that type of mentality. You gotta work hard to maintain to live out here [. . .] and they don't check their children's homework. I check children's homework—kindergarten—you know—and you can tell that the parent didn't check it, and the Afterschool program did it with them. Or they might have not done the homework for three days because their parent didn't check their folder. Why? Because mom is work-

> ing or in school. So, it's still the same. I don't judge the parents or
> anything like that; it's just a struggle, and you have to work to main-
> tain to live out here, to pay your mortgage and get the nice car and,
> you know, have your child fit in. Whereas, uh, in the inner city, you
> have to, you know, work hard to, you know, maintain to put food
> on your table, and you gotta do what you have to do; and, at the
> same time, the children suffer. It's just a struggle all the way around.

Whether families stayed in the city or moved to Waterhaven, they still struggled—but at least in Waterhaven, they had more hope of positive outcomes for their
families. Despite the town's problems, life was safer and better than it had been in
the city.

At Waterhaven Elementary, the children often struggled, feeling misunderstood
by teachers and the principal—especially regarding disciplinary issues. Considering
that many people in Waterhaven, from police officers to middle-aged white women,
perceived African-Americans as potentially threatening, it is unsurprising the girls
felt misunderstood. Unfortunately, they had not a single African-American teacher
or administrator at Waterhaven Elementary to turn to. However, even supervision
by African-American caretakers is no guarantee that children will be protected from
racist discourse: Well-intentioned though she was, during the police visit, Nadine
provided an opening for apparent racism at Nonprofit Aftercare. All these variables
can be understood to have shaped the psyches of the girls in my study, as well as
their peers.

Race Representations in the Media

White people's prejudices against African-Americans reflect assumptions about race
that permeate broader society and, therefore, the mainstream media. On television,
people of color have been stereotyped as criminals and terrorists—at least when
they're not stereotyped as naturally athletic (e.g., Baptista-Fernandez & Greenberg,
1980; Bristor et al., 1995; Zinkhan et al., 1990). Furthermore, people of color have
been marginalized in either non-speaking or passive roles (Riffe et al., 1989; Taylor
et al., 1995; Wilkes & Valencia, 1989; Seiter, 1990). When depicted in professional roles, people of color have been depicted as lacking professionalism and inferi-
or to whites in comparable positions (Hunt, 2005, p. 270). Overall, people of color
have represented significantly less of the television population (Larson, 2002, pp.
224–5) than the 18% of the U.S. population they constituted during the 2000 U.S.
Census. Meanwhile, among television's directors, white males have been significant-

ly overrepresented. They composed about 34% of the U.S. population in 2000, but "accounted for 80 percent of the television directors from the top 40 shows in the 2000–2001 season" (Hunt, 2005). Only 6% were minorities, and their percentage among television's writers was not much better: only 9% in 2001 (Hunt, 2005). This explains television's traditionally white, male perspective on the world, rife with racial and gender biases.

More positive depictions of people of color have appeared on programs spearheaded and written by racial minorities. For example, UPN—one of the least-watched networks—has generally offered a higher number of black-oriented sitcoms; UPN's writers were 30% black in 2001. (All the other networks had 8% or fewer black writers.) The more positive depictions of people of color have tended to be found within predominantly African-American casts, frequently "ghettoized" on less-popular networks within specific time slots (Hunt, 2005, p. 271). Some of these shows—beginning with *The Cosby Show* (1984–1992)—have depicted a parallel world in which racial politics are not an issue. By depicting a vision of successful integration, "issues of racism seem secondary to mainstream quests for middle-class status based on merit and competition" (Matabane, 2005, p. 71). Different audience members interpreted these positive depictions in different ways, however. For example, on *The Cosby Show*, while "black viewers tended to embrace the show for the 'positive' portrayals of blackness Cosby strived to create," many white viewers "absolved themselves of responsibility for racial inequality in the United States in exchange for welcoming the affluent black family into their living rooms every Thursday night" (Hunt, 2005, pp. 14–15; see also Jhally & Lewis, 1992). Hunt (2005) therefore called for moving beyond regarding black characters as "positive" or "negative" representations, as these terms mean "very little in isolation" (p. 15).

Some studies of audience members have supported the idea that calling representations "positive" or "negative" can be meaningless; context is everything. In a meta-analysis, Matabane (2005) noted that television's positive depictions of black people have increased, blacks who heavily viewed television tended to believe more strongly in this integration myth than did lighter viewers (p. 67). This had potentially negative long-term consequences: "The illusion of well-being among the oppressed may lead to reduced political activity and less demand for social justice and equality" (p. 71).

Children's programs have reflected these patterns of representation. For example, while Hispanics comprised 12.6% of the population in the 2000 U.S. census, in the 30 most popular preschool programs in the late 1990s, only 6% of characters were Hispanic (Borzekowski & Poussaint, 1998). Children's programs have too often cast Whites as the good guys, depicting people of color and heavily accent-ed English speakers as villains (Calvert, Huston, & Wright, 1987; Huston et al., 1992). More positive depictions have often been concentrated by race within indi-vidual children's shows rather than integrated into diverse casts—limiting the number of interracial friendships and relationships portrayed (Weigel and Howes, 1982). Studies have documented the same trends in children's television commer-cials, and while advertisements' depictions of people of color have improved on some variables, progress has been uneven. (E.g., see Atkin & Heald, 1977; Bang & Reece, 2003; Barcus, 1977; Bramlett-Solomon & Roeder, 2008; Bristor, Lee, & Hunt, 1995; Henderson & Baldasty, 2003; Larson, 2002; Licata & Biswas, 1993; Li-Vollmer, 2002; Merskin, 2002; Riffe, Goldson, Saxton, & Yu, 1989; Seiter, 1986; Taylor & Stern, 1997).

Research indicates that television shapes young people's beliefs about race and ethnicity, both their own and others' (Graves, 1993). Some may internalize racism—not unlike Gia's heartbreaking claim that she always does "the wrong thing" and is "terrible." As Tobin's (2000) ethnographic study of the intersection of childhood, race, and media reception reminds us, children's individual under-standings of the media's depictions of different races depend on their communi-ties' dynamics (p. 58). For example, whether a child is part of a racial minority or majority can lead him or her to very different interpretations of on-screen racism than other members of the same minority group have.

Although all girls face issues of gender stereotyping and marginalization in the media, white children do not risk developing negative self-concepts about their race. A range of white characters are portrayed on television; in the U.S. and many other nations, white people dominate the small screen. This is a basic manifestation of white privilege: White people, in general, can expect to read books about people who look like them; be taught by people who look like them; regularly encounter leaders and law enforcement officials who look like them; and to see people like themselves depicted in appealing ways on television. (E.g., see Rothenberg, 2012.)

Race Representations in Girl Hero Cartoons

Girl hero cartoons reflected the broader television environment's problematic depictions of race. While some shows like *Dora the Explorer* and *That's So Raven* provided positive depictions of Latinas and African-American girls, most girl hero cartoons failed in this area, primarily telling white girls' stories. As Table 9.1 illus-trates, of the 14 cartoon girl heroes, 10 (72%) were white—including Jenny, the teenage robot, who when wearing her human exoskin presented as a red-headed Caucasian girl. Of the remaining four heroes, one (Alex on *Totally Spies*) was ambiguous—of indeterminate race or ethnicity. Alex spoke without an accent, but her dark hair and tan skin tone rendered her open to interpretation. Some viewers believed her to be a Caucasian character, while others did not. For example, at the Township Public Library group, while Crystal (African-American, age 10) and Franceska (African-American, age 11) asserted Alex was black, Chyna (African-American, age 11) suggested, "I think she's Puerto Rican." Abby (Euro-American, age 10) said, "I think she's an Asian person." Zoë (Euro-American, age 10) wasn't sure of Alex's race, but responding to Abby, she said, "I don't really think she's Chinese, 'cause most Chinese people are white." (To this, Abby replied, "But there—there are some tan ones.") Elizabeth (Euro-American, age 10) suggested Alex was "mixed," while Ellie (Euro-American, age 10) believed Alex was white but "tanned."

The remaining three characters were black, Asian, and Latina, all from a single show, *W.I.T.C.H.* (see Table 9.1). Their depictions were generally positive and well rounded. For example, Taranee, the African-American character, enjoyed basketball, classical music, photography, and math, countering stereotypes about African-American youth.

Table 9.1: Races Represented by the Cartoon Girl Heroes

	White	Black	Asian	Latina	Native American	Ambiguous	TOTAL
Atomic Betty	1	0	0	0	0	0	
Kim Possible	1	0	0	0	0	0	
Powerpuff Girls	3	0	0	0	0	0	
*Teenage Robot**	1	0	0	0	0	0	
Totally Spies	2	0	0	0	0	1	
W.I.T.C.H.	2	1	1	1	0	0	
Frequency	10	1	1	1	0	1	14
Percentage	71.43	7.14	7.14	7.14	0	7.14	100

* When Jenny, the teenage robot, wore an exoskin that made her appear human, she looked like a red-headed Caucasian girl. Her cartoon inventor/mother was also Caucasian.

W.I.T.C.H. was the last girl hero cartoon to debut and had the shortest run, airing 52 episodes in only two seasons (2005–2006). The others ran from three to six seasons (see Table 9.2), and only *My Life as a Teenage Robot* produced fewer episodes than *W.I.T.C.H.* Therefore, many audience members may have viewed *W.I.T.C.H.* less frequently and over a shorter period of time than other shows in the genre.

Table 9.2: Girl Hero Cartoon Statistics

	Years Aired	# of Seasons Produced	# of Episodes Produced
Atomic Betty	2004–2008	3	79
Kim Possible	2002–2007	4	87
Powerpuff Girls	1998–2004	6	78
Teenage Robot	2003–2009	3	40
Totally Spies	2002–2007	5	130
W.I.T.C.H.	2005–2006	2	52
Average		3.83	77.67

With cartoon girls of color underrepresented on children's television, some white, middle-class girls found it difficult to relate to the girls of color in *W.I.T.C.H.* and criticized their deviance from white beauty ideals. For example, after we screened the first episode of *W.I.T.C.H.* together, Kylie (age 8) and Zoë (age 8) commented that they liked "everybody's" hair, "except for that one girl"—Taranee, the African-American character. Taranee wore her hair cropped short around her face with one long side braid, and when using her superpowers, her hair changed, featuring six longer, skinny braids. (See Figure 4.7 in Chapter Four.) Neither Kylie nor Zoë liked Taranee's everyday haircut, and Zoë disliked her superpowered hairstyle as well:

KYLIE: I just don't like her hair because she got it, like, cut right here [indicating around her face], and then she got one, like, braid down there.

ZOË: That's when her hair got, like three, like, a spider [she indicates hair coming down from the top of her head with both hands]—

KYLE: I like her witch hair better.

REBECCA: So you like that.

KYLIE: I like her witch hair better.

ZOË: Yeah, that looks much better.

KYLIE: It looks much better because I don't like the, um, short hair on the top, and right here [she talks about the braid and indicates it with her hands and hair]—

ZOË: Yeah, and then a little weird. It just looks weird kinda. It doesn't make you look, like, kinda like—if she was here, and she was a kid now, they probably wouldn't let her wear it like that.

REBECCA: Who wouldn't let her?

ZOË: The principal.

ANGELA: [at the same time] The principal, the whole school—

REBECCA: Oh.

ANGELA: The other kids would probably, they would probably be her friend if she had, like, longer hair, like, down, and then, like [inaudible word]—ten braids, whatever!

Zoë and Angela (age 8) could not understand Taranee's African-American hairstyles. They thought such hairstyles would be forbidden at their primarily Caucasian school, because they looked strange to them. Angela's next comment about Cornelia—a character with long, straight, flowing blonde hair—drove home the relationship between these feelings and normative white beauty ideals.

ANGELA: I think they all look weird except for Courtney [meaning Cornelia] because their hair's weird. It's like they dyed it, but then they put the shampoo in it and it made it, like, more colorful.

REBECCA: So, but Courtney's hair is OK.

ANGELA: Yeah.

KYLIE: Courtney's the only normal hair.

This underscores that there was an undercurrent of racial bias in the girls' assessment of the characters on *W.I.T.C.H.* The only girl whose hair they perceived to be "normal" was the Caucasian girl whose hair was a Barbie-like ideal. The others—the redhead with the chin-length hair, the African-American character, the Asian character, and the Latina character—had "weird" and off-putting hair, especially Taranee.

Table 9.3: Races Represented by the Cartoon Girl Heroes, Except *W.I.T.C.H.*

	White	Black	Asian	Latina	Native American	Ambiguous	TOTAL
Atomic Betty	1	0	0	0	0	0	
Kim Possible	1	0	0	0	0	1	
Powerpuff Girls	3	0	0	0	0	0	
Teenage Robot	1	0	0	0	0	0	
Totally Spies	2	0	0	0	0	0	
Frequency	8	0	0	0	0	1	9
Percentage	88.89	0	0	0	0	11.11	100

In the other five shows, not including *W.I.T.C.H.*, nearly 89% of girl heroes were Caucasian (see Table 9.3). With Alex's race ambiguous, viewers could interpret all remaining (non-*W.I.T.C.H.*) girl heroes—whose shows generally ran longer and featured more episodes—as Caucasian. The shows arguably presented a white, middle-class perspective on girl power and empowerment then. How did girls outside this demographic engage with these programs?

Within my own study, the African-American girls enjoyed the cartoons well enough. They felt, however, that some had racist undertones—such as *The Powerpuff Girls*, in which villains were sometimes people of color. One day, I asked the focus group members at the Township Public Library to think about what races were represented in the various cartoons. The Township Public Library group was constructed of volunteers from several neighboring towns, with four African-American girls, one Indian-American girl, and six Euro-American girls. (Two Euro-American girls, Kylie and Zoë, had been participants at Suburban Elementary.) In response to my question about race representation, Crystal (African-American, age 10) and Franceska (African-American, age 11) pointed out:

REBECCA: What about *The Powerpuff Girls?*

CRYSTAL: Powerpuff Girls—

FRANCESKA: We don't know.

CRYSTAL: No, not really.

FRANCESKA: Except for that Black person stealing a bank.

REBECCA: There's a Black man stealing from a bank?

CRYSTAL: Yeah, the bill robbers. Some of them are Black.

REBECCA: [with light sarcasm] Oh, *that's* nice.

In consequence, although *The Powerpuff Girls* is about empowered kindergarten girls working together to fight crime and save the world, another reading is possible: That it is about a group of little white girls who work with white authorities to fight crimes perpetuated by people of color and other marginalized individuals. This has been an issue in the broader girl hero genre; for example, regarding *Buffy the Vampire Slayer*, Ono (2000) noted that many characters of color died or failed to reappear on the show, and of the dead, a substantial number were vampires who Buffy—the white, blonde protagonist of the show—defeated violently. Ono wrote, "The question I would ask is, 'To whom is girl power directed?' This study of *Buffy* answers, 'Predominantly, people of color'" (p. 179). The idea that girl power empowers white girls to engage in on-screen violence against people of color is disturbing indeed.

The girls in my studies recognized, however, that other girl hero cartoons depicted race better than *The Powerpuff Girls* did. Some of the minor recurring characters on Nickelodeon's *My Life as a Teenage Robot* were girls of color, and on Disney's *Kim Possible*, Kim's close friend Monique (voiced by Raven-Symoné)—a popular secondary character—was African-American. They also debated Bonnie's racial identity. Like Alex in *Totally Spies*, Bonnie—Kim's high school nemesis, a mean cheerleader—had dark hair and skin that was not as pale or pink-hued as her girl hero counterparts. This made Bonnie's race seem strategically ambiguous (see Eisenberg, 2007), allowing viewers to read the character as a member of various ethnic or racial groups. At the Township Public Library, this led to a few heated discussions. The African-American girls insisted Bonnie was Black; the Indian-American girl thought Bonnie was white; and the Caucasian girls in attendance believed Bonnie was mixed.

CRYSTAL: Bonnie's Black.

ABBY: (Caucasian, age 10): Mostly Black, but a little White.

FRANCESKA: [to Abby]: Bonnie's not White. Bonnie is Black. Bonnie's not Caucasian—please use the proper language.

CRYSTAL: Whatever!

FRANCESKA: Bonnie's not Caucasian; she is African-American.

CRYSTAL: Yes, she is.

JEWEL: (Indian-American, age 11): No, she's not.

CRYSTAL: Bonnie—

FRANCESKA: Bonnie, impossible.

JEWEL: No, she isn't. [She stands up and walks away.]

CRYSTAL: The mean cheerleader. She's Black.

JEWEL: [from across the room]: No, she *isn't.*

FRANCESKA: Jewel, Bonnie's—

ABBY: She's mixed!

CRYSTAL: She is not mixed.

JEWEL: Bonnie is—she's *not even mixed.*

REBECCA: I don't want you girls to get in a fight with everybody, because sometimes people see things different ways, and it's OK.

FRANCESKA: Don't—look. Bonnie—she has black hair, and her—her, um— [Several girls begin talking at once.]

REBECCA: Let her finish, and then it's your turn.

FRANCESKA: When they go to—when Kim Possible—when they were stuck, they went to, um, Bonnie's house. And—her sister's. But, her sister—those are not her real sisters. Bonnie—Bonnie—they—she looks like she's White, but she's not. She's actually Black.

(In the episode in question, Bonnie's sister Connie—who has light brown hair and dresses in a preppy style—is presented as the brains in the family; Lonnie, who has blonde hair and blue eyes, dresses more revealingly and is positioned as the beauty. By saying Lonnie and Connie are not Bonnie's real sisters, I interpret Franceska's comment as suggesting that Bonnie was adopted into a white family.)

REBECCA: So, you think Bonnie is a light-skinned Black person?

FRANCESKA: Yes.

CRYSTAL: [concurrently] Yes. Like my mom. Like, my mom's really, really, really light.

REBECCA: Wow. See, you know what? I have to say that I thought Bonnie was White, but I could just not be seeing things the same way.

UNKNOWN: Wait. Which one's Bonnie?

REBECCA: Bonnie's the mean cheerleader. In *Kim Possible*, right?

ELIZABETH (Caucasian, age 10): Bonnie's the one with the brown, jagged hair.

CRYSTAL: Yes, she's Black.

REBECCA: It's dark hair.

CRYSTAL: Not all—not all, um, not all people with brown hair are White. My sister, she's Black and she has brown hair.

REBECCA: You make a good point, because there are a lot of shades of Black. Like, it's not, like, Black and White at two extremes. Is that a fair way to say it? [Crystal nods her head.] So, Elizabeth, why did you think Bonnie was White?

ELIZABETH: Well, I'm thinking, not exactly that she's White, the extreme, but she's not Black the extreme.

FRANCESKA: She's *not* mixed. Some kids look like they're mixed. I asked—my friend, she—she's Black, and I asked her if she's mixed, and she said no, she's not mixed. She's only mixed with Indian and, um, and something else. She's not White.

REBECCA: Well, so, like, being mixed Indian and Black isn't the same as being mixed, like, Black and White?

FRANCESKA: Yeah.

REBECCA: Jewel, what did you think? Do you have an opinion on—

JEWEL: I don't think she's Black because, um, cuz when you's at her sister's, you could tell that it's not really her sister.

REBECCA: Hmm.

JEWEL: And, I thought she was White because, um, she act like it, too. [giggles]

As this conversation illustrates, girls with different backgrounds read different visual cues regarding cartoon characters' races. At Township Public Library, the white girls saw markers in Bonnie's physical appearance—her dark brown hair and her tan skin—as indicators of mixed race. Although I don't know what Jewel meant about Bonnie's sisters, her concluding comment suggested she read Bonnie's behavior as an important racial identity consideration.

The girls at the Nonprofit Aftercare Program took a different perspective on Bonnie. Although like Franceska and Crystal they believed some visual cues indicated Bonnie was black, they thought Bonnie was of mixed racial heritage. Rhea explained:

RHEA: See, I think that Bonnie is mixed because she's played by a White person. Sometimes White people talk differently from Black people, right? And she's Black. That's why. And she's, like, mixed, with, um, with the—she's Black color.

In this way, Rhea's interest in the actresses who voiced her favorite characters informed her interpretation. Although Bonnie looked Black, she talked "white," like the actress who voiced her—leading Rhea to conclude that Bonnie was mixed. (Her friends agreed with this assessment.)

Race Representation: Broader Patterns in Girls' Media Culture

Although some girl hero cartoons featured a few girls of color or girls of ambiguous race, the overall pattern was underrepresentation. At Township Public Library and Nonprofit Aftercare sites, the African-American girls noted this reflected a broader pattern.

> REBECCA: Do you think that television that kids watch today is diverse enough, meaning enough people of different races and skin colors?
>
> [Several talk at once, particularly Franceska and Crystal.]
>
> CRYSTAL: Most people in shows—they're White.
>
> FRANCESKA: Yeah, I think that, um, every time I see a show, I see White people, and there's—at least there's only one Black person. So, I think that's kind of racial.

When I agreed that most programs we'd watched primarily featured white people, Crystal pulled a library book out of her book bag pointedly. She was interested in becoming a cheerleader and upon taking cheerleading books out of the library, she had noticed that they were dominated by photos of white girls.

> CRYSTAL: Like here. [Flipping through a cheerleading book on her lap and pointing to a page.] Every single person right here is White.
>
> REBECCA: [looking at the book] Wow, those are all White cheerleaders in that, huh?
>
> CRYSTAL: Yeah. But there's, like, some Black—[inaudible comment because Franceska begins talking].
>
> FRANCESKA: But they give her some respect.
>
> REBECCA: [looking at the book] Oh, so they have one in the center of that [inaudible comment]—
>
> CRYSTAL: In there. And, you know where that thing that we were doing? The cheer? [She flips some more pages.] There is a Black girl. And almost all of them were Black right here.

REBECCA: Right. So, you think that what we've been watching, there's enough diversity that—

FRANCESKA: Can you tell us again what that word is?

REBECCA: Diversity means—I'm sorry. Diversity means people of different, like, races and skin colors.

UNKNOWN: Nope.

REBECCA: Like, if we say something's diverse, that means you're seeing a nice mix-up between White people, Black people, Asian people, maybe.

CRYSTAL: In *some* shows, mostly.

In this way, they spoke to the pattern underscored by the scholarly literature on representation in the media. People who looked like these girls were negated across media: included on a token level, portrayed in negative ways, or not included at all.

Similar to the African-American girls at Township Library, the Nonprofit Aftercare girls felt the broader cultural environment depicted fewer African-American characters than it should have. Like Crystal, Madison brought books into our conversation to illustrate her point; because we met in her school's library, she simply pulled familiar examples from the stack.

MADISON: OK. You can tell, all of these Barbie books are [puts them on the table one by one]—

BAILEY: White. I read that one.

MADISON: —*all*—

BAILEY: Read that one.

MADISON: —*White.*

REBECCA: Why are they all White?

MADISON: [still putting books down] All—*all*—

REBECCA: Is that one Black? Maybe?

DESIRÉE: Yeah, *this* girl is Black, but she's [inaudible].

RHEA: She's *purple!*

MADISON: It's an alien!

ZAYONNA: I'm sorry, but she's ugly.

UNKNOWN: Barbie's ugly.

The girls were appalled: The only black Barbie depicted had purple-hued skin, leading some to reject Barbie with a simple, "she's ugly." (Note that misrepresented skin tones had been a concern for the girls in relation to other licensed properties, as well. For example, Bailey once lamented that her Proud Family beach towel depicted their skin tones incorrectly. "On the towels, they make them look really dark," she had said sadly.)

After the general commotion regarding purple Barbie died down, I asked, "So, why are all those Barbie books featuring White Barbies?" Rhea replied, "They normally just show White Barbies, like, the main character." In other words, although all Barbies are supposedly Barbie, the girls realized a hierarchy existed. Black Barbie was not the same as white Barbie. White Barbie was "the main character"—just like whites were the main characters in most girl hero cartoons, with other races made secondary characters. Indeed, as Rand (1998) noted, when Mattel began presenting multicultural Barbie dolls, they never "boot[ed] blond, white Barbie from center stage" (p. 391). Rhea also made this connection in the way Barbies were advertised in children's television commercials:

> RHEA: Sometimes when they show Barbie dolls and everything, they always put the white dolls—they always put the white Barbie dolls—
>
> MADISON: In the front!
>
> RHEA: I know!

Adding insult to injury, when the girls shopped for Barbies, they could never find black Barbies wearing nice fashions. White Barbies' clothes were better, resonating with DuCille's (1994) argument that many multicultural Barbies from the 1980s were basically white Barbies, "modified only by a dash of color [darker skin] and a change of costume" (p. 51).

> RHEA: Like, some people—and for the black Barbie dolls, they give 'em, like, orange and everything before the white, and next one, they give her, like, pink and blue or something. A lot of black people hate orange!
>
> REBECCA: Wait. So, like, when you go to the store and you buy them off the shelves, are they wearing the different clothes that you don't like?
>
> RHEA: I don't buy them no more, but now—
>
> MADISON: I buy Bratz dolls because all of them—all the Bratz dolls are treated right.
>
> SIMONE AND DESIRÉE: Yeah!

While Barbie had fallen from favor with many girls—for example, Megan (Euro-American, age 9) was "embarrassed" to play with them because they were for younger children, while Angela and her sister Jeannine liked dismembering their Barbies—these African-American girls abandoned Barbie to take a stance. In comparison to White Barbies, Black Barbies were presented inferiorly. Black Barbies were "othered"; Black Bratz were normal—dressed as fashionably as other Bratz. Perhaps this was why Kiara (African-American, age 9) passionately rejected the Mattel brand one day, exclaiming, "I *hate* Barbies!"

Given the media's obvious underrepresentation of girls of color, most African-American girls in my study preferred television programs centered on African-American girls. This preference strengthened with time. When I asked during our second set of meetings how often the Nonprofit Aftercare girls watched girl hero cartoons at home, Rhea replied, "I don't normally watch these kinds of shows, and—[pause] I prefer shows that I normally watch." Previously, however, she had been a regular *Kim Possible* viewer. The shows she and the others preferred included *That's So Raven* (2003–2007, The Disney Channel)—Rhea's absolute favorite; *The Proud Family* (2001–2007, The Disney Channel); and *Sister, Sister* (1994–1995, ABC), which all featured African-American girls in the leading roles. The other girls (but not Rhea) were also partial to *Bratz*, which featured diverse characters based on the dolls. They also liked the sitcom *Full House* (1987–1995, ABC), which focused on a Caucasian family headed by a single father. Although *Full House* was older than they were, nearly all the girls at Nonprofit Aftercare, the Township Library, and Suburban Elementary alike watched it on a daily basis in reruns. Most explained they loved its inclusion of the popular Olsen twins during their adorable toddler years—and some also found the girls' Uncle Jesse "cute."

This meant the African-American cohorts in my study preferred television programs with two fundamental characteristics: happy families (*Raven, Proud Family, Sister, Sister,* and *Full House*), and African-American (*Raven, Proud Family, Sister Sister*) and racially diverse (*Bratz*) casts. The settings were everyday, resembling real life, as opposed to the fantasy worlds within which girl hero cartoons like *The Powerpuff Girls* and *W.I.T.C.H.* existed.

Of these shows, three—*Raven, Proud Family,* and *Bratz*—clearly fell under girl power's umbrella, debuting in the Spice Girls' aftermath. Among the late 1990s and early 2000s shows focused on smart, active girls, they presented a number of black subjects, with different experiences, personalities, and ways of negotiating their worlds. As Gray (2005) stated of prime-time programming about African-Americans, such as *The Cosby Show* (NBC, 1984–1992), *A Different World* (NBC, 1987–1993), and *In Living Color* (Fox, 1990–1994), these shows presented "complex, even contradictory, perspectives and representations of black life in America. The guiding sensibility is neither integrationist nor pluralist [. . .]. [T]hese Black Subjects are not so total and monolithic that they become THE BLACK SUB-JECT" (p. 169). Overall, the shows about African-American girls did the same.

Figure 9.2: *That's So Raven.* Raven-Symoné as Raven Baxter of Disney's *That's So Raven.* ©The Disney Channel. Courtesy of PhotoFest.

The *Bratz* cartoon (Fox, 2005–2007) debuted in September 2005, between my two semester-long fieldwork sessions at Nonprofit Aftercare. The first session ran from February to May 2005; the second, from February to May 2006. As discussed in Chapter Five, when I returned to Nonprofit Aftercare, Gia and Simone had changed aftercare programs, so a new girl, Zayonna, joined us.

Figure 9.3: *Bratz*, the animated television show. From left to right: Jade, Sasha, Cloe, and Yasmin. Courtesy of PhotoFest.

Bratz was popular with everyone in this cohort except Rhea. They asked if I would please record *Bratz* on Saturday mornings so they could watch it together. As I was interested in broadening our discussions beyond girl hero cartoons, I had been letting the girls select what we would screen together, so I agreed. I suggested that I could bring a video of the cartoon, and they could bring their favorite Bratz dolls. "We'll do show and tell," I promised. Everyone except Rhea agreed; she wanted no part of it. ("Those Bratz dolls are creepy," she complained.)

Show and Tell: Bratz Dolls and the Importance of Racial Diversity

When our Bratz show-and-tell day arrived, Zayonna, Bailey, Desirée, and Madison were excited to watch Bratz and show me their favorite dolls. I handed my camcorder over, letting them take control of what was being filmed, as I had been doing for some time; this practice added a more collaborative feel to our time together, giving the girls more control. After Rhea left, I asked, "Why don't you give a tour of the Bratz to the camera? Tell them—tell the camera all about them." Desirée took the camcorder and focused on Zayonna (age 10, African-American), who owned most of the dolls.

> ZAYONNA [pointing out each doll and its name]: This [male Bratz doll] is Cameron. This [light-skinned blonde doll] is Cloe. This [small, light-skinned blonde-haired doll] is the baby. That's Sasha [a dark-skinned doll]. That's Felicia [the darker-skinned doll]. Now, Sasha's about to hold the camera—before she goes on a heart attack.
>
> BAILEY (age 10)/FELICIA: [in a different voice] Don't look at me, I'm not beautiful.
>
> ZAYONNA/CLOE: [again in a different voice] You're beautiful in your own way, Felicia. I want a hug!
>
> DESIRÉE (age 9)/SASHA: Hi. My name is Sasha. I'm the cutest one of the Bratz.
>
> ZAYONNA/CLOE: I know. Aren't you?
>
> UNKNOWN: No, she didn't!
>
> ZAYONNA [holding darkest-skinned doll with braided hair]: That's her sister [indicating Felicia]. That's her sister.
>
> DESIRÉE/SASHA: And don't you like my outfit? This is my sister. I know she's a little powerful, but that's OK. Hello, Felicia. Hi! This is—
>
> ZAYONNA: Cameron.
>
> DESIRÉE/SASHA: Cameron.
>
> ZAYONNA/CAMERON: Mwah! [Cameron kisses Felicia.] Smack! [The dolls keep kissing.]
>
> DESIRÉE/SASHA: He's the only boy out of the Bratz. And, OK, I don't wanna see that! [Cameron and Felicia are still kissing.] [The girls laugh.]

In this way, the girls began by both showing and playing with the dolls—speaking for them and having them act out their imagined relationships. This play behavior embodied critics' usual concerns about the Bratz brand: physical appearance ("I'm not beautiful" and "I'm the cutest lot of the Bratz") and mildly racy play (as in Sasha and Cameron's extended make-out session).

When Bailey voiced the darkest-skinned Bratz doll as saying "Don't look at me, I'm ugly" while Zayonna's Caucasian doll insisted that she was "beautiful in her own way"—perhaps meaning she was unaligned with dominant White beauty ideals—Durham's (1999) reflections on her childhood beliefs about race and beauty came to mind. Durham recalled that as an Indian girl being raised in Canada, she remembered

> believing unquestioningly that I was ugly, and knowing with absolute certainty that I would never play 'the princess' in our grade-school plays because of the way I looked. [. . .] We all understood that princesses looked like Barbie; princesses looked like Marcia Brady; princesses looked like my blonde, blue-eyed friends Connie and Lynne. Any girl who looked like me could not be pretty, was in fact the polar opposite of pretty, simply by reason of her coloring. (p. 196)

This moment in the girls' Bratz play passed quickly, however, and different girls lead the conversation. They had become skilled at asking each other the kinds of questions and follow-up questions that I normally asked.

Desirée asked, "What do you think about these Bratz?" to which Zayonna replied, "They're so cool!" When Bailey replied, "Oh, they're so cute," Desirée probed, "What else?" Bailey said, "They have nice hair," continuing to focus on the Bratz dolls' appearance. As Levin and Kilbourne (2008) have argued, Bratz dolls are "highly structured toys" that "keep children's play focused on the theme suggested by the structure of the toy, thereby creating an unhealthy emphasis on their play on sexy appearance (p. 103). (In fact, Bratz were one of the products that the American Psychological Association (2007) singled out as contributing to an unhealthy sexualization of girls in the U.S.) As the girls' conversation continued, it was unsurprising that this emphasis recurred.

DESIRÉE: Madison, interview me. Come on! Come over here!

MADISON (age 9): OK. [Narrating for the camera:] This is Desirée. She has Sasha.

ZAYONNA [teasing Madison playfully]: Madison looks cross-eyed.

MADISON: Shh!

DESIRÉE: When I think of the Bratz, it's because they're so cool because I like their clothes. And their hair is so cool because you can do it and stuff, and give them makeovers. [At this point, Sasha's skimpy shirt has slipped down below one of her breasts; Zayonna says, "Pull it up! Pull it up!" Saying, "Oops!", Desirée does so.] And, I like her skirt. It's real fashionable. They have bracelets. And it's so cool because you can take off their feet to take off the shoes.

MADISON: Let me ask you a question. Um—Love, what do you like—would you like an outfit like the Brat dolls?

DESIRÉE: Yes, I would, but just in, like, a longer skirt [gesturing to make the hem line on Sasha's skirt lower]—

MADISON: I would get it short!

BAILEY: A smaller shirt.

DESIRÉE: —and just—

BAILEY: A smaller shirt.

DESIRÉE: I want a shirt kinda—

BAILEY: Covering the top.

DESIRÉE: Yeah. And it's so cool because you don't—you don't have to use the shoe—you can take it off, and then *change* it. I wish I had one like that. And aren't her shoes so fashionable?

In this way, the girls expressed differing interests in Bratz fashions. Madison would be happy with a short skirt like Sasha's, but Desirée would want hers longer. Desirée also wanted a less revealing top; it was unclear from my recording whether Bailey agreed.

A wish to emulate Bratz fashions was not unusual among Bratz fans (and dressing up in such styles was part of the appeal of Club Libby Lu, discussed in Chapter Two). As Bratz critics, Levin and Kilbourne (2009) reported anecdotes about younger girls who wished to dress like the Bratz dolls, put on fashion shows, and focus on sexiness. McAllister (2007) has argued that the brand carefully cultivated the feeling of a relationship between girls and the Bratz fashions; he explained,

> The connection between the dolls' clothing and their fans is emphasized throughout Bratz media that serve explicitly as fashion guides. The book *Bratz Crazy for Shoes: A Guide for Your "Soles"* (2005) includes the section "Shoe Basics 101: The Top Six Categories," which pairs descriptions of flats, boots, etc. with drawings of Bratz characters in those styles. [. . .] Even more telling of the "lifestyle brand"

strategy is a multipage "fashion-spread" section in which the dolls are dressed in various outfits. Next to these photos are additional photos of an actual piece of clothing or accessory that girls may purchase to match the particular Bratz style. The price of the item and the retail outlet where it is sold is also listed. (p. 250–251)

Although Madison sounded like she would enjoy visiting retail outlets selling Bratz styles, Desirée seemed not to wish to dress revealingly. She wanted to look as fashionable as the Bratz, but she seemed uncomfortable with revealing clothes; she believed it possible to emulate Bratz without cropped shirts and short skirts. Thus, although this part of their play emphasized appearance, mimicking the sexier aspects of the dolls was appealing to only some girls. As they imagined incorporating the Bratz fashions into their own identities, their visions varied. Not all girls had the same experience or wishes.

As the girls' Bratz conversation continued, the topic of race came up repeatedly. It began when Desirée—perhaps thinking about our previous conversations about race representations—asked her friends:

DESIRÉE: Now, what do you think about most of the Bratz being Black? Is that a good thing?

MADISON: [sassily] That *is* a good thing!!! You know how they make Sasha all dark in the cartoon?

DESIRÉE: Yeah.

MADISON: [sounding annoyed] And then she's all light sometimes!

As mentioned earlier, consistency in licensed characters' skin tones was important to the girls. The girls later complained that the darkest-skinned Bratz doll there (for whom the girls didn't offer a name, but whom Zayonna had said was Felicia's sister) had a purple hue to her skin, not unlike the purple-tinged Barbie from the library book. In depicting very dark skin tones, it seems manufacturers sometimes struggle to create a realistic blend.

The Bratz dolls' most salient signifier of race was their skin tones. Their other features—the shape of their eyes, noses, lips, and faces—scarcely varied. Valdivia (2011) has argued that owing to their facial features' configurations, all Bratz dolls look ambiguously Latina, with the main difference their skin tones (p. 98). This was not unlike Barbie and the Disney princesses, which DuCille (1994) noted all had the facial features of "archetypal white American beauty," but were "dye-dipped" to present darker skin tones (p. 49). Unlike Barbies, however, Bratz had several gradations to their skin tones—something Mattel consultants had argued for more than a decade earlier, to make Shani, a black doll presented in 1991 as a Barbie friend, "more than just a Barbie in blackface" (DuCille, 1994, p. 58). (Mattel didn't listen.)

As the girls' Bratz session progressed, the familial relationships the girls imagined between their Bratz dolls proved important. At one point, after complaining that "this one's kinda purple," Desirée commented, "I don't know why she's her sister." Zayonna was eager to explain her rationale. Before the Flava brand dolls (ethnically diverse dolls with an urban hip-hop style, launched by Mattel in 2003) were discontinued in 2004, Zayonna had purchased several, and she noticed how some of their skin tones matched the Bratz dolls' well.

> ZAYONNA: You know Kiyoni Brown, the real dark-skinned Flava doll? I have her, and she, like, the color of—Felicia's color. So, she's Sasha's sister, so Felicia has a big sister. Besides, before I stop playing, I always—
>
> DESIRÉE: [trying to cut Zayonna off]: OK, back to me.
>
> ZAYONNA: [leaning on Desirée to push her out of the camera's frame] Before I stop playing, I always do this thing called Adoption Agency, which means all the families had to adopt a child.

Zayonna's play offered an interesting counterpoint to critical concerns about Bratz and Flavas. Flavas were Mattel's first, short-lived bid to compete with Bratz, roundly condemned as "stereotypes molded into plastic perpetuity" (Kyles, 2003)— misrepresentations of hip-hop culture ("Toys . . . ," 2003), "too edgy" for pre-teen girls (D'Innocenzio, 2003). Although criticized for their skimpy clothing, Zayonna's play with Bratz and Flavas did not focus exclusively on their fashion or stereotypical attributes. Instead, she also enacted scenarios constructing family relationships, typically along race lines. She seemed to enjoy imagining which dolls could go together, which may have helped her work out her ideas about racial identity.

The fact that the girls did not uniformly receive the Bratz discourse on clothing and sexuality—even sometimes playing with them with a disregard for fashion—dovetailed with earlier findings about how children negotiated Barbie dolls. Messner (2000) argued that critics should avoid "simplistic readings of Barbie as simply conveying hegemonic messages about gender to unwitting children" (p. 775), while Rand (1998) found the Barbie brand does not pass "untransformed into [children's] minds" to generate "self-image, feelings, and other ideological constructs" (p. 386). Rather, people of different backgrounds have found various meanings in their Barbie consumption (Rand, 1998). Logically, Bratz consumers would similarly lack a one-size-fits-all mentality towards the dolls.

The Nonprofit Aftercare girls also used Bratz's racial diversity to explore other concepts. Significantly, they used Bratz to explore ideas about race relations and racism—setting aside the dolls' beloved fashionable appearances to do important identity work, as we will see shortly.

Using Bratz Dolls to Explore Modern Race Relations

Immediately after Zayonna explained that she regularly played Adoption Agency with her Bratz and Flava dolls, Desirée reclaimed the floor by telling the camera, "I'm gonna give you an interview how people who treat each other in real life as Caucasians [holding up Cloe] and African-Americans [holding up Sasha]." (Zayonna protested: "But they are best friends!" but Madison—now holding the camera—seemed to like Desirée's idea and told Zayonna, "Hold on! Hold on!")

Desirée's first scenario was in a school setting like her own, with African-Americans the majority and other races the minority. Desirée's first scenario, based on a real experience, featured two black dolls seated together during lunch who were joined by a white doll. One black doll balked when her black friend spoke welcomingly to the white doll.

> DESIRÉE: So then, sometimes she [Sasha] will get up and she will walk around, say if they were, like, friends [Sasha is next to Cloe]—and somebody else—say, if she was her sister [picking up Black doll #2] and she didn't want them to be friends, so she would come up and say, "Why are you messing around with that Caucasian person?" And sometimes she will get mad, and sometimes when people sitting around, like two Black people and a White person just happen to sit down [Black doll #2 is next to Sasha and is facing Sasha and Cloe] next to the Black person, they might be talking. Sometimes she [Sasha] might be talking, and she [Black doll #2] might be talking; and she [#2] be talking, she [#2] be talking to her, and she [Sasha] might say that *she* [shakes #2] were talking like a White person. And she [Cloe] might get offended. That's how—that's how people—that's how my friend got offended at my other friend.
>
> REBECCA: Who would get offended? The White one, or—
>
> DESIRÉE: Yeah. This one. Because she said—
>
> REBECCA: The blonde one?
>
> DESIRÉE: Because she said, "You're talkin' like a White person." And that's rude.

Desirée's second scenario served as a corrective—an expression of how she wished people would behave towards each other.

> DESIRÉE: And this is how people are supposed to treat people. [Cloe is sitting on Desirée's right thigh; Sasha and #2 are seated on her left thigh.] Say if they was friends [moving Sasha next to Cloe.]. If she [#2] walked up to the first one and said, "Why are you sitting next to that White person?" Instead of just sitting there, she could stand up [Sasha stands up] and say, "Because I want to. Because she's my friend. Not like you. That's a rude thing to say."
>
> MADISON: Yeah, that's a rude thing to say!
>
> DESIRÉE: So, yeah, Purple [calling the darker black doll "Purple" for a name elicits laughter from the other girls], back when she's sitting down [she sits down the two Black dolls—#2 with Cloe, Sasha by herself], and she said that she were talking like a little White woman. She could stand up and say [#2 stands up], "That's not cool. That's offending her. Because she's a White person, and that seems like we're all to be all taught the same. Sometimes you have different accents, and that's not right saying that people who talk like different people—cuz all people have different voices. And, so, she, she can say—she could stand up and say, "That's not right. Everybody have different accents."

Desirée's depiction of girls criticizing other girls' speech resonated with experiences some group members had previously shared. Rhea, who was a top student at a different school, had been teased for talking like a "little white girl." When I once made a casual reference to "little white girls" during one of our meetings, she had laughed uncontrollably and later explained that by using that phrase, "You're disrespecting yourself." It was a touchy spot, and the scholarly literature indicates Rhea's experience was not unique. For example, Jiwani (2006) found that when a black girl wished to identify with the white dominant culture, this choice was likely to "make her the object of derision in her group where she would be accused of being 'whitewashed'" among other black girls (p. 80). Not only that, it would "make her the object of ridicule in the dominant group; where she may be conditionally accepted but only through the erasure of her identity as a young Black woman" (p. 80).

Desirée's stories indicated that although Bratz encourage a focus on appearance, fashion, consumerism, and a host of other problematic topics among girls (see McAllister, 2007), these issues did not necessarily trump other forms of play.

Although these girls engaged with the dolls' salient visual cues—as indicated by their starting point during show-and-tell, emphasizing appearance and romance—this was not the *only* way they played. Because the dolls' racial diversity was superior to that in other children's products, Desirée could use race as another entry point into Bratz play.

Madison, who had immediately liked Desirée's idea of using Bratz dolls to tell these stories, asked to do her own "show" next. She too offered stories on race relations, rather than fashion or sexiness: Her first story was "about how White people treat Black people, and how Black people treat White people, back then." Her second story—about race relations "now"—was similar to those told by Desirée; however, rather than centering on a black girl being ridiculed for "talking white," hers centered on a white girl no one wished to befriend. This character alienated her peers by attempting to speak hip-hop style; "Hi, girly-girl! Wanna be, like, yo, pumped up, yeah?" Madison explained the other dolls were repulsed at this effort to do what "Black people do." However, Madison's first story, about how Whites and Blacks treated one another "back then," took a much different tack.

"Pretend They Have Raggedy Clothes": Imagining Slavery with Bratz Dolls

Based on a combination of information she had learned from history and from mainstream media, Madison's first story was long and complex, about slavery and the Underground Railroad. It unfolded collaboratively with the other girls; they played and operated the camcorder for more than ten minutes. Because of their story's complexity and relevance to their use of media texts to negotiate racism and race relations, I would like to share it in detail. It began with Madison's announcement:

> MADISON: [singing] We're going back in time!
>
> MADISON AND REBECCA: [joining in, making a movie-style time-travel noise:] Do-do-do-do-do. [laughs]
>
> MADISON [taking a deep breath and addressing Rebecca]: I trust you.
>
> BAILEY: [reaching for a doll] I want to be the slave. [Madison looks slightly, probably playfully, aghast—then whispers, "OK."]
>
> REBECCA: Do you need that doll, too?
>
> Note: Zayonna is working the camera; Madison, Desirée, and Bailey are seated at the table.

MADISON: Yeah. [She gives a Black doll to Desirée and to Zayonna.]

BAILEY: We can both be slaves.

MADISON: OK. These are slaves, and—

ZAYONNA: They're some *cute* slaves. Look at their clothes! [She laughs]

REBECCA [laughing]: They're really well-dressed slaves.

MADISON: Pretend they have raggedy clothes.

DESIRÉE: *Raggedy* clothes.

REBECCA: OK.

After establishing who was playing which doll and that we should disregard their clothes, Madison portrayed the white Bratz as menacing slave owners.

MADISON/CLOE: [speaking sharply to the Black dolls] Get to work!

BAILEY/BLACK DOLLS: [in fear] No! [The dolls had been lying down; they now stand bolt upright. They begin jumping up and down.]

MADISON/CLOE: [menacingly] Hurry up. Stop playin' around! [The Black dolls had been jumping; they jumped faster.]

MADISON [narrating]: Some people—some White people that they didn't even notice tried to help them.

MADISON/CAMERON: [whispering to the black dolls] Stop doing the work. Stop doing the work! You can go to the Underground Railroad.

BAILEY: [quietly]: With Harriet Tubman.

ZAYONNA: [loudly, directly into the camera]: With Harriet Tubman.

MADISON/CAMERON: Harriet Tubman. She's at the Underground Railroad. She's trying to save people. Go tomorrow! Tomorrow will be— tomorrow will be—

DESIRÉE/SASHA: [whispering] Tomorrow morning at dawn.

MADISON/CAMERON: No, tomorrow *night*. Because then—because it's frozen—

UNKNOWN: In the rivers we get a head start.

MADISON/CAMERON: [whispering] OK.

Desirée then stated that "the sun came down"; it was nightfall. Zayonna noted the white people were asleep, and Desirée and Bailey acted out a meeting between the slaves and an underground railroad conductor.

BAILEY: When the first crow calls, [singing] "Follow the drinking gourd."

DESIRÉE/SASHA [whispering to the black dolls]: We have to hurry up and go. Let's go. [The dolls exit, crossing the table.] OK, here's our first stop. We have to ask somebody how to get to—how to get to the next stop. Who you gonna ask? Her!

BAILEY: Pretend she's a, you know–

REBECCA: Pretend she's a what?

BAILEY: One of the station people.

MADISON/BABY BRATZ DOLL: I'm sorry I'm a midget [everyone laughs], but I live in this house. I will keep you safe, and I will tell you the next house to go to. You keep on going and going until you see front leg, pat leg.

REBECCA: [softly] Until you see what?

MADISON: Front leg, pat leg.

ZAYONNA: [emphatically] *Peg.* [The girls were referring to "Left foot, peg foot," a sign on the Underground Railroad trail said to have been left by a one-legged Railroad organizer known as Peg Leg Joe.]

MADISON/BABY BRATZ DOLL: And sing that "Follow the Drinking Gourd" [in which the line "Left foot, peg foot, goin' on" appears in the second verse].

At this, Bailey started singing "Follow the Drinking Gourd," an American folk-song believed to have been used by runaway slaves to help them head north to freedom in Canada. (The Drinking Gourd was another name for the Big Dipper constellation, which points to the North Star.) After Bailey started, the other girls quickly joined in:

GIRLS: "For the old man's a-waiting / To carry you to freedom / If you follow the drinking gourd."

REBECCA: How do you all know that song?

MADISON: Music.

DESIRÉE: We sing it in Music class.

Next, Desirée said the runaway slaves would take a nap. The dolls lay down until Madison, still playing the Caucasian Bratz Baby doll as an Underground Railroad conductor, shouted with alarm.

MADISON/BABY: OK, it's time to go! I see the hunters! Run! Run!

DESIRÉE [narrating]: You see, the white people wake up, and they look for signs
        of Harriet Tubman.

Madison then picked up Cloe (the blonde Caucasian Bratz doll) to portray a
menacing slave hunter.

MADISON/CLOE: Have you seen any *slaaaaaves*?

MADISON/BABY [in an innocent, high-pitched voice]: No, I haven't.

MADISON/CLOE: Can I look through your house?

MADISON/BABY [breaking character]: Your hair's a *mess*!

Everyone laughed at this comic relief, which eased the tension that built as the
tall Cloe doll—whose long blonde hair was indeed a mess—leaned intimidating-
ly over the Baby Bratz.

MADISON/CLOE: Have you found any *slaaaaves*?

MADISON/BABY: No! [Nervously] Not—that I know of.

ZAYONNA [whispering to Madison]: I wanna see her face.

ZAYONNA/CLOE: Are you sure? Are you *positive*?

ZAYONNA: Look at—look up at the camera. [The dolls are face—to—face, with
        their faces about 2 inches apart.] Looks like she about to kiss her!

Zayonna's joke also prompted laughter—like Madison's, easing the tension as
the slaves seemed on the verge of being caught by the slave hunter.

MADISON/BABY [with more confidence]: Yes. Yes. I'm positive.

ZAYONNA/CLOE: [angrily] Don't lie to me, woman.

MADISON/CLOE: [suspiciously] Can I look at your house?

MADISON/BABY: [hesitantly] Sure. [They go "inside."]

DESIRÉE/SASHA: [whispering to the other black doll] We have to go. Let's go
        now. [The Black dolls run away.]

ZAYONNA [narrating from behind the camera]: Meanwhile. . . .

DESIRÉE/SASHA: Where is the next stop??

MADISON/CLOE: I *heard* something!

At this point, Bailey's mother arrived to take her home. Bailey wailed, "No!!!" Someone asked if her mom might let her stay, but Bailey said sadly, "I've got basketball."

When Madison resumed storytelling, she snapped the detachable plastic ponytail off the Baby Bratz to create a new character, pretending it was a man. (Desirée pointed out that "he" was still wearing earrings and a bikini, and she and Zayonna had a good laugh over it; Madison/Baby, in a deep voice, retorted, "This is my— you know—underclothes," and the girls laughed even harder). Responding to an imagined question about runaway slaves, Madison replied:

MADISON/BABY: [in a deep voice] No, I don't know anything about them.

ZAYONNA [narrating again]: Meanwhile. . . .

MADISON: This is Mister and [snapping the ponytail back on the Baby Bratz] Mrs. Midget. OK.

MADISON/BABY: [snapping the ponytail off and speaking in a deep voice again] So, I haven't seen any. They don't even live upstairs, but we do have an attic. You want to look at it? To *see?*

MADISON/CLOE: Sure. [She goes "upstairs" to the TV cart.] Your attic is humongous! A *lot* of slaves could be here. *Anywhere.* Behind those boxes! [She scoots suddenly across the TV to "look."] No. . . . [quickly] Behind *there!* [She scoots along the side of the TV.] No. . . . [The doll comes back "downstairs" to the table to the other White dolls.] If you find one, contact me at [555–1234].

ZAYONNA: That's your phone number, Madison! You know that? [Laughter]

At this point, I asked where the slaves were. Desirée had been playing with a different Bratz doll during Madison's slave hunting and seemed momentarily lost. I recapped for her:

REBECCA: OK, so this mean White woman [picking up Cloe] just searched Mrs. and Mr. Midget's attic and found no slaves. So what's been going on? Where are the slaves?

DESIRÉE: After that, they hung up some posters about Harriet Tubman and her sister. So meanwhile—

ZAYONNA: No, Harriet Tubman's *children.*

DESIRÉE: Yeah, you could say that. But then they went and they finally made it to the South. So then—

ZAYONNA: You mean North?

DESIRÉE: North.

MADISON: They had to cross the, um, water, the frozen water because it's so
cold.

DESIRÉE: I know.

MADISON: And they're all cold.

REBECCA: I'd be cold in that skirt.

ZAYONNA: I know.

DESIRÉE: So then her sister said, "What about all the other slaves and your husband back there? Don't you want to go and get 'em?"

[other doll] "Yes, I do love my John."

[first doll] "OK, let's go."

When Desirée's dolls had this exchange, I recognized it as dialogue from *Sister,
Sister.*

REBECCA: Isn't that a line from *Sister, Sister?* [Desirée and then the other girls
laugh.] [still laughing]

ZAYONNA: I saw that *Sister, Sister.*

DESIRÉE: [still chuckling] I saw it last night.

Madison then pretended the Baby Bratz was Harriet Tubman's disembodied
voice, inspiring the runaway slaves. Madison/Baby Bratz/Harriet Tubman said,
"Take her to the North." Desirée's doll protested it might be "a little scary," but
Madison's doll reassured her: "You will live! You will live." Along the way, Madison
portrayed the Caucasian male Bratz doll, Cameron, as accompanying his wife, the
blonde Cloe doll, on an expedition searching for their slaves—but then he secretly went against her, wishing to free them. When he suggested they give up the search
and return home, she refused, crying, "No! I need my slaves! I'll hunt them down
with doggies if I have to!" After a close call in which Cloe nearly found the Bratz
dolls behind some trees, Cloe still refused to give up, insisting, "No. I can *feel* them."

MADISON: [explaining] Like, um, back then, they would do anything to get
their slaves. [In an ominous voice] *Anything!* [musing] I don't know
if they would sell their house.

At this point, the girls ended the "show." When asked, they said their performances for the camcorder were fairly typical of their Bratz play:

REBECCA: So, do you play Bratz like this at home? Like, do you play with your Bratz with stories like this?

ZAYONNA: Sometimes I do, sometimes I don't.

MADISON: Sometimes I do, sometimes—

DESIRÉE: Zayonna, have you played with, like, baby dolls at home with, like, slaves before, anything?

ZAYONNA: Yeah. One time I put—I was playing with Sasha and Felicia and the rest of her family. She has—[pauses to count]—five younger sisters. So, um, they were all showed to be different people. Like, the rest of the Bratz dolls were, like,—[hesitates, then says a little softer]—Caucasian. [aloud] So, I made one of the ladies, pretend that they were, um, slave, they made Sasha's mom one of the workers. And Sasha's mom eventually died because she didn't have any food. She was hot and she didn't bathe, and she was really nasty.

Though darker than the girls' collaborative story, Zayonna had played with her Bratz dolls similarly on prior occasions. This seems to have reflected an effort to comprehend through play the horrible realities of slavery.

In considering the girls' Bratz play, I am struck by how useful and important it was to them. As with Desirée's initial stories about black and white children interacting during lunch break, because the dolls were racially diverse, the girls could readily ignore the problematic aspects of Bratz—their emphasis on appearance; their lack of interest in anything besides looking good—to grapple with America's history of slavery. Play's usefulness in socialization is well documented in the literature; citing previous work on how porcelain dolls allowed girls to imagine themselves as mothers, friends, and shoppers, Wertheimer (2006) argued that in the age of Barbie and Bratz, "doll play remains a key tool in helping girls learn the gendered roles and expectations of their cultures and societies" (p. 218). I would argue these expectations and roles encompass not only gender but race, too.

Wertheimer (2006) further argued that doll play provides children "a flexible space to begin experimenting with present and future identities" (p. 219). Desirée and Morgan indeed did this sort of work in their shorter play narratives about interracial friendships. But their imaginations combined with the Bratz dolls' diversity also afforded them the chance to experiment with their collective past—to explore how it might have felt to be a slave on the run: the intense fear experienced by their ancestors, and the heart-wrenching decisions they made about leaving family members behind. They also used Bratz to imagine how black individuals like Harriet Tubman and Peg Leg Joe helped lead the slaves to freedom—and also, in Madison's case, to explore the frightening determination and possessiveness white slave owners felt towards their slaves. As play "offers a key site to begin negotiating certain of the fears and tensions intrinsic to one's cultural and social environment" (Wertheimer, 2006, p. 219), and as the girls knew that prejudice, stereotyping, and discrimination were ongoing issues in the world around them, this play was important work.

Discussion

In contemplating girl hero cartoons in the lives of the Nonprofit Aftercare girls, it is worth considering how much they could identify with the girl heroes and their missions. The cartoon girl heroes' primary activities were fighting crime and saving the day. The girl heroes battled criminals and other villains, and although most worked on their own terms, they often helped local law enforcement. The Powerpuff Girls helped the Mayor of Townsville; the Spies worked with an international agency, WOOHP, that resembled the CIA; and so on. If in my informants' own community their experiences with the police were problematic, and if they experienced the construct of "criminals" as people like themselves, this might lend some distance from the girl heroes' mission objectives.

Girl power was a mediated subculture for girls, but not every girl fit within its boundaries neatly. The intersection of gender, race, and class meant girl power was on target for white girls at Suburban Elementary, but for African-American girls at Nonprofit Aftercare and the Township Public Library, its messages were off center—particularly when depicting little white girls fighting criminals of color with impunity. They watched these shows sometimes but preferred others. Unlike the Hawaiian children in Tobin's (2000) study, who ignored the postcolonialist implications of Disney's *Swiss Family Robinson* and expressed racist ideas towards their own people, the children in my study were wary. Recognizing broader media culture's inherent racism, which marginalized or erased girls of color, they gave their allegiance to the more inclusive media texts, like *The Proud Family*, *That's So Raven*, *Sister, Sister, Full House*, and *Bratz*. Two-thirds of these focused on secure, happy black families, living in materially comfortable circumstances with both parents married. Following in the footsteps of *The Cosby Show*, which changed African-Americans' depictions on television (Gray, 2005), these programs seemed uplifting.

258 I *Growing up with Girl Power: Girlhood on Screen and in Everyday Life*

The girls' preference for more diverse, less segregated shows may have functioned as a type of wish fulfillment. In their everyday experiences, white community members were prejudiced against blacks. Internalized racism among African-Americans also existed, as potentially evidenced by Nadine's request that the white police officers teach the African-American boys in her care about respect—and also by the girls' discourse, including but not limited to their Bratz play, about black children "acting white." Race relations between whites and amongst blacks had relevance to the girls' media consumption, and programs in which everyone got along presented an appealing alternate reality.

Meanwhile, *Bratz* brought the girls' favorite toy line to life—but their doll play did not strictly imitate the fashion- and competition-centered storylines of the cartoon. Instead, the girls drew from elements ranging from *Sister, Sister's* black history month episode on Harriet Tubman to lessons from school (such as "Follow the Drinking Gourd," a song they learned in music class). Adding further ideas from their imaginations, they engaged in play much freer than the imitative forms of play encouraged by structured toys. Although critics and parents rightfully complain that media texts and popular culture have colonized children's fantasy play, Goetz, Lemish, Aidman, & Moon (2005) have argued that children still use their imaginations without media influence or, in some cases, with only traces of media influence.

The African-American girls' Bratz play therefore offered several insights. Bratz dolls have sparked well-founded concerns from a range of critics, including the American Psychological Association, who have explained the potential negative impacts on girls of structured play with sexy dolls. The reality of the girls' play at Nonprofit Aftercare Program demonstrated a more complex situation, however. Perhaps for some girls, imitation—taking pleasure in consumption and sexualized fashions—is the only use for Bratz dolls. For the girls at Nonprofit Aftercare, however, the dolls' racial diversity was extremely salient. Although critics have rightfully noted that Bratz dolls are largely the same—the same exaggerated hair, the same facial features, the same bodily proportions (Valdivia, 2011)—they also have presented something missing from all other truly popular doll brands: a wide range of skin types. Therefore, while the girls' Bratz play could be problematic, Bratz simultaneously opened avenues for play that other toys did not. As with the girls' preferred television programming, Bratz may have functioned as a means to playtime wish fulfillment. The girls could use Bratz to act out their visions for unprejudiced interactions between whites and blacks—and also between blacks in their peer groups, in which children are not chided for "talking white" or befriending white students at their school. The way these girls used their Bratz dolls brings to mind Hunt's (2005) assertion that we must move beyond characterizing television's black characters as "positive" or "negative" (p. 15). With the options Bratz present some girls for play and racial identity negotiation, Bratz—though problematic—are not *entirely* problematic.

This finding is worth bearing in mind in relation to Chapters Six, Seven, and Eight. Although girl hero cartoons depicted girls and girlhood problematically, in ways worthy of critique, girls play active roles in making meaning. For every potential negative outcome we see in a media text or property, girls may find an additional, more fruitful use for it. In an ideal world, the toys and texts provided to children would not be bundled with so many problems; it would not be a surprise when they find alternative negotiations of them. Given the reality, however, it is important to recognize not *all* consequences of problematic media properties are negative. They can be good and bad for children at the same time.

Notes

1. I would like to thank April Logan and Tiffany Chenault for their comments on an earlier draft of this chapter.
2. Note: The town and school names have been changed to ensure the anonymity of all participants.
3. The group was supposed to encompass girls ages 8–11, but the Nonprofit Aftercare Program had accidentally sent home permission slips to all the girls in the program, resulting at first in the involvement of a few girls too young and too old. This worked itself out over the first few meetings.

Conclusion

In the past two decades, we have witnessed a range of discourses about girlhood—some overlapping, some in sequence, and many contradicting each other. The discourse of the girl crisis argued that adolescent girlhood is rife with problems because of structural inequalities in our society. Girls have been shortchanged in every arena, from the educational system to the media to the marketplace. The discourse of the riot grrrls used grassroots, feminist, punk-rock tactics to argue that girls needed to transform girlhood into an empowering status. They argued that girls can subvert the status quo, fight social expectations and ignore other interests—those of adults, would-be boyfriends, and the marketplace—to become their own cultural producers, powered by girl power. Soon afterwards, the discourse of the Spice Girls reframed girl power as the idea that girls can be strong, sassy, and fun while still being normatively feminine—a commodity-driven mode of empowerment available for purchase. And the discourses of the cartoon girl heroes built on that form of girl power, depicting girlhood as something other than the opposite of boyhood: girls can be physically strong, powerful, and intelligent while still maintaining feminine appearances. This discourse, too, celebrated the marketplace as a means to self-expression, with girl power neatly pre-packaged for sale.

In this study of girl power's evolution and its meanings to girls, I have developed a perspective—grounded in contextualized, richly qualitative data—of the benefits and limitations of mainstreamed girl power discourse in girls' lives and identity negotiations. I began this book by asking, What have real girls made of girl power's mixed messages? The studies I shared in this book shed light on this question. By interviewing twenty young feminists from a range of backgrounds, I learned about their recollections of girl power at its moment of mainstreaming by the Spice Girls. Many interviewees spoke of the Spice Girls as celebrators of girls' friendships and fun, which they experienced as a site of consumption—one that, to various interviewees at various times, had been pleasurable and/or tinged with conflict and discontent. Many interviewees shared stories of playtime experiences that pointed to their peer groups' roles in constructing shared meanings and understandings during Spice Girls play—such as who among them could be understood to represent which Spice Girl, and why. Several interviewees credited the Spice Girls with leading them to feminism and/or broadening their cultural horizons, and several also pointed to the important role feminist parenting played in their upbringings and their engagement with the Spice Girls media phenomenon.

Furthermore, by conducting ongoing group interviews and ethnographic fieldwork with preadolescent girls, I was able to document and develop an in-depth perspective of the role of post-Spice-Girls girl power in the lives of preadolescent girls, particularly as articulated through the discourses of girl hero cartoons. Through our group conversations, my interviewees constructed and communicated shared meanings about the media texts we viewed together. Overall, these conversations indicated that there were numerous outcomes of girl hero cartoons' discourses on girlhood. A positive outcome: Thanks in part to the cartoons' positive depictions of girls, many of my interviewees held the category of girls in high esteem. They believed in and spoke passionately about girls' strengths and abilities. When coupled with assertions of boys' inferiority taken from broader girl power culture, however (e.g., "boys drool"), this "girl esteem" seemed to magnify the ingroup/outgroup bias that is common in children's gender identity development. Further research in this area might prove interesting.

Holding the category of "girls" in high esteem is not the same as possessing self-esteem, however. Mainstream girl power's overemphasis upon normatively nice behavior and appearance limited my informants' abilities to draw upon girl power as a source of empowerment. The pattern of depicting girls rigidly—with all girls looking basically the same, with behavior and/or personal style typed into only three rough categories—replicated and reinscribed problems found elsewhere in mainstream media and popular culture. My young informants found it difficult to tease out producers' positive intended meanings within cartoons like *Totally Spies* and *The Powerpuff Girls*. When characters' physical appearances and behaviors did not align with the norm, they were subject to harsh criticism from the girls in my study—a skill which the girls were all too quick to turn inwards, for in some cases, they were painfully aware that they did not measure up to the ideals that dominate our media and culture. Their self-criticisms sometimes bordered on self-loathing. The fact that my interviewees had a high regard for girls as a group but not always for themselves clarified that the construct of the "girl" promoted to supremacy by girl power differed from the lived, embodied reality of being an unmediated girl. This indicates a failure in the mission of girl power to empower individual girls and raise their self-esteem.

The undercurrent of racism within girl power—ranging from the only black Spice Girl being dubbed "Scary" and thus not appealing to many young girls, to the overwhelming lack of girls of color as girl heroes—additionally limited the benefits of some modes of girl power for African-American girls. For some of these girls, girl hero cartoons were yet another reminder of the cultural subjugation of their race—an issue across both media and their everyday lives. Fortunately, some branches of girl power had blossomed into more diverse representations of girls, like those on *That's So Raven* and *Bratz*. The African-American girls in my study often turned to these modes of girl power, which (though far from perfect) they could use to grapple with their growing understandings of the issues of race and racism.

Lessons Learned

In addition to these findings about girls' negotiations of girl power media culture, several other findings emerged.

The importance of feminist parenting. Feminist parenting emerged as a significant factor in children's ability to think critically about media content. As several young feminists who had been Spice Girls fans suggested, their feminist upbringings helped them—as children—recognize the flaws in the Spice Girls' rhetoric and the commercial imperatives of their empowerment messages. Although this recollection might have been informed by hindsight and reflective of some interviewees' current beliefs, a similar case emerged in my study at Suburban Elementary, which lends further insight. There, Angela—whose mother had often spoken with her about sexism in media and society—demonstrated without prompting her ability to notice instances of sexist discourse in girl hero cartoons during our meetings. (Like two of the young feminists who were raised by feminist parents, Angela's mother also taught at the college level.) As the ability to think critically about media messages is an indicator of media literacy and a major goal of media literacy education, I suggest future researchers of children's media studies and/or media education might wish to investigate the relationship between feminist parenting and children's media literacy skills.

The need for characters who defy stereotypes. Although girl power has presented characters who buck the stereotype of girls as passive and weak, girl power characters—from the Spice Girls on—are quite stereotypical in appearance. Furthermore, the variance between sets of girl characters has been poor. Girl characters often have been rigidly "typed," rather than presented as multifaceted, complex people. Thus, several of the young feminists who recalled their girlhood Spice Girls play reflected that stereotyping among friends was used to determine who could play which Spice Girl, which limited the imaginative potential of their play. Considering how much the girls at the Nonprofit Aftercare did with so little—playing productively with Bratz, whose variance was limited to skin tone and hair color only—it seems that unstereotypical characters presented in a favorable light could be highly valued by girl audiences. Their presentation in a favorable light, however, is key. For example, we saw that when *The Powerpuff Girls* presented a story about Bunny, the misfit Powerpuff, as a lesson on judging others by their appearances, the show conflated her non-normative physical appearance with lack of intelligence and poor behavior. As a result, the girls in my study misread the moral of the story; they thought it was to avoid creating something stupid. This seems to be a difficult thing to get right: On *W.I.T.C.H.*, Taranee—the only definitely black girl hero in any of the girl hero cartoons—was presented in a positive, unstereotypical way, but the Euro-American girls I spoke with could not get past her African-American hairstyles. Due to the lack of diversity in their own school, her appearance seemed unintelligible, distancing them from the character.

The need for curriculum-driven pre-teen programming. Given these difficulties, something stands out in my analysis of the presentation of non-stereotypical characters: the need for a true curriculum in programming for this age group. Although girl hero cartoons promoted themselves as serving pedagogical functions for their viewers, bolstering girls' self-esteem and teaching them about empowerment, these goals were not curriculum-backed—and good intentions are not always enough. Popular television programs for pre-school children, such as *The Wonder Pets* and *Dora the Explorer,* are backed by curricula informed by in-house education specialists. The participants in my study easily recognized the difference; as Angela insisted, in the programs targeting her age group, "there's nothing to learn."

What if the girl hero cartoons made it fun to learn about the significance of difference and inclusion in girls' empowerment? What if the cartoons' producers had worked to develop in their audience members an age-appropriate critical apparatus—one that might help them understand some of the sexism, racism, and stereotypes in our society that they find so difficult to understand? Might these strategies have more directly addressed some of the self-esteem and other issues that seemed to exist among the girls in my study? Perhaps they would have. Unfortunately, my contacts within the children's television industry have told me it is virtually impossible to get such shows greenlighted by the networks. Some have tried and failed, for received wisdom is that such shows would not appeal broadly enough. However, considering that twenty years ago network executives firmly believed that children's shows with female protagonists would never compete in the ratings wars, I argue it is time to reconsider this belief. Children in the seven- to eleven-year-old set are still learning about themselves, their potential, the world and their place in it, and how to relate to others. As the usefulness of curriculum-backed television does not magically disappear once children enter grade school—and as programs with good intentions, like the girl hero cartoons, have been shown to fall short of their goals—it is time for parents, educators, and critics to demand more from the networks.

The usefulness of creative and quality interactions in children's media studies. In qualitative studies, it takes time for the researcher to establish relationships and engage in quality interactions with the study's participants. In my research with young girls for this book, I felt that the interactions of the highest quality were those at Suburban Elementary and the Nonprofit Aftercare. At both of these sites, I spent significant amounts of time with girls in their everyday surroundings—whereas at the Township Public Library, I spent less frequent (though longer) blocks of time with girls who were not already part of an established community. In focus group style, they came together only during our meetings. This methodological limitation of the Township group contributed to my emphasis on the Suburban and Nonprofit groups in my chapters on girls' negotiations of girl power cartoons: The latter two were very different research contexts than the former and better suited to the development of a sustained research relationship with the participants.

At Suburban and Nonprofit, a real relationship of trust evolved among the girls and with me, as evidenced by the self-disclosures—some quite sensitive—that they offered later in our time together. For example, the Suburban Elementary girls' drawings of how they thought they looked and how they wished they could look took place towards the end of our time together, as did the Nonprofit Aftercare girls' sharing of their understanding of race relations and slavery through their Bratz dolls. Media researchers have become increasingly interested in creative approaches to their research, and Buckingham (2009) has documented their limitations. In my studies, however, I feel that these creative approaches—the drawings and the video of the Bratz dolls/slaves, in which the girls handed the camera and storytelling independently—worked well. For this success, I credit the the quality of our interactions leading up to that point. Having gotten to know the girls in my study pretty well during our time together, I do not believe that those creative visual methods would have yielded such insights had I only briefly visited their schools. (As Madison said to me before she launched into the story she told with her Bratz dolls, "I trust you.")

The importance of taking on history. This book comprises several studies—historical research, textual analyses, interviews with young feminists, and research with three groups of young girls. Although the time frame is the not-too-distant past, as a whole, these studies offer a longitudinal perspective on girl power's development with a sense of cultural history. The story told in this book begins in the early 1990s and culminates in girl hero cartoons' televisual peak in 2005–2006, bringing significant patterns to light—to a greater degree than an analysis of any one text or cultural moment could.

Mitchell and Reid-Walsh (2002) have noted that when analyses are linked to a specific popular culture text, the findings might seem less relevant when that text or product is no longer trendy (pp. 8–9). As the themes detailed in this book appeared in our culture over time and in various forms, their ongoing relevance is unsurprising. Consider the following:

- In 2010, NPR reported that the wage gap between men and women persists, and noted that occupational segregation—in which women work in lower-paying fields, as decried by the Ms. Foundation in Take Our Daughters to Work Day—is one factor (Ludden, 2010).

- In January 2011, a Toronto police officer speaking at York University offered his audience rape prevention tips—one of which was, "Women should avoid dressing like sluts in order not to be victimized." Outraged women organized "SlutWalks" across Canada, the U.S., England, Australia, South Africa, and several other nations to protest this widespread victim-blaming mentality. "'Slut' is being reappropriated," they said (SlutWalk Toronto, 2011). The ensuing media attention and debate, however, was reminiscent of controversy surrounding the riot grrrls' use of "slut" in performance as a protest.

- On *Feminist Frequency*, a YouTube video series created by *Bitch* magazine, Anita Sarkeesian (2011) criticized the mainstream tokenization of female characters, explaining that Katha Pollitt's Smurfette Principle is still in full play. With teams of girl heroes receding from the mainstream, then, representations appear once more to be business as usual.

- In *Cinderella Ate My Daughter*, Peggy Orenstein (2011) unpacked the dangers of the normatively feminine girly girl culture found in the hugely profitable Disney Princess brand. Even as Disney creates post-girl-power princesses who have agency and are sometimes heroes in their own rights,

for little girls, girls still cherish frilly normative femininity and all the helpless behavior implied therein.

* The scholarly journal *Sex Roles* reported on the prevalence of sexy clothing for young girls from online retailers, with nearly 30% of all items for
  sale having sexualized characteristics (Goodin, Denburg, Murnen, and
  Smolak, 2011).

This book's themes also underscore the usefulness of examining histories of girl
culture and everyday life. Scholars of children's popular culture such as Kearney
(2008) and Mitchell and Reid-Walsh (2002) have encouraged academic researchers
to look backwards, to take cultural history seriously. As I have argued elsewhere
(Hains, 2008b), by turning to the past, we can improve our understandings of the
dilemmas and contradictions we encounter today. I would like to once again make
the call for additional research in this vein.

The importance of talking with girls. Girls are too infrequently given the opportunity to share their perspective on girlhood with adults, as the history of girl power
discourse demonstrates. In the girl crisis discourse, adults—worried about the status of girls—argued for societal changes that would benefit girls. In the riot grrrl
movement, older girls fought to improve their lives themselves. Drawing upon both,
in mainstream girl power, adults told stories about girls' value and worth to girl
audiences, seeking to bolster and empower young girls (for profit).

Prior to my research on girls' negotiation of girl power media, much of the literature praising girl hero cartoons was written by and for adults; very little data
explored what real girls thought. My study, however, indicates that girl hero cartoons were not as uniformly positive for girls as their champions believed them to
be. Likewise, most of the previous critical literature on Bratz dolls, written by and
for adults, has been uniformly critical. My study, however, indicates that because
of their racial diversity, Bratz dolls are not as uniformly harmful to girls as their critics believe them to be, and my findings are quite different than what scholars versed
in the literature might expect. (Indeed, they were quite different than what I was
expecting.)

Therefore, I hope that this book gives real girls better representation in adults'
ongoing conversations about girls' media culture. By choosing to quote girls exten-
sively, rather than summarize their words, I have deliberately foregrounded young
girls' voices. While the specific conversations foregrounded were my selections, and
the conclusions drawn are likewise my own, I have done my best to choose conversations in which the girls were truly engaged and enthused—signals that the conversations were important to them. I fully recognize that if they were in my
position, the girls might have chosen to foreground different data and drawn dif-

ferent conclusions. Nevertheless, I have strived to treat their words and actions with integrity, in a manner worthy of the trust they placed in me during our study. If they were able to comment upon my manuscript, I hope that like the young feminists featured in Chapter Three, they would feel I have accurately represented their perspectives and experiences.

Epilogue

Profiles in Mediated Girlhood

"Over the years, I've just become more mature and stuff."
—*Angela, age 13 (Euro-American)*

"You get a lot more responsibility when you're thirteen than when you're ten."
—*Abby, age 15 (Euro-American)*

In 2010, I traveled to Waterhaven and Claret Park. I wished to interview as many of my original interviewees as possible. With five years passing since my original study's inception, I hoped to learn what these girls in hindsight thought about growing up with girl power. As teenagers, what did girl power now mean to them?

Many of my study's original participants were impossible to reach. Some had moved; others had changed their phone numbers. I reached six girls from Suburban Elementary: Angela, Bobbi, Kelly, Kylie, Maria, and Maura. (Maura had not been a member of our video group at Suburban Elementary, but she was one of the tomboy-identified girls I spoke regularly with on the playground; I had interviewed her at her home twice during my fieldwork, at her request.) I also reached two girls from the Nonprofit Aftercare Program: Simone and Madison. Everyone but Kelly wanted to meet for a follow-up interview, so I scheduled visits to the homes of the remaining seven girls. A few months later, in 2011, I additionally reached Abby and Elizabeth, both from the Township Public Library group, and interviewed them by telephone.

As this epilogue will demonstrate, when asked what they remembered about girl power and girl hero cartoons, most had little to say. I originally hoped to have enough data to write a chapter called "Girl Power, Grown Up," but this was not possible. Unlike the young women who grew up with Spice Girls, who specifically used the phrase "girl power" on their products and media, these younger girls barely remembered the concept. Those who did, however, tended to link girl power with ideas related to empowerment and feminism, though they did not necessarily use those words.

Bobbi

When I met with Bobbi (age 15, Euro-American), she was dressed simply, without much makeup. She wore her hair long with bangs and looked happy. She was a freshman at Claret Park High School (CPHS), a large and diverse public high school comprising nearly 4,000 students from over 55 nationalities. Although like Suburban Elementary CPHS is located in the town of Claret Park, it is shared by several neighboring towns, most of which are significantly more diverse than Claret Park itself. The student body is 44% Caucasian, 41% African-American, 12% Asian, and 2% Latino, and more than a third are eligible for the free lunch program because of their families' socioeconomic situations.

Because of its large size, CPHS has a diverse range of extracurricular options for its students, and Bobbi had become a devoted member of the high school band. She described herself as "the biggest band geek ever," and she said most of her friends were also members. She said this placed her peer group towards the bottom of the school hierarchy, but this didn't bother them. She liked to attend band camp and musical theater camp during the summers.

As Bobbi and I recalled how nearly uniformly white Suburban Elementary had been, which contrasted significantly with CPHS, she reflected on the relationships between groups of students at the high school. She witnessed a lot of racial stereotyping between students at CPHS, overhearing statements like "The Asians are smart; if you need tutoring, you go find an Asian." She also said that according to popular belief, "black people are ghetto. Anybody from the 'hood is ghetto." However, from her perspective as a white, middle-class girl, she didn't characterize these stereotypes as racist or offensive:

> BOBBI: It's not so much of a racist thing or anything like that, as it is of just, like—we accept each other. But [pause] if someone says something, and it's not proper English, it'll be like, "Oh, that's ghetto," or something like that. I guess things aren't taken offensively.

Reflecting on these dynamics, she offered, "It's really weird, because you go two miles up that way, and they're rich; they have huge houses. And you go, like, two miles this way, and people are getting stabbed to death." The students from the wealthy areas, she said, tended to be "snobs."

Given the time-consuming nature of her extracurriculuar interests, Bobbi reported she spends little time watching television. "I'm never home," she said—but she enjoyed watching *Degrassi*, *George Lopez*, *Fresh Prince of Bel Air*, *iCarly*, and *Glee* when she could.

When asked what she remembered about girl power, Bobbi thought there might have been a television show by the same name:

REBECCA: What do you remember about the concept of "girl power," which was kind of popular when you were a kid? Do you—

BOBBI: About the show?

REBECCA: No, there wasn't a show called *Girl Power*, it was just an idea.

BOBBI: I thought there was a show called that. Did we talk about that?

REBECCA: I think that was the context for our discussions a lot of the time. There were all these shows about *girl heroes*, you know.

BOBBI: Right. Okay, that might have been it.

Asked what she thought girl power was all about, Bobbi made a link between *The Powerpuff Girls* and the need for equality between the sexes:

BOBBI: I remember, like, you would look at *The Powerpuff Girls*. And we would be like, "Well, they're superheroes, and they're talented. What do you think that people in our town do?" or something like that that?

REBECCA: Yeah.

BOBBI: Sort of something like that? I don't know. Who knows? But, um [pause], I think that women have come really far in a while, cuz, I mean, we've been talking about that in school a lot lately. And people have definitely [pause], like, developed a lot further. There's still countries today where women don't have any rights at all.

REBECCA: Right.

BOBBI: And I don't think that's right because I think men need to realize that without women they wouldn't exist.

REBECCA: Mm-hm.

BOBBI: And, I mean, like, they can't—we can't exist without each other, so we should be equal.

To her, then, if girl power was a component of the girl hero cartoons she recalled viewing, then girl power was about equality between the sexes, which she communicated as a firmly held belief.

Kylie

Kylie (age 14; Euro-American) was an eighth grader when we met again in 2010. Her hair was long and highlighted, with heavy bangs; she wore a lot of eye make-up. Dressed in the t-shirt of one of her favorite bands, she said most of her t-shirts were band shirts. She attended Claret Park Middle School, which had an enrollment of about 1,500 students, 73% of whom were Caucasian, 18% African-American, 5% Asian, and 2% Latino. Just under a third of all the students were eligible for the school's free lunch program. She didn't feel there were rigid social groups at her middle school; "It's not really particular," she said. "You can talk to someone, like, a different group, and they'll be fine with it. They won't try to be rude to you or anything; they'll just talk to you. It's just, like, everybody talking to everybody else." She noted, however, that she often found it easier to get along with boys than other girls. She explained, "Like, we're—you're better friends with the guys than you are with the girls, cuz the girls start more drama than the guys do. The girls start rumors about you, and you'll not want to get into it, so you talk to the guys. The guys don't do that. They'll mess around with you, but you *know* they're kidding. So you don't get mad at them. You laugh with them."

Despite her stated preference for boys' friendships, Kylie was still friends with Bobbi and Angela. She frequently walked home from the middle school with Angela, and because Kylie's MP3 player was broken, Angela would share hers with Kylie during their walks and introduce new music to her. Kylie appreciated this because, she said, "The most important thing to me is music." She preferred music in which the performers played their own instruments, positioning herself in opposition to her peers' preference for pop acts like Kesha. The kids at her school tended to taunt other kids, however, based on the types of music posters they had in their lockers. "If it's a type of music they think is weird, they'll make fun of you about it," she explained.

A member of her middle school band, Kylie reported that Bobbi had already recruited her for the high school band. "She was begging me to play the tenor saxophone for marching band 'cause we needed more of them, evidently," Kylie explained. "So I was the first one to sign up."

Kylie said that at the moment, her favorite television programs included *Sonny with a Chance, Serious, Endurance, Gilmore Girls, The Secret Life of the American Teenager*, and *10 Things I Hate About You*. She also spent a lot of time on the social networking sites MySpace, Facebook, and myYearbook.

Like Bobbi, Kylie couldn't remember girl power as a concept. When prompted, however, she suddenly recalled the popular sentiment that girls could do anything:

REBECCA: Do you remember anybody using the term "girl power" when you were a kid?

KYLIE: No.

REBECCA: So does the term mean anything to you at all?

KYLIE: No.

REBECCA: That's okay. Well, I remember "girl power" was kind of supposed to be giving girls the message that—

KYLIE WITH REBECCA: —girls can do anything.

KYLIE: Yeah.

REBECCA: Do you remember people saying things like that? Like, "Girls rule, boys drool?"

KYLIE: Yeah, one of my friends used to say that a lot.

When asked what she remembered liking about the girl hero cartoons, Kylie was unsure. She mainly recalled her devotion to them, not the content; she reflected, "It's just, like, a show you get into, and you stay with it till the end."

Angela

At thirteen years old, Angela (Euro-American) was an eighth grader at Claret Park Middle School, like Kylie. She wore a lot of makeup, heavy on the eyeliner, and her once short, curly hair was styled long and straight. She was a year younger than her classmates, because she had started kindergarten a year early. She said this was not a problem socially: "I'm not saying that I'm more intelligent than people, but sometimes I'm more mature than people in *my* grade, so sometimes I seem even older." She looked forward to her fourteenth birthday in September 2010. "Fourteen, for some reason, just appeals to me more than being thirteen," she said. "When you're thirteen—I know seventh graders, and they're all immature. When you're fourteen, you might seem a little more mature. [. . .] Fourteen's a good age to be. Fourteen, fifteen, sixteen, seventeen. When you're a teenager, you can just have fun but not worry about adult responsibilities like taking care of children or paying bills." These issues of adult responsibilities were on her mind because her parents had divorced recently. The oldest of four children, Angela was a witness to how hard her mother was working to raise them.

Asked to describe herself, Angela noted music was very important to her. She also felt like she had "different personalities." Some days, she felt "normal" and "happy," but other days, she felt "really insecure—like, how everybody feels, especially girls. Every girl is insecure about themselves. Sometimes, I'll wake up in the morning and hate the way my hair is. Then if I straighten it, I'll think I look really pretty, so I'll just walk out and be happy." She also described feeling stressed about her grades; I recalled her being an excellent student in elementary school, but she had recently been grounded for earning a C in science. "I'm not *really* intelligent," she insisted, "but I am pretty smart." She often wished that she could just "do over" her bad days.

Music was very important to her. She liked finding interesting, "unique" new bands to listen to. She also enjoyed attending the same summer musical theater camp as Bobbi, and she was a member of her middle school band as well.

When asked what she remembered about our group, she replied, "I remember that we used to watch little clips from TV shows, what now seem like old TV shows. I don't know if they were old then, when we watched them, but we watched *Jenny, the Teenage Robot*. I don't know if we watched *The Powerpuff Girls*, but we watched a lot of shows encouraging girls to do good things and just to know that we can do anything. Shows with superhero girls, encouraging girls to want to be a superhero of reality—to go out and do whatever they can, and prove that they could be as smart as anybody—or smarter."

Angela was more directly familiar with the concept of feminism than girl power, in part because she had been learning about it lately in school. Noting that she wasn't sure of the "actual dictionary definition," she described feminism as "the actual power that girls have."

> ANGELA: We just went over this thing in our class; there's a worksheet, and it said things we need to improve with women's rights. And it had that men's salary, [. . .] men would be making more than women, and that got me kinda aggravated. Every girl put their little post-it note thing of "that needs improvement." I thought that, even if it's one dollar difference—like, it wasn't, it was thousands of dollars differences—but, I mean, like—

REBECCA: Yeah, it's, um, women—for every dollar that a man makes—on average—in the United States, a women only makes seventy cents. So, you have to work a whole extra four months to make what a guy makes in a year for the same job.

ANGELA: Exactly. That's just, like, why? I don't understand why that has to happen. It just shows how people are ignoring it. They talk about it, but they don't really do anything.

REBECCA: Right.

ANGELA: And if there was a woman president, I don't know what they would do, because, just because there's a woman, doesn't mean you should automatically elect them. I'm not saying I wasn't for Hillary Clinton or whatever, but a lot of women just went to vote for her because she was a woman. I'm not for her or against her, but a lot of women would just be like, "Oh, she's a woman, so I'm gonna vote for her; she's gonna go for women's rights." But she really didn't emphasize anything like that.

Angela spoke with passion about this subject and clearly paid attention to this unit in school. Unlike Angela, Kylie and Bobbi could not remember studying similar units; perhaps their teachers had not covered it, or perhaps they had forgotten. Angela had always been quick to comment upon issues of gender inequality in the media as a young girl, so it was interesting to see that she had sustained this interest in a more general sense.

Maria

Maria (age 13, Euro-American) was a seventh grader at the time of our follow-up interview. Like Angela and Kylie, she too attended Claret Park Middle School, though she didn't talk with Angela anymore. A member of the school band (playing flute) and the orchestra (playing violin), she was still dressed in her school uniform of a polo shirt and khakis during our visit. She wore simple hoop earrings and no makeup.

Maria played softball and several other sports, and her school's student athletes were her primary peer group. When at home, she still watched Nickelodeon, ABC Family, and the Disney Channel. Asked about favorite shows, she said with a bashful pause, "This may sound silly, but I like *SpongeBob* still." She also listened to a lot of music on YouTube, and she enjoyed Facebook and playing games on her Nintendo Wii.

Like Kylie, Maria witnessed difficulties between girls at school. When asked about this, she explained, "People will talk about each other to other people, or they'll make up something about someone. And a lot of times now, there's actual fights. Like, a fistfight." She had never witnessed any of the girls' fistfights, however—she'd just heard about them. She said a lot of fights were started because of rumors that had been spread over IM or text messages. She said that cyberbullying did not happen within her sports-oriented peer group, though. She also commented that a major difference between the middle school and her elementary school was that "people try to act more grown up now. Especially with their makeup. They try to look like they're grown up, but it's kinda bad. They'll put all the eyeliner and everything."

Maria had no specific recollections about girl power. What came to mind "for some reason," she said, "is *The Powerpuff Girls.*" When prompted, she could not recall encountering any merchandise featuring slogans like "Girls rule." When I asked if she had ever heard of feminism, she replied,

MARIA: Yeah. Do you mean when they're discriminating against, like—you're a woman, so it's like you're not strong or anything?

REBECCA: Yeah. Yeah, what's your understanding of what feminism actually means?

MARIA: Like [pause], you're not [pause] strong, or important or something.

REBECCA: Mmm. Right. Part of why I ask is that some of those cartoons that we used to watch together, like *The Powerpuff Girls*, some people think that they were good examples of TV shows that were feminist, because they were trying to say, "Girls are important, and girls are strong."

MARIA: Mmm.

REBECCA: And some people say they weren't really. So I don't know if you would have any opinion of that, based on what you can remember about those shows. Like, if you think Girl Power is related to feminism at all.

MARIA: I think it kinda is because, they have the three different attitudes of a girl, but they're all the same strength. Bubbles is the kind of girl—like, not girlie, but quiet or shy-ish. Then there was the pretty one, and there's the tomboy one. But they're all the same still?

REBECCA: Right.

MARIA: So they can all do the same thing.

In other words, to Maria, the girl power discourse found in *The Powerpuff Girls* was not necessarily about equality to boys. Rather, she recalled it as an empowering message about all girls being equal and strong, regardless of what type of identity they conveyed.

Maura

When we met, she was dressed simply and wore little makeup. Still an excellent student, she said she could be "*kind* of a perfectionist" with her school projects, boasting a 100% average in math. Her mother complained that the school was not challenging Maura enough, and that their efforts to have her switched into a higher level course of study had failed. Maura said she rarely had to study for her tests. "I focus more on my academics than my social life," she said. "You can describe me as strange or quirky."

Maura was interested in art and shared a sketchbook filled with drawings. She did not watch much television, as her parents had no cable subscription (and never had); she explained, "We're more of an intellectual family." She also said she didn't watch movies "as much as other people." Her main pop culture interest was anime, which influenced her drawings.

As had been the case during my fieldwork, Maura still had some challenges relating to her peers. For example, she reported difficulty working in groups; she would "get angry" because "nobody listens to me." "I would definitely be better as a leader than a follower," she reflected.

Unlike the other girls from Suburban Elementary, Maura could conceptualize girl power in detail.

REBECCA: If you hear the term "girl power," what does that mean to you?

MAURA: [thinking] Well, definitely a feminist kind of person that would, um, they don't always need someone to depend on. Also, it kind of brings to mind a group of women that can kind of work together and they don't need help. That would definitely be feminist kind of stuff.

REBECCA: Right. Well, so what does "feminist" mean to you? Like, what is feminism?

MAURA: I guess it's kind of someone who can do a lot of things independently without the help of—like, in the past, what people would think that only a man could do. And it's also being able to stand up for your rights as a woman. For instance, in the fifties they would have different pay rates for men and women. Standing up for your rights to get the same pay for doing the same job.

REBECCA: Yeah. So, do you think that feminism has much application for girls like you today?

MAURA: Definitely.

REBECCA: In what ways?

MAURA: Uh, well, there's definitely harassment at work. Things like that. There's at school, and just in general, working together to overcome something. Things like that.

To Maura, then, the concept of girl power evoked feminism and the fight for equality.

Maura could not recall where she had learned about feminism, but it seemed her mother had played a significant role. Maura explained that when her language arts class had read *On Women's Right to the Suffrage*, she was one of the few students who comprehended it, because her mother was always encouraging her to read "classic books that are written in an older style." She respected her mother's suggestions in intellectual pursuits, noting that her mother worked in a male-dominated scientific field where she had recently faced harassment. "My mom is *definitely* courageous," Maura said proudly. "I mean, with all the work harassment, she had to be defiant and courageous to stand up for herself. I definitely admire that in her."

Simone

Simone (African-American, age 12) had participated in the group at the Nonprofit Aftercare during its first year only. The reason: Her parents had transferred her out of Waterhaven Elementary to a new private Catholic school, where she was now a seventh grader. Unlike Waterhaven, which was predominantly black, her private school was 80% Caucasian and 20% "other races," making Simone a racial minority. Although the school was Catholic, the student body was not uniformly so; 20% were affiliated with other religions. The school boasted much smaller numbers than the local public schools, with only 230 students and an 8 to 1 student/teacher ratio. Asked her thoughts on the diversity at her school, Simone replied, "Not much. It's mostly Caucasian." She never felt treated unfairly by the other kids, though: "Since I've been in third grade, I kind of grew up with them, so it's pretty much like we're family."

When Simone and I met, it was a Sunday morning, and her family was getting dressed for church. She got up early to meet with me and was already wearing a pretty dress. As we caught up and chatted about school, she said her favorite subjects were Art and Gym and that she was very involved extracurricularly. She was both an elected member of her student council and a member of several sports teams: "I do basketball, volleyball, softball, track, and soccer," she said. Her weekends were typically taken up with four or five different sports games, and during the summer, she often attended basketball and golf camps.

Simone explained her current media interests included *Full House*, which she said she enjoyed watching as she got ready for school, and a variety of web sites, which she said she spent more time with than television. Favorite sites included Facebook and Sport Goal, which featured lots of sport trivia quizzes. A fan of Taylor Swift, she enjoyed downloading music to her telephone, a Samsung Rogue, on which she said, "I have a really wide range, from hip-hop to pop to rock to techno." While doing her homework, she typically listened to music on YouTube.

Asked about her recollections of our group, Simone remembered we watched *The Powerpuff Girls* together. She thought that her favorite show had probably been *That's So Raven*, however (which indeed it was; she selected her pseudonym, Simone, based on the *Raven* star's last name). Simone had no recollection of "girl power" as a concept, and when asked if she'd ever heard anybody say "Girls rule" or "Girls rule, boys drool," she said uncertainly, "I've heard of it, but I've never really talked about it that much."

Madison

Madison (age 13, African-American) and I held our follow-up interview late one evening. She looked polished and pretty in a layered tank top and a white swing sweater. She wore some makeup and blue contact lenses, and her medium-length hair was styled smooth. She struck me as poised.

Two years prior, Madison's family had moved an hour north of Waterhaven. There, she was an eighth grader in a public high school that ran from grades eight through twelve. Madison explained that when her mother found a better job as a manager for a not-for-profit institution, "We moved over here for a bigger house and a better education for me and my little brother." As was the case for Simone, her new school had significantly different demographics than did Waterhaven; its student body was 76% Caucasian, 19% African-American, 3% Asian, and 2% Latino. Only 7% of students were from socioeconomic situations that qualified them for a free lunch; the area was significantly more affluent than either Waterhaven or Claret Park.

Madison did not fit in completely at her new school. "I guess people here are a little more complicated," she said. "I don't know. They're just different over here than they are in Waterhaven." She said most people were "nice—just different," but that some were definitely racist. She complained that the passageway between her high school and middle school had many stickers on the walls reading "White Pride Worldwide." Madison was worried about the impact of their predominantly white schools and social contexts on her 5-year-old brother, Frederick; he had internalized racism in a way that she had not at his age, given that she had attended a predominantly black school at the time. According to my field notes:

> I was sharing with Madison some synopses of our conversations from our group meetings, and asking her if she could remember the day they all cracked up because I talked about "little white girls." She started saying it sounded familiar when Frederick, who at that point had joined us, declared sullenly, "I don't want to be black. I hate brown and black. Light is better than dark." I told him that made me very sad to hear. Madison explained that he is the only African-American child in his kindergarten class, and he came home one day upset. I said that he shouldn't listen to what anybody else says, because there is nothing wrong with being black, and Madison said it wasn't anything anyone had said—it was just something he had picked up.

Despite these problems, Madison preferred her new location for its safety. She said that in the past year, a cousin and a close family friend "who was like an uncle" to her had been killed in the nearby major city. Both were shot. Her new town was much safer for her immediate family.

Madison was involved in three extracurricular groups. One based at her school focused on raising money for medical research. Another group taught students leadership skills and promised to help its graduates with college expenses, such as books, upon graduation; and the third group was travel-oriented, also preparing students for college. "My family wants me to go to college," she explained. "My older brothers, they didn't go to college, but they want *me* to go to college."

In her spare time, Madison enjoyed watching *Criminal Minds* and *CSI*, which she said "I'm pretty much addicted to." She enjoyed playing her Nintendo Wii—especially Wii Fit and Rock Band—and she loved using Facebook; she often IMed her friends using Facebook chat. She also listened to a lot of music, citing her favorites as being Beyonce, Eric Bana, jazz, and even classical music, which she attributed to her parents. She enjoyed receiving music recommendations from her friend's brother, who she said was good at introducing her to new music. She also played the clarinet and piano, and she said she was currently studying guitar. "I want to play the violin, too," she added. Her father and his family are very musically inclined, everyone in his family plays an instrument or sings. She said proudly, "My dad said if I learn how to play the piano, I can play anything."

Madison remembered watching *Kim Possible* and *That's So Raven* during our group meetings; she still had a Raven pin that I gave to each of the girls in the group on her book bag. She couldn't recall "girl power" or the phrase "girls rule," but when prompted, she did fondly and vividly recall her love for *The Powerpuff Girls:*

REBECCA: I think *The Powerpuff Girls* were supposed to be "girl power."

MADISON: Oh, I loved *The Powerpuff Girls!*

REBECCA: Oh, you did?

MADISON: Yeah. I had "girl"—I had Powerpuff Girl everything. I just had, like, my whole room Powerpuff Girl. And then I would love to draw them.

REBECCA: Oh, you did?

MADISON: Then I was disappointed when they didn't show it anymore.

REBECCA: Yeah. What—what do you remember liking about *The Powerpuff Girls?*

MADISON: It was just funny. And then, I liked the Momo [sic] Jojo, the whole monkey thing.

REBECCA: Right.

MADISON: And then I just loved the characters. It was interesting to watch.

To Madison, then, girl power had little meaning—but she had a fondness for the girl power media and products of her childhood.

Abby

Abby (age 15, Euro-American) had been a member of the Township Public Library group. When I conducted her follow-up interview by phone in 2011, she was in the tenth grade at her public high school, whose student body was 88% white, 6% Asian, 5% African-American, and 1% Latino. She said the school was well integrated; "It's not like the Asian kids are only friends with the Asian kids and whatnot. Everyone is kind of friends with different people."

Abby was part of a circle of friends who enjoyed computer games, especially Sims; she said they all wished their Sims could "hang out and connect together." She characterized her friends as being "loud." When I asked how, she laughed and said, "Just like when we're hanging out, we'll scream or something, or do something obnoxiously stupid." She reported she was still a tomboy in some ways but not as much as she used to be: "I will wear dresses and skirts occasionally now," she explained. Abby had long-standing interests in sports and music (her instrument was the cello), but due to a serious shoulder injury, she had been unable to do either for some time.

When I asked Abby about girl power, she recognized the phrase, saying, "I remember I had a shirt I got from a friend that said girl power on it." She could not pinpoint any meaning behind it, however. When asked whether she remembered people saying things like "girls rule" and "boys drool," she replied, "Yes. I would definitely hear them at recess. Like on the school playground. There was a lot of 'girls rule, boys drool.'" During the timeframe of the Township Library group, her favorite television shows had been *Kim Possible* and *Totally Spies*; she remembered *Totally Spies* was popular enough among her friends that they used to play it at recess. "We had to have a hideout, and we would run around doing different missions," she explained.

REBECCA: Now did you guys assign who was which spy?

ABBY: Yeah, we always had one that we always were.

REBECCA: So which spy did you get to be?

ABBY: I was thinking that something I did Clover or Daffodil for one of them.

REBECCA: So you were probably the blonde one.

ABBY: Probably.

REBECCA: So can you tell me anything more about the way you would play *Totally Spies*?

ABBY: Well, I remember that we would always have one person that would stay back at the headquarters or whatever, and make sure no one else took it. And then we would often run to a willow tree as a back up, and we would just go on various missions to find different things across the playground.

In this way, for Abby and her peers, *Totally Spies* seems to have served a similar function as the Spice Girls did for an earlier generation of girls: fodder for imaginative play on the schoolyard.

Elizabeth

Elizabeth (Euro-American, age 15) attended the same public school as Abby. At the time of our phone interview in 2011, she was also a tenth grade student. Elizabeth and Abby were still on friendly terms, but they were in different classes, so they did not see much of one another. Elizabeth continued to be actively involved in the performing arts; she was a singer and dancer who had performed with community organizations since she was a child. She had also attended the same summer musical theater camp as Bobbi and Kylie, which though located in Waterhaven drew children from surrounding towns. Elizabeth was already thinking about colleges, and music was a factor in her thinking; she was especially interested in Oberlin and Yale because both "have good liberal arts academics, as well as a music school." She hoped to attend a college with a dual enrollment option in both areas.

Elizabeth described herself as having grown "a little more introverted" than she was in elementary and middle school, "but I also feel like I have better friendships because I'm more comfortable in social situations." She said high school had thrown her into more social situations, "so that I really need to fend for myself and interact with new people. It's kind of annoying, but its really helping me in interactions with my peers, because I've always seemed to have better interactions with people who are older than I."

An avid reader, Elizabeth didn't watch as much television as she used to. She occasionally watched *The Nanny* and *Glee*, and she was pleased that her parents—who had been very strict about her television viewing throughout her childhood—trusted her to make her own decisions about television now. However, television was not much of a draw. She said that at the moment, she was re-reading Susan Cooper's *The Dark Is Rising* series, and she also enjoyed playing computer games. She was especially drawn to games that "are time management- and creativity-type games, where I get to design my own fashions and design my own candy. And there's an interior design game. Things like that, I tend to move towards."

Elizabeth remembered watching *The Powerpuff Girls* and *Kim Possible*, which she said was "my favorite one. I continued watching it for a really long time, as long as it was on Disney Channel." She explained, "As a character, she was not the typical vapid teenager; she was a little more intelligent than that, so I think I related to her more than some of the other characters. Some of the humor with her parents—who are a rocket scientist and a brain surgeon—and her younger twin brothers also was fun for me."

When asked what, if anything, she remembered about the phrase "girl power," Elizabeth linked it to empowerment:

ELIZABETH: [pause] That was sort of what the group was based around. Most of the TV shows we watched sort of had that theme. Uh, a lot of the shows were about girls with either super powers or some other way of making a big difference in the world and saving people. And it was sort of [pause] breaking out of the stereotypes while still remaining in them, if you can sort of understand what that means. Um, they had—some of them had stereotypical characters and personalities, but they did unstereotypical things. So it was supposed to be—I—it felt like it was empowering to the typical teenager, pre-teenage girl, that it's, like, you-can-be-normal-and-still-do-something-extraordinary-and-cool type of shows. Type of phrase. Type of ideal.

Like Maura, Elizabeth also independently brought up the concept of feminism, which at first she called "women's lib," which she defined as "women's liberation movements. And women's suffrage. And all of the things that have been done thus far to promote male and female equality." Elizabeth felt these things were important, though she lamented, "Women's lib is sort of giving all-women's colleges a bad reputation, at this point." When I asked if she had ever heard the terms "feminism" or "feminist" to describe these sorts of things, she replied after a long pause:

ELIZABETH: I have heard the term. I know the term. [pause] I wouldn't call myself a feminist necessarily, [pause] but [sigh], I don't know, I guess I am because I believe that women can do anything that men can do [slight pause] mostly. I believe that they're equal but different. There are things that guys are better at than girls; there are things that girls are better at than guys. There are just—there are—even if you get down to a strictly biological and anatomical level, there are differences between men and women, and [pause] they exist, and I accept that fact. But I think that, as far as jobs, as far as intelligence, as far as education, it should be fairly even.

REBECCA: Right. OK. So you want people treated equally in terms of, like, employment and education, but you're recognizing that there are underlying differences that you think are, you know, legitimate. Right? Am I translating that right?

ELIZABETH: Mm-hm. [. . .]

REBECCA: Now, you said you wouldn't call yourself feminist necessarily, but you guess you sort of are one. But what are your impressions of people who identify themselves as "feminists"?

ELIZABETH: Um, I don't really want to make judgments because, really, what I know of it is the stereotypical, diehard feminists that you see on television, for example. They'll stop at nothing to affirm the equality between men and women, and it comes up in their everyday conversation, in everything they do. And I feel like [pause]—I don't feel like I talk about it all the time.

REBECCA: That makes sense. So—there are sort of three terms we've been discussing, right? "Girl Power" and "women's lib" or "women's liberation" and "feminism." And I was wondering, what relationships do you see between Girl Power and the other two, if any?

ELIZABETH: [pause] Um [pause], I think they're definitely interrelated. Women's lib and feminism are sort of the more developed [pause], possibly more mature ways of thinking about the same topics. I mean [pause], girl power is sort of the way I thought of it when I was in middle school or even late elementary school. And now [slight chuckle]—the cliché has come into play, and a little bit of higher education has come into play, so I think of it differently. But I think the concepts are in essence the same.

Thus, like Maura's idea that girl power was about gender equality, Elizabeth thought of it in a similar way; but whereas Maura considered girl power and feminism roughly synonymous, Elizabeth saw them on a continuum, with feminism a more developed form of girl power. However, unlike Maura, who saw feminism as "definitely" relevant to girls' everyday lives, Elizabeth did not:

ELIZABETH: It doesn't come into my everyday life too much because, every now and then I come across someone who's prejudiced gender-wise; but most of the people I interact with on a daily basis—like, my teachers and my fellow students—don't have those kinds of prejudices. They've not been raised in a time where gender—gender prejudice was rampant.

As one final methodological note, it is worth mentioning that in addition to infrequently recalling the phrase "girl power," the girls I re-interviewed five years later could recall little about our group conversations. What they did remember was a general positive feeling about the time we spent conversing together; several volunteered that they remembered liking me and our group, which I was glad to hear, given that I worked hard to make the groups positive experiences for the girls who participated. Elizabeth explained:

ELIZABETH: I remember us discussing the shows, discussing life in general, just talking about what was going on in our lives in an environment where not very many of us actually went to the same school, and so we felt—we felt a little bit [slight pause] safer. Um, I don't remember being really close with any of the girls, but I definitely felt safe talking about it with people who weren't necessarily gonna know the people that I know; so probably weren't gonna be able to tell anybody about it.

The girls' general lack of specific recollections about the content and focus of our groups—the numerous girl hero cartoons we watched together—was in many ways unsurprising. After all, I cannot remember many details about the activities I participated in during third, fourth, and fifth grade either. (I remember a summer in which I participated in a reading group for fourth-graders across my town, which in structure was probably the most similar activity I had to these "video clubs"—and I have only the faintest recollections about what we read or discussed.) They shared different things with me during our five-year follow-up interviews than they shared when they were elementary school children—a good reminder that in Chapter Three, my young feminist interviewees' recollections—though often clear and vibrant—were indubitably filtered by time, interest, and patterns of memory construction.

In short, discussing media with children *while they are still children* is an important objective for scholars in this area. By bringing specific texts to young audiences for discussion, we can learn much more—and with much greater nuance—than we can by conversing about texts with children in the abstract or in hindsight.

Works Cited

Aaker, D. A. (2004). *Brand strategy: Creating relevance, differentiation, energy, leverage, and clarity.* New York, NY: Simon & Schuster.

Aaker, D.A., & Joachimsthaler, E. (2000). *Brand leadership.* New York, NY: Simon & Schuster.

Aapola, S., Gonick, M., and Harris, A. (2005). *Young femininity: Girlhood, power and social change.* New York, NY: Palgrave Macmillan.

AAUW Online Museum. (n.d.). Retrieved from https://svc.aauw.org/museum/history/1990_1999/index.cfm

Advertiser Staff. (2000, August 29). For Powerpuffs, whomping the bad guys is girl stuff. *The Honolulu Advertiser.* Retrieved May 1, 2003 from http://the.honoluluadvertiser.com/2000/Aug/29/829islandlife14.html

Aisenberg, N. (1994). *Ordinary heroines: Transforming the male myth.* New York, NY: Continuum.

Allard, A. C. (2002). "Aussies" and "wogs" and the "group-in-between": Year 10 students' constructions of cross-cultural friendships. *Discourse: Studies in the Cultural Politics of Education, 23*(2): 193–209.

American Association of University Women (1991). *Shortchanging girls, shortchanging America.* Washington, DC: AAUW, Analysis Group, Greenberg-Lake.

American Association of University Women (1992). *The AAUW report: How schools short-change girls.* Washington, DC: AAUW Educational Foundation, The Wellesley College Center for Research on Women.

American Association of University Women (1993). *Hostile hallways: The AAUW survey on sexual harassment in American schools.* Washington, DC: American Association of University Women Educational Foundation.

American Association of University Women (2001). *Hostile hallways: Bullying, teasing, and sexual harassment in School.* Washington, DC: American Association of University Women Educational Foundation.

American Psychological Association (2007). *Report of the APA task force on the sexualization of girls.* Retrieved from http://www.apa.org/pi/women/programs/girls/report-full.pdf

Associated Press. (1992, Oct. 21). Company news: Mattel says it erred: Teen Talk Barbie turns silent on math. *The New York Times,* p. D4.

Atkin, C., & Heald, G. (1977). The content of children's toy and food commercials. *Journal of Communication, 27*(4), 107–114.

Bandura, A. (1977). *Social learning theory.* New York, NY: General Learning Press.

Bang, H.-K., & Reece, B. (2003). Minorities in children's television commercials: New, improved, and stereotyped. *Journal of Consumer Affairs, 37*(1), 42–67.

Banet-Weiser, S. (2004). Girls rule! Gender, feminism, and Nickelodeon. *Critical Studies in Media Communication, 21,* 119–139.

Banet-Weiser, S. (2007). *Kids rule!: Nickelodeon and consumer citizenship.* Durham: Duke University Press.

Banks, C. A. (2005). Black girls/white spaces: Managing identity through memories of schooling. In P. J. Bettis & N. G. Adams (Eds.), *Geographies of girlhood: Identities in-between* (pp. 177–194). Mahwah, NJ: Lawrence Erlbaum Associates.

Baptista-Fernandez, & Greenberg, B. (1980).The context, characteristics and communication behaviors of blacks on television. In B. Greenberg (Ed.), *Life on television: Content analyses of U.S. television drama* (pp. 13–21). Norwood, NJ: Ablex.

Barcus, F. (1977). *Children's television: An analysis of programming and advertising.* New York: Praeger.

Barner, M. R. (1999). Sex-role stereotyping in FCC-mandated children's educational television. *Journal of Broadcasting & Electronic Media, 43,* 551–564.

Barthes, R. (1972). *Mythologies.* London: Paladin.

Baumgardner, J., & Richards, A. (2000). *Manifesta: Young women, feminism, and the future.* New York, NY: Farrar, Straus & Giroux.

Bentley, M. K. (1999). The body of evidence: Dangerous intersections between development and culture in the lives of adolescent girls. In S. R. Mazzarella & N. Pecora (Eds.), *Growing up girls: Popular culture and the construction of identity* (pp. 209–221). New York: Peter Lang.

Bettis, P. J., Jordan, D., & Montgomery, D. (2005). Girls in groups: The preps and the sex mob try out for womanhood. In P. J. Bettis & N. G. Adams (Eds.), *Geographies of girlhood: Identities in-between* (pp. 69–84). Mahwah, NJ: Lawrence Erlbaum Associates.

Bhana, D. (2005). "Show me the panties:" Girls play games in the school ground. In C. Mitchell and J. Reid-Walsh (Eds.) *Seven going on seventeen: Tween studies in the culture of girlhood* (pp. 163–172). New York: Peter Lang.

Bikini Kill (1991). *Revolution Girl Style Now!* [Cassette]. Olympia, OR: Kill Rock Stars.

Boettcher, S. (2004, Feb. 6). Suddenly, boy-bashing is all the rage for teenage girls. *Edmonton Journal,* n.p. Retrieved from http://www.canadiancrc.com/Newspaper_Articl es/Edmonton_Journal_Boys_stink_06FEB04.aspx

Bonilla-Silva, E. (2002). The linguistics of color blind racism: How to talk nasty about blacks without sounding "racist." *Critical Sociology, 28*(1–2): 41–64.

Bonilla-Silva, E., and Embrick, D. G. (2007). "Every place has a ghetto . . ." The signifi- cance of whites' social and residential segregation. *Symbolic Interaction, 30*(3): 323– 345.

Bonilla-Silva, E., Goar, C., and Embrick, D. G. (2006). When whites flock together: The social psychology of white habitus. *Critical Sociology, 32*(2–3): 229–253.

Bordo, S. (1995). *Unbearable weight: Feminism, western culture, and the body.* Berkeley, CA: University of California Press.

Borzekowski, D. L. G., & Poussaint, A. F. (1998). *Latino American preschoolers and the media.* University of Pennsylvania, Annenberg Public Policy Center.

Bourgoyne, J.E. (1993, March 27). Steinem turns 59, pushes program to take girls to work. *Times-Picayune,* p. A23.

Bramlett-Solomon, S., and Roeder, Y. (2008). Looking at race in children's television: Analysis of Nickelodeon commercials. *Journal of Children and Media, 2*(1): 56–66.

Briefs. (2000, June 19). *Multichannel News, 21*(25): n.p. Retrieved from http://www. multichannel.com/article/59802-Atlanta.php

Bristor, J. M., Lee, R. G., & Hunt, M. (1995). African-American images in television adver- tising: Progress or prejudice? *Journal of Public Policy and Marketing, 14,* 48–62.

Brown, L. M. (1998). *Raising their voices: The politics of girls' anger.* Cambridge, MA: Harvard University Press.

Brown, L. M. (2008). The "girls" in girls' studies. *Girlhood Studies: An Interdisciplinary Journal, 1*(1), 1–12.

Brown, L. M., & Gilligan, C. (1992). *Meeting at the crossroads: Women's psychology and girls' development.* New York, NY: Ballantine.

Browne, B. A. (1998). Gender stereotypes in advertising on children's television in the 1990s: A cross-national analysis. *Journal of Advertising, 27,* 83–96.

Brumberg, J. J. (1997). *The body project: An intimate history of American girls.* New York: Vintage.

Brush, S. (1991). Women in science and engineering. *American Scientist, 79,* 404–419.

Buckingham, D. (1993). *Children talking television: The making of television literacy.* London: The Falmer Press.

Buckingham, D. (1996). *Moving images: Understanding children's emotional responses to tele- vision.* Manchester, England: Manchester University Press.

Buckingham, D. (2009). "Creative" visual methods in media research: Possibilities, problems and proposals. *Media, Culture & Society, 31*(4): 633–652.

Burgess, A. (2002, April 1). Marathon totally spies global music and merch potential in its tween girl toon. *Kidscreen* 8(4), 51.

Busico, M. (1992, Oct. 4). Riot grrrls: Angry punk rock sisterhood leaving boys' rules behind for "Revolution Girl Style Now." *The Houston Chronicle*, p. 3.

Calvert, S. L., Huston, A. C., & Wright, J. C. (1987). Effects of television preplay formats on students' attention and story comprehension. *Journal of Applied Developmental Psychology, 8,* 329–342.

Carter, B. (1991, May 1). Children's TV, where boys are king. *The New York Times,* p. A1.

Cartoon Network (1998). Saving the world before bedtime, *The Powerpuff Girls* kicks off as half-hour series on Cartoon Network. Press release retrieved from http://www.CartoonNetwork.com

Casey, B., Casey, N., Calvert, B., French L., & Lewis, J. (2002). Discourse/discourse analysis. *Television studies: The key concepts.* (pp. 64–67). London: Routledge.

Castleman, L. (2004, May 1). Marathon has U.S. retail opps for *Totally Spies!* in its crosshairs. *Kidscreen*, p. 27.

Ceccarelli, L. (1998). Polysemy: Multiple meanings in rhetorical criticism. *Quarterly Journal of Speech, 84*(4): 395–415.

Center for Communication. (2005, July). *Bios: Betty Cohen.* Retrieved from http://www.cencom.org/bios.aspx?id=890

Chen, S. (2010, Feb. 18). Girl's arrest for doodling raises concerns about zero tolerance. CNN. Retrieved from http://articles.cnn.com/2010–02–18/justice/new.york.doodle.ar rest_1_zero-tolerance-schools-police-precinct?_s=PM:CRIME

Cherland, M. (2005). Reading Elisabeth's girlhood: History and popular culture at work in the subjectivity of a tween. In C. Mitchell & J. Reid-Walsh (Eds.), *Seven Going on Seventeen: Tween studies in the culture of girlhood.* (pp. 95–116). New York, NY: Peter Lang.

Chevalier, M. & Mazzalovo, G. (2004). *Pro logo: Brands as a factor of progress.* New York, NY: Palgrave Macmillan.

Chideya, F., with Rossi, M. & Hannah, D. (1992, Nov. 23). Revolution, girl style. *Newsweek*, p. 84.

Chira, S. (1992). Bias against girls is found rife in schools, with lasting damage. *The New York Times,* p. A1.

Corliss, R. (2001, April 16). Go ahead, make her day. *Time.* Retrieved from http://www.time.com/time/magazine/article/0,9171,999541,00.html

Correll, J., Park, B., Judd, C., & Wittenbrink, B. (2002). The police officer's dilemma: Using ethnicity to disambiguate potentially threatening individuals. *Journal of Personality and Social Psychology, 83,* 1314–1329.

Coulter, N. (2005). The consumption chronicles: Tales from suburban Canadian tweens in the 1980s. In C. Mitchell & J. Reid-Walsh (Eds.), *Seven Going on Seventeen: Tween studies in the culture of girlhood.* (pp. 330–346). New York, NY: Peter Lang.

Critics question Barbie's self-esteem (or lack thereof). (1992, Oct. 2). *The New York Times,* p. D3.

Currie, D. H., & Kelly, D. M. (2005) "I'm going to crush you like a bug": Understanding girls' agency and empowerment. In Y. Jiwani, C. Steenbergen, & C. Mitchell (Eds.) *Girlhood: Redefining the limits* (pp. 173–190). Montreal, Canada: Black Rose Books.

Currie, D. H., Kelly, D. M., and Pomerantz, S. (2009). *"Girl power": Girls reinventing girlhood.* New York: Peter Lang.

D'Innocenzio, A. (2003, October 18). Toy companies and stores try to win back tween girls. *Star-News,* p. 8C.

Daley, S. (1991, January 9). Little girls lose their self-esteem on way to adolescence, study finds. *The New York Times,* p. B6.

Davison, T. E., & McCabe, M. P. (2006). Adolescent body image and psychosocial functioning. *Journal of Social Psychology, 146*(1), 15–30.

Dean, G.A. (1991, January 31). TV damages girls' self-esteem. *The New York Times,* p. A22.

DeMott, R. (2000). The Powerpuff Girls' phenomenal merchandising mantra. *Animation World Magazine, 5* (7). Retrieved from http://www.awn.com/mag/issue5.07/5.07pages/ demottppg.php3

DeRogatis, J. (2002, July 3). 'Powerpuff Girls' fight the good fight. *The Chicago Sun-Times,* p. 43.

Dicker, R., & Piepmeier, A (2003). *Catching a Wave: Reclaiming Feminism for the 21st Century.* Boston, MA: Northeastern University Press.

Dix, L. (Ed.). (1987). *Women: Their underrepresentation and career differentials in science and engineering.* Washington, DC: National Research Council.

Douglas, S. J. (1995). *Where the Girls Are: Growing up Female with the Mass Media.* New York, NY: Three Rivers Press.

Dowling, C. (1981). *The Cinderella complex: Women's hidden fear of independence.* New York, NY: Summit.

Dowling, C. (2000). *The frailty myth: Redefining the physical potential of women and girls.* New York, NY: Random House.

Driscoll, C. (1999). Girl culture, revenge and global capitalism: Cybergirls, riot grrls, Spice Girls. *Australian Feminist Studies, 14*(29), 173–193.

Driscoll, C. (2002). *Girls: Feminine adolescence in popular culture and cultural theory.* New York, NY: Columbia University Press.

DuCille, A. (1994). Dyes and dolls: Multicultural Barbie and the merchandizing of difference. *Differences: A Journal of Feminist Cultural Studies, 6*(1): 47–68.

Duke, L.L. & Kreshel, P.J. (1998). Negotiating femininity: Girls in early adolescence read teen magazines. *Journal of Communication Inquiry,* 22(1): 48–71.

Durham, M. G. (1999). Out of the Indian diaspora: Mass media, myths of femininity, and the negotiation of adolescence between two cultures, In S. R. Mazzarella and N. O. Pecora (Eds.), *Growing up girls: Popular culture and the construction of identity,* pp. 193–208. New York, NY: Peter Lang.

Durham, M. G. (2003). The girling of America: Critical reflections on gender and popular communication. *Popular Communication, 1*(1), 23–31.

Durham, M. G. (2008). *The Lolita effect: The media sexualization of young girls and what we can do about it.* Woodstock, NY: Overlook Press.

Ebenkamp, B. (2001, June 11). Power to the puff people. *Brandweek*, 42(24), pp. 36, 38, 40, 42.

Eccles, J. (1984). Sex differences in mathematics participation. In M. Steinkamp & M. Maehr (Eds.), *Advances in motivation and achievement: Women in science* (*Vol. 2*, pp. 93–137). Greenwich, CT: JAI Press.

Eccles, J. (1987). Gender roles and women's achievement-related decisions. *Psychology of Women Quarterly, 11*, 135–172.

Eccles, J., Adler, T., & Meece, J. L. (1984). Sex differences in achievement: A test of alternate theories. *Journal of Personality and Social Psychology, 46*, 26–43.

Eco, U. (1986). *Faith in fakes: Essays.* Translated by William Weaver. London: Secker and Warburg.

Eder, D., Evans, C. C., & Parker, S. (1995). *School talk, gender and adolescent culture.* New Brunswick, NJ: Rutgers University Press.

Eisenberg, E. M. (2007). *Strategic ambiguities: Essays on communication, organization, and identity.* Thousand Oaks, CA: Sage.

Ellerbee, L. (1994, April 5). Taking our daughters to work is worth doing. *The Seattle Post-Intelligencer*, p. A13.

Ellwood, I. (2002). *The essential brand book: Over 100 techniques to increase brand value.* London: Kogan Page Publishers.

Ervelles, N. & Mutua, K. (2005). "I am a woman now!": Rewriting cartographies of girlhood from the critical standpoint of disability. In P. J. Bettis and N. G. Adams (Eds.) *Geographies of girlhood: Identities in-between*, pp. 253–269. Mahwah, NJ: Lawrence Erlbaum.

Evans, S. M. (2004). *Tidal wave: How women changed America at century's end.* New York: The Free Press.

Faludi, S. (1992). *Backlash: The undeclared war against American women.* New York, NY: Crown Publishers.

Farmer, H., Anderson, M., & Brock, K. (1991, April). *Factors differentiating college science majors.* Paper presented at the annual meeting of the American Educational Research Association, Chicago.

Fisherkeller, J. (2002). *Growing up with television: Everyday learning among young adolescents.* Philadelphia: Temple University Press.

Forum Analytics (n.d.). Testimonials. [Web site]. Retrieved September 15, 2010 from http://www.forumanalytics.com/testimonials.html

France, K. (1993, July 8–22). Grrrls at war. *Rolling Stone*, pp. 23–4.

Gardner, M. (1993, April 1). Girls to preview careers firsthand. *Christian Science Monitor*, p. 11.

Gerbner, G. (1998). Casting the American scene: A look at the characters on prime time and daytime television from 1994–1997. *The 1998 Screen Actors Guild report: Casting the American scene, Dec. 1998.* Retrieved April 26, 2007, from http://www.media-awareness.ca/english/resources/research_documents/reports/diversity/american_scene.cfm

Gerbner, G. and Gross, L. (1976). Living with television: The violence profile. *Journal of Communication, 26:* 172–199.

Gerbner, G., & Signorielli, S. (1979, October). *Women and Minorities in Television Drama, 1969–1978.* Philadelphia: University of Pennsylvania, Annenberg School of Communications.

Gilligan, C. (1982), *In a different voice: Psychological theory and women's development.*Cambridge, MA: Harvard University Press.

Gills, S., Howie, G., & Munford, R. (2007). *Third wave feminism: A critical exploration.* New York, NY: Palgrave Macmillan.

Goetz, M., D. Lemish, A. Aidman and H. Moon (2005) *Media and the make-believe worlds of children.* Mahwah, NJ: Erlbaum.

Goetz, T. (Sept. 1997). For the Spice Girls, Girl Power = Selling Power. *Spin,* p. 90.

Goffman, E. (1959). *The presentation of self in everyday life.* New York, NY: Anchor Press.

Goldenberg, S. (2009, April 17). British woman hideously ugly. Sings song. *The adventures of Jacques Cousteau* [Web log post.] Retrieved from http://www.jackcousteau.com/2009/04/british-woman-hideously-ugly-sings-song.html

Goldman, R., Heath, D., & Smith, S.L. (1991). Commodity feminism. *Critical Studies in Mass Communication, 8,* 333–351.

Gonick, M. (2006). Sugar and spice and something more than nice? Queer girls and transformations of social exclusion. In Y. Jiwani, C. Steenbergen, and C. Mitchell (Eds.), *Girlhood: Redefining the limits,* 122–137. Montreal: Black Rose Books.

Goodale, G. (1999, Feb. 5). Television's superwomen. *Christian Science Monitor,* p. 13.

Goodin, S. M., Denburg, A., Murnen, S. K., and Smolak, L. (2011). "Putting on" Sexiness: A Content Analysis of the Presence of Sexualizing Characteristics in Girls' Clothing. *Sex Roles,* DOI 10.1007/s11199–011–9966–8.

Goodman, M. (2005). Dr. Toon: Nuts and bolts with Rob Renzetti. *Animation World Network.* Retrieved from http://www.awn.com/articles/drtoon/dr-toon-nuts-and-bolts-rob-renzetti/page/2%2C1

Gottschalk, L. (2003). Same-sex sexuality and childhood gender non-conformity: A spurious connection. *Journal of Gender Studies, 12*(1), 35–50.

Graves, S. (1993).Television, the portrayal of African Americans, and the development of children's attitudes. In G. Berry & J. Asamen (Eds.), *Children and television: Images in a changing sociocultural world* (pp. 179–190). Newbury Park, CA: Sage.

Gray, H. (2005). The politics of representation in network television. In Hunt, D. M. (Ed.) *Channeling blackness: Studies on television and race in America* (pp. 155–174). New York: Oxford University Press.

Gunelius, S. (2009). *Building brand value the Playboy way.* New York, NY: Palgrave Macmillan.

Gurian, M. and Stevens, K. (2005). *The minds of boys: Saving our sons from falling behind in school and life.* San Francisco, CA: Jossey-Bass.

Guthrie, M.R. (2005). Somewhere in-between: Tween queens and the marketing machine. Doctoral Dissertation, Bowling Green State University.

Hager, L. (2002, October). What little girls are really made of: The Powerpuff Girls, citizenship, and quantum mechanics or, "Better pray for the girls." Paper presented at Cultivating Knowledge(s): A Conference and a Celebration, University of Florida, Gainesville, FL.

Hains, R. C. (2004). The problematics of reclaiming the girlish: *The Powerpuff Girls* and girl power. *Femspec*, 5(2), 1–39.

Hains, R. C. (2007a). Inventing the teenage girl: The construction of female identity in Nickelodeon's *My Life as a Teenage Robot. Popular Communication*, 5(3), 191–213.

Hains, R. C. (2007b). Pretty smart: Subversive intelligence in girl power cartoons. In S.A. Inness (Ed.), *Geek chic: Smart women in popular culture.* New York, NY: Palgrave Macmillan, pp. 65–84.

Hains, R. C. (2008a). Power(puff) feminism: The Powerpuff Girls as a site of strength and collective action in the third wave. In M. Meyers (Ed.) *Women in popular culture: Meaning and representation.* Cresskill, NJ: Hampton Press, pp. 211–235.

Hains, R. C. (2008b). The origins of the girl hero: Shirley Temple, child star and commodity. *Girlhood Studies, 1*(1): 60–80.

Hains, R. C. (2009). Power feminism, mediated: Girl power and the commercial politics of change. *Women's Studies in Communication, 32*(1), 89–113.

Halberstam, D. (1994, Sept. 11). Popular, pretty, polite, not too smart. *The New York Times Review of Books.* Retrieved from http://peggyorenstein.com/books/reviews/schoolgirls_nytimes.html

Halberstam, J. (1998). *Female masculinity.* Durham, NC: Duke University Press.

Halpin, M. (2010, June/July). The revolution continues: Remembering riot grrrl with Kathleen Hanna. *Bust*, p. 73.

Harris, A. (2005). In a girlie world: Tweenies in Australia. In C. Mitchell and J. Reid-Walsh (Eds.) *Seven going on seventeen: Tween studies in the culture of girlhood* (pp. 209–223). New York, NY: Peter Lang Publishing.

Havrilesky, H. (2002, July 2). Powerpuff Girls meet world. *Salon.* Retrieved from http://www.salon.com/life/feature/2002/07/02/powerpuff

Henderson, J. J., & Baldasty, G. J. (2003). Race, advertising, and prime-time television. *Howard Journal of Communication, 14*, 97–112.

Henry, A. (2004). *Not my mother's sister: Generational conflict and third-wave feminism.* Bloomington, IN: University of Indiana Press.

Hey, V. (1997). *The company she keeps: An ethnography of girls' friendship.* Buckingham: Open University Press.

Heywood, L. & Drake, J. (Eds.) (1997). *Third Wave Feminism: Being Feminist, Doing Feminism.* Minneapolis, MN: University of Minnesota Press.

Hilton, T., Miller, J., & Brown, K. (1991, February). *Tomorrow's scientists, mathematicians, and engineers.* Paper presented to the 1991 annual meeting of the American Association for the Advancement of Science, Washington, DC.

Hochschild, A. R. (1994.) The commercial spirit of intimate life and the abduction of feminism: Signs from women's advice books. *Theory, Culture & Society, 11*: 1–24.

Holden, S. (2002, July 3). They have a tantrum, then save the world. *The New York Times,* p. E3.

Holewa, L. (2011, Feb. 27). Florida boy, 8, arrested at school for 5th time. AOL News. Retrieved from http://www.aolnews.com/2011/02/27/florida-boy-8-arrested-at-school-for-5th-time/

Hopkins, S. (2002, February 19). Bam! Crash! Kapow! Girls are heroes now. *Sydney Morning Herald,* p. 11.

Hopkins, S. (2002). *Girl heroes: The new force in popular culture.* Sydney: Pluto Press.

Hunt, D. M. (2005). *Channeling blackness: Studies on television and race in America.* New York, NY: Oxford University Press.

Huston, A. C., Donnerstein, E., Fairchild, H., Feshbach, N., Katz, P., Murray, J., Rubinstein, E., Wilcox, B., & Zuckerman, D. (1992). *Big world, small screen: The role of television in American society.* Lincoln: University of Nebraska Press.

Inness, S. A. (1999). *Tough girls: Women warriors and wonder women in popular culture.* Philadelphia, PA: University of Pennsylvania Press.

James, A. (2006, January 25). Cartoon Network draws "Team." *Daily Variety, 290*(18), p.6.

Japenga, A. (1995, November 15). Punk's girls groups are putting the self back into self esteem. *New York Times,* p. 30.

Jen Smith (n.d.) In *ZineWiki: The Independent Media Wikipedia.* Retrieved February 19, 2011 from http://zinewiki.com/Jen_Smith

Jervis, L. (2004). The end of feminism's third wave: The cofounder of *Bitch* magazine says goodbye to the generational divide. *Ms. Magazine.* Retrieved from http://www.msmagazine.com/winter2004/thirdwave.asp

Jhally, S. & Lewis, J. (1992). *Enlightened Racism:* The Cosby Show, *audiences, and the myth of the American Dream.* Boulder, CO: Westview Press.

Jiwani, Y. (2005). Tween worlds: Race, gender, age, identity, and violence. In C. Mitchell and J. Reid-Walsh (Eds.) *Seven going on seventeen: Tween studies in the culture of girlhood,* 173–190. New York, NY: Peter Lang.

Jiwani, Y. (2006). Racialized violence and girls and young women of colour. In Y. Jiwani, C. Steenbergen, and C. Mitchell (Eds.) *Girlhood: Redefining the limits.* (pp. 70–88). Montreal: Black Rose Books.

Kalson, S. (1993, April 12). Today, a visit to the office; tomorrow . . . *The Pittsburgh Post-Gazette,* p. D1.

Kearney, M. C. (1998). "Don't need you": Rethinking identity politics and separatism from a grrrl perspective. In J.S. Epstein (Ed.) *Youth culture: Identity in a postmodern world*, 148–188. Malden, MA: Blackwell Publishers.

Kearney, M. C. (2006). *Girls make media*. New York, NY: Routledge.

Kearney, M. C. (2008). New directions: Girl-centered media studies for the twenty-first century. *Journal of Children and Media, 2*(1): 82–83.

Kearney, M. C. (2011). *Mediated girlhoods: New explorations of girls' media culture*. New York: Peter Lang.

Kiley, D. (2005, July 5). Not every brand is a lifestyle brand. *Bloomberg Business Week*. Retrieved from http://nybw.businessweek.com/the_thread/brandnewday/archives/2005/07/not_every_brand_is_a_lifestyle_brand.html

Kindlon & Thompson (1999). *Raising Cain: Protecting the emotional life of boys*. New York, NY: Ballantine.

Klein, N. (2000). *No logo: Taking aim at the brand bullies*. New York, NY: Macmillan.

Kleinfeld, J. (1998). *The myth that schools shortchange girls: Social science in the service of deception*. Washington, D.C.: The Women's Freedom Network. Retrieved from http://education.nmsu.edu/ci/morehead/documents/the-myth-that-schools-shortchange-girls.pdf

Kohlberg, L. (1969). Stage and sequence: The cognitive-development approach to socialization. In D. A. Goslin (Ed.), *Handbook of socialization theory and research* (pp. 347–480). Chicago: Rand McNally.

Koji, S. and Fernandes, M. (2010). Does it matter where we meet? The role of emotional context in evaluative first impressions. *Canadian Journal of Experimental Psychology, 64*(2): 107–116.

Kurtzman, J. (1992, October 25). Business diary/October 18–23: No more math phobia for Barbie. *The New York Times*, p. C2.

Kyles, K. (2003, August 14). Mattel's hip-hop Flava dolls flop. *The Chicago Tribune*. Retrieved from http://articles.chicagotribune.com/2003–08–14/news/0308140373_1_hip-hop-dolls-flava

Lamb, S. (2002). *The secret lives of girls: What good girls really do—sex play, aggression, and their guilt*. New York: The Free Press.

Lamb, S., & Brown, L. M. (2006). *Packaging Girlhood: Rescuing our daughters from marketers' schemes*. New York, NY: St. Martin's Press.

Larson, M. S. (2001). Interactions, activities, and gender in children's television commercials: A content analysis. *Journal of Broadcasting & Electronics, 45*(1), 41–56.

Larson, M. S. (2002). Race and interracial relationships in children's television commercials. *The Howard Journal of Communication, 13*: 223–235.

Lemish, D. (1998). Spice Girls' talk: A case study in the development of gendered identity. In S. A. Inness (Ed.) *Millennium girls: Today's girls around the world*, pp. 145–168. Lanham, MD: Rowman & Littlefield.

Lemish, D. (2003) Spice World: Constructing femininity the popular way. *Popular Music and Society, 26*(1): 17–29.

Leonard, M. (2007). *Gender in the music industry: Rock, discourse and girl power*. Burlington, VT: Ashgate Publishing Company.

Lesko, N. (1988). The curriculum of the body: Lessons from a Catholic high school. In L. Roman, L. Christian-Smith and E. Ellsworth (Eds.) *Becoming feminine: The politics of popular culture*, 123–42. London: Falmer Press.

Levin, D. E. and Kilbourne, J. (2008). *So sexy so soon: The new sexualized childhood and what parents can do to protect their kids*. New York: Ballantine.

Lewis, A. E. (2003). Everyday race-making: Navigating racial boundaries in schools. *American Behavioral Scientist, 47*(3): 283–305.

Li-Vollmer, M. (2002). Race representation in child-targeted television commercials. *Mass Communication and Society, 5*(2), 207–228.

Licata, J., & Biswas, A. (1993). Representation, roles and occupational status of Black models in television advertisements. *Journalism Quarterly, 70*(4), 868–882.

Lichty, L. F., Torres, J. M. C., Valenti, M. C., and Buchanan, N. T. (2008). Sexual harassment policies in K-12 schools: Examining accessibility to students and content. *Journal of School Health, 78*(11): 607–614.

Linn, S. (2004) *Consuming kids: The hostile takeover of childhood*. New York, NY: New Press.

Lombardi, K.S. (1993, March 14). Easing bias against girls in the classroom. *The New York Times*, Section 13WC, p. 1.

Ludden, J. (2010, April 19). Despite new law, gender salary gap persists. The Morning Edition. NPR & WBUR. Retrieved from http://www.wbur.org/npr/125998232

Malik, F. (2005). Mediated consumption and fashionable selves: Tween girls, fashion magazines, and shopping. In C. Mitchell & J. Reid-Walsh (Eds.), *Seven going on seventeen: Tween studies in the culture of girlhood* (pp. 257–277). New York: Peter Lang.

Mandell, N. (1988). The least-adult role in studying children. *Journal of Contemporary Ethnography*, 16: 433–467.

Mann, J. (1994). *The difference: Discovering the hidden ways we silence girls*. New York, NY: Warner.

Martin, C. L., and Ruble, D. N. (2009). Patterns of gender development. *Annual Review of Psychology, 61*: 353–81.

Matabane, P. W. (2005). Television and the black audience: Cultivating moderate perspectives on racial integration. In D. M. Hunt (Ed.) *Channeling blackness: Studies on television and race in America* (pp. 64–73). New York: Oxford University Press.

Mayville, S., Katz, R. C., Gipson, M. T., & Cabral, K. (1999). Assessing the prevalence of body dysmorphic disorder in an ethnically diverse group of adolescents. *Journal of Child and Family Studies, 8*(3): 357–362.

Mazzarella, S. R., and Pecora, N. O. (2007). Girls in crisis: Newspaper coverage of adolescent girls. *Journal of Communication Inquiry, 31*(1): 6–27.

McAlister, N. (2002, July 2). Powerpuff Girls battle villains on big screen. *Florida Times-Union*, p. C1.

McAllister, M. P. (2007). "Girls with a passion for fashion": The Bratz brand as integrated spectacular consumption. *Journal of Children and Media, 1*(3): 244–258.

McDonnell, E. (1993, August 7). Women rockers create their own alternatives. *Billboard: The Billboard Report*, p. 1.

McNeal, J.U. (1987). *Children as consumers: Insights and implications*. Lexington, MA: Lexington Books.

McNeal, J.U. (1992). *Kids as customers: A handbook of marketing to children*. Lexington, MA: Lexington Books.

McRobbie, A. (2000). *Jackie* magazine: Romantic individualism and the teenage girl. In A. McRobbie (Ed.), *Feminism and youth culture* (pp. 67–117). New York, NY: Routledge.

Meltzer, M. (2010). *Girl power: The nineties revolution in music*. New York, NY: Faber and Faber, Inc.

Merskin, D. (2002). Boys will be boys: A content analysis of gender and race in children's advertisements on the Turner Cartoon Network. *Journal of Current Issues and Research in Advertising, 24*(1), 51–59.

Merten, D.E. (1997). The meaning of meanness: Popularity, competition, and conflict among junior high school girls. *Sociology of Education, 70*: 175–91.

Messner, M. A. (2000). Barbie Girls versus Sea Monsters: Children constructing gender. *Gender and Society, 14*(6): 765–784.

Mitchell, C. and Reid-Walsh, J. (2002). *Researching children's popular culture: The cultural spaces of childhood*. New York: Routledge.

Mitchell, C. and Reid-Walsh, J. (2007). *Girl culture: An encyclopedia*. Westport, CT: Greenwood Publishing Group.

Michman, R.D., Mazze, E.M., and Greco, A.J. (2003). *Lifestyle marketing: Reaching the new American consumer*. Greenwood Publishing Group.

Moorhead, J. (2007, Oct. 24). Girl power comes of age. *The Guardian*, p. 14. Retrieved from http://www.guardian.co.uk/world/2007/oct/24/gender.pop

Morris, E. W. (2005). From "middle class" to "trailer trash": Teachers' perceptions of white students in a predominately minority school. *Sociology of Education, 78*: 99–121.

Moss, L. (2000, October 9). 'Powerpuff' Quarter. *Multichannel News 21*(41), 1, 58.

Munk, N. (1997, December 8). Girl power! *Fortune*. Retrieved from http://www.nina-munk.com/articleDetails.htm?doc=GirlPower

Murnen, S. K., and Smolak, L. (2000). The experience of sexual harassment among grade-school students: early socialization of female subordination? *Sex Roles, 43*(1/2): 1–17.

Napoli, M. (2003). If only I was like Mary-Kate and Ashley: Constructing girlhood through representation and consumption. (Doctoral dissertation, The Pennsylvania State University, 2003). *Dissertation Abstracts International, 64*, 4654.

Napoli, M. (2004). "I want to be just like Mary-Kate and Ashley": Young girls talk about popular teen icons in an after-school book club. *Women in Literacy and Life Assembly, 13*. Retrieved from http://scholar.lib.vt.edu/ejournals/WILLA/fall04/napoli.html

National Science Foundation. (1990). *Selected data on science and engineering doctorate awards: 1990*. (Report NSF 91–310). Washington, DC: Author.

Netter, S. (2008, Jan. 14). Parents consider legal action after autistic girl, 8, arrested at school. ABC News. Retrieved from http://abcnews.go.com/US/story?id=6640478

Neu, T.W., and Weinfeld, R. (2007). *Helping boys succeed in school: A practical guide for parents and teachers.* Waco, TX: Prufrock.

Neumark-Sztainer, D., Croll, J., Story, M., Hannan, P. J., French, S. A., & Perry, C. (2002). Ethnic/racial difference in weight-related concerns and behaviors among adolescent girls and boys: Findings from Project EAT. *Journal of Psychosomatic Research, 53*(5): 963–74.

Newcomb, H. M. (1988). One night of prime time: An analysis of television's multiple voices. In J. W. Carey (Ed.) *Media, myths, and narrative: Television and the press.* Thousand Oaks, CA: Sage.

Newcomb, H. M. (1991). On the dialogic aspects of mass communication. In R. K. Avery & D. Eason (Eds.), *Critical perspectives on media and society* (pp. 69–87). New York, NY: Guilford Press.

Newsom, V. A. (2004). Young females as super heroes: Superheroines in the animated sailor moon. *Femspec,5*(2): 57–81.

Nguyen, M. (2010, March 28). Punk Planet 40. *Thread & Circuits: An Archive of a Wayward Youth* [blog]. Retrieved October 14, 2010 from http://threadandcircuits.wordpress.com/2010/03/28/58/

Noble, B. P. (1993, April 4). At work; when daughters invade the office. *The New York Times,* p. C25.

Oliver, M. B. (2003). African American men as "criminal and dangerous": Implications of media portrayals of crime on the "criminalization" of African American men. *Journal of African American Studies, 7*(2): 3–18.

Ono, K. (2000). To be a vampire on *Buffy the Vampire Slayer:* Race and ("other") socially marginalizing positions on horror TV. In E. Helford (Ed.) *Fantasy Girls: Gender in the New Universe of Science Fiction and Fantasy Television* (163–186). Lanham, MD: Rowman & Littlefield Publishers.

Orenstein, P. (1994). *Schoolgirls: Young women, self-esteem, and the confidence gap* (in association with the American Association of University Women). New York, NY: Anchor Books.

Orenstein, P. (2011). *Cinderella ate my daughter: Dispatches from the front lines of the new girlie-girl culture.* New York: HarperCollins.

Ormrod, J.E. (1999). *Human learning* (3rd ed.). Upper Saddle River, NJ: Prentice-Hall.

Ostrow, J. (2003, November 23). Why big tween spenders have retailers and TV execs peddling sexed-up products to exploit the new hot-pink power. *The Denver Post,* p. F-01.

Padel, R. (1997, June 10). Puppy power for the nineties. *The Independent,* p. 19.

Paoletta, M. (2006, Sept. 2). MTV's "Juice": Shaping lifestyles and attitudes around the world. *Billboard,* p. 46.

Payne, B.K. (2006). Weapon bias: Split-second decisions and unintended stereotyping. *Current Directions in Psychological Science, 15,* 287–291.

Perlmutter, P. (2002). Minority group prejudice. *Society, 39*(3): 59–65.

Petrovic, J. E. and Ballard, R. (2005). Unstraightening the ideal girl: lesbians, high school, and spaces to be. In P. Bettis and N. Adams (Eds.), *Geographies of girlhood: Identity in between,* pp. 195–209. Mahwah, NJ: Lawrence Erlbaum Associates.

Pipher, M. (1994). *Reviving Ophelia: Saving the selves of adolescent girls.* New York, NY: Random House.

Pollack (1999). *Real boys: Rescuing our sons from the myths of boyhood.* New York: Henry Holt.

Pollitt, K. (1991, April 7). The Smurfette principle. *The New York Times Magazine.* Retrieved June 25, 2011 from http://www.nytimes.com/1991/04/07/magazine/hers-the-smurfette-principle.html

Pomerantz, S. (2008). Style and girl culture. In Mitchell and Reid-Walsh (Eds.) *Girl culture: An encyclopedia,* Vol. 1 (pp. 64–72). Westport, CT: Greenwood Press.

Pozner, J.L. (1998, April). Makes me wanna grrrowl: Spice Girls' pre-packaged power speak reduces feminism to skintight soundbites. *Sojourner: The Women's Forum.*

Rand, E. (1998). Older head on younger bodies. In H. Jenkins (Ed.) *The children's culture reader* (pp. 382–93). New York: New York University Press.

Renold, E. (2006). "They won't let us play . . . unless you're going out with one of them": Girls, boys, and Butler's "heterosexual matrix" in the primary years. *British Journal of Sociology of Education, 27*(4): 489–509.

Riffe, D., Goldson, H., Saxton, K., & Yu,Y. (1989). Females and minorities in TV ads in 1987 Saturday children's programs. *Journalism Quarterly, 66*(1),129–136.

Riordan, E. (2001, July). Commodified agents and empowered girls: Consuming and producing feminism. *Journal of Communication Inquiry, 25*(3): 279–297.

Riot Grrrl (n.d.) In *ZineWiki: The Independent Media Wikipedia.* Retrieved February 19, 2011 from http://zinewiki.com/Riot_Grrrl

Rothenberg, P. S. (2012). *White privilege: Essential readings on the other side of racism.* New York: Worth.

Rushkoff, D. (Producer). (2001, Feb. 27). *Frontline: The merchants of cool* (2001). [Television broadcast.] Boston, MA: PBS.

Russell, R. and Tyler, M. (2002). Thank heaven for little girls: "Girl Heaven" and the commercial context of feminine childhood. *Sociology, 36*: 619–637.

Sadker, M. & Sadker, D. (1994). *Failing at fairness: How our schools cheat girls.* New York, NY: Touchstone.

Sailer, S. (2002, July 3). Powerpuff Girls Movie. *United Press International.* Retrieved from http://www.isteve.com/Film_Powerpuff_Girls.htm

Sarkeesian, A. (2011, April 21). Tropes vs. Women: #3 The Smurfette Principle. Retrieved from http://www.feministfrequency.com/2011/04/tropes-vs-women-3-the-smurfette-principle/

Sax, L. (2007). *Boys adrift: The five factors driving the growing epidemic of unmotivated boys and underachieving young men.* New York, NY: Basic Books.

Schraw, E.H. (1992, October 11). Grrrl look out, guys talk. *Portland Oregonian,* p. 10.

Schrum, K. (1998). "Teena means business": Teenage girls' culture and "Seventeen" magazine, 1944–1950. In S.A. Inness (Ed.) *Delinquents and debutantes: Twentieth-century American girls' cultures.* New York, NY: New York University Press, pp. 134–163.

Seiter, E. (1986). Stereotypes and the media: A re-evaluation. *Journal of Communication, 1,* 14–26.

Seiter, E. (1990). Different children, different dreams: Racial representation in advertising. *Journal of Communication Inquiry, 14*(1), 31–47.

Seiter, E. (1992). Semiotics, structuralism, and television. In R. C. Allen (Ed.), *Channels of discourse, reassembled* (pp. 31–66). Chapel Hill, NC: University of North Carolina Press.

Selig, J. (2010, Dec. 14). Yes, Virginia, there is a CP team. *Planet Preschool.* [Web log post.] Retrieved from http://kidscreen.com/2010/12/14/yes-virginia-there-is-a-cp-team/

Sellers, P. (1989, May 8). The ABC's of marketing to kids. *Fortune.* 119: 114.

The Sentinel (2002). The Powerpuff Girls Movie. p. 27.

Shinew, D. M., and Jones, D. T. (2005). Girl talk: Adolescent girls' perceptions of leadership. In P. J. Bettis and N. G. Adams (2005) *Geographies of girlhood: Identities in-between,* 55–68. Mahwah, NJ: Lawrence Erlbaum.

Siegel, D. L., Coffey, T. J., and Livingston, G. (2004). *The great tween buying machine: Capturing your share of the multibillion dollar tween market.* Chicago, IL: Dearborn Trade Publishing.

Signorielli, N. (1989). Television and conceptions about sex roles: Maintaining conventionality and the status quo. *Sex Roles,* 21, 341–360.

Simmons, R. (2002). *Odd girl out: The hidden culture of aggression in girls.* New York: Harcourt.

Simpson, A. (2009, Jan. 16). Powerpuff Girls 10th anniversary interview with creator Craig McCracken. *Cold Hard Flash.* Retrieved October 12, 2010 from http://coldhardflash.com/2009/01/powerpuff-girls-10th-anniversary-interview-with-creator-craig-mccracken.html

Sinclair, D. (2004). *Wannabe: How the Spice Girls reinvented pop fame.* New York, NY: Omnibus Press.

SlutWalk Toronto. (2011). Because we've had enough. Retrieved from slutwalktoronto.com

Smith, K. (2003, July 8). The 25 greatest girl power movies ever made. *MovieMaker Magazine*(51). Retrieved from http://www.moviemaker.com/directing/article/the_25_greatest_girl_power_movies_ever_made_3004/

Snead, E. (1992, August 7). Feminist riot grrls don't just wanna have fun. *USA Today,* p. 5D.

Spice Girls. (1996). *Spice* [CD]. Beverly Hills, CA: Virgin.

Spice Girls.(1997). *Girl power.* Secaucus, NJ: Carol Pub. Group.

Spice Girls. (1998). *Spiceworld: The official book of the movie.* New York, NY: Three Rivers Press.

Sternglanz, S. H., & Serbin, L. (1974). Sex role stereotyping in children's television programs. *Developmental Psychology,* 10, 710–715.

Swystun, J. (2007). *The brand glossary.* New York, NY: Palgrave Macmillan.

Tanenbaum, L. (2000). *Slut! Growing up female with a bad reputation.* New York: Perennial.

Tannen, D. (1990). *You just don't understand: Women and men in conversation.* New York, NY: Ballantine Books.

Taylor, C., Lee, J., & Stern, B. (1995). Portrayals of African, Hispanic, and Asian Americans in magazine advertising. *American Behavioral Scientist, 38*(4), 608–620.

Taylor, C., & Stern, B. (1997). Asian-Americans: Television advertising and the "model minority" stereotype. *Journal of Advertising,* 26(2), 47–61.

Thompson, A. (1998). Not the color purple: Black feminist lessons for educational caring. *Harvard Educational Review, 68*(4): 522–44.

Thorne, B. (1993.) *Gender play: Girls and boys in school.* New Brunswick, NJ: Rutgers University Press.

Tobin, J. (2000). *"Good guys don't wear hats": Children's talk about the media.* New York: Teachers College Press.

Tolman, D. (2002) *Dilemmas of desire: Teenage girls talk about sexuality.* Cambridge, MA: Harvard University Press.

"Totally Spies!" line hits Kmart (2006, April 10). *DSN Retailing Today,* 45(7), 15.

"Toys: Flavas of the week." (2003, August 4). *Newsweek.* Retrieved from http://www.newsweek.com/2003/08/04/toys-flavas-of-the-week.html

Trigg, M., and Wittenstrom, K. (1996). That's the way the world really goes: sexual harassment and New Jersey teenagers. *Initiatives, 57*(2): 55–65.

Tuchman, G. (1978). Introduction: The symbolic annihilation of women by the mass media. In G. Tuchman, A.K. Daniels, and J. Benet (Eds.) *Hearth and Home: Images of women in the mass media* (p. 3–38). New York, NY: Oxford University Press.

Tyre, P. (2006). The trouble with boys. (Cover story: The Boy Crisis. At every level of education, they're falling behind. What to do?) *Newsweek.* Retrieved from http://www.newsweek.com/2006/01/29/the-trouble-with-boys.html

Tyre, P. (2008). *The trouble with boys.* New York, NY: Crown.

Tyreman, D. (2009). *World famous: How to give your business a kick-ass brand identity.* New York, NY: AMACOM.

U.S. Department of Education. (1984). Science and mathematics education in American high schools: Results from the high school and beyond study. *National Center for Education Statistics Bulletin*

U.S. Department of Health and Human Services (2001). *Girl power!* [Web site]. Retrieved from http://web.archive.org/web/20010515060637/http://www.girlpower.gov/

Vail, T. (2010, September 28). In the beginning there was rhythm! *Jigsaw* [Web log post]. Retrieved from http://jigsawunderground.blogspot.com/2010/09/in-beginning-there-was-rhythm.html

Vail, T. (2010, October 13). Girls to the Front book tour at the Olympia Library! *Jigsaw* [Web log post]. Retrieved from http://jigsawunderground.blogspot.com/2010/10-/girls-to-front-book-tour.html

Valdivia, A. N. (2008). Mixed race on Disney Channel: From *Johnnie Tsunami* to *The Cheetah Girls*. In M. Beltran and C. Fojas (Eds.) *Mixed race Hollywood: Multiraciality in film and culture*, 269–89. New York, NY: New York University Press.

Valdivia, A. N. (2011). This tween bridge over my Latina girl back: The U.S. mainstream negotiates ethnicity. In M.-C. Kearney (Ed.) *Mediated girlhoods: New explorations of girls' media culture*, 93–112. New York, NY: Peter Lang.

Van Tassel, P. (1992, April 5). New move to combat sex bias in classroom. *The New York Times*, Section 12NJ, p. 1.

Walkerdine, V. (1997). *Daddy's girl: Young girls and popular culture*. Cambridge, MA: Harvard University Press.

Wardle, J., & Watters, R. (2004). Sociocultural influences on attitudes to weight and eating: Results of a natural experiment. *International Journal of Eating Disorders, 34*(4), 589–596.

Weigel, R. H. & Howes, P. W. (1982). Race relations on children's television. *The Journal of Psychology, 111*, 109–112.

Weinkauf, G. (2002, July 4). Powerpuff 'n' stuff: Animator Craig McCracken discusses his little whoopass chargettes. *New Times Los Angeles*. Retrieved May 6, 2003, from LexisNexis database.

Weldon, F. (2007, Dec. 5). Girl power? *The Daily Mail*, p. 23.

Wertheimer, S. (2006). Pretty in panties: Moving beyond the innocent child paradigm in reading preteen modeling websites. In Y. Jiwani, C. Steenbergen, and C. Mitchell (Eds.) *Girlhood: Redefining the limits* (pp. 208–226). Montreal, Canada: Black Rose Press.

West, L. (n.d.) The Spice Girls Collection [Web site]. Retrieved February 19, 2011 from http://spicegirlscollection.co.uk/

White, E. (2002). *Fast girls: Teenage tribes and the myth of the slut*. New York: Scribner.

Wilkes, R., & Valencia, H. (1989). Hispanics and blacks in television commercials. *Journal of Advertising, 18*(1),19–25.

Willett, R. (2005). Constructing the digital tween: Market discourse and girls' interests. In C. Mitchell & J. Reid-Walsh (Eds). *Seven going on seventeen: Tween studies in the culture of girlhood* (pp. 278–293). New York, NY: Peter Lang Press.

Willis, J. and Todorov, A. (2005). First impressions: Making up your mind after a 100-ms exposure to a face. *Psychological Science, 17*(7): 592–598.

Wingfield, A. H. (2007). The modern mammy and the angry black man: African American professionals' experiences with gendered racism in the workplace. *Race, Gender, & Class, 14*(1–2): 196–212.

Wiseman, R. (2002). *Queen bees and wannabes: Helping your daughter survive cliques, gossip, boyfriends, and other realities of adolescence*. New York: Three Rivers Press.

Wolf, N. (1991). *The Beauty Myth*. New York. NY: Anchor Books.

World Health Organization (2007). Global strategy on diet, physical activity and health. Retrieved April27, 2007, from http://www.who.int/dietphysicalactivity/publications/facts/obesity/en/

Zaslow, E. (2009). *Feminism, Inc.: Coming of age in girl power media culture.* New York, NY: Palgrave Macmillan.

Zebrowitz, L. (1997) *Reading faces: Window to the soul?* Boulder, CO: Westview Press.

Zinkhan, G., Qualls, W., & Biswas, A. (1990). The use of blacks in magazine and television advertising: 1946 to 1986. *Journalism Quarterly, 67*(3), 547–553.

Index

mediated youth

Sharon R. Mazzarella
General Editor

Grounded in cultural studies, books in this series will study the cultures, artifacts, and media of children, tweens, teens, and college-aged youth. Whether studying television, popular music, fashion, sports, toys, the Internet, self-publishing, leisure, clubs, school, cultures/activities, film, dance, language, tie-in merchandising, concerts, subcultures, or other forms of popular culture, books in this series go beyond the dominant paradigm of traditional scholarship on the effects of media/culture on youth. Instead, authors endeavor to understand the complex relationship between youth and popular culture. Relevant studies would include, but are not limited to studies of how youth negotiate their way through the maze of corporately-produced mass culture; how they themselves have become cultural producers; how youth create "safe spaces" for themselves within the broader culture; the political economy of youth culture industries; the representational politics inherent in mediated coverage and portrayals of youth; and so on. Books that provide a forum for the "voices" of the young are particularly encouraged. The source of such voices can range from in-depth interviews and other ethnographic studies to textual analyses of cultural artifacts created by youth.

For further information about the series and submitting manuscripts, please contact:

SHARON R. MAZZARELLA
School of Communication Studies
James Madison University
Harrisonburg, VA 22807

To order other books in this series, please contact our Customer Service Department at:

(800) 770-LANG (within the U.S.)
(212) 647-7706 (outside the U.S.)
(212) 647-7707 FAX

Or browse online by series at WWW.PETERLANG.COM